Physics for Game Developers

Physics for Game Developers

David M. Bourg

O'REILLY®

Beijing · Cambridge · Farnham · Köln · Paris · Sebastopol · Taipei · Tokyo

Physics for Game Developers
by David M. Bourg

Copyright © 2002 O'Reilly Media, Inc. All rights reserved.
Printed in the United States of America.

Published by O'Reilly Media, Inc., 1005 Gravenstein Highway North, Sebastopol, CA 95472.

O'Reilly Media, Inc. books may be purchased for educational, business, or sales promotional use. On-line editions are also available for most titles (*safari.oreilly.com*). For more information contact our corporate/institutional sales department: 800-998-9938 or *corporate@oreilly.com*.

Editor:	Robert Denn
Production Editor:	Darren Kelly
Cover Designer:	Ellie Volckhausen
Interior Designer:	David Futato

Printing History:

January 2002:	First Edition.

 This book uses RepKover™, a durable and flexible lay-flat binding.

ISBN: 0-596-00006-5
[M]   [3/05]

Table of Contents

Preface

Who Is This Book For?

Simply put, this book is targeted at computer game developers who do not have a strong mechanics or physics background but are charged with the task of incorporating *real physics* in their games.

As a game developer, and very likely as a gamer yourself, you've seen products being advertised as "ultra-realistic" or as using "real-world physics." At the same time you, or perhaps your company's marketing department, are wondering how you can spice up your own games with such realism. Or perhaps you want to try something completely new that requires you to explore real physics. The only problem is that you threw your college physics textbook in the lake after final exams and haven't touched the subject since. Maybe you licensed a really cool physics engine but you have no idea how the underlying principles work and how they will affect what you're trying to model. Or perhaps you are charged with the task of tuning someone else's physics code but you really don't understand how it works. Well then, this book is for you.

Sure you could scour the Internet, trade journals, and magazines for information and how-to's on adding physics-based realism to your games. You could even fish out that old physics text and start from scratch. However, you're likely to find that the material is either too general to be applied directly or too advanced, requiring you to search for other sources to get up to speed on the basics. This book will pull together the information you need and will serve as the starting point for you, the game developer, in your effort to enrich your game's content with physics-based realism.

This book is not a recipe book that simply gives sample code for a miscellaneous set of problems. The Internet is full of such example programs (including some very good ones, I might add). Rather than giving you a collection of specific solutions to specific problems, my aim is to arm you with a thorough and fundamental understanding of the relevant topics so that you can formulate your own solutions to a variety of problems. I'll do this by explaining, in detail, the principles of physics applicable to game development and by providing complementary hand calculation examples in addition to sample programs.

What I Assume You Know

Although I don't assume that you are a physics expert, I do assume that you have at least a basic college-level understanding of classical physics typical of non-physics and non-engineering majors. It is not essential that your physics background is fresh in your mind, as the first several chapters of this book review the subjects relevant to game physics.

I also assume that you are proficient in trigonometry, vector math, and matrix math, although I do include reference material in the appendices. Further, I assume that you have at least a basic college-level understanding of calculus, including integration and differentiation of explicit functions. Numerical integration and differentiation are a different story, and I cover these techniques in detail in the later chapters of this book.

Mechanics

Most people that I've talked to when I was developing the concept for this book immediately thought of flight simulators when the phrases "real physics" and "real-time simulation" came up. Certainly, cutting-edge flight simulations are relevant in this context; however, many different types of games and specific game elements stand to benefit from physics-based realism.

Consider this example: you're working on the next blockbuster hunting game, complete with first-person 3D, beautiful textures, and an awesome soundtrack to set the mood, but something is missing. That something is realism. Specifically, you want the game to "feel" more real by challenging the gamer's marksmanship, and you want to do this by adding considerations such as distance to target, wind speed and direction, and muzzle velocity, among others. Moreover, you don't want to fake these elements; rather, you would like to model them realistically based on the principles of physics. Gary Powell, with MathEngine Plc, put it like this: "The illusion and immersive experience of the virtual world, so carefully built up with high polygon models, detailed textures and advanced lighting, is so often shattered as soon as objects start to move and interact."[*] "It's all about interactivity and immersiveness," says Dr. Steven Collins, CEO of Havok.com.[†] I think both these guys are right on target. Why invest so much time and effort making your game world look as realistic as possible but not take the extra step to make it behave just as realistically?

---

[*] Gary Powell works for MathEngine Plc. Their products include Dynamics Toolkit 2 and Collision Toolkit 1, which handle single- and multiple-body dynamics. Their web site is at *www.mathengine.com* if you'd like more information about their products.

[†] Dr. Collins is the CEO of Havok.com. Their technology handles rigid body, soft body, cloth, and fluid and particle dynamics. You can check their stuff out at *www.havok.com*.

Here are a few examples of specific game elements that stand to benefit, in terms of realism, from the use of real physics:

- The trajectory of rockets and missiles, including the effects of fuel burn-off
- The collision of objects such as billiard balls
- The effects of gravitation between large objects such as planets and battle stations
- The stability of cars racing around tight curves
- The dynamics of boats and other waterborne vehicles
- The flight path of a baseball after it is struck by a bat
- The flight of a playing card being tossed into a hat

This is by no means an exhaustive list, but just a few examples to get you in the right frame of mind. Pretty much anything in your games that bounces around, flies, rolls, slides, or isn't sitting dead still can be realistically modeled to create compelling, believable content for your games.

So how can this realism be achieved? By using physics, of course, which brings us back to the title of this section: the subject of *mechanics*. Physics is a vast field of science that covers many different, but related subjects. The subject most applicable to realistic game content is the subject of mechanics, which is really what's meant by "real physics."

By definition, mechanics is the study of bodies at rest and in motion and of the effect of forces on them. The subject of mechanics is subdivided into *statics,* which specifically focuses on bodies at rest, and *dynamics,* which focuses on bodies in motion. One of the oldest and most studied subjects of physics, the formal origins of mechanics, can be traced back more than 2000 years to Aristotle. An even earlier treatment of the subject was formalized in *Problems of Mechanics,* but the origins of this work are unknown. Although some of these early works attributed some physical phenomena to magical elements, the contributions of such great minds as Galileo, Kepler, Euler, Lagrange, d'Alembert, Newton, and Einstein, to name a few, have helped to develop our understanding of this subject to such a degree that we have been able to achieve the remarkable state of technological advancement that we see today.

Because you want your game content to be alive and active, I'll look primarily at bodies in motion and will therefore delve into the details of the subject of dynamics. Within the subject of dynamics there are even more specific subjects to investigate, namely, *kinematics,* which focuses on the motion of bodies without regard to the forces that act on the body, and *kinetics*, which considers both the motion of bodies and the forces that act on or otherwise affect bodies in motion. I'll be taking a very close look at these two subjects throughout this book.

Arrangement of this Book

Physics-based realism is not new to gaming; in fact, many games on the shelves these days advertise their physics engines. Also, many 3D modeling and animation tools have physics engines built in to help realistically animate specific types of motion. Naturally, magazine articles appear every now and then that discuss various aspects of physics-based game content. In parallel, but at a different level, research in the area of real-time *rigid body** simulation has been active for many years, and the technical journals are full of papers that deal with various aspects of this subject. You'll find papers on subjects ranging from the simulation of multiple, connected rigid bodies to the simulation of cloth. However, while these are fascinating subjects and valuable resources, as I hinted earlier, many of them are of limited immediate use to the game developer, as they first require a solid understanding of the subject of mechanics, requiring you to learn the basics from other sources. Furthermore, many of them focus primarily on the mathematics involved in solving the equations of motion and don't address the practical treatment of the forces acting on the body or system being simulated. I asked John Nagle, with Animats, what is, in his opinion, the most difficult part of developing a physics-based simulation for games, and his response was developing numerically stable, robust code.† Gary Powell echoed this when he told me that minimizing the amount of parameter tuning to produce stable, realistic behavior was one of the most difficult challenges. I agree that speed and robustness in dealing with the mathematics of bodies in motion are crucial elements of a simulator. On top of that, so are completeness and accuracy in representing the interacting forces that initiate and perpetuate the simulation in the first place. As you'll see later in this book, forces govern the behavior of objects in your simulation, and you need to model them accurately if your objects are to behave realistically.

This prerequisite understanding of mechanics and the real-world nature of forces that may act on a particular body or system have governed the organization of this book.

Chapters 1 through 5 are essentially a mechanics primer and will start off by reviewing basic concepts and progress by gradually building on these concepts addressing the more challenging aspects of rigid body dynamics. The aim here is to give you enough of a refresher course in mechanics that you can move on to more advanced reading where these fundamentals are prerequisite. If you are already up to speed on the subject of mechanics, you might want to skip directly to Chapter 6.

Chapter 1, Basic Concepts
> This warm-up chapter covers the most basic of principles that are used and referred to throughout this book. The specific topics addressed include mass and center of mass, Newton's laws, inertia, units and measures, and vectors.

Chapter 2, Kinematics
> This chapter covers such topics as linear and angular velocity, acceleration, momentum, and the general motion of particles and rigid bodies in two and three dimensions.

---

* A rigid body is formally defined as a body, composed of a system of particles, whose particles remain at fixed distances from each other with no relative translation or rotation among particles. Although the subject of mechanics deals with flexible bodies and even fluids such as water, we'll focus our attention on bodies that are rigid.

† John Nagle is the developer of Falling Bodies, a dynamics plug-in for Softimage 3D. You can check out his patented technology at *www.animats.com.*

Chapter 3, Force

The principles of force and torque are covered in this chapter, which serves as a bridge from the subject of kinematics to that of kinetics. General categories of forces are discussed, including drag forces, force fields, and pressure.

Chapter 4, Kinetics

This chapter combines elements of Chapters 2 and 3 to address the subject of kinetics and explains the difference between kinematics and kinetics. Further discussion treats the kinetics of particles and rigid bodies in two and three dimensions.

Chapter 5, Collisions

In this chapter I cover particle and rigid body collision response, that is, what happens after two objects run in to each other.

Chapters 6 through 10 take a look at some real-world problems. These chapters focus on modeling with the aim of arming you with a solid understanding of the nature of certain physical systems, specifically the forces involved, such that these systems can be accurately modeled in real-time simulators if you choose to pursue that subject further. The example topics in this part are not meant to be all-inclusive of every system you might try to model in a game. Rather, they were selected to best illustrate the specific physical phenomenon and concepts that are relevant to a wide variety of problems.

Chapter 6, Projectiles

Chapter 6 is the first in a series of chapters addressing specific problems that can be modeled in a game to provide physically realistic content. This first chapter addresses the subject of projectiles and discusses the forces acting on projectiles in flight as well as factors that influence speed and trajectory.

Chapter 7, Aircraft

This chapter focuses on the elements of flight, including propulsor forces, drag, geometry, mass, and, most important, lift. It also serves as the starting point for a working 3D real-time simulation that will be developed in Chapter 15.

Chapter 8, Ships

The fundamental elements of floating vehicles are discussed in this chapter, including floatation, stability, volume, drag, and speed.

Chapter 9, Hovercraft

Hovercraft have some of the characteristics of both aircraft and boats. This chapter considers the characteristics that distinguish the hovercraft as a unique vehicle. Topics covered include hovering flight, aerostatic lift, and directional control.

Chapter 10, Cars

In this chapter, specific aspects of automobile performance are addressed, including aerodynamic drag, rolling resistance, skidding distance, and roadway banking.

Chapters 11 through 17, along with the three appendices, offer an introduction to real-time simulations. These chapters introduce the subject of real-time simulations and discuss various aspects of this field as applicable to computer games. The subject of real-time simulators is vast and deserves an entire book on its own, so this book focuses on the fundamentals. I walk you through the development of a 2D simulation of a couple of hovercraft, a 3D flight simulation, a generic multibody simulation in 3D with collision response, and a simulation of cloth using particles and springs.

Chapter 11, Real-Time Simulations
> This chapter introduces the subject of real-time simulations and covers several numerical integration methods for solving the differential equations of motion.

Chapter 12, 2D Rigid Body Simulator
> This chapter addresses the practical aspects of implementing a simple 2D particle and rigid body simulator. A simple real-time simulation of a couple of hovercraft is developed in this chapter.

Chapter 13, Implementing Collision Response
> This chapter shows you how to implement collision response, as discussed in Chapter 5, in a real-time simulation. Specifically, collision response is added to the hovercraft simulation developed in Chapter 12.

Chapter 14, Rigid Body Rotation
> Before moving to 3D simulators, the issue of representing rotational orientation for rigid bodies in three dimensions is addressed. Here, Euler angles, rotation matrices, and quaternions are considered.

Chapter 15, 3D Rigid Body Simulator
> This chapter combines all of the material contained in Chapters 11 through 14 and looks at the practical aspects of implementing a simple 3D rigid body simulator. Here, I show you how to develop a simple flight simulator based on the aerodynamic model discussed in Chapter 7.

Chapter 16, Multiple Bodies in 3D
> This chapter extends the example program presented in Chapter 15 by adding the ability to handle several rigid bodies as well as collision detection and response in 3D. The example presented here consists of a car crashing into a couple of test blocks.

Chapter 17, Particle Systems
> This chapter illustrates what you can achieve with simple particle simulations. Specifically, this chapter presents an example simulation that uses a system of particles and springs to mimic cloth. The example program simulates a cloth flag fluttering in the wind while hanging from a flagpole.

Appendix A, Vector Operations
> This appendix shows you how to implement a C++ class that captures all of the vector operations that you'll need when writing 2D or 3D simulations.

Appendix B, Matrix Operations
> This appendix implements a class that captures all of the operations you need to handle 3×3 matrices.

Appendix C, Quaternion Operations
> This appendix implements a class that captures all of the operations you need to handle quaternions when writing 3D rigid body simulations.

In addition to resources pertaining to real-time simulations, the bibliography at the end of this book provides sources of information on mechanics, mathematics, and other specific technical subjects, such as books on aerodynamics.

Conventions in This Book

The following typographical conventions are used in this book:

Constant width

> is used to indicate command-line computer output, code examples, and keyboard accelerators.

Constant width italic

> is used to indicate variables in code examples.

Italic

> is used to introduce new terms and to indicate URLs, variables, filenames and directories, commands, and file extensions.

Bold

> is used to indicate vector variables.

We'd Like to Hear from You

We have tested and verified the information in this book to the best of our ability, but you may find that features have changed (or even that we have made mistakes!). Please let us know about errors you may find, as well as your suggestions for future editions, by writing to:

O'Reilly & Associates, Inc.
1005 Gravenstein Highway North
Sebastopol, CA 95472
(800) 998-9938 (in the U.S. or Canada)
(707) 829-0515 (international/local)
(707) 829-0104 (fax)

We have a web page for the book, where we list examples, errata, and any plans for future editions. You can access this information at:

http://www.oreilly.com/catalog/physicsgame

You can also send messages using email. To be put on our mailing list or request a catalog, send email to:

info@oreilly.com

To comment on the book, send email to:

bookquestions@oreilly.com

Acknowledgments

I want to thank Robert Denn, the editor of this book, for his skillful review of my writing and his insightful comments and suggestions, not to mention his patience. I also want to express my appreciation to O'Reilly & Associates for agreeing to take on this project, giving me the opportunity to develop an idea I had been tossing around for over a year. Further, special thanks goes to all of the production and technical staff at O'Reilly.

Thanks goes to Gary Powell, with MathEngine Plc, Dr. Steven Collins, with Havok.com, and John Nagle, with Animats, for their expert comments and answers my various questions regarding game physics and real-time simulators. I can't forget the technical reviewers, Sam Kalat, Mike Keith, and Michelle McDonald, for their thoughtful and expert comments and suggestions. Also, special thanks goes to my business partner and long-time friend, Glenn Seemann, who got me started in computer game development. Finally, I want to thank my loving wife and best friend, Helena, for her endless support and encouragement, and our new baby girl, Natalia, for making every day special.

CHAPTER 1

Basic Concepts

As a warm-up, this chapter will cover the most basic of principles that will be used and referred to throughout the remainder of this book. First, I'll introduce Newton's laws of motion, which are very important in the study of mechanics. Then I'll discuss units and measures and explain the importance of keeping track of units in your calculations. You'll also have a look at the units associated with various physical quantities that you'll be studying. After discussing units, I'll define our general coordinate system, which will serve as our standard frame of reference. Then I'll explain the concepts of mass, center of mass, and moment of inertia and show you how to calculate these quantities for a collection, or combination, of masses. Finally, I'll discuss Newton's second law of motion in greater detail and take a quick look at vectors.

Newton's Laws of Motion

In the late 1600s (around 1687), Sir Isaac Newton put forth his philosophies on mechanics in his *Philosophiae Naturalis Principia Mathematia*. In this work, Newton stated the now-famous laws of motion, which are summarized here:

Law I
> A body tends to remain at rest or continue to move in a straight line at constant velocity unless it is acted upon by an external force. This is the concept of inertia.

Law II
> The acceleration of a body is proportional to the resultant force acting on the body, and this acceleration is in the same direction as the resultant force.

Law III
> For every force acting on a body (action) there is an equal and opposite reacting force (reaction) in which the reaction is collinear to the acting force.

These laws form the basis for much of the analysis in the field of mechanics. Of particular interest to us in the study of dynamics is the second law, which is written

$$F = ma$$

where F is the resultant force acting on the body, m is the mass of the body, and a is the linear acceleration of the body's center of gravity. I'll discuss this second law in greater detail later in this chapter, but before that there are some more fundamental issues that must be addressed.

Units and Measures

Over the years of teaching various engineering courses, I've observed that one of the most common mistakes my students make when performing calculations is using the wrong units for a quantity, thus failing to maintain consistent units, resulting in some pretty wacky answers. For example, in the field of ship performance the most commonly misused unit is that for speed, when people forget to convert speed in knots to speed in ft/s or m/s. One knot is equal to 1.69 ft/s, and considering that many quantities of interest in this field are proportional to speed squared, this mistake could result in answers that are as much as 185% off target! So if some of your results look suspicious later on, the first thing you need to do is go back to your formulas and check their dimensional consistency.

To check dimensional consistency, you must take a closer look at your units of measure and consider their component dimensions. I am not talking about 2D or 3D type dimensions here, but rather the basic measurable dimensions that will make up various *derived* units for the physical quantities that we will be using. These basic dimensions are *mass*, *length*, and *time*.

It is important for you to be aware of these dimensions, as well as the combinations of these dimensions that make up the other derived units, so that you can ensure dimensional consistency in your calculations. For example, you know that the weight of an object is measured in units of force, which can be broken down into component dimensions:

$$F = (M)(L/T^2)$$

where M is mass, L is length, and T is time. Does this look familiar? Well, if you consider that the component units for acceleration are (L/T^2), let a be the symbol for acceleration, and let m be the symbol for the mass of an object, you get

$$F = ma$$

which is the famous expression of Newton's second law of motion. I will take a closer look at this equation later.

By no means did I just derive this famous formula. What I did was check its dimensional consistency, albeit in reverse. All it means is that any formulas you develop to represent a force acting on a body had better come out to a consistent set of units in the form of $(M)(L/T^2)$. This might seem trivial at the moment; however, when you start looking at more complicated formulas for the forces acting on a body, you'll want to be able to break down these formulas into their component dimensions so that you can check their dimensional consistency. Later, we will be using actual units, either the English system or the SI (Système International), for our physical quantities, and unless you want to show these values to your gamers, it really does not matter which system you use in your games. Again, what is important is consistency.

To help clarify this point, consider the formula for the friction drag on a body moving through a fluid, such as water:

$$R_f = 1/5 \rho V^2 S C_f$$

In this formula, R_f represents resistance (a force) due to friction, ρ is the density of water, V is the speed of the moving body, S is the submerged surface area of the body, and C_f is an empirical (experimentally determined) drag coefficient for the body. Now rewriting this formula in terms of basic dimensions instead of variables will show that the dimensions on the left side of the formula match exactly the dimensions on the right side. Since R_f is a force, its basic dimensions are of the form

$$(M)(L/T^2)$$

as discussed earlier, which implies that the dimensions of all the terms on the right side of the equation, when combined, must yield an equivalent form. Considering the basic units for density, speed, and surface area:

Density

$$(M)/(L^3)$$

Speed

$$(L)/(T)$$

Area

$$(L^2)$$

and combining these dimensions for the terms $\rho V^2 S$ as follows:

$$[(M)/(L^3)][(L)/(T)]^2[L^2]$$

and collecting the dimensions in the numerator and denominator, we get the following form:

$$(ML^2L^2)/(L^3T^2)$$

Canceling dimensions that appear in both the numerator and denominator yields

$$M(L/T^2)$$

which is consistent with the form shown earlier for resistance, R_f. This exercise also reveals that the empirical term, C_f, for the coefficient of friction must be nondimensional, that is, it is a constant number with no units.

With that, let's take a look at some more common physical quantities that you will be using, along with their corresponding symbols, component dimensions, and units in both the English and SI systems. This information is summarized in Table 1-1.

Table 1-1. *Common Physical Quantities and Units*

Quantity	Symbol	Dimensions	Units, English	Units, SI
Acceleration, linear	a	L/T^2	ft/s^2	m/s^2
Acceleration, angular	α	$radian/T^2$	$radian/s^2$	$radian/s^2$
Density	ρ	M/L^3	$slug/ft^3$	kg/m^3
Force	F	$M(L/T^2)$	pound, lb	newton, N
Kinematic viscosity	ν	L^2/T	ft^2/s	m^2/s
Length	L (or x, y, z)	L	feet, ft	meters, m
Mass	m	M	Slug	kilogram, kg
Moment (torque)	M (see footnote[a])	$M(L^2/T^2)$	ft-lb	N-m
Mass Moment of Inertia	I	ML^2	lb-ft-s²	kg-m²
Pressure	P	$M/(LT^2)$	lb/ft^2	N/m^2
Time	T	T	seconds, s	seconds, s
Velocity, linear	V	L/T	ft/s	m/s
Velocity, angular	ω	$radian/T$	radian/s	radian/s
Viscosity	M	$M/(LT)$	lb s/ft²	N s/m²

[a] In general, I will use a capital M to represent a moment (torque) acting on a body and a lowercase m to represent the mass of a body. If I'm referring to the basic dimension of mass in a general sense, that is, referring to the dimensional components of derived units of measure, I'll use a capital M. Usually, the meanings of these symbols will be obvious based on the context in which they are used; however, I will specify their meanings in cases in which ambiguity may exist.

Coordinate System

Throughout this book I will refer to a standard *right-handed* Cartesian coordinate system when specifying position in 2D or 3D space. In two dimensions I will use the coordinate system shown in Figure 1-1a, in which rotations are measured positive counterclockwise.

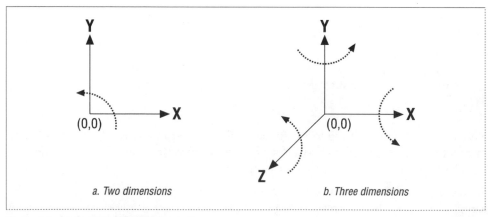

a. Two dimensions   b. Three dimensions

Figure 1-1. *Right-Handed Coordinate System*

In three dimensions I will use the coordinate system shown in Figure 1-1b, in which rotations about the x-axis are positive from positive y to positive z, rotations about the y-axis are positive from positive z to positive x, and rotations about the z-axis are positive from positive x to positive y.

Vectors

Let me take you back for a moment to your high school math class and review the concept of *vectors*. Essentially, a vector is a quantity that has both magnitude and direction. Recall that a *scalar*, unlike a vector, has only magnitude and no direction. In mechanics, quantities such as force, velocity, acceleration, and momentum are vectors, and you must consider both their magnitude and direction. Quantities such as distance, density, and viscosity are scalars.

With regard to notation, I'll use boldface type to indicate a vector quantity, such as force, **F**. When referring to the magnitude only of a vector quantity, I'll use lightface type. For example, the magnitude of the vector force, **F**, is F with components along the coordinate axes, F_x, F_y, and F_z. In the code samples throughout the book, I'll use the * symbol to indicate vector dot product or scalar product operations, depending on the context, and I'll use the ^ symbol to indicate vector cross product operations.

Because we will be using vectors throughout this book, it is important that you refresh your memory on the basic vector operations, such as vector addition, dot product, and cross product. For your convenience, so that you don't have to drag out that old math book, I've included a summary of the basic vector operations in Appendix A. This appendix provides code for a Vector class that contains all the important vector math functionality. Further, I explain how to use specific vector operations, such as the dot product and cross product operations, to perform some common and useful calculations. For example, in dynamics you'll often have to find a vector perpendicular, or *normal*, to a plane or contacting surface; you use the cross product operation for this task. Another common calculation involves finding the shortest distance from a point to a plane in space; here you use the dot product operation. Both of these tasks are described in Appendix A, and I encourage you to review it before delving too deeply in the example code presented throughout the remainder of this book.

Mass, Center of Mass, and Moment of Inertia

The properties of a body, *mass*, *center of mass*, and *moment of intertia*, collectively called *mass properties*, are absolutely crucial to the study of mechanics, as the linear and angular* motion of a body and a body's response to a given force are functions of these mass properties. Thus, to accurately model a body in motion, you need to

---

* Linear motion refers to motion in space without regard to rotation; angular motion specifically refers to the rotation of a body about any axis (the body may or may not be undergoing linear motion at the same time).

know or be capable of calculating these mass properties. Let's look at a few definitions first.

In general, people think of mass as a measure of the amount of matter in a body. For our purposes in the study of mechanics, we can also think of mass as a measure of a body's resistance to motion or a change in its motion. Thus, the greater a body's mass, the harder it will be to set it in motion or change its motion.

In laymen's terms, the center of mass (also known as *center of gravity*) is the point in a body around which the mass of the body is evenly distributed. In mechanics, the center of mass is the point through which any force can act on the body without resulting in a rotation of the body.

Although most people are familiar with the terms *mass* and *center of gravity*, the term *moment of inertia* is not so familiar; however, in mechanics it is equally important. The mass moment of inertia of a body is a quantitative measure of the radial distribution of the mass of a body about a given axis of rotation. Analogous to mass being a measure of a body's resistance to linear motion, mass moment of inertia is a measure of a body's resistance to rotational motion.

Now that you know what these properties mean, let's look at how to calculate each.

For a given body made up of a number of particles, the total mass of the body is simply the sum of the masses of all elemental particles making up the body, where the mass of each elemental particle is its mass density times its volume. Assuming that the body is of uniform density, then the total mass of the body is simply the density of the body times the total volume of the body. This is expressed in the following equation:

$$m = \int \rho \, dV = \rho \int dV$$

In practice, you rarely need to take the volume integral to find the mass of a body, especially considering that many of the bodies we will consider, for example, cars and planes, are not of uniform density. You will simplify these complicated bodies by breaking them down into an ensemble of component bodies of known or easily calculable mass and simply sum the masses of all components to arrive at the total mass.

The calculation of the center of gravity of a body is a little more involved. First, divide the body into an infinite number of elemental masses with the center of each mass specified relative to the reference coordinate system axes. Next, take the *first moment* of each mass about the reference axes and then add up all of these moments. The first moment is the product of the mass times the distance along a given coordinate axis from the origin to the center of mass. Finally, divide this sum of moments by the total mass of the body, yielding the coordinates to the center of mass of the body relative to the reference axes. You must perform this calculation once for each dimension, that is, twice when working in 2D and three times when working in 3D. Here are the equations for the 3D coordinates of the center of mass of a body:

$$x_c = \left\{ \int x_o\, dm \right\} \Big/ m$$

$$y_c = \left\{ \int y_o\, dm \right\} \Big/ m$$

$$z_c = \left\{ \int z_o\, dm \right\} \Big/ m$$

where $(x, y, z)_c$ are the coordinates of the center of mass for the body and $(x, y, z)_o$ are the coordinates to the center of mass of each elemental mass. The quantities $x_o\, dm$, $y_o\, dm$, and $z_o\, dm$ represent the first moments of the elemental mass, dm, about each of the coordinate axes.

Here again, don't worry too much about the integrals in these equations. In practice you will be summing finite numbers of masses, and the formulas will take on the friendlier forms shown here:

$$x_c = \left\{ \sum x_o\, m \right\} \Big/ \left\{ \sum m \right\}$$

$$y_c = \left\{ \sum y_o\, m \right\} \Big/ \left\{ \sum m \right\}$$

$$z_c = \left\{ \sum z_o\, m \right\} \Big/ \left\{ \sum m \right\}$$

Note that you can easily substitute weights for masses in these formulas since the constant acceleration due to gravity, g, would appear in both the numerators and denominators, thus dropping out of the equations. Recall that the weight of an object is its mass times the acceleration due to gravity, g, which is 32.174 ft/s^2 (9.8 m/s^2) at sea level.

The formulas for calculating the total mass and center of gravity for a system of discrete point masses can conveniently be written in vector notation as follows:

$$m_t = \sum m_i$$

$$\mathbf{CG} = \left[\sum (\mathbf{cg_i})(m_i) \right] \Big/ m_t$$

where m_t is the total mass, m_i is the mass of each point mass in the system, $\mathbf{CG}$ is the combined center of gravity, and $\mathbf{cg_i}$ is the location of the center of gravity of each point mass in design, or reference, coordinates. Notice that $\mathbf{CG}$ and $\mathbf{cg_i}$ are shown as vectors, since they denote position in Cartesian coordinates. This is a matter of convenience, since it allows you to take care of the x, y, and z (or just x and y in two dimensions) components in one shot.

In the code samples that follow, let's assume that the point masses making up the body are represented by an array of structures in which each structure contains the point mass's design coordinates and mass. The structure will also contain an element to hold the coordinates of the point mass relative to the combined center of gravity of the rigid body, which will be calculated later.

```
typedef struct _PointMass
{
     float mass;
     Vector designPosition;
     Vector correctedPosition;
} PointMass;

// Assume that _NUMELEMENTS has been defined
PointMass Elements[_NUMELEMENTS];
```

Here's some code that illustrates how to calculate the total mass and combined center of gravity of the elements:

```
int    i;
float  TotalMass;
Vector CombinedCG;
Vector FirstMoment;

TotalMass = 0;
for(i=0; i<_NUMELEMENTS; i++)
     TotalMass+= Elements[I].mass;

FirstMoment = Vector(0, 0, 0);
for(i=0; i<_NUMELEMENTS; i++)
{
     FirstMoment += Element[i].mass * Element[i].designPosition;
}
CombinedCG = FirstMoment / TotalMass;
```

Now that the combined center of gravity location has been found, you can calculate the relative position of each point mass as follows:

```
for(i=0; i<_NUMELEMENTS; i++)
{
     Element[i].correctedPosition = Element[i].designPosition -
                                    CombinedCG;
}
```

To calculate the mass moment of inertia, you need to take the second moment of each elemental mass making up the body about each coordinate axis. Here, the lever is not the distance to the elemental mass centroid along the coordinate axis, as in the calculation for center of mass; it is the perpendicular distance from the coordinate axis, about which we want to calculate the moment of inertia, to the elemental mass centroid. The second moment is then the product of the mass times this distance squared.

Referring to Figure 1-2 for an arbitrary body in three dimensions, when calculating moment of inertia about the x-axis, I_{xx}, this distance, r, will be in the yz-plane such that $r_x^2 = y^2 + z^2$. Similarly, for the moment of inertia about the y-axis, I_{yy}, $r_y^2 = z^2 + x^2$, and for the moment of inertia about the z-axis, I_{zz}, $r_z^2 = x^2 + y^2$.

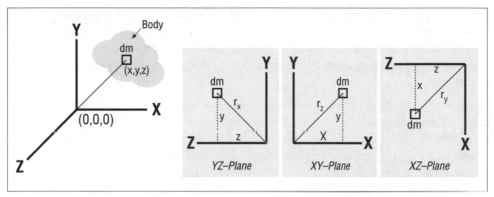

Figure 1-2. Arbitrary Body in 3D

The equations for mass moment of inertia about the coordinate axes in 3D are:

$$I_{xx} = \int r_x^2 \, dm = \int (y^2 + z^2) \, dm$$

$$I_{yy} = \int r_y^2 \, dm = \int (z^2 + x^2) \, dm$$

$$I_{zz} = \int r_z^2 \, dm = \int (x^2 + y^2) \, dm$$

Let's look for a moment at a common situation that arises in practice. Say you are given the moment of inertia, I_o, of a body about an axis, called the *neutral axis*, passing through the center of mass of the body, but you want to know the moment of inertia, I, about an axis some distance from, but parallel to, this neutral axis. In this case, you can use the transfer of axes, or *parallel axis theorem*, to determine the moment of inertia about this new axis. The formula to use is

$$I = I_o + md^2$$

where m is the mass of the body and d is the perpendicular distance between the parallel axes.

There is an important practical observation to make here: the new moment of inertia is a function of the distance separating the axes squared. This means that in cases in which I_o is known to be relatively small and d relatively large, you can safely ignore I_o, since the md^2 term will dominate. You must use your judgment here, of course. This formula for transfer of axes also indicates that the moment of inertia of a body will be at its minimum when calculated about an axis passing through the body's center of gravity. The body's moment of inertia about any parallel axis will always increase by an amount md^2 when calculated about an axis that does not pass through the body's center of mass.

In practice, calculating mass moment of inertia for all but the simplest shapes of uniform density is a complicated endeavor, so we will often approximate the moment of inertia of a body about axes passing through its center of mass by using simple formulas for basic shapes that approximate the object. Further, we will break down complicated bodies into smaller components and take advantage of the fact that I_o may be negligible for certain components, considering its md^2 contribution to the total body's moment of inertia.

Figures 1-3 through 1-7 show some simple solid geometries for which you can easily calculate mass moments of inertia. The mass moment of inertia formulas for each of these simple geometries of homogenous density about the three coordinate axes are shown in the figure captions. Similar formulas for other basic geometries can readily be found in college-level dynamics texts (see the bibliography at the end of this book for a few sources).

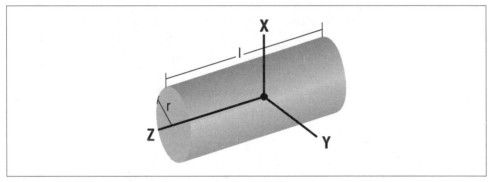

Figure 1-3. Circular Cylinder; $I_{xx} = I_{yy} = (1/4)mr^2 + (1/12)ml^2$; $I_{zz} = (1/2)mr^2$

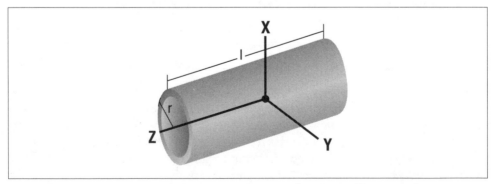

Figure 1-4. Circular Cylindrical Shell; $I_{xx} = I_{yy} = (1/2)mr^2 + (1/12)ml^2$; $I_{zz} = mr^2$

As you can see, these formulas are relatively simple to implement. The trick here is to break up a complex body into a number of smaller, simpler representative geometries whose combination will approximate the complex body's inertia properties. This exercise is largely a matter of judgment considering the desired level of accuracy.

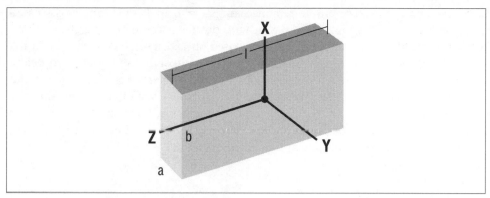

Figure 1-5. Rectangular Cylinder; $I_{xx} = (1/12)m(a^2 + l^2)$; $I_{yy} = (1/12)m(b^2 + l^2)$; $I_{zz} = (1/12)$ $m(a^2 + b^2)$

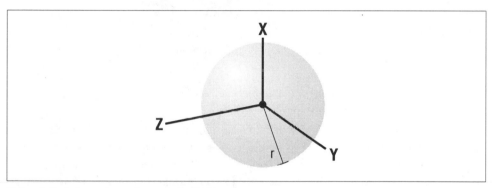

Figure 1-6. Sphere; $I_{xx} - I_{yy} - I_{zz} - (2/5)mr^2$

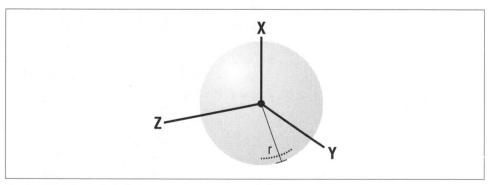

Figure 1-7. Spherical Shell; $I_{xx} = I_{yy} = I_{zz} = (2/3)mr^2$

Let's look at a simple 2D example demonstrating how to apply the formulas discussed in this section. Suppose you're working on a top-down view auto racing game in which you want to simulate the automobile sprite based on 2D rigid body dynamics. At the start of the game the player's car is at the starting line, full of fuel and ready to go. Before starting the simulation, you need to calculate the mass properties of the car, driver, and fuel load at this initial state. In this case, the *body* is made up of three components: the car, driver, and full load of fuel. Later on during the game, however, the mass of this body will change as fuel burns off and the driver gets thrown after a crash. For now, let's focus on the initial condition as illustrated in Figure 1-8.

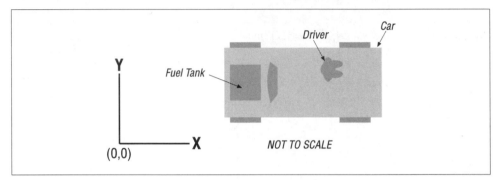

Figure 1-8. Example Body Consisting of Car, Driver, and Fuel

The properties of each component in this example are given in Table 1-2. Note that length is measured along the *x*-axis, width is measured along the *y*-axis, and height would be coming out of the paper. Also note that the coordinates, in the form (x, y), to the centroid of each component are referenced to the global origin.

Table 1-2. Example Properties

Car	Driver (seated)	Fuel
Length = 15.5 ft	Length = 3.0 ft	Length = 1.5 ft
Width = 6.0 ft	Width = 1.5 ft	Width = 3.0 ft
Height = 4.1 ft	Height = 3.5 ft	Height = 1.0 ft
Weight = 3913.0 lb	Weight = 190.0 lb	Density of Fuel = 1.45 slug/ft^3
Centroid = (100, 100) ft	Centroid = (103, 105) ft	Centroid = (93, 100) ft

The first mass property we want to calculate is the mass of the body. This is a simple calculation, since we are already given the weight of the car and the driver. The only other component of weight we need is that of the fuel. Since we are given the mass density of the fuel and the geometry of the tank, we can calculate the volume of the tank and multiply by the density and the acceleration due to gravity to get the weight of the fuel in the tank. This yields 210 lb of fuel as shown here:

$$W_{\text{fuel}} = \rho v g = (1.45 \, \text{slug/ft}^3)(1.5 \, \text{ft})(3 \, \text{ft})(1 \, \text{ft})(32.174 \, \text{ft/s}^2) = 210 \, \text{lb}$$

Now, the total weight of the body is

$$W_{\text{total}} = W_{\text{car}} + W_{\text{driver}} + W_{\text{fuel}}$$
$$W_{\text{total}} = 3913 \, \text{lb} + 190 \, \text{lb} + 210 \, \text{lb} = 4317 \, \text{lb}$$

To get the mass of the body, you simply divide the weight by the acceleration due to gravity:

$$M_{\text{total}} = W_{\text{total}}/g = 4317 \, \text{lb}/(32.174 \, \text{ft/s}^2) = 134.2 \, \text{slugs}$$

A slug is a strange-sounding unit that you might not feel comfortable using, so converting to SI units for mass, we get 1958.2 kg, nearly 2 metric tons.

The next mass property we want is the location of the center of gravity of the body. In this example we will calculate the centroid relative to the global origin and will apply the first moment formula twice, once for the x-coordinate and again for the y-coordinate, as shown here:

$$X_{\text{cg body}} = \{(x_{\text{cg car}})(W_{\text{car}}) + (x_{\text{cg driver}})(W_{\text{driver}}) + (x_{\text{cg fuel}})(W_{\text{fuel}})\}/W_{\text{total}}$$
$$X_{\text{cg body}} = \{(100 \, \text{ft})(3913 \, \text{lb}) + (103 \, \text{ft})(190 \, \text{lb}) + (100 \, \text{ft})(210 \, \text{lb})\}/4317 \, \text{lb}$$
$$X_{\text{cg body}} = 99.7 \, \text{ft}$$

$$Y_{\text{cg body}} = \{(y_{\text{cg car}})(W_{\text{car}}) + (y_{\text{cg driver}})(W_{\text{driver}}) + (y_{\text{cg fuel}})(W_{\text{fuel}})\}/W_{\text{total}}$$
$$Y_{\text{cg body}} = \{(100 \, \text{ft})(3913 \, \text{lb}) + (105 \, \text{ft})(190 \, \text{lb}) + (100 \, \text{ft})(210 \, \text{lb})\}/4317 \, \text{lb}$$
$$Y_{\text{cg body}} = 100.1 \, \text{ft}$$

Notice that we used weight in these equations instead of mass. Remember that we can do this because the acceleration due to gravity built into the weight value is constant and appears in both the numerator and denominator, thus canceling out.

Now it's time to calculate the mass moment of inertia of the body. This is easy enough in this 2D example, since we have only one rotational axis, coming out of the paper, and therefore need to perform the calculation only once. The first step is to calculate the local moment of inertia of each component about its own neutral axis. Given the limited information we have on the geometry and mass distribution of each component, we will make a simplifying approximation by assuming that each component can be represented by a rectangular cylinder and will therefore use the corresponding formula for moment of inertia. In the equations that follow, I'll use a lowercase

w to represent width so as to not confuse it with weight, for which I've been using a capital W.

$$I_{o\,car} = (m/12)(w^2 + L^2)$$
$$I_{o\,car} = ((3913\,\text{lb}/32.174\,\text{ft/s}^2)/12)((6.0\,\text{ft})^2 + (15.5\,\text{ft})^2) = 2800\,\text{lb-s}^2\text{-ft}$$
$$I_{o\,driver} = (m/12)(w^2 + L^2)$$
$$I_{o\,driver} = ((190\,\text{lb}/32.174\,\text{ft/s}^2)/12)((1.5\,\text{ft})^2 + (3.0\,\text{ft})^2) = 5.5\,\text{lb-s}^2\text{-ft}$$
$$I_{o\,fuel} = (m/12)(w^2 + L^2)$$
$$I_{o\,fuel} = ((210\,\text{lb}/32.174\,\text{ft/s}^2)/12)((3.0\,\text{ft})^2 + (1.5\,\text{ft})^2) = 6.1\,\text{lb-s}^2\text{-ft}$$

Since these are the moments of inertia of each component about its own neutral axis, we now need to use the parallel axis theorem to transfer these moments to the neutral axis of the body, which is located at the body center of gravity that we recently calculated. To do this, the distance from the body center of gravity to each component's center of gravity must be found. The distances squared from each component to the body center of gravity are

$$d_{car}^2 = (x_{cg\,car} - X_{cg})^2 + (y_{cg\,car} - Y_{cg})^2$$
$$d_{car}^2 = (100\,\text{ft} - 99.7\,\text{ft})^2 + (100\,\text{ft} - 100.1\,\text{ft})^2 = 0.1\,\text{ft}^2$$
$$d_{driver}^2 = (x_{cg\,driver} - X_{cg})^2 + (y_{cg\,driver} - Y_{cg})^2$$
$$d_{driver}^2 = (103\,\text{ft} - 99.7\,\text{ft})^2 + (105\,\text{ft} - 100.1\,\text{ft})^2 = 34.9\,\text{ft}^2$$
$$d_{fuel}^2 = (x_{cg\,fuel} - X_{cg})^2 + (y_{cg\,fuel} - Y_{cg})^2$$
$$d_{fuel}^2 = (93\,\text{ft} - 99.7\,\text{ft})^2 + (100\,\text{ft} - 100.1\,\text{ft})^2 = 44.9\,\text{ft}^2$$

Now we can apply the parallel axis theorem as follows:

$$I_{cg\,car} = I_o + md^2$$
$$I_{cg\,car} = 2800\,\text{lb-s}^2\text{-ft} + (3913\,\text{lb}/32.174\,\text{ft/s}^2)(0.1\,\text{ft}^2) = 2812\,\text{lb-s}^2\text{-ft}$$
$$I_{cg\,driver} = I_o + md^2$$
$$I_{cg\,driver} = 5.5\,\text{lb-s}^2\text{-ft} + (190\,\text{lb}/32.174\,\text{ft/s}^2)(34.9\,\text{ft}^2) = 211.6\,\text{lb-s}^2\text{-ft}$$
$$I_{cg\,fuel} = I_o + md^2$$
$$I_{cg\,fuel} = 6.1\,\text{lb-s}^2\text{-ft} + (210\,\text{lb}/32.174\,\text{ft/s}^2)(44.9\,\text{ft}^2) = 299.2\,\text{lb-s}^2\text{-ft}$$

Notice the obvious relatively large contribution to I_{cg} for the driver and the fuel due to the md^2 terms. In this example, the local inertia of the driver and fuel are only 2.7% and 2.1%, respectively, of their corresponding md^2 terms.

Finally, we can obtain the total moment of inertia of the body about its own neutral axis by summing the I_{cg} contributions of each component as follows:

$$I_{cg\,total} = I_{cg\,car} + I_{cg\,driver} + I_{cg\,fuel}$$

$$I_{cg\,total} = 2812\,\text{lb-s}^2\text{-ft} + 211.6\,\text{lb-s}^2\text{-ft} + 299.2\,\text{lb-s}^2\text{-ft} = 3322.8\,\text{lb-s}^2\text{-ft}$$

In summary, the mass properties of the body, that is, the combination of the car, driver and full tank of fuel, are shown in Table 1-3.

Table 1-3. Example Summary of Mass Properties

Property	Computed Value
Total Mass (weight)	134.2 slugs (4317 lb)
Combined Center of Mass Location	$(x, y) = (99.7\,\text{ft}, 100.1\,\text{ft})$
Mass Moment of Inertia	3322.8 lb-s^2-ft

It is important that the concepts illustrated in this example are well understood because as we move on to more complicated systems and especially to general motion in 3D, these calculations are only going to get more complicated. Moreover, the motion of the bodies to be simulated are functions of these mass properties, in that mass will determine how these bodies are affected by forces, center of mass will be used to track position, and mass moment of inertia will determine how these bodies rotate under the action of noncentroidal forces.

So far, we have looked at moments of inertia about the three coordinate axes in 3D space. However, in general 3D rigid body dynamics, the body may rotate about any axis, not necessarily one of the coordinate axes, even if the local coordinate axes pass through the body center of mass. This complication implies that we must add a few more terms to our set of I's for a body to handle this generalized rotation. I will address this topic further in the last section of this chapter, but before I do that, I need to go over Newton's second law of motion in detail.

Newton's Second Law of Motion

As I stated in the first section of this chapter, Newton's second law of motion is of particular interest in the study of mechanics. Recall that the equation form of Newton's second law is

$$F = ma$$

where F is the resultant force acting on the body, m is the mass of the body, and a is the linear acceleration of the body center of gravity.

If you rearrange this equation as

$$F/m = a$$

you can see how the mass of a body acts as measure of resistance to motion. Observe here that as mass increases in the denominator for a constant applied force, the resulting acceleration of the body will decrease. It can be said that the body of greater mass offers greater resistance to motion. Similarly, as the mass decreases for a constant applied force, the resulting acceleration of the body will increase, and it can be said that the body of smaller mass offers lower resistance to motion.

Newton's second law also states that the resulting acceleration is in the same direction as the resultant force on the body; therefore, force and acceleration must be treated as vector quantities. In general, there may be more than one force acting on the body at a given time, which means that the resultant force is the vector sum of all forces acting on the body. Thus, you can now write

$$\sum \mathbf{F} = m\mathbf{a}$$

where **a** represents the acceleration vector.

In 3D, the force and acceleration vectors will have x, y, and z components in the Cartesian reference system. In this case, the component equations of motion are written as follows:

$$\sum F_x = ma_x$$
$$\sum F_y = ma_y$$
$$\sum F_z = ma_z$$

An alternative way to interpret Newton's second law is that the sum of all forces acting on a body is equal to the rate of change of the body's momentum over time, which is the derivative of momentum with respect to time. Momentum equals mass times velocity, and since velocity is a vector quantity, so is momentum. Thus,

$$\mathbf{G} = m\mathbf{v}$$

where **G** is linear momentum of the body, m is the body's mass, and **v** is velocity of the center of gravity of the body. The time rate of change of momentum is the derivative of momentum with respect to time:

$$d\mathbf{G}/dt = d/dt(m\mathbf{v})$$

Assuming that the body mass is constant (for now), you can write

$$d\mathbf{G}/dt = m\,d\mathbf{v}/dt$$

Observing that the time rate of change of velocity, $d\mathbf{v}/dt$, is acceleration, we arrive at

$$d\mathbf{G}/dt = m\mathbf{a}$$

and

$$\sum \mathbf{F} = d\mathbf{G}/dt = m\mathbf{a}$$

So far, we have considered only translation of the body without rotation. In generalized 3D motion, you must account for the rotational motion of the body and will therefore need some additional equations to fully describe the body's motion. Specifically, you will require analogous formulas relating the sum of all moments (torque) on a body to the rate of change in its angular momentum over time or the derivative of angular momentum with respect to time. Thus,

$$\sum \mathbf{M}_{cg} = d/dt(\mathbf{H}_{cg})$$

where $\sum \mathbf{M}_{cg}$ is the sum of all moments about the body center of gravity, and $\mathbf{H}$ is the angular momentum of the body. $\mathbf{M}_{cg}$ can be expressed as

$$\mathbf{M}_{cg} = \mathbf{r} \times \mathbf{F}$$

where $\mathbf{F}$ is a force acting on the body, $\mathbf{r}$ is the distance vector from $\mathbf{F}$, perpendicular to the line of action of $\mathbf{F}$, to the center of gravity of the body, and $\times$ is the vector cross product operator.

The angular momentum of the body is the sum of the moments of the momentum of all particles in the body about the axis of rotation, which in this case we assume passes through the center of gravity of the body. This can be expressed as

$$\mathbf{H}_{cg} = \sum \mathbf{r_i} \times m_i(\omega \times \mathbf{r_i})$$

where i represents the ith particle making up the body, ω is the angular velocity of the body about the axis under consideration, and $(\omega \times \mathbf{r_i})$ is the angular momentum of the ith particle, which has a magnitude of $\omega \mathbf{r_i}$. For rotation about a given axis this equation can be rewritten in the form

$$H_{cg} = \int \omega \mathbf{r}^2 \, dm$$

Given that the angular velocity is the same for all particles making up the rigid body, we have

$$H_{cg} = \omega \int \mathbf{r}^2 dm$$

and recalling that moment of inertia, I, equals $\int \mathbf{r}^2 \, dm$, we get

$$H_{cg} = I\omega$$

Taking the derivative with respect to time, we obtain

$$dH_{cg}/dt = d/dt(I\omega) = I d\omega/dt = I\alpha$$

where α is the angular acceleration of the body about a given axis.

Finally we can write

$$\sum \mathbf{M}_{cg} = \mathbf{I}\alpha$$

As I stated in our discussion on mass moment of inertia, we will have to further generalize our formulas for moment of inertia and angular moment to account for general rotation about any body axis. Generally, $\mathbf{M}$ and α will be vector quantities, while $\mathbf{I}$ will be a tensor,* since the magnitude of moment of inertia for a body may vary depending on the axis of rotation.

---

* In this case, $\mathbf{I}$ will be a second rank tensor, which is essentially a 3 × 3 matrix. A vector is actually a tensor of rank 1, and a scalar is actually a tensor of rank zero.

Tensors

A tensor is a mathematical expression that has magnitude and direction, but its magnitude might not be unique, depending on the direction. Tensors are usually used to represent properties of materials when these properties have different magnitudes in different directions. Materials with properties that vary depending on direction are called *anisotropic* (*isotropic* implies the same magnitude in all directions). For example, consider the elasticity (or strength) of two common materials, a sheet of plain paper and a piece of woven or knitted cloth. Take the sheet of paper and, holding it flat, pull on it softly from opposing ends. Try this lengthwise, widthwise, and then along a diagonal. You should observe that the paper seems just as strong, or stretches about the same, in all directions. It is isotropic; therefore, only a single scalar constant is required to represent its strength for all directions.

Now try to find a piece of cloth with a simple, relatively loose weave in which the threads in one direction are perpendicular to the threads in the other direction. Most neckties will do. Try the same pull test that you conducted with the sheet of paper, pulling the cloth along each thread direction and then at a diagonal to the threads. You should observe that the cloth stretches more when you pull it along a diagonal to the threads than when you pull it along the direction of the run of the threads. The cloth is anisotropic in that it exhibits different elastic (or strength) properties depending on the direction of pull; thus, a collection of vector quantities (a tensor) is required to represent its strength for all directions.

In the context of the subject of this book, the property under consideration is a body's moment of inertia, which in 3D requires nine components to fully describe it for any arbitrary rotation. Moment of inertia is not a strength property as in the paper and cloth example, but it is a property of the body that varies with the axis of rotation. Since nine components are required, moment of inertia will be generalized in the form of a 3×3 matrix (*second-rank* tensor) later in this book.

I need to mention a few things at this point regarding coordinates, which will become important when you're writing your real-time simulator. Both the equations of motion have, so far, been written in terms of global coordinates and not body-fixed coordinates. That's okay for the linear equation of motion, in which you can track the body's location and velocity in the global coordinate system. However, from a computational point of view, you don't want to do that for the angular equation of motion for bodies that rotate in three dimensions.* The reason why is because the moment of inertia term, when calculated with respect to global coordinates, actually changes depending on the body's position and orientation. This means that during your simulation you'll have to recalculate the inertia matrix (and its inverse) a lot, which is computationally inefficient. It's better to rewrite the equations of motion in terms of local (attached to the body) coordinates so that you have to calculate the inertia matrix (and its inverse) only once, at the start of your simulation.

---

* In two dimensions it's okay to leave the angular equation of motion as it is shown here, since the moment of inertia term is simply a constant scalar quantity.

In general, the time derivative of a vector, **V**, in a fixed (nonrotating) coordinate system is related to its time derivative in a rotating coordinate system by the following equation:

$$(d\mathbf{V}/dt)_{\text{fixed}} = (d\mathbf{V}/dt)_{\text{rot}} + (\boldsymbol{\omega} \times \mathbf{V})$$

The $(\boldsymbol{\omega} \times \mathbf{V})$ term represents the difference between **V**'s time derivative as measured in the fixed coordinate system and **V**'s time derivative as measured in the rotating coordinate system. We can use this relation to rewrite the angular equation of motion in terms of local, or body-fixed, coordinates. Further, the vector to consider is the angular momentum vector $\mathbf{H}_{\text{cg}}$. Recall that $\mathbf{H}_{\text{cg}} = \mathbf{I}\boldsymbol{\omega}$, and its time derivative is equal to the sum of moments about the body's center of gravity. These are the pieces you need for the angular equation of motion, and you can get to that equation by substituting $\mathbf{H}_{\text{cg}}$ in place of **V** in the derivative transform relation as follows:

$$\sum \mathbf{M}_{\text{cg}} = d\mathbf{H}_{\text{cg}}/dt = \mathbf{I}(d\boldsymbol{\omega}/dt) + (\boldsymbol{\omega} \times (\mathbf{I}\boldsymbol{\omega}))$$

where the moments, inertia tensor, and angular velocity are all expressed in local (body) coordinates. Although this equation looks a bit more complicated than the one I showed you earlier, it is much more convenient to use, since **I** will be constant throughout your simulation (unless your body's mass or geometry changes for some reason during your simulation) and the moments are relatively easy to calculate in local coordinates. You'll put this equation to use later, in Chapter 15, when I show you how to develop a simple 3D rigid body simulator.

Inertia Tensor

Take another look at the angular equation of motion and notice that I wrote the inertia term, **I**, in bold, implying that it is a vector. You've already seen that for 2D problems, this inertia term reduces to a scalar quantity representing the moment of inertia about the single axis of rotation. However, in three dimensions there are three coordinate axes about which the body can rotate. Moreover, in generalized three dimensions the body can rotate about any arbitrary axis. Thus, for 3D problems, **I**, is actually a 3 × 3 matrix, a second-rank tensor.

To understand where this inertia matrix comes from, you must look again at the angular momentum equation:

$$\mathbf{H}_{\text{cg}} = \int (\mathbf{r} \times (\boldsymbol{\omega} \times \mathbf{r}))dm$$

where $\boldsymbol{\omega}$ is the angular velocity of the body, **r** (see Figure 1-9) is the distance from the body's center of gravity to each elemental mass, dm, and $(\mathbf{r} \times (\boldsymbol{\omega} \times \mathbf{r}))dm$ is the angular momentum of each elemental mass. The term in parentheses is called a triple vector product and can be expanded by taking the vector cross products; **r** and $\boldsymbol{\omega}$ are vectors that can be written as follows:

$$\mathbf{r} = x\mathbf{i} + y\mathbf{j} + z\mathbf{k}$$
$$\boldsymbol{\omega} = \omega_x\mathbf{i} + \omega_y\mathbf{j} + \omega_z\mathbf{k}$$

Expanding the triple vector product term yields

$$\mathbf{H}_{cg} = \int \{[(y^2 + z^2)\boldsymbol{\omega}_x - xy\boldsymbol{\omega}_y - xz\boldsymbol{\omega}_z]\mathbf{i} + [-yx\boldsymbol{\omega}_x + (z^2 + x^2)\boldsymbol{\omega}_y - yz\boldsymbol{\omega}_z]\mathbf{j}$$
$$+ [-zx\boldsymbol{\omega}_x - zy\boldsymbol{\omega}_y + (x^2 + y^2)\boldsymbol{\omega}z]\mathbf{k}\} \, dm$$

To simplify this equation, let's replace a few terms by letting

$$I_{xx} = \int (y^2 + z^2) \, dm$$

$$I_{yy} = \int (z^2 + x^2) \, dm$$

$$I_{zz} = \int (x^2 + y^2) \, dm$$

$$I_{xy} = I_{yx} = \int (xy) \, dm$$

$$I_{xz} = I_{zx} = \int (xz) \, dm$$

$$I_{yz} = I_{zy} = \int (yz) \, dm$$

Substituting these I-variables, some of which should look familiar to you, back into the expanded equation yields

$$\mathbf{H}_{cg} = [I_{xx}\boldsymbol{\omega}_x - I_{xy}\boldsymbol{\omega}_y - I_{xz}\boldsymbol{\omega}_z]\mathbf{i} + [-I_{yx}\boldsymbol{\omega}_x + I_{yy}\boldsymbol{\omega}_y - I_{yz}\boldsymbol{\omega}_z]\mathbf{j}$$
$$+ [-I_{zx}\boldsymbol{\omega}_x - I_{zy}\boldsymbol{\omega}_y + I_{zz}\boldsymbol{\omega}_z]\mathbf{k}$$

Simplifying this a step further by letting $\mathbf{I}$ be a matrix:

$$\mathbf{I} = \begin{matrix} I_{xx} - I_{xy} - I_{xz} \\ -I_{yx} \; I_{yy} - I_{yz} - I_{zx} - I_{zy} \; I_{zz} \end{matrix}$$

yields the following equation:

$$\mathbf{H}_{cg} = \mathbf{I}\boldsymbol{\omega}$$

You already know that $\mathbf{I}$ represents the moment of inertia, and the terms that should look familiar to you already are the moment of inertia terms about the three coordinate axes, I_{xx}, I_{yy}, and I_{zz}. The other terms are called *products of inertia*:

$$I_{xy} = I_{yx} = \int (xy) \, dm$$

$$I_{xz} = I_{zx} = \int (xz) \, dm$$

$$I_{yz} = I_{zy} = \int (yz) \, dm$$

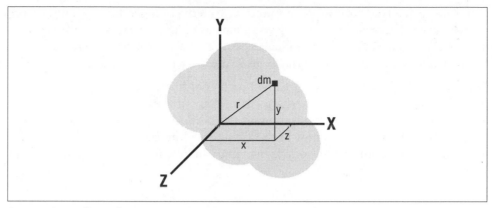

Figure 1-9. Products of Inertia

Just like the parallel axis theorem, there's a similar transfer of axis formula that applies to products of inertia:

$$I_{xy} = I_{o(xy)} + md_x d_y$$
$$I_{xz} = I_{o(xz)} + md_x d_z$$
$$I_{yz} = I_{o(yz)} + md_y d_z$$

where the I_o terms represent the local products of inertia, that is, the products of inertia of the object about axes that pass through its own center of gravity, m is the object's mass, and the d terms are the distances between the coordinate axes that pass through the object's center of gravity and a parallel set of axes some distance away (see Figure 1-10).

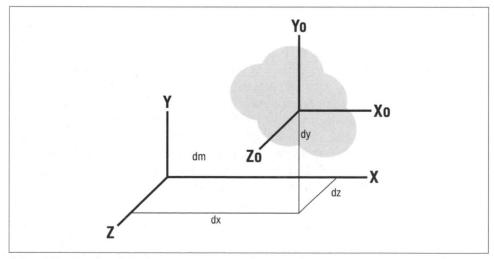

Figure 1-10. Transfer of Axes

You'll notice that I did not give you any product of inertia formulas for the simple shapes shown earlier. The reason is that the given moments of inertia were about the *principal axes* for these shapes. For any body there exists a set of axes oriented with respect to the body such that the product of inertia terms in the inertia tensor are all zero.

For the simple geometries shown earlier, each coordinate axis represented a plane of symmetry, and products of inertia go to zero about axes that represent planes of symmetry. You can see this by examining the product of inertia formulas, where, for example, all of the (xy) terms in the integral will be cancelled out by each corresponding $-(xy)$ term if the body is symmetric about the y-axis as illustrated in Figure 1-11.

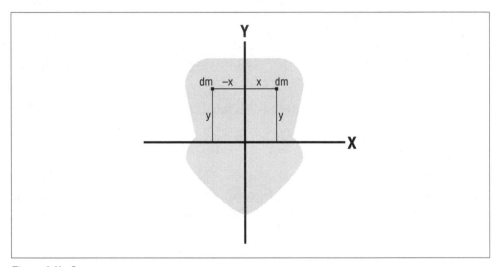

Figure 1-11. Symmetry

For composite bodies, however, there might not be any planes of symmetry, and the orientation of the principal axes will not be obvious. Further, you might not even want to use the principal axes as your local coordinate axes for a given rigid body, since it might be awkward to do so. For example, take the airplane in the `FlightSim` example that I discuss in Chapter 7, in which you'll have the local coordinate design axes running, relative to the pilot, fore and aft, up and down, and left and right. This orientation is convenient for locating the parts of the wings, tail, elevators, and so on with respect to each other, but these axes don't necessarily represent the principal axes of the airplane. The result is that you'll use axes that are convenient and deal with the nonzero products of inertia (which, by the way, can be either positive or negative).

I already showed you how to calculate the combined moments of inertia for a composite body made up of a few smaller elements. Accounting for the product of inertia terms follows the same procedure except that, typically, your elements are such that their local product of inertia terms are zero. This is the case only if you represent your elements by simple geometries such as point masses, spheres, rectangles, and the like. That being the case, the main contribution to the rigid body's products of inertia will be due the transfer of axes terms for each element.

Before looking at some sample code, let's first revise the element structure to include a new term to hold the element's local moment of inertia as follows:

```
typedef struct _PointMass
{
    float mass;
    Vector designPosition;
    Vector correctedPosition;
    Vector localInertia;
} PointMass;
```

Here, I'm using a vector to represent the three local moment of inertia terms, and I'm also assuming that the local products of inertia are zero for each element.

The following code sample shows how to calculate the inertia tensor given the component elements:

```
float       Ixx, Iyy, Izz, Ixy, Ixz, Iyz;
Matrix3x3   InertiaTensor;

Ixx = 0;    Iyy = 0;    Izz = 0;
Ixy = 0;    Ixz = 0;    Iyz = 0;

for (i = 0; i<_NUMELEMENTS; i++)
{
    Ixx += Element[i].LocalInertia.x +
        Element[i].mass * (Element[i].correctedPosition.y *
        Element[i].correctedPosition.y +
        Element[i].correctedPosition.z *
        Element[i].correctedPosition.z);

    Iyy += Element[i].LocalInertia.y +
        Element[i].mass * (Element[i].correctedPosition.z *
        Element[i].correctedPosition.z +
        Element[i].correctedPosition.x *
        Element[i].correctedPosition.x);

    Izz += Element[i].LocalInertia.z +
        Element[i].mass * (Element[i].correctedPosition.x *
        Element[i].correctedPosition.x +
        Element[i].correctedPosition.y *
        Element[i].correctedPosition.y);

    Ixy += Element[i].mass * (Element[i].correctedPosition.x *
        Element[i].correctedPosition.y);

    Ixz += Element[i].mass * (Element[i].correctedPosition.x *
        Element[i].correctedPosition.z);

    Iyz += Element[i].mass * (Element[i].correctedPosition.y *
        Element[i].correctedPosition.z);
}

// e11 stands for element on row 1 column 1, e12 for row 1 column 2, etc.
```

```
InertiaTensor.e11 = Ixx;
InertiaTensor.e12 = -Ixy;
InertiaTensor.e13 = -Ixz;

InertiaTensor.e21 = -Ixy;
InertiaTensor.e22 = Iyy;
InertiaTensor.e23 = -Iyz;

InertiaTensor.e31 = -Ixz;
InertiaTensor.e32 = -Iyz;
InertiaTensor.e33 = Izz;
```

Note that the inertia tensor is calculated about axes that pass through the combined center of gravity for the rigid body, so be sure to use the corrected coordinates for each element relative to the combined center of gravity when applying the transfer of axes formulas.

I should also mention that this calculation is for the inertia tensor in body-fixed coordinates, or local coordinates. As I discussed earlier in this chapter, it is better to rewrite the angular equation of motion in terms of local coordinates and use the local inertia tensor to save some number crunching in your real-time simulation.

CHAPTER 2

Kinematics

In this chapter I'll explain the fundamental aspects of the subject of kinematics. Specifically, I'll explain the concepts of linear and angular displacement, velocity, and acceleration. I've prepared an example program for this chapter that shows you how to implement the kinematic equations for particle motion. After discussing particle motion, I go on to explain the specific aspects of rigid body motion. This chapter, along with the next chapter on force, are prerequisites to understanding the subject of kinetics, which you'll study in Chapter 4.

Introduction

In the preface I told you that kinematics is the study of the motion of bodies without regard to the forces acting on the body. Therefore, in kinematics attention will be focused on position, velocity, and acceleration of a body; how these properties are related; and how they change over time.

Here, you'll look at two types of bodies: particles and rigid bodies. In the preface I stated that a rigid body is a system of particles that remain at fixed distances from each other with no relative translation or rotation among them. In other words, a rigid body does not change its shape as it moves, or any changes in the body's shape are so small or unimportant that they can safely be neglected. When considering a rigid body, its dimensions and orientation are important, and you must consider both the body's linear motion and its angular motion.

On the other hand, a particle is a body that has mass, but its dimensions are negligible or unimportant in the problem being investigated. For example, when considering the path of a projectile or a rocket over a great distance, you can safely ignore the body's dimensions in analyzing its trajectory. When you are considering a particle, its linear motion is important, but the angular motion of the particle itself is not. It's as though, when looking at a problem, you are zooming way out, looking at the big picture, so to speak, as opposed to zooming in on the body as you do when looking at the rotation of rigid bodies.

Whether you are looking at problems involving particles or rigid bodies, there are some important kinematic properties common to both. These are, of course, the object's position, velocity, and acceleration. The next section discusses these properties in detail.

Velocity and Acceleration

In general, velocity is a vector quantity that has magnitude and direction. The magnitude of velocity is speed. Speed is a familiar term: it's how fast your speedometer says you're going when you drive your car down the highway. Formally, speed is the rate of travel, or the ratio of distance traveled to the time it took to travel that distance. In math terms you can write

$$v = \Delta s / \Delta t$$

where v is speed, the magnitude of velocity $\mathbf{v}$, and Δs is distance traveled over the time interval Δt. Note that this relation reveals that the units for speed are composed of the basic dimensions length divided by time, L/T. Some common units for speed are feet per second, *ft/s*; miles per hour, *mi/h*; and meters per second, *m/s*.

Here's a simple example: A car is driving down a straight road; it passes marker 1 at time t_1 and marker 2 at time t_2, where t_1 equals 0 s and t_2 equals 1.136 s. The distance between these two markers, s, is 100 ft (see Figure 2-1). Calculate the speed of the car.

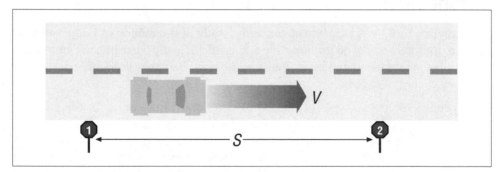

Figure 2-1. Example: Car Speed

You are given that s equals 100 ft; therefore, Δs equals 100 ft, and Δ_t equals $t_2 - t_1$, or 1.136 s. The speed of the car over this distance is

$$v = \Delta s / \Delta t = 100\,\text{ft}/1.136\,s = 88.03\ \text{ft/s}$$

which is approximately 60 mi/h. This is a simple one-dimensional example, but it brings up an important point, which is that the speed just calculated is the average speed of the car over that distance. You don't know anything at this point about the car's acceleration or whether or not it is traveling at a constant 60 mi/h. It could very well be that the car was accelerating (or decelerating) over that 100-ft distance.

To more precisely analyze the motion of the car in this example, you need to understand the concept of *instantaneous* velocity. Instantaneous velocity is the specific velocity at a given instant in time, not over a large time interval as in the car example. This means that you need to look at very small Δt's. In math terms, you must consider the limit as Δt approaches zero, that is, as Δt gets infinitesimally small. This is written as follows:

$$v = \lim_{\Delta t \to 0}(\Delta s / \Delta t)$$

In differential terms, velocity is the derivative of displacement (change in position) with respect to time,

$$v = ds/dt$$

You can rearrange this relationship and integrate over the intervals from s_1 to s_2 and t_1 to t_2 as shown here:

$$v \, dt = ds$$
$$\int_{s_1}^{s_2} ds = \int_{t_1}^{t_2} v \, dt$$
$$s_2 - s_1 = \Delta s = \int_{t_1}^{t_2} v \, dt$$

This relation shows that displacement is the integral of velocity over time. This gives you a way of working back and forth between displacement and velocity.

In kinematics an important distinction is made between displacement and distance traveled. In one dimension, displacement is the same as distance traveled; however, when considering vectors in space, displacement is actually the vector from the initial position to the final position without regard to the path traveled; displacement is the difference between the starting position coordinates and the ending position coordinates. Thus, you need to be careful when calculating average velocity given displacement if the path from the starting position to the final position is not a straight line. When Δt is very small (as it approaches zero), displacement and distance traveled are the same.

Another important kinematic property is acceleration, which should also be familiar to you. Referring to your driving experience, you know that acceleration is the rate at which you can increase your speed. Your friend who boasts that his brand-new XYZ 200I can go from *0 to 60* in 4.2 seconds is referring to acceleration. Specifically, he is referring to average acceleration.

Formally, average acceleration is the rate of change in velocity, or Δv over Δt:

$$a = \Delta v / \Delta t$$

Taking the limit as Δt goes to zero gives the instantaneous acceleration:

$$a = \lim_{\Delta t \to 0} \Delta v / \Delta t$$
$$a = dv/dt$$

Thus, acceleration is the time rate of change in velocity, or the derivative of velocity with respect to time.

Rearranging and integrating yield

$$dv = a\,dt$$

$$\int_{v_1}^{v_2} dv = \int_{t_1}^{t_2} a\,dt$$

$$v_2 - v_1 = \Delta v = \int_{t_1}^{t_2} a\,dt$$

This relationship provides a means to work back and forth between velocity and acceleration.

Thus, the relationships between displacement, velocity, and acceleration are

$$a = dv/dt = d^2s/dt^2$$

and

$$v\,dv = a\,ds$$

This is the kinematic differential equation of motion. In the next few sections you'll have a look at some examples of the application of these equations for some common classes of problems in kinematics.

Constant Acceleration

One of the simplest classes of problems in kinematics involves constant acceleration. A good example of this sort of problem involves the acceleration due to gravity, g, on objects moving relatively near the earth's surface where the gravitational acceleration is a constant 32.174 ft/s^2 (9.8 m/s^2). Having constant acceleration makes integration over time relatively easy, since you can pull the acceleration constant out of the integrand, leaving just dt.

Integrating the relationship between velocity and acceleration described earlier when acceleration is constant yields the following equation for instantaneous velocity:

$$\int_{v_1}^{v_2} dv = \int_{t_1}^{t_2} a\,dt$$

$$\int_{v_1}^{v_2} dv = a \int_{t_1}^{t_2} dt$$

$$v_2 - v_1 = a \int_{t_1}^{t_2} dt$$

$$v_2 - v_1 = a(t_2 - t_1)$$

$$v_2 = at_2 - at_1 + v_1$$

When t_1 equals zero, you can rewrite this equation in the following form:

$$v_2 = at_2 + v_1$$

$$v_2 = v_1 + at_2$$

This simple equation allows you to calculate the instantaneous velocity at any given time by knowing the elapsed time, the initial velocity, and the constant acceleration.

You can also derive an equation for velocity as a function of displacement instead of time by considering the kinematic differential equation of motion:

$$v \, dv = a \, ds$$

Integrating both sides of this equation yields an alternative function for instantaneous velocity as follows:

$$\int_{v_1}^{v_2} v \, dv = a \int_{s_1}^{s_2} ds$$
$$(v_2^2 - v_1^2)/2 = a(s_2 - s_1)$$
$$v_2^2 = 2a(s_2 - s_1) + v_1^2$$

You can derive a similar formula for displacement as a function of velocity, acceleration, and time by integrating the differential equation

$$v \, dt = ds$$

with the formula derived earlier for instantaneous velocity,

$$v_2 = v_1 + at$$

substituted for v. Doing so yields the formula

$$s_2 = s_1 + v_1 t + (at^2)/2$$

In summary, the three kinematic equations derived above are

$$v_2 = v_1 + at_2$$
$$v_2^2 = 2a(s_2 - s_1) + v_1^2$$
$$s_2 = s_1 + v_1 t + (at^2)/2$$

Remember, these equations are valid only when acceleration is constant. Note that acceleration can be zero or even negative in cases in which the body is decelerating.

You can rearrange these equations by algebraically solving for different variables, and you can also derive other handy equations using the same approach that I just showed you. For your convenience I've provided some other useful kinematic equations, for constant acceleration problems, in Table 2-1.

In cases in which acceleration is not constant but is some function of time, velocity, or position, you can substitute the function for acceleration into the differential equations shown earlier to derive new equations for instantaneous velocity and displacement. The next section considers such a problem.

Table 2-1. Constant Acceleration Kinematic Formulas

To Find	Given These	Use This
a	$\Delta t, v_1, v_2$	$a = (v_2 - v_1)/\Delta t$
a	$\Delta t, v_1, \Delta s$	$a = (2\Delta s - 2v_1\Delta t)/(\Delta t)^2$
a	$v_1, v_2, \Delta s$	$a = (v_2^2 - v_1^2)/(2\Delta s)$
Δs	a, v_1, v_2	$\Delta s = (v_2^2 - v_1^2)/(2a)$
Δs	$\Delta t, v_1, v_2$	$\Delta s = (\Delta t / 2)(v_1 + v_2)$
Δt	a, v_1, v_2	$\Delta t = (v_2 - v_1)/a$
Δt	$a, v_1, \Delta s$	$\Delta t = \left(\sqrt{v_1^2 + 2a\Delta s} - v_1 \right) \Big/ a$
Δt	$v_1, v_2, \Delta s$	$\Delta t = (2\Delta s)/(v_1 + v_2)$
v_1	$\Delta t, a, v_2$	$v_1 = v_2 - a\Delta t$
v_1	$\Delta t, a, \Delta s$	$v_1 = \Delta s / \Delta t - (a\Delta t)/2$
v_1	$a, v_2, \Delta s$	$v_1 = \sqrt{v_2^2 - 2a\Delta s}$

Nonconstant Acceleration

A common situation that arises in real-world problems is one in which drag forces act on a body in motion. Typically, drag forces are proportional to velocity squared. Recalling the equation of Newton's second law of motion, $F = ma$, you can deduce that the acceleration induced by these drag forces is also proportional to velocity squared.

Later, I'll show you some techniques that will allow you to calculate this sort of drag force, but for now, let the functional form of drag-induced acceleration be

$$a = -kv^2$$

where k is a constant and the negative sign indicates that this acceleration acts in the direction opposing the body's velocity. Now substituting this formula for acceleration into the equation above and then rearranging yields

$$a = dv/dt$$
$$-kv^2 = dv/dt$$
$$-k\,dt = dv/v^2$$

If you integrate the right side of this equation from v_1 to v_2 and the left side from 0 to t and then solve for v_2, you'll get a formula for the instantaneous velocity as a function of the initial velocity and time as shown here:

$$-k \int_0^t dt = \int_{v_1}^{v_2} (1/v^2)\, dv$$
$$-kt = 1/v_1 - 1/v_2$$
$$v_2 = v_1/(1 + v_1kt)$$

If you substitute this equation for v in the relation $v = ds/dt$ and integrate again, you'll end up with a new equation for displacement as a function of initial velocity and time. This procedure is shown below:

$$v \, dt = ds, \quad \text{where} \quad v = v_1/(1 + v_1 kt)$$

$$\int_0^t v \, dt = \int_{s_1}^{s_2} ds$$

$$\int_0^t [v_1/(1 + v_1 kt)] \, dt = \int_{s_1}^{s_2} ds$$

$$\ln(1 + v_1 kt)/k = s_2 - s_1$$

If s_1 equals zero, then

$$s = \ln(1 + v_1 kt)/k$$

Note that in this equation ln is the natural logarithm operator.

This example demonstrates the relative complexity of nonconstant acceleration problems versus constant acceleration problems. It's a fairly simple example in which you are able to derive closed-form equations for velocity and displacement. In practice, however, there may be several different types of forces acting on a given body in motion, which could make the expression for induced acceleration quite complicated. This complexity would render a closed-form solution like the one above impossible to obtain unless you impose some simplifying restrictions on the problem, forcing you to rely on other solution techniques such as numerical integration. I'll talk about this sort of problem in greater depth in Chapter 11.

2D Particle Kinematics

When considering motion in one dimension, that is, when the motion is restricted to a straight line, it is easy enough to directly apply the formulas derived earlier to determine instantaneous velocity, acceleration, and displacement. However, in two dimensions, with motion possible in any direction in a given plane, you must consider the kinematic properties of velocity, acceleration, and displacement as vectors.

Using rectangular coordinates in the standard Cartesian coordinate system, you must account for the x- and y-components of displacement, velocity, and acceleration. Essentially, you can treat the x- and y-components separately and then superimpose these components to define the corresponding vector quantities.

To help keep track of these x- and y-components, let $\mathbf{i}$ and $\mathbf{j}$ be unit vectors in the x- and y-directions, respectively. Now you can write the kinematic property vectors in terms of their components as follows:

$$\mathbf{v} = v_x \mathbf{i} + v_y \mathbf{j}$$
$$\mathbf{a} = a_x \mathbf{i} + a_y \mathbf{j}$$

If x is the displacement in the $x$direction and y is the displacement in the $y$direction, then the displacement vector is

$$\mathbf{s} = x\mathbf{i} + y\mathbf{j}$$

It then follows that

$$\mathbf{v} = d\mathbf{s}/dt = dx/dt\,\mathbf{i} + dy/dt\,\mathbf{j}$$
$$\mathbf{a} = d\mathbf{v}/dt = d^2\mathbf{s}/dt = d^2x/dt\,\mathbf{i} + d^2y/dt\,\mathbf{j}$$

Consider a simple example in which you're writing a hunting game and you need to figure out the vertical drop in a fired bullet from its aim point to the point at which it actually hits the target. In this example, assume that there is no wind and no drag on the bullet as it flies through the air (I'll deal with wind and drag on projectiles in Chapter 6). These assumptions reduce the problem to one of constant acceleration, which in this case is that due to gravity. It is this gravitational acceleration that is responsible for the drop in the bullet as it travels from the rifle to the target. Figure 2-2 illustrates the problem.

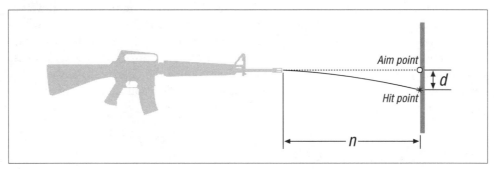

Figure 2-2. 2D Kinematics Example Problem

Let the origin of the 2D coordinate system be at the end of the rifle, with the x-axis pointing toward the target and the y-axis pointing upward. Positive displacements along the x-axis are toward the target, and positive displacements along the y-axis are upward. This implies that the gravitational acceleration will act in the negative y-direction.

Treating the x- and y-components separately allows you to break the problem up into small, easy-to-manage pieces. Looking at the x-component first, you know that the bullet will leave the rifle with an initial muzzle velocity v_m in the x-direction, and since we are neglecting drag, this speed will be constant. Thus,

$$a_x = 0$$
$$v_x = v_m$$
$$x = v_x t = v_m t$$

Now looking at the y-component, you know that the initial speed in the y-direction, as the bullet leaves the rifle, is zero, but the y acceleration is $-g$ (due to gravity). Thus,

$$a_y = -g = dv_y/dt$$
$$v_y = a_y t = -gt$$
$$y = (1/2)a_y t^2 = -(1/2)gt^2$$

The displacement, velocity, and acceleration vectors can now be written as follows:

$$\mathbf{s} = (v_m t)\mathbf{i} - (1/2gt^2)\mathbf{j}$$
$$\mathbf{v} = (v_m)\mathbf{i} - (gt)\mathbf{j}$$
$$\mathbf{a} = -(g)\mathbf{j}$$

These equations give the instantaneous displacement, velocity, and acceleration for any given time instant between the time the bullet leaves the rifle and the time it hits the target. The magnitudes of these vectors give the total displacement, velocity, and acceleration at a given time. For example,

$$s = \sqrt{(v_m t)^2 + (1/2gt^2)^2}$$
$$v = \sqrt{(v_m)^2 + (gt)^2}$$
$$a = \sqrt{g^2} = g$$

To calculate the bullet's vertical drop at the instant the bullet hits the target, you must first calculate the time required to reach the target, and then you can use that time to calculate the y-component of displacement, which is the vertical drop. Here are the formulas to use:

$$t_{hit} = x_{hit}/v_m = n/v_m$$
$$d = y_{hit} = -(1/2)g(t_{hit})^2$$

where n is the distance from the rifle to the target and d is the vertical drop of the bullet at the target.

If the distance to the target, n, equals 500 meters (m) and the muzzle velocity, v_m, equals 800 m/s, then the equations for t_{hit} and d give

$$t_{hit} = 0.625 \text{ s}$$
$$d = 1.9 \text{ m}$$

These results tell you that to hit the intended target at that range, you'll need to aim for a point about 2 m above it.

3D Particle Kinematics

Extending the kinematic property vectors to three dimensions is not very difficult. It simply involves the addition of one more component to the vector representations shown in the previous section on 2D kinematics. Introducing **k** as the unit vector in the z-direction, you can now write

$$\mathbf{s} = x\mathbf{i} + y\mathbf{j} + z\mathbf{k}$$
$$\mathbf{v} = d\mathbf{s}/dt = dx/dt\,\mathbf{i} + dy/dt\,\mathbf{j} + dz/dt\,\mathbf{k}$$
$$\mathbf{a} = d^2\mathbf{s}/dt = d^2x/dt\,\mathbf{i} + d^2y/dt\,\mathbf{j} + d^2z/dt\,\mathbf{k}$$

Instead of treating two components separately and then superimposing them, you now treat three components separately and superimpose these. This is best illustrated by an example.

Suppose that instead of a hunting game, you're now writing a game that involves the firing of a cannon from, say, a battleship onto a target some distance away, for example, another ship or an inland target such as a building. To add complexity to this activity for your user, you'll want to give him control of several factors that affect the shell's trajectory, namely, the firing angle of the cannon, both horizontal and vertical angles, and the muzzle velocity of the shell, which is controlled by the amount of powder packed behind the shell when it is loaded into the cannon. The situation is set up in Figure 2-3.

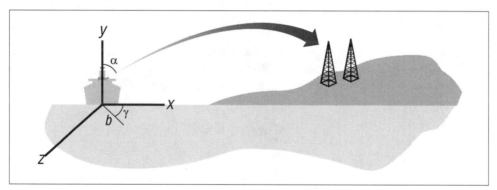

Figure 2-3. 3D Kinematics Example Problem

I'll show you how to set up the kinematic equations for this problem by treating each vector component separately at first and then combining these components.

x-Components

The x-components here are similar to that shown in the rifle example of the previous section in that there is no drag force acting on the shell; thus, the x-component of acceleration is zero, which means that the x-component of velocity is constant and equal to the x-component of the muzzle velocity as the shell leaves the cannon. Note that since the cannon barrel may not be horizontal, you'll have to compute the x-component of the muzzle velocity, which is a function of the direction in which the cannon is aimed.

The muzzle velocity vector is

$$\mathbf{v}_m = v_{mx}\mathbf{i} + v_{my}\mathbf{j} + v_{mz}\mathbf{k}$$

and you are given only the direction of $\mathbf{v}_m$ as determined by the direction in which the user points the cannon and its magnitude as determined by the amount of powder the user chooses to pack into the cannon. To calculate the components of the muzzle velocity, you need to develop some equations for these components in terms of the direction angles of the cannon and the magnitude of the muzzle velocity.

You can use the direction cosines of a vector to determine the velocity components as follows:

$$\cos\theta_x = v_{mx}/v_m$$
$$\cos\theta_y = v_{my}/v_m$$
$$\cos\theta_z = v_{mz}/v_m$$

Refer to *Appendix A* for a description and illustration of vector direction cosines.

Since the initial muzzle velocity vector direction is the same as the direction in which the cannon is aimed, you can treat the cannon as a vector with a magnitude of L, its length, and pointing in a direction defined by the angles given in this problem. Using the cannon length, L, and its components instead of muzzle velocity in the equations for direction cosines gives

$$\cos\theta_x = L_x/L$$
$$\cos\theta_y = L_y/L$$
$$\cos\theta_z = L_z/L$$

In this example you are given the angles α and γ (see Figure 2-4) that define the cannon orientation.

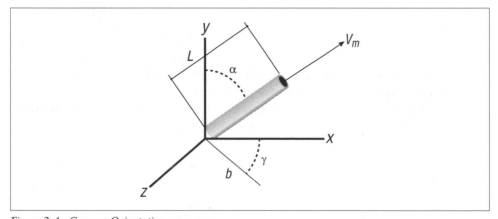

Figure 2-4. Cannon Orientation

Using these angles, it follows that the projection, b, of the cannon length, L, onto the xz-plane is

$$b = L \cos(90° - \alpha)$$

and the components of the cannon length, L, on each coordinate axis are =

$$L_x = b \cos \gamma$$
$$L_y = L \cos \alpha$$
$$L_z = b \sin \gamma$$

Now that you have the information required to compute direction cosines, you can write equations for the initial muzzle velocity components as follows:

$$v_{mx} = v_m \cos \theta_x$$
$$v_{my} = v_m \cos \theta_y$$
$$v_{mz} = v_m \cos \theta_z$$

Finally, you can write the x-components of displacement, velocity, and acceleration as follows:

$$a_x = 0$$
$$v_x = v_{mx} = v_m \cos \theta_x$$
$$x = v_x t = (v_m \cos \theta_x)\, t$$

y-Components

The y-components are just like the previous rifle example, again with the exception here of the initial velocity in the y-direction:

$$v_{my} = v_m \cos \theta_y$$

Thus,

$$a_y = -g$$
$$v_y = v_{my} + at = (v_m \cos \theta_y) - gt$$

Before writing the equation for the y-component of displacement, you need to consider the elevation of the base of the cannon, plus the height of the end of the cannon barrel to calculate the initial y-component of displacement when the shell leaves the cannon. Let y_b be the elevation of the base of the cannon, and let L be the length of the cannon barrel; then the initial y-component of displacement, y_o is

$$y_o = y_b + L \cos \alpha$$

Now you can write the equation for y as

$$y = y_o + v_{my}t + (1/2)at^2$$
$$y = (y_b + L \cos \alpha) + (v_m \cos \theta_y)t - (1/2)gt^2$$

z-Components

The z-components are largely analogous to the x-components and can be written as follows:

$$a_z = 0$$

$$v_z = v_{mz} = v_m \cos \theta_z$$

$$z = v_z t = (v_m \cos \theta_z)t$$

The Vectors

With the components all worked out, you can now combine them to form the vector for each kinematic property. Doing so for this example gives the displacement, velocity, and acceleration vectors shown here:

$$\mathbf{s} = [(v_m \cos \theta_x)t]\mathbf{i} + [(v_b + L \cos \alpha) + (v_m \cos \theta_y)t - (1/2)gt^2]\mathbf{j} + [(v_m \cos \theta_z)t]\mathbf{k}$$

$$\mathbf{v} = [v_m \cos \theta_x]\mathbf{i} + [(v_m \cos \theta_y) - gt]\mathbf{j} + [v_m \cos \theta_z]\mathbf{k}$$

$$\mathbf{a} = -g\mathbf{j}$$

Observe here that the displacement vector essentially gives the position of the center of mass of the shell at any given instant in time; thus, you can use this vector to plot the trajectory of the shell from the cannon to the target.

Hitting the Target

Now that you have the equations fully describing the shell's trajectory, you need to consider the location of the target to determine when a direct hit occurs. To show how this is done, I've prepared a sample program that implements these kinematic equations along with a simple bounding box collision detection method for checking whether or not the shell has struck the target. Basically, at each time step at which I calculate the position of the shell after it has left the cannon, I check to see whether this position falls within the bounding dimensions of the target object represented by a cube.

The sample program is set up such that you can change all of the variables in the simulation and view the effects of your changes. This program is a simple dialog-based application, written in standard C, using the Windows API functions. The executable file name is *cannon.exe*. There is only one source file, *cannon.c*, and one header file, *cannon.h*, for this example. I used Microsoft's Developer Studio to compile and build this application.

Figure 2-5 shows the main screen for the cannon example program, in which the governing variables are shown on the left. The upper illustration is a bird's-eye view looking down on the cannon and the target; the lower illustration is a profile (side) view.

You can change any of the variables shown in the main window and press the fire button to see the resulting flight path of the shell. A message box will appear when

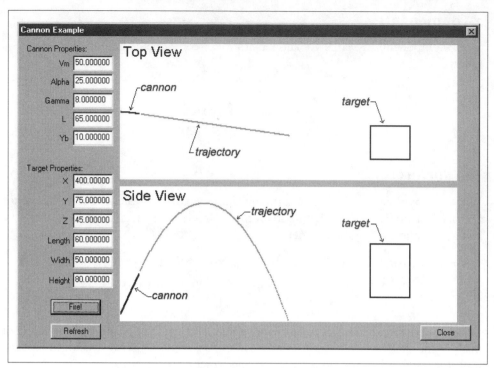

Figure 2-5. Cannon Sample Program Main Window

you hit the target or when the shell hits the ground. The program is set up so that you can repeatedly change the variables and press fire to see the result without erasing the previous trial. This allows you to gauge how much you need to adjust each variable to hit the target. Press the refresh button to redraw the views when they get too cluttered.

Figure 2-6 shows a few trial shots that I made before finally hitting the target.

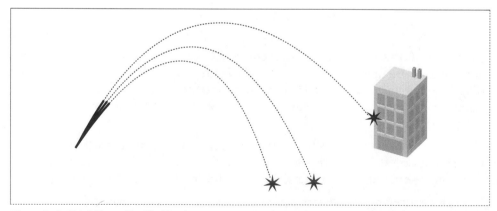

Figure 2-6. Trial Shots (Profile View)

The code for this example is really quite simple. Aside from the overhead of setting up the window, controls, and illustrations, all of the action takes place when the *fire* button is pressed. Here's the event handler that gets executed when the fire button is pressed; it's contained in the main window message handler function, DemoDlgProc:

```
case IDC_FIRE:
        // update the variables with
        // the values shown in the edit controls
        GetDlgItemText(hDlg, IDC_VM, str, 15);
        Vm = atof(str);

        GetDlgItemText(hDlg, IDC_ALPHA, str, 15);
        Alpha = atof(str);

        GetDlgItemText(hDlg, IDC_GAMMA, str, 15);
        Gamma = atof(str);

        GetDlgItemText(hDlg, IDC_L, str, 15);
        L = atof(str);

        GetDlgItemText(hDlg, IDC_YB, str, 15);
        Yb = atof(str);

        GetDlgItemText(hDlg, IDC_X, str, 15);
        X = atof(str);

        GetDlgItemText(hDlg, IDC_Y, str, 15);
        Y = atof(str);

        GetDlgItemText(hDlg, IDC_Z, str, 15);
        Z = atof(str);

        GetDlgItemText(hDlg, IDC_LENGTH, str, 15);
        Length = atof(str);

        GetDlgItemText(hDlg, IDC_WIDTH, str, 15);
        Width = atof(str);

        GetDlgItemText(hDlg, IDC_HEIGHT, str, 15);
        Height = atof(str);

        // initialize the time and status variables
        status = 0;
        time = 0;

        // start stepping through time for the sim.
        // until the target is hit, the shell hits
        // the ground, or the sim. times out.
        while(status == 0)
        {
                // do the next time step
                status = DoSimulation();

                // update the views
                hdc = GetDC(hTopView);
                GetClientRect(hTopView, &r);
                DrawTopView(hdc, &r);
                ReleaseDC(hTopView, hdc);
```

```
                hdc = GetDC(hSideView);
                GetClientRect(hSideView, &r);
                DrawSideView(hdc, &r);
                ReleaseDC(hSideView, hdc);
        }

        // Report results
        if (status == 1)
                MessageBox(NULL, "Direct Hit", "Score!", MB_OK);

        if (status == 2)
                MessageBox(NULL, "Missed Target", "No Score.", MB_OK);

        if (status == 3)
                MessageBox(NULL, "Timed Out", "Error", MB_OK);
        break;
```

The first several lines simply get the new values for the variables shown on the main window. After that the program enters a `while` loop, stepping through increments of time and recalculating the position of the shell projectile using the formula for the displacement vector, s, shown earlier. The shell position at the current time is calculated in the function `DoSimulation`. Immediately after calling `DoSimulation`, the program updates the illustrations in the main window showing the shell's trajectory. `DoSimulation` returns 0, keeping the `while` loop going, if there has not yet been a collision or if the time has not yet reached the preset time-out value.

Once the `while` loop terminates, by `DoSimulation` returning nonzero, the return value from this function call is checked to see whether a hit has occurred between the shell and the ground or the shell and the target. Just so that the program does not get stuck in this `while` loop, `DoSimulation` will return a value of 3, indicating that it is taking too long.

Now let's take a look at what's happing in the function `DoSimulation` (I've also included here the global variables that are used in `DoSimulation`).

```
//------------------------------------------------------------------------------//
// Define a custom type to represent
// the three components of a 3D vector, where
// i represents the x-component, j represents
// the y-component, and k represents the z-
// component
//------------------------------------------------------------------------------//
typedef struct TVectorTag
{
    double i;
    double j;
    double k;
} TVector;


//------------------------------------------------------------------------------//
// Now define the variables required for this simulation
//------------------------------------------------------------------------------//
double          Vm;     // Magnitude of muzzle velocity, m/s
double          Alpha;  // Angle from y-axis (upward) to the cannon.
                        // When this angle is zero, the cannon is pointing
                        // straight up; when it is 90 degrees, the cannon
                        // is horizontal
```

```
double       Gamma;   // Angle from x-axis, in the xz-plane to the cannon.
                      // When this angle is zero the cannon is pointing in
                      // the positive x-direction; positive values of this angle
                      // are toward the positive z-axis
double       L;       // This is the length of the cannon, m
double       Yb;      // This is the base elevation of the cannon, m

double       X;       // The x-position of the center of the target, m
double       Y;       // The y-position of the center of the target, m
double       Z;       // The z-position of the center of the target, m
double       Length,  // The length of the target measured along the x-axis, m
double       Width;   // The width of the target measured along the z-axis, m
double       Height;  // The height of the target measure along the y-axis, m

TVector      s;       // The shell position (displacement) vector

double       time;    // The time from the instant the shell leaves
                      // the cannon, seconds
double       tInc;    // The time increment to use when stepping through
                      // the simulation, seconds

double       g;       // acceleration due to gravity, m/s^2

//-----------------------------------------------------------------------------//
// This function steps the simulation ahead in time. This is where the kinematic
// properties are calculated. The function will return 1 when the target is hit
// and 2 when the shell hits the ground (xz-plane) before hitting the target;
// otherwise, the function returns 0.
//-----------------------------------------------------------------------------//
int DoSimulation(void)
//-----------------------------------------------------------------------------//
{
    double cosX;
    double cosY;
    double cosZ;
    double xe, ze;
    double b, Lx, Ly, Lz;
    double tx1, tx2, ty1, ty2, tz1, tz2;

    // step to the next time in the simulation
    time+=tInc;

    // First calculate the direction cosines for the cannon orientation.
    // In a real game you would not want to put this calculation in this
    // function, since it is a waste of CPU time to calculate these values
    // at each time step as they never change during the sim. I put them
    // here in this case only so that you can see all the calculation steps in a
    // single function.
    b = L * cos((90-Alpha) *3.14/180); // projection of barrel onto xz-plane
    Lx = b * cos(Gamma * 3.14/180);    // x-component of barrel length
    Ly = L * cos(Alpha * 3.14/180);    // y-component of barrel length
    Lz = b * sin(Gamma * 3.14/180);    // z-component of barrel length

    cosX = Lx/L;
    cosY = Ly/L;
    cosZ = Lz/L;

    // These are the x- and z-coordinates of the very end of the cannon barrel
    // we'll use these as the initial x and z displacements
    xe = L * cos((90-Alpha) *3.14/180) * cos(Gamma * 3.14/180);
    ze = L * cos((90-Alpha) *3.14/180) * sin(Gamma * 3.14/180);
```

```
// Now we can calculate the position vector at this time
s.i = Vm * cosX * time + xe;
s.j = (Yb + L * cos(Alpha*3.14/180)) + (Vm * cosY * time) -
      (0.5 * g * time * time);
s.k = Vm * cosZ * time + ze;

// Check for collision with target
// Get extents (bounding coordinates) of the target
tx1 = X - Length/2;
tx2 = X + Length/2;
ty1 = Y - Height/2;
ty2 = Y + Height/2;
tz1 = Z - Width/2;
tz2 = Z + Width/2;

// Now check to see whether the shell has passed through the target
// I'm using a rudimentary collision detection scheme here in which
// I simply check to see whether the shell's coordinates are within the
// bounding box of the target. This works for demo purposes, but
// a practical problem is that you might miss a collision if for a given
// time step the shell's change in position is large enough to allow
// it to "skip" over the target.
// A better approach is to look at the previous time step's position data
// and to check the line from the previous position to the current position
// to see whether that line intersects the target bounding box.
if( (s.i >= tx1 && s.i <= tx2) &&
    (s.j >= ty1 && s.j <= ty2) &&
    (s.k >= tz1 && s.k <= tz2) )
    return 1;

// Check for collision with ground (xz-plane)
if(s.j <= 0)
    return 2;

// Cut off the simulation if it's taking too long
// This is so the program does not get stuck in the while loop
if(time>3600)
    return 3;

    return 0;
}
```

I've commented the code so that you can readily see what's going on. This function essentially does four things:

- increments the time variable by the specified time increment;
- calculates the initial muzzle velocity components in the x-, y-, and z-directions;
- calculates the shell's new position;
- checks for a collision with the target, using a bounding box scheme or the ground.

Here is the code that computes the shell's position:

```
// Now we can calculate the position vector at this time
s.i = Vm * cosX * time + xe;
s.j = (Yb + L * cos(Alpha*3.14/180)) + (Vm * cosY * time) -
      (0.5 * g * time * time);
s.k = Vm * cosZ * time + ze;
```

This code calculates the three components of the displacement vector, s, using the formulas that I gave you earlier. If you wanted to compute the velocity and acceleration vectors as well, just to see their values, you should do so in this section of the program. You can set up a couple of new global variables to represent the velocity and acceleration vectors, just as I did with the displacement vector, and apply the velocity and acceleration formulas that I gave you.

That's all there is to it. It's obvious by playing with this sample program that the shell's trajectory is parabolic in shape, which is typical *projectile motion*. You'll take a more detailed look at this sort of motion in Chapter 6.

Even though I put a comment in the source code, I must reiterate a warning here regarding the collision detection scheme that I used in this example. Because I'm checking the current position coordinate only to see whether it falls within the bounding dimensions of the target cube, I run the risk of skipping over the target if, for a given time step, the change in position is too large. A better approach would be to keep track of the shell's previous position and check to see whether the line connecting the previous position to the new one intersects the target cube.

Kinematic Particle Explosion

At this point you might be wondering how particle kinematics can help you create realistic game content unless you're writing a game that involves shooting a gun or a cannon. If you are, let me offer you a few ideas and then show you an example. Say you're writing a football simulation game. You can use particle kinematics to model the trajectory of the football after it is thrown or kicked. You can also treat the wide receivers as particles when calculating whether or not they'll be able to catch the thrown ball. In this scenario you'll have two particles, the receiver and the ball, traveling independently, and you'll have to calculate when a collision occurs between these two particles, indicating a catch (unless, of course, your player is all thumbs and fumbles the ball after it hits his hands). You can find similar applications for other sports-based games as well.

What about a 3D shoot-'em-up game? How could you use particle kinematics in this genre aside from bullets, cannons, grenades, and the like? Well, you could use particle kinematics to model your player when he or she jumps into the air either running or standing still. For example, your player reaches the middle of a catwalk only to find a section missing, and you have the player immediately back up a few paces to get a running head start before leaping into the air, hoping to clear the gap. This long jump scenario is perfect for using particle kinematics. All you really need to do is define your player's initial velocity, both speed and take-off angle, and then apply the vector formula for displacement to calculate whether or not he or she makes the jump. You can also use the displacement formula to calculate the player's trajectory so that you can move the player's viewpoint accordingly, giving the illusion of leaping into the air. You may in fact already be using these principles to model this action in your games, or at least you've seen it done if you play games of this genre. If your player happens to fall short on the jump, you can use the formulas for velocity to calculate the impact velocity of the player when he or she hits the ground below. On the basis of this impact velocity you can determine an appropriate amount of damage to deduct from the player's health score, or if the velocity is over a certain threshold, you can say goodbye to your would-be adventurer!

Another use for simple particle kinematics is for certain special effects such as particle explosions. This sort of effect is quite simple to implement and really adds a sense of realism to explosion effects. The particles don't just fly off in random, straight-line trajectories. Instead, they rise and fall under the influence of their initial velocity, angle, and the acceleration due to gravity, which gives the impression that the particles have mass.

So let me show you an example of a kinematic particle explosion. The code for this example is taken from the cannon example discussed previously, so a lot of it should look familiar to you. Figure 2-7 shows this program's main window.

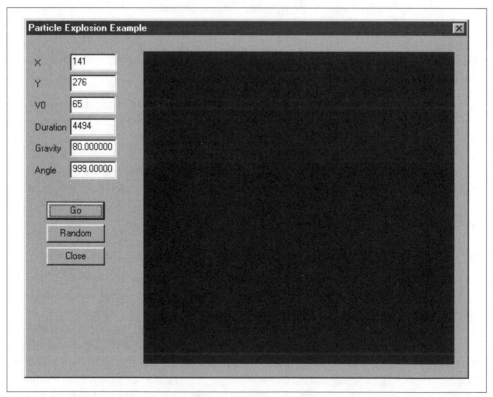

Figure 2-7. Particle Explosion Program

The explosion effect takes place in the large rectangular area on the right. I didn't show the explosion in this screen shot, since all you would see are a bunch of dots, which don't do justice to the effect; it's the motion of those dots that make the effect.

In the edit controls on the left, you specify an *x*- and a *y*-position for the effect, along with the initial velocity of the particles, which is a measure of the explosion's strength, a duration in milliseconds, a gravity factor, and finally an angle. The angle parameter can be any number between 0 and 360 degrees or 999. When you specify an angle in the range of 0 to 360 degrees, all the particles in the explosion will be launched generally in that direction. If you specify a value of 999, then all the particles will shoot off in random directions. The duration parameter is essentially the life of the effect. The particles will fade out as they approach that life.

The first thing you need to do for this example is set up some structures and global variables to represent the particle effect and the individual particles making up the effect along with the initial parameters describing the behavior of the effect as discussed in the previous paragraph. Here's the code:

```
//---------------------------------------------------------------------------//
// Define a custom type to represent each particle in the effect.
//---------------------------------------------------------------------------//
typedef     struct _TParticle
{
    float       x;          // x-coordinate of the particle
    float       y;          // y-coordinate of the particle
    float       vi;         // initial velocity
    float       angle;      // initial trajectory (direction)
    int         life;       // duration in milliseconds
    int         r;          // red component of particle's color
    int         g;          // green component of particle's color
    int         b;          // blue component of particle's color
    int         time;       // keeps track of the effect's time
    float       gravity;    // gravity factor
    BOOL        Active;     // indicates whether this particle
                            // is active or dead
} TParticle;

#define      _MAXPARTICLES 50

typedef struct _TParticleExplosion
{
    TParticle           p[_MAXPARTICLES];   // list of particles
                                            // making up this effect
    int         V0; // initial velocity, or strength, of the effect
    int         x;  // initial x location
    int         y;  // initial y location
    BOOL        Active;     // indicates whether this effect is
                            //active or dead
} TParticleExplosion;

//---------------------------------------------------------------------------//
// Now define the variables required for this simulation
//---------------------------------------------------------------------------//
TParticleExplosion      Explosion;

int         xc;          // x-coordinate of the effect
int         yc;          // y-coordinate of the effect
int         V0;          // initial velocity
int         Duration;    // life in milliseconds
float       Gravity;     // gravity factor (acceleration)
float       Angle;       // indicates particles' direction
```

You can see from this code that the particle explosion effect is made up of a collection of particles. The behavior of each particle is determined by kinematics and the initial parameters set for each particle.

Whenever you press the GO button, the initial parameters that you specified are used to initialize the particle explosion (if you press the Random button, the program randomly selects these initial values for you). This takes place in the function called CreateParticleExplosion:

```
///////////////////////////////////////////////////////////////////
/*      This function creates a new particle explosion effect.

        x,y:      starting point of the effect
        Vinit:    a measure of how fast the particles will be sent flying
                  (it's actually the initial velocity of the particles)
        life:     life of the particles in milliseconds; particles will
                  fade and die out as they approach their specified life
        gravity:  the acceleration due to gravity which controls the
                  rate at which particles will fall as they fly
        angle:    initial trajectory angle of the particles,
                  specify 999 to create a particle explosion
                  that emits particles in all directions; otherwise,
                  0 right, 90 up, 180 left, etc.
*/
void CreateParticleExplosion(int x, int y, int Vinit, int life,
                             float gravity, float angle)
{
    int    i;
    int    m;
    float  f;

    Explosion.Active = TRUE;
    Explosion.x = x;
    Explosion.y = y;
    Explosion.V0 = Vinit;

    for(i=0; i<_MAXPARTICLES; i++)
    {

        Explosion.p[i].x = 0;
        Explosion.p[i].y = 0;
        Explosion.p[i].vi = tb_Rnd(Vinit/2, Vinit);

        if(angle < 999)
        {
            if(tb_Rnd(0,1) == 0)
                m = -1;
            else
                m = 1;
            Explosion.p[i].angle = -angle + m * tb_Rnd(0,10);
        } else
            Explosion.p[i].angle = tb_Rnd(0,360);

        f = (float) tb_Rnd(80, 100) / 100.0f;
        Explosion.p[i].life = tb_Round(life * f);
        Explosion.p[i].r = 255;//tb_Rnd(225, 255);
        Explosion.p[i].g = 255;//tb_Rnd(85, 115);
        Explosion.p[i].b = 255;//tb_Rnd(15, 45);
```

```
            Explosion.p[i].time = 0;
            Explosion.p[i].Active = TRUE;
            Explosion.p[i].gravity = gravity;
        }
    }
```

Here you can see that all the particles are set to start off in the same position as specified by the x- and y-coordinates that you provide; however, you'll notice that the initial velocity of each particle is actually randomly selected from a range of `Vinit/2` to `Vinit`. I do this to give the particle behavior some variety. I do the same thing for the life parameter of each particle so that they don't all fade out and die at the exact same time.

After the particle explosion is created, the program enters a loop to propagate and draw the effect. The loop is a `while` loop as shown here:

```
    while(status)
    {
        DrawRectangle(hBufferDC, &r, 1, RGB(0,0,0));
        status = DrawParticleExplosion(hBufferDC);
        hdc = GetDC(hSideView);
        if(!BitBlt(hdc, 0, 0, r.right, r.bottom, hBufferDC, 0, 0, SRCCOPY))
        {
            MessageBox(NULL, "BitBlt failed", "Error", MB_OK);
            status = FALSE;
        }
        ReleaseDC(hSideView, hdc);
    }
```

The `while` loop continues as long as `status` remains `true`, which indicates that the particle effect is still alive. After all the particles in the effect reach their set life, then the effect is dead and `status` will be set to `false`. All the calculations for the particle behavior actually take place in the function called `DrawParticleExplosion`; the rest of the code in this `while` loop is for clearing the offscreen buffer and then copying it to the main window.

`DrawParticleExplosion`, updates the state of each particle in the effect by calling another function, `UpdateParticleState`, and then draws the effect to the offscreen buffer passed in as a parameter. Here's what these two functions look like:

```
    //---------------------------------------------------------------------------------//
    // Draws the particle system and updates the state of each particle.
    // Returns false when all of the particles have died out.
    //---------------------------------------------------------------------------------//
    BOOL    DrawParticleExplosion(HDC hdc)
    {
        int     i;
        BOOL    finished = TRUE;
        float           r;
        COLORREF    clr;

        if(Explosion.Active)
          for(i=0; i<_MAXPARTICLES; i++)
          {
              if(Explosion.p[i].Active)
```

```
                {
                    finished = FALSE;
            r = ((float)(Explosion.p[i].life-
                    Explosion.p[i].time)/(float)(Explosion.p[i].life));
            clr = RGB(tb_Round(r*Explosion.p[i].r),
                    tb_Round(r*Explosion.p[i].g),
                    tb_Round(r*Explosion.p[i].b));
            DrawCircle(    hdc,
                        Explosion.x+tb_Round(Explosion.p[i].x),
                        Explosion.y+tb_Round(Explosion.p[i].y),
                        2,
                        clr);
            Explosion.p[i].Active = UpdateParticleState(&(Explosion.p[i]),
                                                10);
                }
            }

        if(finished)
            Explosion.Active = FALSE;

        return !finished;
    }

    //-----------------------------------------------------------------------------//
    /* This is generic function to update the state of a given particle.
        p:          pointer to a particle structure
        dtime:      time increment in milliseconds to
                    advance the state of the particle

        If the total elapsed time for this particle has exceeded the particle's
        set life, then this function returns FALSE, indicating that the particle
        should expire.
    */
    BOOL    UpdateParticleState(TParticle* p, int dtime)
    {
        BOOL retval;
        float    t;

        p->time+=dtime;
        t = (float)p->time/1000.0f;
        p->x = p->vi * cos(p->angle*PI/180.0f) * t;
        p->y = p->vi * sin(p->angle*PI/180.0f) * t + (p->gravity*t*t)/2.0f;

        if (p->time >= p->life)
            retval = FALSE;
        else
            retval = TRUE;

        return retval;
    }
```

UpdateParticleState uses the kinematic formulas that I've already shown you to update
the particle's position as a function of its initial velocity, time, and the acceleration due to
gravity. After UpdateParticleState is called, DrawParticleExplosion scales each particle's
color down, fading it to black, based on the life of each particle and elapsed time. The
fade effect is to show the particles dying slowly over time instead of simply disappearing
from the screen. The effect resembles the behavior of fireworks as they explode in the
night sky.

Rigid Body Kinematics

The formulas for displacement, velocity, and acceleration discussed in the previous sections apply as well for rigid bodies as for particles. The difference is that when considering rigid bodies, the point on the rigid body that you track, in terms of linear motion, is the body's center of mass (gravity).

When a rigid body translates with no rotation, all of the particles making up the rigid body move on parallel paths, since the body does not change its shape. Further, when a rigid body does rotate, it generally rotates about axes that pass through its center of mass, unless the body is hinged at some other point about which it is forced to rotate. These facts make the center of mass a convenient point to use to track its linear motion. This is good news for you because you can use all of the material you learned on particle kinematics here in your study of rigid body kinematics.

The procedure for dealing with rigid bodies involves two distinct aspects:

- tracking the translation of the body's center of mass and
- tracking the body's rotation.

The first aspect is old hat by now—just treat the body as a particle; however, the second aspect requires you to consider a few more concepts, namely, local coordinates, angular displacement, angular velocity, and angular acceleration.

For most of the remainder of this chapter I'll discuss *plane* kinematics of rigid bodies. Plane motion simply means that the body's motion is restricted to a flat plane in space where the only axis of rotation about which the body can rotate is perpendicular to the plane. Plane motion is essentially two-dimensional. This allows us to focus on the new kinematic concepts of angular displacement, velocity, and acceleration without getting lost in the math required to describe arbitrary rotation in three dimensions.

You might be surprised by how many problems lend themselves to plane kinematic solutions. For example, in some popular 3D shoot-'em-up games, your character is able to push objects, such as boxes and barrels, around on the floor. Although the game world is three dimensions, these particular objects are restricted to sliding on the floor, a plane, and thus can be treated like a 2D problem. Even if the player pushes on these objects at some angle instead of straight on, you'll be able to simulate the sliding and rotation of these objects using 2D kinematics (and kinetics) techniques.

Local Coordinate Axes

Earlier, I defined the Cartesian coordinate system to use for your fixed global reference, or world coordinates. This world coordinate system is all that's required when you're treating particles; however, for rigid bodies you'll also use a set of local coordinates fixed to the body. Specifically, this local coordinate system will be fixed at the body's center of mass location. You'll use this coordinate system to track the orientation of the body as it rotates.

For plane motion we require only one scalar quantity to describe the body's orientation. This is illustrated in Figure 2-8.

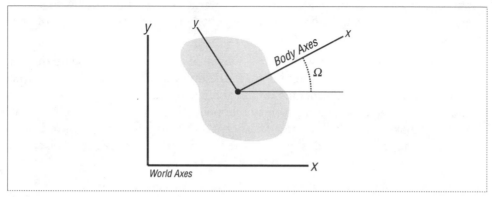

Figure 2-8. *Local Coordinate Axes*

Here, the orientation, Ω, is defined as the angular difference between the two sets of co-ordinate axes: the fixed world axes and the local body axes. This is the so-called Euler angle. In general 3D motion there is a total of three Euler angles, which are usually called *yaw*, *pitch*, and *roll* in aerodynamic and hydrodynamic jargon. While these angular representations are easy to visualize in terms of their physical meaning, they aren't so nice from a numerical point of view, and you'll have to look for alternative representations when writing your 3D real-time simulator. These issues are addressed in Chapter 14.

Angular Velocity and Acceleration

In 2D plane motion, as the body rotates, Ω will change, and the rate at which Ω changes is the angular velocity, ω. Likewise, the rate at which ω changes is the angular acceleration, α. These angular properties are analogous to the linear properties of displacement, velocity, and acceleration. The units for angular displacement, velocity, and acceleration are radians (rad), radians per second (rad/s), and radians per second-squared (rad/s^2), respectively.

Mathematically, you can write these relations between angular displacement, angular velocity, and angular acceleration:

$$\omega = d\Omega/dt$$
$$\alpha = d\omega/dt = d^2\Omega/dt^2$$
$$\omega = \int \alpha \, dt$$
$$\Omega = \int \omega \, dt$$
$$\omega \, d\omega = \alpha \, d\Omega$$

In fact, you can substitute the angular properties, Ω, ω, and α for the linear properties, s, v and a in the equations derived earlier for particle kinematics to obtain similar kinematic equations for rotation. For constant angular acceleration you'll end up with the following equations:

$$\omega_2 = \omega_1 + \alpha t$$
$$\omega_2^2 = \omega_1^2 + 2\alpha(\Omega_2 - \Omega_1)$$
$$\Omega_2 = \Omega_1 + \omega_1 t + (1/2)\alpha t^2$$

When a rigid body rotates about a given axis, every point on the rigid body sweeps out a circular path around the axis of rotation. You can think of the body's rotation as causing additional linear motion of each particle making up the body. This linear motion is in addition to the linear motion of the body's center of mass. To get the total linear motion of any particle or point on the rigid body, you must be able to relate the angular motion of the body to the linear motion of the particle or point as it sweeps its circular path about the axis of rotation.

Before I show you how to do this, let me first explain why you would even want to perform such a calculation. Basically, in dynamics, knowing that two objects have collided is not always enough, and you'll often want to know how hard, so to speak, these two objects have collided. When you're dealing with interacting rigid bodies that may at some point make contact with one another or with other fixed objects, you need to determine not only the location of the points of contact, but also the relative velocity or acceleration between the contact points. This information will allow you to calculate the interaction forces between the colliding bodies.

The arc length of the path swept by a particle on the rigid body is a function of the distance from the axis of rotation to the particle and the angular displacement, Ω. I'll use c to denote arc length and r to denote the distance from the axis of rotation to the particle, as shown in Figure 2-9. The formula relating arc length to angular displacement is

$$c = r\Omega$$

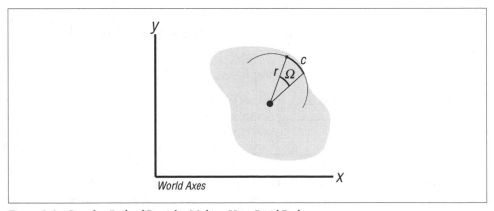

Figure 2-9. *Circular Path of Particles Making Up a Rigid Body*

where Ω must be in radians, not degrees. If you differentiate this formula with respect to time:

$$dc/dt = r \, d\Omega/dt$$

you get an equation relating the linear velocity of the particle as it moves along its circular path to the angular velocity of the rigid body. This equation is written as follows:

$$v = r\omega$$

This velocity as a vector is tangent to the circular path swept by the particle. If you can imagine this particle as a ball at the end of a rod whose other end is fixed to a rotating axis, then if the ball is released from the end of the rod as it rotates, the ball will fly off in a direction tangent to the circular path it was taking when attached to the rod. This is in the same direction as the tangential linear velocity given by the above equation. Figure 2-10 illustrates the tangential velocity.

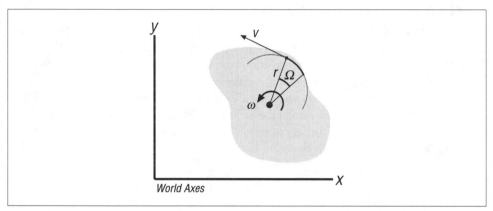

Figure 2-10. Linear Velocity Due to Angular Velocity

Differentiating the equation, $v = r\omega$:

$$dv/dt = r \, d\omega/dt$$

yields a formula for the tangential linear acceleration as a function of angular acceleration:

$$a_t = r\alpha$$

Note that there is another component of acceleration for the particle that results from the rotation of the rigid body. This component is normal, or perpendicular, to the circular path of the particle and is the so-called *centripetal* acceleration, which is always directed toward the axis of rotation (see Figure 2-11). Remember that velocity is a vector, and since acceleration is the rate of change in the velocity vector, there are two ways in which acceleration can be produced. One way is by a change in the magnitude of the velocity vector, that is, a change in speed; the other way is a change in the direction of the velocity vector. The change in speed gives rise to the tangential acceleration component, while the direction change gives rise to the centripetal acceleration component. The resultant acceleration vector is the vector sum of the tangential and centripetal accelerations. Centripetal acceleration is what you feel when you take your car around a tight curve even though your speed is constant.

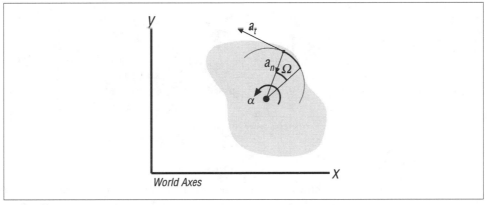

Figure 2-11. Tangential and Centripetal Acceleration

The formula for the magnitude of centripetal acceleration, a_n, is

$$a_n = v^2/r$$

where v is the tangential velocity. Substituting the equation for tangential velocity into this equation for centripetal acceleration gives the following alternative form:

$$a_n = r\omega^2$$

In two dimensions you can easily get away with using these scalar equations; however, in three dimensions you'll have to use the vector forms of these equations. Angular velocity as a vector is parallel with the axis of rotation. In Figure 2-10 the angular velocity would be pointing out of the page directly at you. Its sense, or direction of rotation, is determined by the *righthand rule*. If you take your right hand and curl your fingers in an arc around the axis of rotation with your fingers pointing toward the direction in which the body is rotating, your thumb will stick up in the direction of the angular velocity vector.

If you take the vector cross product (refer to *Appendix A* for a review of vector math) of the angular velocity vector and the vector from the axis of rotation to the particle under consideration, you'll end up with the linear, tangential velocity vector. This is written as

$$\mathbf{v} = \omega \times \mathbf{r}$$

Note that this gives both the magnitude and direction of the linear, tangential velocity. Also, be sure to preserve the order of the vectors when taking the cross product, that is, ω cross $\mathbf{r}$, not the other way around, which would give the wrong direction for $\mathbf{v}$.

Vector Cross Product

Given any two vectors **A** and **B**, the cross product **A** × **B** is defined by a third vector **C** with a magnitude equal to $AB \sin \theta$, where θ is the angle between the two vectors **A** and **B**.

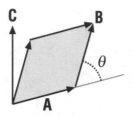

$$\mathbf{C} = \mathbf{A} \times \mathbf{B}$$
$$C = AB \sin \theta$$

The direction of **C** is determined by the righthand rule. The righthand rule is a simple trick to help keep track of vector directions. Assume that **A** and **B** lie in a plane, and let an axis of rotation extend perpendicular to this plane through a point located at the tail of **A**. Take your right hand and pretend to curl your fingers around the axis of rotation from vector **A** toward **B**. Now extend your thumb, as though you are giving a thumbs up, while keeping your fingers curled around the axis. The direction in which your thumb is pointing indicates the direction of vector **C**.

In the figure above, a parallelogram is formed by **A** and **B** (the shaded region). The area of this parallelogram is the magnitude of **C**, which is $AB \sin \theta$.

There are two equations that you'll need in order to determine the vectors for tangential and centripetal acceleration:

$$\mathbf{a}_n = \boldsymbol{\omega} \times (\boldsymbol{\omega} \times \mathbf{r})$$
$$\mathbf{a}_t = \boldsymbol{\alpha} \times \mathbf{r}$$

Another way to look at the quantities **v**, $\mathbf{a}_n$, and $\mathbf{a}_t$ is that they are the velocity and acceleration of the particle under consideration on the rigid body relative to the point about which the rigid body is rotating, for example, the body's center of mass location. This is very convenient, since, as I said earlier, you'll want to track the motion of the rigid body as a particle when looking at the big picture without having to worry about what each particle making up the rigid body is doing all the time. Therefore, you treat the rigid body's linear motion and its angular motion separately. When you do need to take a close look at specific particles of, or points on, the rigid body, you can do so by taking the motion of the rigid body as a particle and then adding to it the relative motion of the point under consideration.

Figure 2-12 shows a rigid body that is traveling at a speed $\mathbf{v}_{cg}$, where $\mathbf{v}_{cg}$ is the speed of the center of mass (or center of gravity) of the rigid body. Remember, the center of mass is the point to track when treating a rigid body as a particle. This rigid body is also rotating with an angular velocity $\boldsymbol{\omega}$ about an axis that passes through the center of mass of the body. The vector $\mathbf{r}$ is the vector from the center of mass of the rigid body to the particular point of interest, P, located on the rigid body.

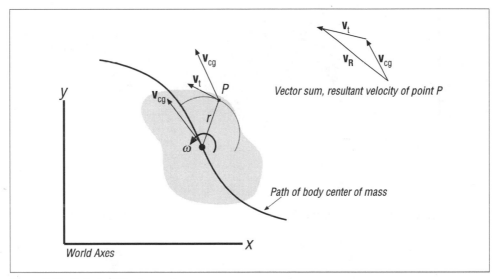

Figure 2-12. Relative Velocity

In this case the resultant velocity of point P can be found by taking the vector sum of the velocity of the center of mass of the body and the tangential velocity of point P due to the body's angular velocity $\boldsymbol{\omega}$. Here's what the vector equation looks like:

$$\mathbf{v}_R = \mathbf{v}_{cg} + \mathbf{v}_t$$

or

$$\mathbf{v}_R = \mathbf{v}_{cg} + (\boldsymbol{\omega} \times \mathbf{r})$$

You can do the same thing with acceleration to determine point $P's$ resultant acceleration. Here, you'll take the vector sum of the acceleration of the rigid body's center of mass, the tangential acceleration due to the body's angular acceleration, and the centripetal acceleration due to the change in direction of the tangential velocity. In equation form, this looks like

$$\mathbf{a}_R = \mathbf{a}_{cg} + \mathbf{a}_n + \mathbf{a}_t$$

Figure 2-13 illustrates what's happening here.

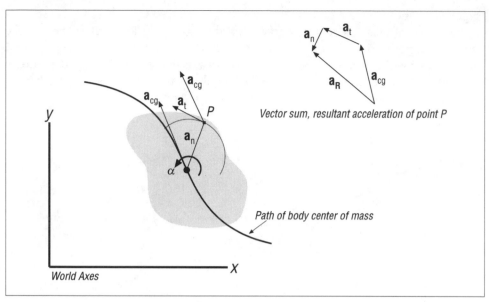

Figure 2-13. Relative Acceleration

You can rewrite the equation for the resultant acceleration in the following form:

$$\mathbf{a_R} = \mathbf{a_{cg}} + (\boldsymbol{\omega} \times (\boldsymbol{\omega} \times \mathbf{r})) + (\boldsymbol{\alpha} \times \mathbf{r})$$

As you can see, using these principles of relative velocity and acceleration allows you to calculate the resultant kinematic properties of any point on your rigid body at any given time by knowing what the center of mass of the body is doing along with how the body is rotating.

CHAPTER 3

Force

This chapter is prerequisite for Chapter 4, which addresses the subject of kinetics. The aim here is to provide you with enough of a background on forces that you can readily appreciate the subject of kinetics. This chapter is not meant to be the final word on the subject of force. In fact, I believe that the subject of force is so important to realistic simulations that I'll revisit the subject several times in various contexts throughout the remainder of this book. In this chapter I'll discuss the two fundamental categories of force and briefly explain some important specific types of force. I'll also explain the relationship between force and torque.

Introduction

As I mentioned at the end of Chapter 2, you need to understand the concept of force before you can fully understand the subject of kinetics. Kinematics is only half the battle. You are already familiar with the concept of force from your daily experiences. You exert a force on this book as you hold it in your hands counteracting gravity. You exert force on your mouse as you move it from one point to another. When you play soccer, you exert force on the ball as you kick it. In general, force is that which makes an object move or, more precisely, changes the acceleration of the object. Even as you hold this book, although it might not be moving, you have effectively changed its acceleration from that due to gravity to zero. When you kick that soccer ball, you change its acceleration from, say, zero when the ball is at rest to some positive value as the ball leaves your foot. These are some examples of externally applied *contact* forces.

There's another broad category of forces, in addition to contact forces, called *field* forces or sometimes *force-at-a-distance* forces. These forces can act on a body without actually having to make contact with it. A good example of this is the gravitational attraction between objects. Another example is the electromagnetic attraction between charged particles. The concept of a force field was developed long ago to help visualize the interaction between objects subject to forces at a distance. You can say that an object is subjected to the gravitational field of another object. Thinking in terms of force fields is supposed to help you grasp the fact that an object can exert a force on another object without having to physically touch it.

Within these two broad categories of forces, there are specific types of forces related to various physical phenomena—forces due to friction, buoyancy, and pressure among others. I discuss idealizations of several of these types of forces in this chapter. Later in this book, I'll revisit these forces from a more practical point of view.

Before going further, I need to explain the implications of Newton's third law as introduced in Chapter 1. Remember, Newton's third law states that for every force acting on a body, there is an equal and opposite reacting force. This means that forces must exist in pairs: a single force can't exist by itself.

Consider the gravitational attraction between the earth and yourself. The earth is exerting a force—your weight—on you, accelerating you toward its center. Likewise, you are exerting a force on the earth, accelerating it toward you. The huge difference between your mass and the earth's makes the acceleration of the earth in this case so small that it's negligible. Earlier, I said that you are exerting a force on this book to hold it up; likewise, this book is exerting a force on your hands equal in magnitude but opposite in direction to the force you are exerting on the book. You feel this reaction force as the book's weight.

This phenomenon of action-reaction is the basis for rocket propulsion. A rocket engine exerts force on the fuel molecules that are accelerated out of the engine exhaust nozzle. The force that is required to accelerate these molecules is exerted back against the rocket as a reaction force called thrust. Throughout the remainder of this book you'll see many other examples of action-reaction, which is an important phenomenon in rigid body dynamics. It is especially important in dealing with collisions and objects in contact, as you'll see later.

Force Fields

The best example of a force field or force at a distance is the gravitational attraction between objects. *Newton's law of gravitation* states that the force of attraction between two masses is directly proportional to the product of the masses and inversely proportional to the square of the distances separating the centers of each mass. Further, this law states that the line of action of the force of attraction is along the line that connects the centers of the two masses. This is written as follows:

$$F_a = (Gm_1m_2)/r^2$$

where G is the gravitational constant, Newton's so-called *universal constant*. G was first measured experimentally by Sir Henry Cavendish in 1798 and equals 6.673×10^{-11} (N-m^2)/kg^2 in metric units or 3.436×10^{-8} ft^4/(lb-s^4) in English units.

So far in this book I've been using the acceleration due to gravity, g, as a constant 9.8 m/s^2 (32.174 ft/s^2). This is true when you are near the earth's surface, for example, at sea level. In reality, g varies with altitude—maybe not by much for our purposes, but it does. Consider Newton's second law along with the law of gravitation for a body near the earth. Equating these two laws, in equation form, yields

$$ma = (GM_em)/(R_e + h)^2$$

where m is the mass of the body, a is the acceleration of the body due to the gravitational attraction between it and the earth, M_e is the earth's mass, R_e is the radius of the earth, and h is the altitude of the body. If you solve this equation for a, you'll have a formula for the acceleration due to gravity as a function of altitude:

$$a = g' = (GM_e)/(R_e + h)^2$$

The radius of the earth is approximately 6.38×10^6 m, and its mass is about 5.98×10^{24} kg. Substituting these values in the above equation and assuming zero altitude (sea level) yields the constant g that we've been using so far, that is, g at sea level equals 9.8 m/s^2.

Friction

Frictional forces (friction) always resist motion and are due to the interaction between contacting surfaces. Thus, friction is a contact force. Friction is always parallel to the contacting surfaces at the point of contact, that is, it is tangential to the contacting surfaces. The magnitude of the frictional force is a function of the normal force between the contacting surfaces and the surface roughness.

This is easiest to visualize by looking at a simple block on a horizontal surface as shown in Figure 3-1.

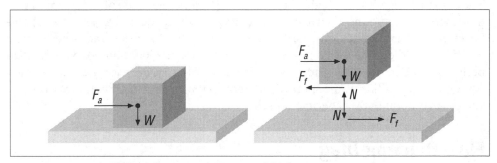

Figure 3-1. Friction, Block in Contact with Horizontal Surface

In this figure the block is resting on the horizontal surface with a small force, F_a, applied to the block on a line of action through the block's center of mass. As this applied force increases, a frictional force will develop between the block and the horizontal surface tending to resist the motion of the block. The maximum value of this frictional force is

$$F_{fmax} = \mu_s N$$

where μ_s is the experimentally determined coefficient of static* friction and N is the normal (perpendicular) force between the block and the surface, which equals the weight of the block in this case. As the applied force increases but is still less than F_{fmax}, the block will remain static, and F_f will be equal in magnitude to the applied force. The block is in static equilibrium. When the applied force becomes greater than F_{fmax}, the frictional force can no longer impede the block's motion, and the block will accelerate under the influence of the applied force. Immediately after the block starts its motion, the frictional force will decrease from F_{fmax} to F_{fk}, where F_{fk} is

$$F_{fk} = \mu_k N$$

Here, k means kinetic, since the block is in motion, and μ_k, the coefficient of kinetic friction,[†] is less than μ_s. Like the static coefficient of friction, the kinetic coefficient of friction is determined experimentally. Table 3-1 shows typical coefficients of friction for several surfaces in contact.

Table 3-1. Coefficients of Friction of Common Surfaces

Surface Condition	M_s	M_k	% Difference
Dry glass on glass	0.94	0.4	54%
Dry iron on iron	1.1	0.15	86%
Dry rubber on pavement	0.55	0.4	27%
Dry steel on steel	0.78	0.42	46%
Dry Teflon on Teflon	0.04	0.04	—
Dry wood on wood	0.38	0.2	47%
Ice on ice	0.1	0.03	70%
Oiled steel on steel	0.10	0.08	20%

The data in Table 3-1 are provided here to show you the magnitude of some typical friction coefficients and the relative difference between the static and kinetic coefficients for certain surface conditions. Other data are available for these and other surface conditions in the technical literature (see the bibliography for sources). Note that experimentally determined friction coefficient data will vary, even for the same surface conditions, depending on the specific condition of the material used in the experiments and the execution of the experiment itself.

Fluid Dynamic Drag

Fluid dynamic drag forces oppose motion as friction does. In fact, a major component of fluid dynamic drag is friction that results from the relative flow of the fluid over (and in contact with) the body's surface. Friction is not the only component of fluid dynamic drag, though. Depending on the shape of the body, its speed, and the nature of the

---

* *Static* here implies that there is no motion; the block is sitting still with all forces balancing.
† The term *dynamic* is sometimes used here instead of *kinetic*.

fluid, fluid dynamic drag will have additional components due to pressure variations in the fluid as it flows around the body. If the body is located at the interface between two fluids (like a ship on the ocean, where the two fluids are air and water), an additional component of drag will exist due to the wave generation.

In general, fluid dynamic drag is a complicated phenomenon that is a function of several factors. I won't go into detail in this section on all these factors, since I'll be revisiting this subject later. However, I do want to discuss how the *viscous* (frictional) component of these drag forces is typically idealized.

Ideal viscous drag is a function of velocity and some experimentally determined *drag coefficient* that is supposed to take into account the surface conditions of the body, the fluid properties (density and viscosity), and the flow conditions. You'll typically see a formula for viscous drag force in the form

$$F_v = -C_f v$$

where C_f is the drag coefficient, v the body's speed, and the minus sign means that the force opposes motion. This formula is valid for slow-moving objects in a viscous fluid. *Slow-moving* implies that the flow around the body is *laminar*, which means that the flow streamlines are undisturbed and parallel.

For fast-moving objects, you'll use the formula for F_v written as function of speed squared as follows:

$$F_v = -C_f v^2$$

Fast-moving implies that the flow around the object is *turbulent*, which means that the flow streamlines are no longer parallel and there is a sort of mixing effect in the flow around the object. Note that the values of C_f are generally not the same for these two equations. In addition to the factors mentioned earlier, C_f depends significantly on whether the flow is laminar or turbulent.

Both of these equations are very simplified and are not adequate for practical analysis of fluid flow problems. However, they do offer certain advantages in computer game simulations. Most obviously, these formulas are easy to implement; you need only know the velocity of the body under consideration, which you get from your kinematic equations, and an assumed value for the drag coefficient. This is convenient, as your game world will typically have many different types of objects of all sizes and shapes that would make rigorous analysis of each of their drag properties impractical. If the illusion of realism is all you need, and not real-life accuracy, then these formulas might be all you need.

Another advantage of using these idealized formulas is that you can tweak the drag coefficients as you see fit to help reduce numerical instabilities when solving the equations of motion while still maintaining the illusion of realistic behavior. If real-life accuracy is what you're going for, then you'll have no choice but to consider a more involved (read "complicated") approach for determining fluid dynamic drag. I'll talk more about drag in Chapters 6 through 10.

A Note on Pressure

Many people confuse pressure with force. I've often heard people say, when explaining a phenomenon, something like "It pushed with a force of 100 pounds per square inch." Although you understand what they mean, technically speaking they are referring to pressure not force. Pressure is force per unit area; therefore, the units are pounds per square inch (psi) or pounds per square foot (psf) and so on. Given the pressure, you'll need to know the total area acted on by this pressure to determine the resultant force. Force equals pressure times area:

$$F = PA$$

This formula tells you that for constant pressure, the greater the area acted upon, the greater the resultant force. If you rearrange this equation, solving for pressure, you'll see that pressure is inversely proportional to area; that is, the greater the area for a given applied force, the smaller the resulting pressure and vice versa:

$$P = F/A$$

An important characteristic of pressure is that it always acts normally (perpendicularly) to the surface of the body or object it is acting on. This fact gives you a clue as to the direction of the resultant force vector.

I wanted to mention pressure here because you'll be working with pressure to calculate forces when you get to the chapters in this book that cover the mechanics of ships, boats, and hovercraft. There, the pressures that you'll consider are hydrostatic pressure (buoyancy) and aerostatic lift. You'll also take a brief look at buoyancy in this chapter.

Buoyancy

You have no doubt felt the effects of buoyancy when immersing yourself in the bathtub. Buoyancy is why you feel lighter in water than you do in air and why some people can float on their backs in a swimming pool.

Buoyancy is a force that develops when an object is immersed in a fluid. It's a function of the volume of the object and the density of the fluid and results from the pressure differential between the fluid just above the object and the fluid just below the object. Pressure increases, the deeper you go in a fluid; thus, the pressure is greater at the bottom of an object of a given height than it is at the top of the object. Consider the cube shown in Figure 3-2.

Let s denote the cube's length, width, and height, which are all equal. Further, let h_t denote the depth to the top of the cube and h_b the depth to the bottom of the cube. The pressure at the top of the cube is $P_t = \rho g h_t$, which acts over the entire surface area of the top of the cube, normal to the surface in the downward direction. The pressure at the bottom of the cube is $P_b = \rho g h_b$, which acts over the entire surface area of the bottom of the cube, normal to the surface in the upward direction. Note that the pressure acting on the sides of the cube increases linearly with submergence, from P_t to P_b. Also, note that

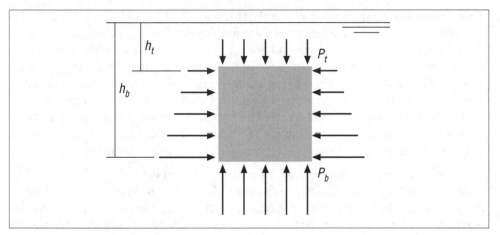

Figure 3-2. Immersed Cube

since the side pressure is symmetric, equal, and opposite, the net side pressure is zero, which means that the net side force (due to pressure) is also zero. The same is not true of the top and bottom pressures, which are obviously not equal, although they are opposite.

The force acting down on the top of the cube is equal to the pressure at the top of the cube times the surface area of the top. This can be written as follows:

$$F_t = P_t A_t$$
$$F_t = (\rho g h_t)(s^2)$$

Similarly, the force acting up on the bottom of the cube is equal to the pressure at the bottom times the surface area of the bottom:

$$F_b = P_b A_b$$
$$F_b = (\rho g h_b)(s^2)$$

The net vertical force (buoyancy) equals the difference between the top and bottom forces:

$$F_B = F_b - F_t$$
$$F_B = (\rho g h_b)(s^2) - (\rho g h_t)(s^2)$$
$$F_B = (\rho g)(s^2)(h_b - h_t)$$

This formula gives the magnitude of the buoyancy force. Its direction is straight up, counteracting the weight of the object.

There is an important observation to be made here. Notice that $(h_b - h_t)$ is simply the height of the cube, which is s in this case. Substituting s in place of $(h_b - h_t)$ reveals that the buoyancy force is a function of the volume of the cube:

$$F_B = (\rho g)(s^3)$$

This is great, since it means that all you need to do to calculate buoyancy is first calculate the volume of the object and then multiply that volume by the specific weight* (ρg) of the fluid. In truth, that's a little easier said than done for all but the simplest geometries. If you're dealing with spheres, cubes, cylinders, and the like, then calculating volume is easy. However, if you're dealing with any arbitrary geometry, then the volume calculation becomes more difficult. There are two ways to handle this difficulty. The first way is to simply divide the object into a number of smaller objects of simpler geometry, calculate their volumes, and then add them all up. The second way is to use numerical integration techniques to calculate volume by integrating over the surface of the object.

You should also note that buoyancy is a function of fluid density, and you don't have to be in a fluid as dense as water to experience the force of buoyancy. In fact, there are buoyant forces acting on you right now, although they are very small, due to the fact that you are immersed in air. Water is many times more dense than air, which is why you notice the force of buoyancy when in water and not when in air. Keep in mind, though, that for very light objects with relatively large volumes, the buoyant forces in air may be significant. For example, consider simulating a large balloon.

Springs and Dampers

Springs are structural elements that, when connected between two objects, apply equal and opposite forces to each object. This spring force follows Hook's law and is a function of the stretched or compressed length of the spring relative to the rest length of the spring and the spring constant of the spring. The spring constant is a quantity that relates the force exerted by the spring to its deflection:

$$F_s = k_s(L - r)$$

Here, F_s is the spring force, k_s is the spring constant, L is the stretched or compressed length of the spring, and r is the rest length of the spring. In the metric system of units, F_s would be measured in newtons (1 N = 1 kg-m/s^2), with L and r in meters and k_s in kg/s^2. If the spring is connected between two objects, it exerts a force of F_s on one object and $-F_s$ on the other; these are *equal and opposite* forces.

Dampers are usually used in conjunction with springs in numerical simulations. They act like viscous drag in that dampers act against velocity. In this case, if the damper is connected between two objects that are moving toward or away from one another, the damper acts to slow the relative velocity between the two objects. The force developed by a damper is proportional to the relative velocity of the connected objects and a damping constant, k_d, that relates relative velocity to damping force:

$$F_d = k_d(v_1 - v_2)$$

This equation shows the damping force, F_d, as a function of the damping constant and the relative velocity of the connected points on the two connected bodies. In metric

---

* Specific weight is density times the acceleration due to gravity. Typical units are lb/ft^3 and N/m^3.

units, where the damping force is measured in newtons and velocity in m/s, k_d has units of kg/s.

Typically, springs and dampers are combined into a single spring-damper element in which a single formula is used to represent the combined force. Using vector notation, the formula for a spring-damper element connecting two bodies is as follows:

$$\mathbf{F}_1 = -\{k_s(L-r) + k_d[(\mathbf{v}_1 - \mathbf{v}_2) \cdot \mathbf{L}]/L\}\mathbf{L}/L$$

Here, $\mathbf{F}_1$ is the force exerted on body 1, and the force $\mathbf{F}_2$ exerted on body 2 is

$$\mathbf{F}_2 = -\mathbf{F}_1$$

L is the length of the spring-damper (L, not in bold print, is the magnitude of the vector $\mathbf{L}$), which is equal to the vector difference in position between the connected points on bodies 1 and 2. If the connected objects are particles, then $\mathbf{L}$ is equal to the position of body 1 minus the position of body 2. Similarly, $\mathbf{v}_1$ and $\mathbf{v}_2$ are the velocities of the connected points on bodies 1 and 2. The quantity $(\mathbf{v}_1 - \mathbf{v}_2)$ represents the relative velocity between the connected bodies.

Springs and dampers are useful when you want to simulate collections of connected particles or rigid bodies. The spring force provides the structure, or glue, that holds the bodies together (or keeps them separated by a certain distance), while the damper helps smooth out the motion between the connected bodies so that it's not too jerky or springy. These dampers are also very important from a numerical stability point of view in that they help keep your simulations from blowing up. I'm getting a little ahead of myself here, but I'll show you how to use these spring-dampers in a real-time simulation of cloth in Chapter 17.

Force and Torque

I need to make the distinction here between force and torque.* Force is that which causes linear acceleration, while torque is that which causes rotational acceleration. Torque is force times distance. Specifically, to calculate the torque applied by a force acting on an object, you need to calculate the perpendicular distance from the axis of rotation to the line of action of the force and then multiply this distance by the magnitude of the force. This calculation gives the magnitude of the torque. Typical units for force are pounds, newtons, and tons. Since torque is force times a distance, its units take the form of a length unit times a force unit such as foot-pounds, newton-meters, or foot-tons.

Since both force and torque are vector quantities, you must also determine the direction of the torque vector. The force vector is easy to visualize: its line of action passes through the point of application of the force with its direction determined by the direction in which the force is applied. As a vector, the line of action of torque is along the axis of rotation, with the direction determined by the direction of rotation and the *righthand rule* (see Figure 3-3). The *righthand* rule is a simple trick to help keep track of vector

---

* Another common term for torque is *moment*.

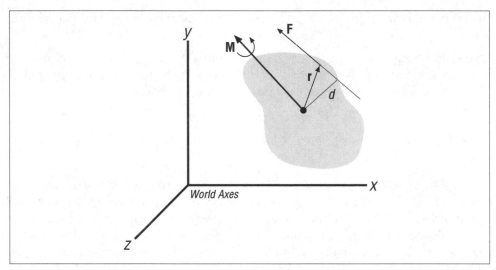

Figure 3-3. Force and Torque

directions—in this case the torque vector. Take your right hand and pretend to curl your fingers around the axis of rotation with your finger tips pointing in the direction of rotation. Now extend your thumb, as though you are giving a thumbs up, while keeping your fingers curled around the axis. The direction in which your thumb is pointing indicates the direction of the torque vector. Note that this makes the torque vector perpendicular to the applied force vector, as shown in Figure 3-3.

I said earlier that the magnitude of torque is found by multiplying the magnitude of the applied force times the perpendicular distance between the axis of rotation and the line of action of the force. This calculation is easy to perform in two dimensions, where the perpendicular distance (*d* in Figure 3-3) is readily calculable.

However, in three dimensions you'll want to be able to calculate torque by knowing only the force vector and the coordinates of its point of application on the body relative to the axis of rotation. You can accomplish this by using the following formula:

$$\mathbf{M} = \mathbf{r} \times \mathbf{F}$$

The torque, $\mathbf{M}$, is the vector cross product of the position vector, $\mathbf{r}$, and the force vector, $\mathbf{F}$.

In rectangular coordinates you can write the distance, force, and torque vectors as follows:

$$\mathbf{r} = x\mathbf{i} + y\mathbf{j} + z\mathbf{k}$$
$$\mathbf{F} = F_x\mathbf{i} + F_y\mathbf{j} + F_z\mathbf{k}$$
$$\mathbf{M} = M_x\mathbf{i} + M_y\mathbf{j} + M_z\mathbf{k}$$

The scalar components of $\mathbf{r}$ (*x*, *y*, and *z*) are the coordinate distances from the axis of rotation to the point of application of the force, $\mathbf{F}$. The scalar components of the torque vector, **M**, are defined by the following:

$$M_x = yF_z - zF_y$$
$$M_y = zF_x - xF_z$$
$$M_z = xF_y - yF_x$$

Consider the rigid body shown in Figure 3-4 acted upon by the force **F** at a point away from the body's center of mass.

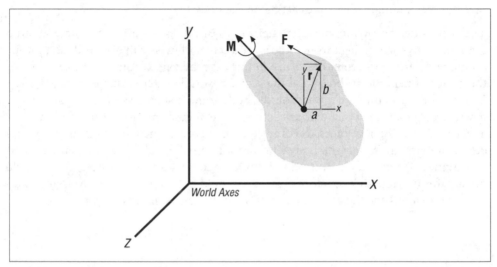

Figure 3-4. Torque Example

In this example **F**, a, and b are given and are as follows:

$$\mathbf{F} = (-90\,\text{lb})\mathbf{i} + (156\,\text{lb})\mathbf{j} + (0)\mathbf{k}$$
$$a = 0.66\,\text{ft}$$
$$b = 0.525\,\text{ft}$$

Calculate the torque about the body's center of mass due to the force **F**.

The first step is to put together the distance vector from the point of application of **F** to the body's center of mass. Since the local coordinates a and b are given, **r** is simply

$$\mathbf{r} = (0.66\,\text{ft})\mathbf{i} + (0.525\,\text{ft})\mathbf{j} + (0)\mathbf{k}$$

Now, using the formula $\mathbf{M} = \mathbf{r} \times \mathbf{F}$ (or the formulas for the components of the torque vector shown earlier), you can write

$$\mathbf{M} = [(0.66\,\text{ft})\mathbf{i} + (0.525\,\text{ft})\mathbf{j} + (0)\mathbf{k}] \times [(-90\,\text{lb})\mathbf{i} + (156\,\text{lb})\mathbf{j} + (0)\mathbf{k}]$$
$$\mathbf{M} = [(0.66\,\text{ft})(156\,\text{lb}) - (0.525\,\text{ft})(-90\,\text{lb})]\mathbf{k}$$
$$\mathbf{M} = (150.2\,\text{ft-lb})\mathbf{k}$$

Note that the x- and y-components of the torque vector are zero; therefore, the torque moment is pointing directly along the z-axis. The torque vector would be pointing out of the page of this book in this case.

In dynamics you need to consider the sum, or total, of all forces acting on an object separately from the sum of all torques acting on a body. When summing forces, you simply add, vectorally, all of the forces without regard to their point of application. However, when summing torques, you must take into account the point of application of the forces to calculate the torques as shown in the previous example. Then you can take the vector sum of all torques acting on the body.

When considering rigid bodies that are not physically constrained to rotate about a fixed axis, any force acting through the body's center of mass will not produce a torque on the body about its center of gravity. In this case the axis of rotation passes through the center of mass of the body, and the vector **r** would be zero (all components zero). When a force acts through a point on the body some distance away from its center of mass, a torque on the body will develop, and the angular motion of the body will be affected. Generally, field forces, forces at a distance, are assumed to act through a body's center of mass; thus, only the body's linear motion will be affected unless the body is constrained to rotate about a fixed point. Other contact forces, however, generally do not act through a body's center of mass (they could but aren't necessarily assumed to) and tend to affect the body's angular motion as well as its linear motion.

CHAPTER 4

Kinetics

Recall that kinetics is the study of the motion of bodies, including the forces that act on them. It's now time that I combine the material presented in the earlier chapters, namely, kinematics and forces, to study the subject of kinetics. As in the chapter on kinematics, I'll first discuss particle kinetics and then go on to discuss rigid body kinetics.

In kinetics the most important equation that you must consider is Newton's second law:

$$\mathbf{F} = m\mathbf{a}$$

When rigid bodies are involved, you must also consider that the forces acting on the body will tend to cause rotation of the body in addition to translation. The basic relationship here is

$$\mathbf{M}_{\text{cg}} = \mathbf{I}\alpha$$

where $\mathbf{M}_{\text{cg}}$ is the vector sum of all moments (torques) acting on the body, $\mathbf{I}$ is the body moment of inertia tensor, and α is the angular acceleration.

Collectively, these two equations are referred to as the *equations of motion*.

You will encounter two types of problems in kinetics. One type is when you know the body's acceleration or it can be readily determined by using kinematics, and you must solve for the force(s) acting on the body. The other type is when you know the force(s) acting on the body or you can estimate these, and you must solve for the resulting acceleration of the body (and subsequently its velocity and displacement). Obviously, it's this second type of problem that is most applicable to game physics, so that's primarily what I'll be discussing from here on.

Let me stress that you must consider the sum of *all* of the forces acting on the body when solving kinetics problems. These include all applied forces and all reaction forces. Aside from the computational difficulties in solving the equations of motion, one of the more challenging aspects of kinetics is identifying and properly accounting for all of these forces. In the next several chapters you'll look at specific problems in which the particular forces involved will be investigated. For now, and for the purpose of generality, let's stick with the idealized forces introduced in the previous chapter.

The general procedure for solving kinetics problems of interest to us is as follows:

1. Calculate the body's mass properties (mass, center of mass, and moment of inertia).
2. Identify and quantify all forces and moments acting on the body.
3. Take the vector sum of all forces and moments.
4. Solve the equations of motion for linear and angular accelerations.
5. Integrate with respect to time to find linear and angular velocity.
6. Integrate again with respect to time to find linear and angular displacement.

This outline makes the solution to kinetics problems seem easier than it actually is because there are a number of complicating factors that you'll have to overcome. For example, in many cases the forces acting on a body are functions of displacement, velocity, or acceleration. This means that you'll have to use iterative techniques to solve the equations of motion. Further, since you most likely will not be able to derive closed-form solutions for acceleration, you'll have to numerically integrate to estimate velocity and displacement at each instant of time under consideration. These computational aspects will be addressed further in Chapters 11 through 17.

Particle Kinetics in 2D

As in particle kinematics, in particle kinetics you need to consider only the linear motion of the particle. Thus, the equations of motion will consist of equations of the form $\mathbf{F} = m\mathbf{a}$, in which motion in each coordinate direction will have its own equation. The equations for 2D particle motion are

$$\sum F_x = ma_x$$
$$\sum F_y = ma_y$$

where $\sum F_x$ means the sum of all forces in the x-direction, $\sum F_y$ means the sum of all forces in the y-direction, a_x is the acceleration in the x-direction, and a_y is the acceleration in the y-direction.

The resultant force and acceleration vectors are

$$\mathbf{a} = a_x\mathbf{i} + a_y\mathbf{j}$$
$$a = \sqrt{a_x^2 + a_y^2}$$
$$\sum \mathbf{F} = \sum F_x\mathbf{i} + \sum F_y\mathbf{j}$$
$$\sum F = \sqrt{\left(\sum F_x\right)^2 + \left(\sum F_y\right)^2}$$

Let's look at a simple illustrative example. A ship floating in water, initially at rest, starts up its propeller, generating a thrust T, which starts the ship moving forward.

Assume that the ship's forward speed is slow and the resistance to its motion can be approximated by

$$R = -Cv$$

where R is the total resistance, C is a drag coefficient, v is the ship speed, and the minus sign indicates that this resistive force opposes the forward motion of the ship. Find formulas for the ship's speed, acceleration, and distance traveled as functions of time, assuming that the propeller thrust and resistance force vectors act on a line of action passing through the center of gravity of the ship. (This assumption lets you treat the ship as a particle instead of a rigid body.)

The first step in solving this problem is to identify all of the forces acting on the ship. Figure 4-1 shows a *free-body diagram* of the ship with all of the forces acting on it, namely, the propeller thrust, T; resistance, R; the ship's weight, W; and buoyancy, B.

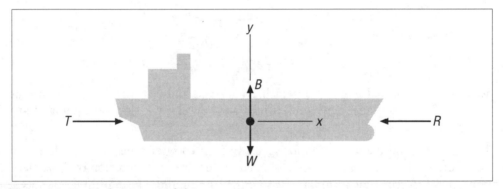

Figure 4-1. Free-Body Diagram of Ship

Notice here that the buoyancy force is exactly equal in magnitude to the ship's weight and opposite in direction; thus, these forces cancel each other, and there will be no motion in the y-direction. This must be the case if the ship is to stay afloat. This observation effectively reduces the problem to a one-dimensional problem with motion in the x-direction only where the forces acting in the x-direction are the propeller thrust and resistance.

Now you can write the equation (for motion in the x-direction), using Newton's second law, as follows:

$$\sum F = ma$$
$$T - R = ma$$
$$T - (Cv) = ma$$

where a is the acceleration in the x-direction and v is the speed in the x-direction.

The next step is to take this equation of motion and integrate it to derive a formula for the speed of the ship as a function of time. To do this, you must make the substitution $a = dv/dt$, rearrange, integrate, and then solve for speed as follows:

$$T - (Cv) = m(dv/dt)$$

$$dt = [m/(T - Cv)]\, dv$$

$$\int_0^t dt = \int_{v_1}^{v_2} [m/(T - Cv)]\, dv$$

$$t - 0 = -(-(m/C)\ln(T - Cv))\big|_{v_1}^{v_2}$$

$$t = -(m/C)\ln(T - Cv_2) + (m/C)\ln(T - Cv_1)$$

$$t = (m/C)[\ln(T - Cv_1) - \ln(T - Cv_2)]$$

$$(C/m)t = \ln[(T - Cv_1)/(T - Cv_2)]$$

$$e^{(C/m)t} = e^{\ln[(T-Cv_1)/(T-Cv_2)]}$$

$$e^{(C/m)t} = (T - Cv_1)/(T - Cv_2)$$

$$(T - Cv_2) = (T - Cv_1)e^{-(C/m)t}$$

$$v_2 = (T/C) - e^{-(C/m)t}(T/C - v_1)$$

where v_1 is the initial ship speed (which is constant) and v_2 is the ship speed at time t. v_2 is what you're after here, since it tells you how fast the ship is traveling at any instant of time.

Now that you have an equation for speed as a function of time, you can derive an equation for displacement (distance traveled in this case) as a function of time. Here, you'll have to recall the formula $v\, dt = ds$, substitute the above formula for speed, integrate, rearrange, and solve for distance traveled. These steps are shown below:

$$v\, dt = ds$$

$$v_2\, dt = ds$$

$$[(T/C) - e^{-(C/m)t}(T/C - v_1)]\, dt = ds$$

$$\int_0^t (T/C) - e^{-(C/m)t}(T/C - v_1)\, dt = \int_{s_1}^{s_2} ds$$

$$(T/C)\int_0^t dt - (T/C - v_1)\int_0^t e^{-(C/m)t} dt = s_2 - s_1$$

$$\left\{(T/C)t + [(T/C) - v_1](m/C)e^{-(C/m)t}\right\}_0^t = s_2 - s_1$$

$$\left\{(T/C)t + [(T/C) - v_1](m/C)e^{-(C/m)t}\right\} - \{0 + [(T/C) - v_1](m/C)\} = s_2 - s_1$$

$$(T/C)t + (T/C - v_1)(m/C)e^{-(C/m)t} - (T/C - v_1)(m/C) = s_2 - s_1$$

$$s_2 = s_1 + (T/C)t + (T/C - v_1)(m/C)e^{-(C/m)t} - (T/C - v_1)(m/C)$$

Finally, you can write an equation for acceleration by going back to the original equation of motion and solving for acceleration:

$$T - (Cv) = ma$$
$$a = (T - (Cv))/m$$
$$\text{where } v = v_2 = (T/C) - e^{-(C/m)t}(T/C - v_1)$$

In summary, the equations for velocity, distance traveled, and acceleration are as follows:

$$v_2 = (T/C) - e^{-(C/m)t}(T/C - v_1)$$
$$s_2 = s_1 + (T/C)t + (T/C - v_1)(m/C)e^{-(C/m)t} - (T/C - v_1)(m/C)$$
$$a = [T - (Cv)]/m$$

To illustrate the motion of the ship further, I've plotted the ship's speed, distance traveled, and acceleration versus time as shown in Figures 4-2, 4-3, and 4-4. To facilitate these illustrations, I've assumed the following:

- The initial ship speed and displacement are zero at time zero.
- The propeller thrust is 20,000 thrust units.
- The ship's mass is 10,000 mass units.
- The drag coefficient is 1000.

You'll notice that the ship's speed approaches the steady state speed of 20 speed units, assuming that the propeller thrust remains constant. This corresponds to a reduction in acceleration from a maximum acceleration at time zero to no acceleration once the steady speed is achieved.

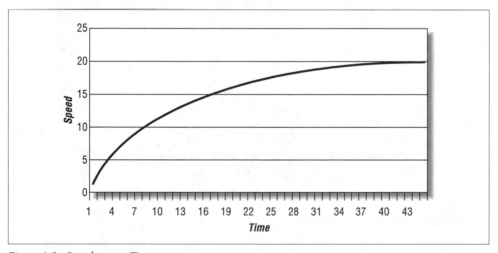

Figure 4-2. Speed versus Time

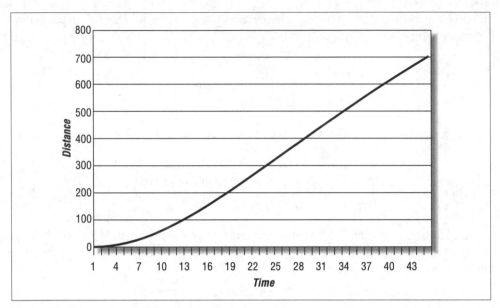

Figure 4-3. Distance versus Time

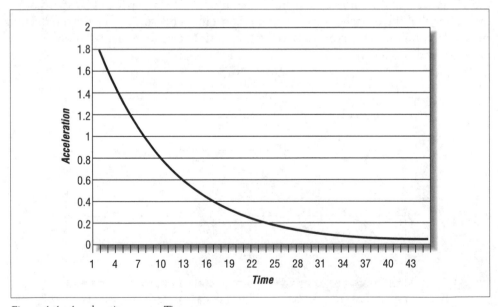

Figure 4-4. Acceleration versus Time

This example illustrates how to set up the differential equations of motion and integrate them to find velocity, displacement, and acceleration. In this case you were able to find a closed-form solution; that is, you were able to integrate the equations symbolically to derive new ones. You could do this because I imposed enough constraints on the problem to make it manageable. But you can readily see that if there were more forces acting on the ship, or if the thrust were not held constant but was some function of speed, or if the resistance were a function of speed squared, and so on, the problem would get increasingly complicated, making a closed-form solution much more difficult if possible at all.

Particle Kinetics in 3D

As in kinematics, extending the equations of motion for a particle to three dimensions is easy to do. You simply need to add one more component and will end up with three equations as follows:

$$\sum F_x = ma_x$$
$$\sum F_y = ma_y$$
$$\sum F_z = ma_z$$

The resultant force and acceleration vectors are now

$$\mathbf{a} = a_x\mathbf{i} + a_y\mathbf{j} + a_z\mathbf{k}$$
$$a = \sqrt{a_x^2 + a_y^2 + a_z^2}$$
$$\sum \mathbf{F} = \sum F_x\mathbf{i} + \sum F_y\mathbf{j} + \sum F_z\mathbf{k}$$
$$\sum F = \sqrt{\left(\sum F_x\right)^2 + \left(\sum F_y\right)^2 + \left(\sum F_z\right)^2}$$

To hammer these concepts home, I want to present another example.

Let's go back to the cannon program discussed in Chapter 2. In that example I made some simplifying assumptions so that I could focus on the kinematics of the problem without complicating it too much. One of the more significant assumptions I made was that there was no drag acting on the projectile as it flew through the air. Physically, this would be valid only if the projectile were moving through a vacuum, which of course, is unlikely here on the earth. Another significant assumption I made was that there was no wind to act on the projectile, affecting its course. These two considerations, drag and wind, are important in real-life projectile problems, so to make this example a little more interesting, and more challenging to the user if this were an actual game, I'll now go ahead and add these two considerations.

First, assume that the projectile is a sphere and that the drag force acting on it as it flies through the air is a function of some drag coefficient and the speed of the projectile.

This drag force can be written as follows:

$$\mathbf{F}_d = -C_d \mathbf{v}$$
$$\mathbf{F}_d = -C_d v_x \mathbf{i} - C_d v_y \mathbf{j} - C_d v_z \mathbf{k}$$

where C_d is the drag coefficient, v is the velocity of the projectile (v_x, v_y, and v_z are its components), and the minus sign means that this drag force opposes the projectile's motion. Actually, I'm cheating a bit here, since in reality the fluid dynamic drag would be more a function of speed squared. I'm doing this here to facilitate a closed-form solution.

Second, assume that the projectile is subjected to a blowing wind and that the force of this wind on the projectile is a function of some drag coefficient and the wind speed. This force can be written as follows:

$$\mathbf{F}_w = -C_w \mathbf{v}_w$$
$$\mathbf{F}_w = -C_w \mathbf{v}_{wx} \mathbf{i} - C_w \mathbf{v}_{wz} \mathbf{k}$$

where C_w is the drag coefficient, v_w is the wind speed, and the minus sign means that this force opposes the projectile's motion when the wind is blowing in a direction opposite of the projectile's direction of motion. When the wind is blowing with the projectile, say, from behind it, then the wind will actually help the projectile along instead of impede its motion. In general, C_w is not necessarily equal to C_d shown in the drag formula. Referring to Figure 2-3, I'll define the wind direction as measured by the angle γ. The x- and z-components of the wind force can now be written in terms of the wind direction, γ, as follows:

$$F_{wx} = F_w \cos \gamma = -(C_w v_w) \cos \gamma$$
$$F_{wz} = F_w \cos \gamma = -(C_w v_w) \sin \gamma$$

Finally, let's apply a gravitational force to the projectile instead of specifying the effect of gravity as a constant acceleration, as was done in Chapter 2. This allows you to include the force due to gravity in the equations of motion. Assuming that the projectile is relatively close to sea level, the gravitational force can be written as

$$\mathbf{F}_g = -mg\mathbf{j}$$

where the minus sign indicates that it acts in the negative y-direction (pulling the projectile toward the earth), and g on the right side of this equation is the acceleration due to gravity at sea level.

Now that all of the forces have been identified, you can write the equations of motion in each coordinate direction:

$$\sum F_x = F_{wx} + F_{dx} = m(dv_x/dt)$$
$$\sum F_y = F_{dy} + F_{gy} = m(dv_y/dt)$$
$$\sum F_z = F_{wz} + F_{dz} = m(dv_z/dt)$$

Note here that I already made the substitution *dv/dt* for acceleration in each equation. Following the same procedure shown in the previous section, you now need to integrate each equation of motion twice: once to find an equation for velocity as a function of time and again to find an equation for displacement as a function of time. As before, I'll show you how this is done component by component.

You might be asking yourself now, "Where's the thrust force from the cannon that propels the projectile in the first place?" In this example I'm looking specifically at the motion of the projectile after it has left the muzzle of the cannon where there is no longer a thrust force acting on the projectile (it isn't self-propelled). To account for the effect of the cannon thrust force, which acts over a very short period of time while the projectile is within the cannon, you have to consider the muzzle velocity of the projectile when it initially leaves the cannon. The components of the muzzle velocity in the coordinate directions will become initial velocities in each direction, and they will be included in the equations of motion once they have been integrated. The initial velocities will show up in the velocity and displacement equations just as they did in the example in Chapter 2. You'll see this in the following sections.

x-Components

The first step is to make the appropriate substitutions for the force terms in the equation of motion and then integrate to find an equation for velocity:

$$-F_{wx} - F_{dx} = m(dv_x/dt)$$

$$-(C_w v_w \cos \gamma) - C_d v_x = m \, dv_x/dt$$

$$dt = m \, dv_x/[-(C_w v_w \cos \gamma) - C_d v_x]$$

$$\int_0^t dt = \int_{vx_1}^{vx_2} -m/[(C_w v_w \cos \gamma) + C_d v_x] \, dv_x$$

$$t = -(m/C_d) \ln[(C_w v_w \cos \gamma) + C_d v_x]\Big|_{vx_1}^{vx_2}$$

$$t = -(m/C_d) \ln[(C_w v_w \cos \gamma) + C_d v_{x_2}] + (m/C_d) \ln[(C_w v_w \cos \gamma) + C_d v_{x_1}]$$

$$(C_d/m)t = \ln\{[(C_w v_w \cos \gamma) + C_d v_{x_1}]/[(C_w v_w \cos \gamma) + C_d v_{x_2}]\}$$

$$e^{(C_d/m)t} = e^{\ln\{[(C_w v_w \cos \gamma) + C_d v_{x_1}]/[(C_w v_w \cos \gamma) + C_d v_{x_2}]\}}$$

$$e^{(C_d/m)t} = [(C_w v_w \cos \gamma) + C_d v_{x_1}]/[(C_w v_w \cos \gamma) + C_d v_{x_2}]$$

$$[(C_w v_w \cos \gamma) + C_d v_{x_2}] = [(C_w v_w \cos \gamma) + C_d v_{x_1}]e^{-(C_d/m)t}$$

$$v_{x_2} = (1/C_d)\big[e^{(-C_d/m)t}(C_w v_w \cos \gamma + C_d v_{x_1}) - (C_w v_w \cos \gamma)\big]$$

To get an equation for displacement as a function of time, you need to recall the equation *v dt = ds*, make the substitution for *v* (using the above equation), and then integrate one more time:

$$v_{x_2}dt = ds_x$$

$$(1/C_d)\big[e^{(-C_d/m)t}(c_w v_w \cos\gamma + C_d v_{x_1}) - (c_w v_w \cos\gamma)\big]dt = ds_x$$

$$\int_0^t (1/C_d)\big[e^{(-C_d/m)t}(c_w v_w \cos\gamma + C_d v_{x_1}) - (c_w v_w \cos\gamma)\big]dt = \int_{s_{x_1}}^{s_{x_2}} ds_x$$

$$s_{x_2} = \big\{(m/C_d)e^{(-C_d/m)t}[-(c_w v_w \cos\gamma)/C_d - v_{x_1}] - [(c_w v_w \cos\gamma)/C_d]t\big\}$$
$$-\{(m/C_d)[-(c_w v_w \cos\gamma)/C_d - v_{x_1}]\} + s_{x_1}$$

Yes, these equations are ugly. Just imagine if I hadn't made the simplifying assumption that drag is proportional to speed and not speed squared! You would have ended up with some really nice equations with an arctan term or two thrown in.

y-Components

For the y-components you need to follow the same procedure shown earlier for the x-components, but with the appropriate y-direction forces. Here's what it looks like:

$$-F_{dy} - F_{gy} = m(dv_y/dt)$$

$$-(C_d v_y) - mg = m(dv_y/dt)$$

$$\int_0^t dt = -m \int_{v_{y_1}}^{v_{y_2}} 1/(C_d v_y + mg)dv_y$$

$$v_{y_2} = (1/C_d)e^{(-C_d/m)t}(C_d v_{y_1} + mg) - (mg)/C_d$$

Now that you have an equation for velocity, you can proceed on to get an equation for displacement as before:

$$v_{y_2}\,dt = ds_y$$

$$\big[(1/C_d)e^{(-C_d/m)t}(C_d v_{y_1} + mg) - (mg)/C_d\big]dt = ds_y$$

$$\int_0^t \big[(1/C_d)e^{(-C_d/m)t}(C_d v_{y_1} + mg) - (mg)/C_d\big]dt = \int_{s_{y_1}}^{s_{y_2}} ds_y$$

$$s_{y_2} = s_{y_1} + \big\{-[v_{y_1} + (mg)/C_d](m/C_d)e^{(-C_d/m)t} - t(mg)/C_d\big\}$$
$$+\{(m/C_d)[v_{y_1} + (mg)/C_d]\}$$

Okay, that's two down and only one more to go.

z-Components

With the z-component you get a break. You'll notice that the equations of motion for the x- and z-components look almost the same with the exception of the x and z subscripts and the sine versus cosine terms. Taking advantage of this fact you can simply copy the x-component equations and replace the x subscript with a z and the cosine terms with sines and be done with it:

$$v_{z_2} = (1/C_d)\left[e^{(-C_d/m)t}(c_w v_w \sin\gamma + C_d v_{z_1}) - (c_w v_w \sin\gamma)\right]$$

$$s_{z_2} = \{(m/C_d)e^{(-C_d/m)t}[-(C_w v_w \sin\gamma)/C_d - v_{z_1}] - [(C_w v_w \sin\gamma)/C_d]t\}$$
$$-\{(m/C_d)[-(C_w v_w \sin\gamma)/C_d - v_{z1}]\} + s_{z1}$$

Cannon Revised

Now that you have some new equations for the projectile's displacement in each coordinate direction, you can go to the *cannon* example source code and replace the old displacement calculation formulas with the new ones. Make the changes in the DoSimulation function as follows:

```
//-----------------------------------------------------------------------------
//
int      DoSimulation(void)
//-----------------------------------------------------------------------------
//
{
    .
    .
    .

    // new local variables:
    double    sx1, vx1;
    double    sy1, vy1;
    double    sz1, vz1;
    .
    .
    .

    // Now we can calculate the position vector at this time

    // Old position vector commented out:
    //s.i = Vm * cosX * time + xe;
    //s.j = (Yb + L * cos(Alpha * 3.14/180)) + (Vm * cosY * time) -
    //    (0.5 * g * time * time);
    //s.k = Vm * cosZ * time + ze;

    // New position vector calculations:
    sx1 = xe;
    vx1 = Vm * cosX;
    sy1 = Yb + L * cos(Alpha * 3.14/180);
    vy1 = Vm * cosY;

    sz1 = ze;
    vz1 = Vm * cosZ;

    s.i = ( (m/Cd) * exp(-(Cd * time)/m) * ((-Cw * Vw * cos(GammaW * 3.14/180))/Cd -

        vx1) - (Cw * Vw * cos(GammaW * 3.14/180) * time) / Cd ) -
          ( (m/Cd) * ((-Cw * Vw * cos(GammaW * 3.14/180))/Cd - vx1) ) + sx1;
```

```
        s.j = sy1 + ( -(vy1 + (m * g)/Cd) * (m/Cd) * exp(-(Cd*time)/m) -
            (m * g * time) / Cd ) + ( (m/Cd) * (vy1 + (m * g)/Cd) );

        s.k = ( (m/Cd) * exp(-(Cd * time)/m) * ((-Cw * Vw * sin(GammaW * 3.14/180))/Cd -

            vz1) - (Cw * Vw * sin(GammaW * 3.14/180) * time) / Cd ) -
            ( (m/Cd) * ((-Cw * Vw * sin(GammaW * 3.14/180))/Cd - vz1) ) + sz1;
        .
        .
        .
        .
    }
```

To take into account the cross wind and drag, you'll need to add some new global variables to store the wind speed and direction, the mass of the projectile, and the drag coefficients. You'll also have to add some controls in the dialog window so that you can change these variables when you run the program. Figure 4-5 shows how I added these interface controls in the upper right corner of the main window.

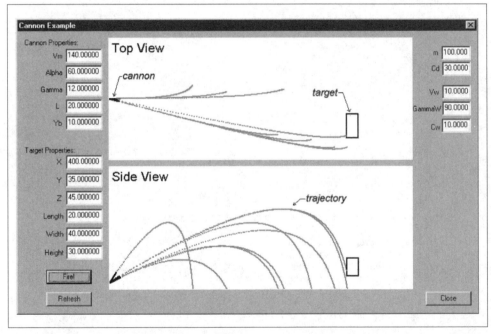

Figure 4-5. Revised Cannon Example Screen Shot

I also added these lines to the DemoDlgProc function to handle the new wind speed and direction values:

```
//----------------------------------------------------------------------------
//
LRESULT CALLBACK DemoDlgProc(HWND hDlg, UINT message, WPARAM wParam, LPARAM lParam)
//----------------------------------------------------------------------------
//
```

```
{
       •
       •
       •

       case WM_INITDIALOG:

       •
       •
       •

              // New variables:
              sprintf( str, "%f", m );
              SetDlgItemText(hDlg, IDC_M, str);

              sprintf( str, "%f", Cd );
              SetDlgItemText(hDlg, IDC_CD, str);

              sprintf( str, "%f", Vw );
              SetDlgItemText(hDlg, IDC_VW, str);

              sprintf( str, "%f", GammaW );
              SetDlgItemText(hDlg, IDC_GAMMAW, str);

              sprintf( str, "%f", Cw );
              SetDlgItemText(hDlg, IDC_CW, str);

       •
       •
       •

              case IDC_REFRESH:

       •
       •
       •

                     // New variables:
                     GetDlgItemText(hDlg, IDC_M, str, 15);
                     m = atof(str);

                     GetDlgItemText(hDlg, IDC_CD, str, 15);
                     Cd = atof(str);

                     GetDlgItemText(hDlg, IDC_VW, str, 15);
                     Vw = atof(str);

                     GetDlgItemText(hDlg, IDC_GAMMAW, str, 15);
                     GammaW = atof(str);

                     GetDlgItemText(hDlg, IDC_CW, str, 15);
                     Cw = atof(str);

       •
       •
       •

              case IDC_FIRE:

       •
       •
       •

                     // New variables:
                     GetDlgItemText(hDlg, IDC_M, str, 15);
                     m = atof(str);

                     GetDlgItemText(hDlg, IDC_CD, str, 15);
                     Cd = atof(str);
```

```
GetDlgItemText(hDlg, IDC_VW, str, 15);
Vw = atof(str);

GetDlgItemText(hDlg, IDC_GAMMAW, str, 15);
GammaW = atof(str);

GetDlgItemText(hDlg, IDC_CW, str, 15);
Cw = atof(str);

        .
        .
        .
}
```

After playing with this example program, you should readily see that the trajectory of the projectile is noticeably different from that typically obtained in the original example. By adjusting the values of wind speed, direction, and the drag coefficients, you can dramatically affect the projectile's trajectory. If you set the wind speed to zero and the drag coefficients to 1, the trajectory will look like that obtained in the original example, in which wind and drag were not taken into account. Be careful though; don't set the drag coefficient to zero because this will result in a divide-by-zero error. I didn't put the exception handler in the program, but you can see that it will happen by looking at the displacement vector formulas where the drag coefficient appears in the denominator of several terms.

From a user's perspective, if this were a video game, the problem of hitting the target becomes much more challenging when wind and drag are taken into account. The wind element is particularly interesting because you can change the wind speed and direction during game play, forcing the user to pay careful attention to the wind in order to hit the target accurately.

Rigid Body Kinetics

You already know from your study of kinematics in Chapter 2 that dealing with rigid bodies adds rotation, or angular motion, into the mix of things to consider. As I stated earlier, the equations of motion now consist of a set of equations relating forces to linear accelerations and another set of equations relating moments to angular accelerations. Alternatively, you can think of the equations of motion as relating forces to the rate of change in linear momentum and moments to the rate of change in angular momentum as discussed in Chapter 1.

As in kinematics, the procedure for dealing with rigid body kinetics problems involves two distinct aspects: tracking the translation of the body's center of mass, where the body is treated as a particle, and tracking the body's rotation, in which you'll utilize the principles of local coordinates and relative angular velocity and acceleration as discussed in Chapter 2. Really, the only difference between rigid body kinematics and kinetics problems is that in kinetics problems we have forces to consider (including their resulting moments).

The vector equations are repeated here for convenience:

$$\mathbf{F} = m\mathbf{a}$$

$$\mathbf{M}_{cg} = I\boldsymbol{\alpha}$$

where, in two dimensions,

$$\sum \mathbf{F} = \sum F_x \mathbf{i} + \sum F_y \mathbf{j}$$

$$\sum F = \sqrt{\left(\sum F_x\right)^2 + \left(\sum F_y\right)^2}$$

Going from two-dimensional particle problems to two-dimensional rigid body problems involves only the addition of one more equation. This equation is, of course, the moment equation relating the sum of all moments acting on the body to the body's moment of inertia and its angular acceleration. In plane motion the axis of rotation of the rigid body is always perpendicular to the coordinate plane. And since there is only one axis of rotation, there is only one inertia term and one angular acceleration term to consider. Thus, you can write

$$M_{cg} = I\alpha$$

where M_{cg} is the total moment and is calculated by using the formulas discussed in the section entitled "Force and Torque" in Chapter 3 and I is calculated about the axis of rotation using the techniques discussed in the section entitled "Mass, Center of Mass, and Moment of Inertia" in Chapter 1.

In their component forms, the set of equations of motion for two-dimensional kinetics problems are

$$\sum F_x = ma_x$$

$$\sum F_y = ma_y$$

$$\sum M_{cg} = I\alpha$$

Since these equations indicate linear motion on the xy-plane, the angular acceleration will be about the z-axis perpendicular to the xy-plane. Likewise, the moment of inertia, I, will be taken about the z-axis.

Recall (from Chapter 3) that moment is calculated by taking the cross product of the position vector for the force under consideration and the force vector. This means that, unlike in particle kinetics, you now have to keep track of exactly where on the body each force is applied. This is best illustrated with an example.

Consider the box of uniform density shown in Figure 4-6. Uniform density means that its center of gravity is at the box's geometric center. Find the value of the minimum force, F_p, applied at the upper edge of the box, required to start tipping the box over.

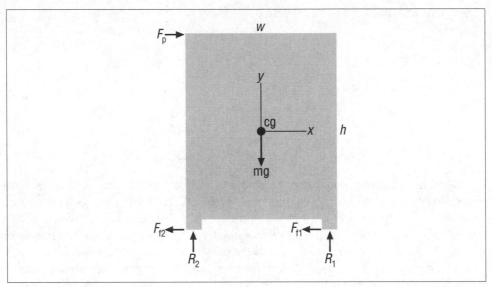

Figure 4-6. Box Free-Body Diagram

In this figure, F_p is the applied force, R_1 and R_2 are the reaction forces at supports 1 and 2, F_{f1} and F_{f2} are the forces due to friction at points 1 and 2, and mg is the weight of the box.

This is an example of the type of problem in which you know something about the motion of the object and have to find the value of one or more forces acting on it. To find the value of the force that will be just enough to start the box tipping, you need to look at the instant when the reaction force at support 2 is zero. This implies that all of the weight of the box is now supported at point 1 and the box is starting to rotate over. At this instant, just before it starts to rotate, the angular acceleration of the box is zero. Note that the box's linear acceleration isn't necessarily zero; that is, you can push on the box and it may slide without actually tipping over.

The equations of motion for this problem are

$$\sum F_x = F_p = ma_x$$
$$\sum F_y = R_1 + R_2 - mg = ma_y = 0$$
$$\sum M_{cg} = F_p(h/2) + R_2(w/2) - R_1(w/2) + F_{f_2}(h/2) + F_{f_1}(h/2) = I\alpha = 0$$

Rewriting the second equation (above) when R_2 is zero shows that R_1 is equal to the weight of the box. Further, when R_2 is zero, the $R_2(w/2)$ term drops out of the moment equation, which can be rewritten by solving for F_p in terms of R_1. Note that when R_2 goes to zero, so does F_{f_2}. After some algebra the equation looks as follows:

$$F_p = mg(w/h) - F_{f_1}$$

Here, you can see that the tipping force, applied to the upper edge, is proportional to the weight and size of the box (actually, the ratio of its width to its height), which you can readily appreciate from a physical point of view. The friction term is important here because the existence of the friction force actually helps the box to tip. If the box were on a frictionless surface, it would tend to slide rather than tip.

Let's take a look at another example. Consider a circular cylinder on an inclined plane, as shown in Figure 4-7. If the cylinder is set at the top of the plane and released, it will start rolling down the plane. Develop equations for the cylinder's linear acceleration and angular velocity as it rolls down. Note that the cylinder will roll because of the torque created by the friction force that's developed between the cylinder and the plane. If this were a frictionless problem, then the cylinder would not roll down the plane; it would simply slide down the plane, and its angular velocity would be zero.

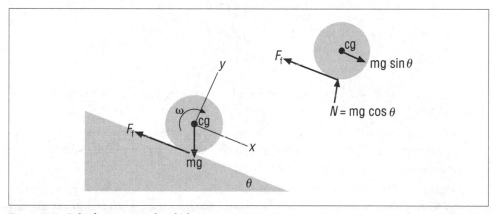

Figure 4-7. Cylinder on an Inclined Plane

In this problem I've set up the coordinate system with the x-axis parallel to the inclined plane. This makes the equations cleaner and allows you to effectively eliminate the y-component, since the cylinder is not moving into or away from (perpendicularly) the plane. Setting up the equations of motion in the y-direction indicates that the two y-direction forces, in this case the component of the weight of the cylinder in the y-direction and the reaction force normal to the plane, are equal and opposite and thus cancel out:

$$\sum F_y = mg \cos \theta - mg \cos \theta = 0$$

That was easy. Now look at the forces in the x-direction. The equation of motion is

$$\sum F_x = (mg \sin \theta) - F_f = ma_x$$

where F_f is the force due to friction, and a_x is the linear acceleration (in the x-direction) of the center of gravity of the cylinder. Assuming that the cylinder rolls without slipping, the friction force is equal to $\mu_s N$, where μ_s is the coefficient of static friction and N is the normal reaction force between the cylinder and the plane.* Making this substitution for F_f and solving for a_x yields

$$(mg \sin \theta) - \mu_s N = ma_x$$
$$a_x = g(\sin \theta - \mu_s \cos \theta)$$

Notice that this acceleration is constant for a given plane angle and coefficient of friction.

To find the angular velocity, you need to sum all of the moments (torques) about the center of gravity, make the substitution $d\omega/dt$ for α, integrate and solve for ω, the angular velocity:

$$\sum M_{cg} = F_f r = I_{cg} \alpha$$
$$F_f r = I_{cg} \, d\omega/dt$$
$$dt = I_{cg}/(F_f r) \, d\omega$$
$$\int_0^t dt = I_{cg}/(F_f r) \int_{\omega_1}^{\omega_2} d\omega$$
$$\omega_2 = [(F_f r)/I_{cg}]t + \omega_1$$

You could have skipped the integration here by observing that this is a constant acceleration problem and recalling the equation (from Chapter 2) $\omega_2 = \alpha t + \omega_1$.

These two examples illustrate a very important aspect of rigid body kinetics: you must consider the point of application of forces in addition to their magnitudes and directions to properly account for angular motion.

In the case of plane motion, or 2D motion, of rigid bodies as discussed here, you are able to readily set up the equations of motion and investigate both the linear and angular motion of the body. In generalized 3D motion the linear motion of rigid bodies is no different from that of particles; you simply track the motion of the rigid body's center of gravity. In three dimensions, however, rotation gives us some grief, as it is no longer a simple matter of treating rotation about a single axis as in plane motion. In 3D you'll have to consider rotation about any axis, which leads to some difficulties in representing arbitrary rotations (Euler angles won't work for us) as well as to complications determining moments of inertia for rotation about any axis. I'll discuss these issues in Chapters 11 through 15.

---

* If the cylinder were rolling and slipping, then you would use the coefficient of kinetic friction instead of the coefficient of static friction.

CHAPTER 5

Collisions

Now that you understand the motion of particles and rigid bodies, you next need to consider what happens when they run into each other. That's what I'll address in this chapter. Specifically, I'll show you how to handle particle and, more interestingly, rigid body collision response.

Before moving forward, I need to make a distinction between collision *detection* and collision *response*. Collision detection is a computational geometry problem involving the determination of whether and where two or more objects have collided. Collision response is a physics problem involving the motion of two or more objects after they have collided. Although the two problems are intimately related, in this chapter I'll be focusing solely on the problem of collision response.

I must say, however, that collision detection is not to be taken lightly; it is a crucial aspect of any real-time simulation in which objects are not supposed to be able to pass through each other. Your collision response algorithms rely on the results of your collision detection algorithms to accurately determine the appropriate response to any collision; therefore, you should take care in making sure your collision detection schemes are accurate and reliable. That said, collision detection is no easy task. I personally find it much more difficult to implement robustly than the physics aspects of rigid body simulations. For game applications, speed is also a major issue, as I'm sure you are aware, and very accurate collision detection can be slow. For the sake of speed and simplicity I'll use a bounding sphere scheme along with bounding box and vertex edge and vertex face collision detection schemes in the examples that you'll see later in this book. I'll talk more about this subject in Chapters 13 and 16 when I show you some example simulations.

My treatment of rigid body collision response in this chapter is based on classical (Newtonian) impact principles. Here, bodies that are colliding are treated as rigid irrespective of their construction and material. As in earlier chapters, the rigid bodies discussed here do not change shape even upon impact. This, of course, is an idealization. You know from your everyday experience that when objects collide, they dent, bend, compress, or crumple. For example, when a baseball strikes a bat, the ball may compress as much as three quarters of an inch during the millisecond of impact. Notwithstanding this reality, we'll rely on well established analytical and empirical methods to approximate rigid body collisions.

This classical approach is widely used in engineering machine design, analysis, and simulations; however, for rigid body simulations there is another class of methods, known as *penalty methods,* at your disposal.* In penalty methods the force at impact is represented by a temporary spring that gets compressed between the objects at the point of impact. This spring compresses over a very short time and applies equal and opposite forces to the colliding bodies to simulate collision response. Proponents of this method say that it has the advantage of ease of implementation. However, one of the difficulties encountered in its implementation is numerical instability. There are other arguments for and against the use of penalty methods, but I won't get into the debate here. Instead, I've included several references in the bibliography for you to review if you are so inclined.

Impulse-Momentum Principle

Impulse is defined as a force that acts over a very short period of time. For example, the force exerted on a bullet when fired from a gun is an impulse force. The collision forces between two colliding objects are impulse forces, as when you kick a football or hit a baseball with a bat.

More specifically, impulse is a vector quantity equal to the change in momentum. The so-called *impulse-momentum* principle says that the change in moment is equal to the applied impulse. For problems involving constant mass and moment of inertia, you can write

$$\text{Linear impulse} = \int_{t-}^{t+} \mathbf{F} \, dt = m(\mathbf{v}_+ - \mathbf{v}_-)$$

$$\text{Angular impulse} = \int_{t-}^{t+} \mathbf{M} \, dt = \mathbf{I}(\omega_+ - \omega_-)$$

In these equations $\mathbf{F}$ is the impulsive force, $\mathbf{M}$ is the impulsive torque (or moment), t is time, $\mathbf{v}$ is velocity, the subscript $-$ refers to the instant just prior to impact, and the subscript $+$ refers to the instant just after impact. You can calculate the average impulse force and torque using the following equations:

$$\mathbf{F} = m(\mathbf{v}_+ - \mathbf{v}_-)/(t_+ - t_-)$$

$$\mathbf{M} = \mathbf{I}(\omega_+ - \omega_-)/(t_+ - t_-)$$

---

* I use the classical approach in this book and am mentioning penalty methods only to let you know that the method I'm going to show is not the only one. Roughly speaking, the "penalty" in "penalty methods" refers to the numerical spring constants, which are usually large, that are used to represent the stiffness of the springs and thus the hardness (or softness) of the colliding bodies. These constants are used in the system of equations of motion describing the motion of all the bodies under consideration before and after the collision.

Consider this simple example: A 150-g (0.01028-slug) bullet is fired from a gun at a muzzle velocity of 2480 ft/s. The bullet takes 0.008 s to travel through the 24-in. rifle barrel. Calculate the impulse and the average impulsive force exerted on the bullet. In this example the bullet's mass is a constant 150 g, and its initial velocity is zero; thus, its initial momentum is zero. Immediately after the gun is fired, the bullet's momentum is its mass times the muzzle velocity of 2480 ft/s, which yields a momentum of 25.5 slug-ft/s. The impulse is equal to the change in momentum and is simply 25.5 slug-ft/s. The average impulse force is equal to the impulse divided by the duration of application of the force, or, in this case,

$$\text{Average impulse force} = (25.5 \text{ slug-ft/s})/(0.0008 \text{ s})$$

$$\text{Average impulse force} = 3187 \text{ lb}$$

This is a simple but important illustration of the concept of impulse, and you'll use the same principle when dealing with rigid body impacts. During impacts, the forces of impact are usually very high, and the duration of impact is usually very short. When two objects collide, each applies an impulse force to the other; these forces are equal in magnitude but opposite in direction. In the gun example the impulse that is applied to the bullet to set it in motion is also applied in the opposite direction to the gun to give you a nice kick in the shoulder. This is simply Newton's third law in action.

Impact

In addition to the impulse momentum principle discussed in the previous section, our classical impact, or collision response, analysis relies on another fundamental principle: Newton's principle of conservation of momentum, which states that when a system of rigid bodies collide, momentum is conserved. This means that for bodies of constant mass, the sum of their masses times their respective velocities before the impact is equal to the sum of their masses times their respective velocities after the impact:

$$m_1 v_{1-} + m_2 v_{2-} = m_1 v_{1+} + m_2 v_{2+}$$

Here, m refers to mass, v refers to velocity, subscript 1 refers to body 1, subscript 2 refers to body 2, subscript $-$ refers to the instant just before impact, and subscript $+$ refers to the instant just after impact.

A crucial assumption of this method is that during the instant of impact, the only force that matters is the impact force; all other forces are assumed to be negligible over that very short duration. Remember this assumption because later, in Chapter 13, I'll rely on it when implementing collision response in an example 2D real-time simulation.

I've already stated that rigid bodies don't change shape during impacts, and you know from your own experience that real objects do change shape during impacts. What's happening in real life is that *kinetic energy* is being converted to strain energy, causing the objects to deform. When the deformation in the objects is permanent, energy is lost, and thus kinetic energy is not conserved.

Kinetic Energy

Kinetic energy is a form of energy associated with moving bodies. Kinetic energy is equal to the energy required to accelerate the body from rest, which is also equal to the energy required to bring the moving body to a stop. As you might expect, kinetic energy is a function of the body's speed, or velocity, in addition to its mass. The formula for linear kinetic energy is

$$KE_{\text{linear}} = (1/2)mv^2$$

Angular, or rotational, kinetic energy is a function of the body's inertia and angular velocity:

$$KE_{\text{angular}} = (1/2)I\omega^2$$

Conservation of kinetic energy between two colliding bodies means that the sum of kinetic energy of both bodies before impact is equal to the sum of the kinetic energy of both bodies after impact:

$$m_1 v_{1-}^2 + m_2 v_{2-}^2 = m_1 v_{1+}^2 + m_2 v_{2+}^2$$

Collisions that involve losses in kinetic energy are said to be *inelastic*, or *plastic*, collisions. For example, if you throw two clay balls against each other, their kinetic energy is converted to permanent strain energy in deforming the clay balls, and their collision response, that is, their motion after impact, is less than spectacular. If the collision is *perfectly inelastic*, then the two balls of clay will stick to each other and move together at the same velocity after impact. Collisions in which kinetic energy is conserved are called perfectly *elastic*. In these collisions the sum of kinetic energy of all objects before the impact is equal to the sum of kinetic energy of all objects after the impact. A good example of elastic impact (though not *perfectly* elastic) is the collision between two billiard balls, in which the ball deformation is negligible and certainly not permanent under normal circumstances.

Of course, in reality, impacts are somewhere between perfectly elastic and perfectly inelastic. This means that for rigid bodies, which don't change shape at all, we'll have to rely on an empirical relation to quantify the degree of elasticity of the impact(s) that we're trying to simulate. The relation that we'll use is the ratio of the relative separation velocity to the relative approach velocity of the colliding objects:

$$e = -(v_{1+} - v_{2+})/(v_{1-} - v_{2-})$$

Here, e is known as the *coefficient of restitution* and is a function of the colliding objects' material, construction, and geometry. This coefficient can be experimentally determined for specific impact scenarios, for example, the collision between a baseball and bat or a golf club and ball. For perfectly inelastic collisions, e is zero; and for perfectly elastic collisions, e is 1. For collisions that are neither perfectly inelastic nor perfectly elastic, e can be any value between zero and 1. In this regard, the velocities that are considered are along the *line of action* of the collision.

In frictionless collisions the line of action of impact is a line perpendicular (or normal) to the colliding surfaces. When the velocity of the bodies is along the line of action, the impact is said to be *direct*. When the line of action passes through the center of mass of the bodies, the collision is said to be *central*. Particles and spheres of uniform mass distribution always experience central impact. *Direct central* impact occurs when the line of action passes through the centers of mass of the colliding bodies and their velocity is along the line of action. When the velocities of the bodies are not along the line of action, the impact is said to be *oblique*. You can analyze oblique impacts in terms of component coordinates where the component parallel to the line of action experiences the impact, but the component perpendicular to the line of action does not. Figure 5-1 illustrates these impacts.

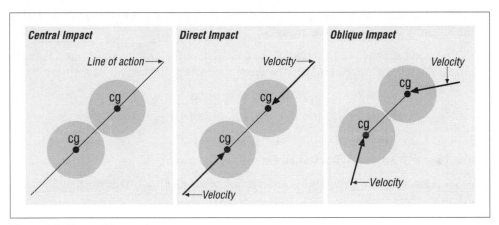

Figure 5-1. Types of Impact

As an example, consider the collision between two billiard balls as illustrated in Figure 5-2.

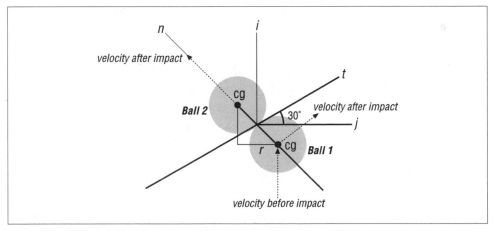

Figure 5-2. Billiard Ball Collision Example

Both balls are a standard 2.25 in. in diameter, and each weighs 5.5 oz. Assume that the collision is nearly perfectly elastic and that the coefficient of restitution is 0.9. If the velocity of ball 1 when it strikes ball 2 is 20 ft/s in the x-direction as shown in Figure 5-2, calculate the velocities of both balls after the collision, assuming that this is a frictionless collision.

The first thing you need to do is recognize that the line of action of impact is along the line connecting the centers of gravity of both balls, which, since these are spheres, is also normal to both surfaces. You can then write the unit normal vector as follows:

$$\mathbf{n} = \left(\sqrt{((2r)^2 - r^2)} \, \mathbf{i} - r\mathbf{j} \right)/|\mathbf{n}|$$
$$\mathbf{n} = (0.866)\mathbf{i} - (0.5)\mathbf{j}$$

where $\mathbf{n}$ is the unit normal vector, r is the ball radius, and $\mathbf{i}$ and $\mathbf{j}$ represent unit vectors in the x- and y-directions, respectively.

Now that you have the line of action of the collision, or the unit normal vector, you can calculate the relative normal velocity between the balls at the instant of collision:

$$v_{rn} = [\mathbf{v}_{1-} - \mathbf{v}_{2-}] \cdot \mathbf{n}$$
$$v_{rn} = [(20 \text{ ft/s})\mathbf{i} + (0 \text{ ft/s})\mathbf{j}] \cdot [(0.864)\mathbf{i} - (0.5)\mathbf{j}]$$
$$v_{rn} = 17.28 \text{ ft/s}$$

Notice here that since ball 2 is initially at rest, v_{2-} is zero.

Now you can apply the principle of conservation of momentum in the normal direction as follows:

$$m_1 v_{1n-} + m_2 v_{2n-} = m_1 v_{1n+} + m_2 v_{2n+}$$

Noting that m_1 equals m_2, since the balls are identical, and that v_{2n-} is zero and then solving for v_{1n+} yields

$$v_{1n+} = v_{1n-} - v_{2n+}$$

To actually solve for these velocities, you need to use the equation for coefficient of restitution and make the substitution for v_{1n+}. Then you'll be able to solve for v_{2n+}. Here's how to proceed:

$$e = (-v_{1n+} + v_{2n+})/(v_{1n-} - v_{2n-})$$
$$e v_{1n-} = -(v_{1n-} - v_{2n+}) + v_{2n+}$$
$$v_{2n+} = v_{1n-}(e + 1)/2$$
$$v_{2n+} = (17.28 \text{ ft/s})(1.9)/2 = 16.43 \text{ ft/s}$$

Using this result and the formula for v_{1n+} yields

$$v_{1n+} = 17.28 \text{ ft/s} - 16.42 \text{ ft/s} = 0.86 \text{ ft/s}$$

Since the collision is frictionless, there is no impulse acting in the tangential direction. This means that momentum is conserved in that direction too and that the final tangential speed of ball 1 is equal to its initial tangential speed, which in this case is equal to 10 ft/s (this equals (20 ft/s) sin 30°). Since ball 2 had no initial tangential speed, its velocity after impact is solely in the normal direction. Converting these results back to *xy*-coordinates instead of normal and tangential coordinates yields the following velocities for each ball after impact:

$$\mathbf{v}_{2+} = (16.42 \text{ ft/s}) \sin 60° \, \mathbf{i} - (16.42 \text{ ft/s}) \cos 60° \, \mathbf{j}$$
$$\mathbf{v}_{1+} = [(0.86 \text{ ft/s}) \cos 30° + (10 \text{ ft/s}) \sin 30°]\mathbf{i}$$
$$+ [(-0.86 \text{ ft/s}) \sin 30° + (10 \text{ ft/s}) \cos 30°)]\mathbf{j}$$
$$\mathbf{v}_{1+} = (5.43 \text{ ft/s})\mathbf{i} + (8.23 \text{ ft/s})\mathbf{j}$$

To further illustrate the application of these collision response principles, consider another example, this time the collision between a baseball bat and baseball as shown in Figure 5-3.

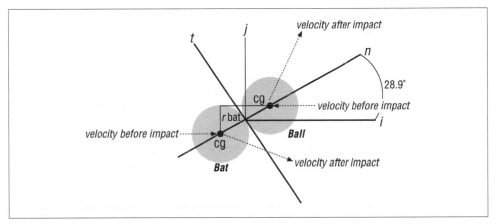

Figure 5-3. Baseball and Bat Collision Example

To a reasonable degree of accuracy the motion of a baseball bat at the instant of collision can be described as independent of the batter; that is, you can assume that the bat is moving freely and pivoting about a point located near the handle end of the bat. Assume that the ball strikes the bat on the sweet spot, that is, a point near the center of percussion.* Further assume that the bat is swung in the horizontal plane and that the baseball is traveling in the horizontal plane when it strikes the bat. The bat is of standard dimensions with a maximum diameter of 2.75 in. and a weight of 36 oz (mass equals 0.07 slug). The ball is also of standard dimensions with a radius of 1.47 in. and a weight of 5.125 oz (mass equals 9.96×10^{-3} slug). The ball reaches a speed of 132 ft/s (90 mph) at the instant it strikes the bat, and the speed of the bat at the point of impact is 103 ft/s (70.2 mph). For this collision the coefficient of restitution is 0.46. In the millisecond of

---

* The center of percussion is a point located near one of the nodes of natural vibration and is the point at which, when the bat is struck by the ball, no force is transmitted to the handle of the bat. If you have ever hit a baseball incorrectly and experienced a painful vibrating sensation in your hands, then you know what it feels like to miss the center of percussion.

impact that occurs, the baseball compresses quite a bit; however, in this analysis assume that both the bat and the ball are rigid. Finally, assume that this impact is frictionless.

As in the previous example, the line of action of impact is along the line connecting the centers of gravity of the bat and ball; thus, the unit normal vector is

$$\mathbf{n} = \left(\sqrt{(r_1 + r_2)^2 - r_1^2}\, \mathbf{i} - r_1 \mathbf{j} \right)/|\mathbf{n}|$$
$$\mathbf{n} = (0.875)\mathbf{i} + (0.484)\mathbf{j}$$

Here the subscripts 1 and 2 denote the bat and ball, respectively.

The relative normal velocity between the bat and ball is

$$v_{rn} = [\mathbf{v}_{1-} - \mathbf{v}_{2-}] \cdot \mathbf{n}$$
$$v_{rn} = [(235 \text{ ft/s})\mathbf{i} + (0 \text{ ft/s})\mathbf{j}] \cdot [(0.875)\mathbf{i} - (0.484)\mathbf{j}]$$
$$v_{rn} = 205.6 \text{ ft/s}$$

The velocity components of the bat and ball in the normal direction are

$$v_{1n-} = \mathbf{v}_{1-} \cdot \mathbf{n} = 90.125 \text{ ft/s}$$
$$v_{2n-} = \mathbf{v}_{2-} \cdot \mathbf{n} = -115.5 \text{ ft/s}$$

Applying the principle of conservation of momentum in the normal direction and solving for v_{1n+} yields

$$m_1 v_{1n-} + m_2 v_{2n-} = m_1 v_{1n+} + m_2 v_{2n+}$$
$$(0.07 \text{ slug})(90.125 \text{ ft/s}) + (9.96 \times 10^{-3} \text{ slug})(-115.5 \text{ ft/s})$$
$$= (0.07 \text{ slug})v_{1n+} + (9.96 \times 10^{-3} \text{ slug})v_{2n+}$$
$$v_{1n+} = 73.691 \text{ ft/s} - (0.142 \text{ ft/s})v_{2n+}$$

As in the previous example, applying the formula for coefficient of restitution with the above formula for v_{1n+} yields

$$e = (-v_{1n+} + v_{2n+}/(v_{1n-} - v_{2n-})$$
$$0.46 = [-73.691 \text{ ft/s} + (0.142 \text{ ft/s})v_{2n+} + v_{2n+}/([90.125 \text{ ft/s} + 115.5 \text{ ft/s})$$
$$v_{2n+} = 147.34 \text{ ft/s} \qquad \text{and} \qquad v_{1n+} = 52.77 \text{ ft/s}$$

Here again, since this impact is frictionless, each object retains its original tangential velocity component. For the bat this component is 49.78 ft/s; for the ball it's −63.8 ft/s. Taking these normal and tangential components and converting them to xy-coordinates yields the following bat and ball velocities for the instant just after impact:

$$\mathbf{v}_{1+} = 70.25\mathbf{i} - 18\mathbf{j}$$
$$\mathbf{v}_{2+} = 98.2\mathbf{i} + 127\mathbf{j}$$

Both of these examples illustrate fundamental impact analysis using the classical approach. They also share an important assumption: that the impacts are frictionless. In reality you know that billiard balls and baseballs and bats collide with friction;

otherwise, you would not be able to apply English in billiards or create lift-generating spin on baseballs. Later in this chapter I'll discuss how to include friction in your impact analysis.

Linear and Angular Impulse

In the previous section you were able to work through the specific examples by hand, using the principle of conservation of momentum and the coefficient of restitution. This approach will suffice if you're writing games in which the collision events are well defined and anticipated. However, if you're writing a real-time simulation in which objects, especially arbitrarily shaped rigid bodies, may or may not collide, then you'll want to use a more general approach. This approach involves the use of formulas to calculate the actual impulse between colliding objects so that you can apply this impulse to each object, instantly changing its velocity. In this section I'll derive the equations for impulse, both linear and angular, and I'll show you how to implement these equations in code in Chapter 13.

In dealing with particles or spheres, the only impulse formula that you'll need is that for linear impulse, which will allow you to calculate the new linear velocities of the objects after impact. So the first formula that I'll derive for you is that for linear impulse between two colliding objects as shown in Figure 5-4.

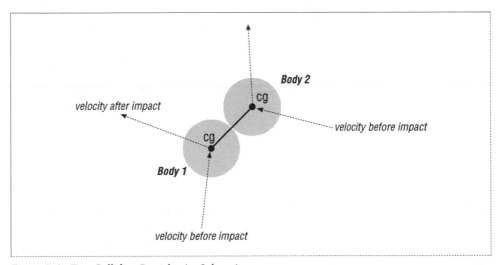

Figure 5-4. Two Colliding Particles (or Spheres)

For now, assume that the collision is frictionless and that the line of action of the impulse is along the line connecting the centers of mass of the two objects. This line is normal to the surfaces of both objects.

To derive the formula for linear impulse, you have to consider the formula from the definition of impulse along with the formula for coefficient of restitution. Here, let *J* represent the impulse:

$$J = m(v_+ - v_-)$$
$$e = -(v_{1+} - v_{2+})/(v_{1-} - v_{2-})$$

In these equations the velocities are those along the line of action of the impact, which in this case is a line connecting the centers of mass of the two objects. Since the same impulse applies to each object, just in opposite directions, you actually have three equations to deal with:

$$J = m_1(v_{1+} - v_{1-})$$
$$-J = m_2(v_{2+} - v_{2-})$$
$$e = -(v_{1+} - v_{2+})/(v_{1-} - v_{2-})$$

Notice I've assumed that J acts positively on body 1 and that its negation, $-J$, acts on body 2. Also notice that there are three unknowns in these equations: the impulse and the velocities of both bodies after the impact. Since there are three equations and three unknowns, you can solve for each unknown by rearranging the two impulse equations and substituting them into the equation for e. After some algebra you'll end up with a formula for J that you can then use to determine the velocities of each body just after impact. Here's how that's done:

$$\text{For body 1:} \quad v_{1+} = J/m_1 + v_{1-}$$
$$\text{For body 2:} \quad v_{2+} = -J/m_2 + v_{2-}$$

Substituting v_{1+} and v_{2+} into the equation for e yields

$$e(v_{1-} - v_{2-}) = -[(J/m_1 + v_{1-}) - (-J/m_2 + v_{2-})]$$
$$e(v_{1-} - v_{2-}) + v_{1-} - v_{2-} = -J(1/m_1 + 1/m_2)$$

Let $v_r = (v_{1-} - v_{2-})$; then

$$ev_r + v_r = -J(1/m_1 + 1/m_2)$$
$$J = -v_r(e + 1)/(1/m_1 + 1/m_2)$$

Since the line of action is normal to the colliding surfaces, v_r is the relative velocity along the line of action of impact and J acts along the line of action of impact, which in this case is normal to the surfaces, as I've already stated.

Now that you have a formula for the impulse, you can use the definition of impulse along with this formula to calculate the change in linear velocity of the objects involved in the impact. Here's how that's done in the case of two objects colliding:

$$v_{1+} = v_{1-} + (J\mathbf{n})/m_1$$
$$v_{2+} = v_{2-} + (-J\mathbf{n})/m_2$$

Notice that for the second object, the negative of the impulse is applied, since it acts on both objects equally but in opposite directions.

When dealing with rigid bodies that rotate, you'll have to derive a new equation for impulse that includes angular effects. You'll use this impulse to calculate new linear and angular velocities of the objects just after impact. Consider the two objects colliding at point P as shown in Figure 5-5.

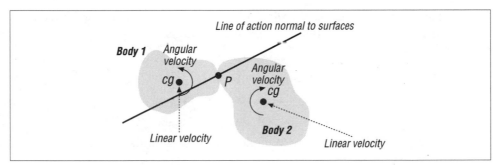

Figure 5-5. Two Colliding Rigid Bodies

There's a crucial distinction between this collision and that discussed earlier. In this case the velocity at the point of contact on each body is a function of not only the objects' linear velocity but also their angular velocities, and you'll have to recall the following formula to calculate the velocities at the impact point on each body:

$$\mathbf{v}_p = \mathbf{v}_g + (\boldsymbol{\omega} \times \mathbf{r})$$

In this relation, $\mathbf{r}$ is the vector from the body's center of gravity to the point P.

Using this formula, you can rewrite the two formulas relating the linear velocity after impact to the impulse and initial velocity as follows:

For body 1: $\mathbf{v}_{1g+} + (\boldsymbol{\omega}_{1+} \times \mathbf{r}_1) = \mathbf{J}/m_1 + \mathbf{v}_{1g-} + (\boldsymbol{\omega}_{1-} \times \mathbf{r}_1)$

For body 2: $\mathbf{v}_{2g+} + (\boldsymbol{\omega}_{2+} \times \mathbf{r}_2) = -\mathbf{J}/m_2 + \mathbf{v}_{2g-} + (\boldsymbol{\omega}_{2-} \times \mathbf{r}_2)$

There are two additional unknowns here, the angular velocities after impact, which means that you need two additional equations. You can get these equations from the definition of angular impulse:

For body 1: $(\mathbf{r}_1 \times \mathbf{J}) = \mathbf{I}_1(\boldsymbol{\omega}_{1+} - \boldsymbol{\omega}_{1-})$

For body 2: $(\mathbf{r}_2 \times -\mathbf{J}) = \mathbf{I}_2(\boldsymbol{\omega}_{2+} - \boldsymbol{\omega}_{2-})$

Here, the moment due to the impulse is calculated by taking the vector cross product of the impulse with the distance from the body's center of gravity to the point of application of the impulse.

By combining all of these equations with the equation for e and following the same procedure that's used in deriving the linear impulse formula, you'll end up with a formula for J that takes into account both linear and angular effects, which you can then use to find the linear and angular velocities of each body immediately after impact.

Here's the result:

$$J = -\mathbf{v}_r(e + 1)/\{1/m_1 + 1/m_2 + \mathbf{n} \cdot [(\mathbf{r}_1 \times \mathbf{n})/\mathbf{I}_1] \times \mathbf{r}_1 + \mathbf{n} \cdot [(\mathbf{r}_2 \times \mathbf{n})/\mathbf{I}_2] \times \mathbf{r}_2\}$$

Here $\mathbf{v}_r$ is the relative velocity along the line of action at the impact point P, and $\mathbf{n}$ is a unit vector along the line of action at the impact point pointing out from body l.

With this new formula for J, you can calculate the change in linear and angular velocities of the objects involved in the collision using these formulas:

$$\mathbf{v}_{1+} = \mathbf{v}_{1-} + (J\mathbf{n})/m_1$$
$$\mathbf{v}_{2+} = \mathbf{v}_{2-} + (-J\mathbf{n})/m_2$$
$$\omega_{1+} = \omega_{1-} + (\mathbf{r}_1 \times J\mathbf{n})/\mathbf{I}_{cg}$$
$$\omega_{2+} = \omega_{2-} + (\mathbf{r}_2 \times -J\mathbf{n})/\mathbf{I}_{cg}$$

As I said earlier, I'll show you how to implement these formulas for impulse in code when you get to Chapter 13.

Friction

Friction acts between contacting surfaces to resist motion. When objects collide in any type of collision except direct impact, for that very brief moment of contact they will experience a friction force that acts tangentially to the contacting surfaces. Not only will this tangential force change the linear velocities of the colliding objects in the tangential direction, it will also create a moment (torque) on the objects tending to change their angular velocities. This tangential impulse combined with the normal impulse results in an effective line of action of the total collision impulse that is no longer perpendicular to the contacting surfaces.

In practice, it is very difficult to quantify this collision friction force due to the fact that the friction force is not necessarily constant if the collision is such that the friction force does not develop beyond the maximum static friction force. Further complications stem from the fact that objects do tend to deform when they collide, creating an additional source of resistance. That said, since the friction force is a function of the normal force between the contacting surfaces, you know that the ratio of the normal force to the friction force is equal to the coefficient of friction. If you assume that the collisions are such that the kinetic coefficient of friction is applicable, then this ratio is constant:

$$\mu = F_f/F_n$$

Here, F_f is the tangential friction force and F_n is the normal impact force. You can extend this to say that the ratio of the tangential impulse to normal impulse is equal to the coefficient of friction.

Consider the collision between the club head of a golf club and a golf ball as illustrated in Figure 5-6.

In the velocity diagram on the left, v_- represents the relative velocity between the ball and club head at the instant of impact, v_+ represents the velocity of the ball just after

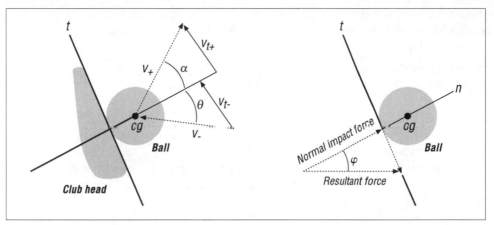

Figure 5-6. Golf Club–Ball Collision

impact, and v_{t-} and v_{t+} represent the tangential components of the ball velocity at and just after the instant of impact, respectively.

If this were a frictionless collision, v_{t-} and v_{t+} would be equal, as would the angles α and θ. However, with friction the tangential velocity of the ball is reduced, making v_{t+} less than v_{t-}, which also means that α will be less than θ.

The force diagram on the right in Figure 5-6 illustrates the forces involved in this collision with friction. Since the ratio of the tangential friction force to the normal collision force is equal to the coefficient of friction, you can develop an equation relating the angle ϕ to the coefficient of friction:

$$\tan\phi = F_f/F_n = \mu$$

In addition to this friction force changing the linear velocity of the ball in the tangential direction, it will also change the angular velocity of the ball. Since the friction force is acting on the ball's surface some distance from its center of gravity, it creates a moment (torque) about the ball's center of gravity that causes the ball to spin. If you use an approach similar to the rolling cylinder example back in Chapter 4, you can develop an equation for the new angular velocity of the ball in terms of the normal impact force or impulse:

$$\sum M_{cg} = F_f r = I_{cg}\, d\omega/dt$$
$$\mu F_n r = I_{cg}\, d\omega/dt$$
$$\mu F_n r\, dt = I_{cg}\, d\omega$$
$$\int_{t-}^{t+} F_n\, dt = I_{cg}/(\mu r) \int_{\omega-}^{\omega+} \omega\, dt$$

Notice here that the integral on the left is the normal impulse; thus,

$$\text{Impulse} = I_{cg}/(\mu r)(\omega_+ - \omega_-)$$
$$\omega_+ = (\text{Impulse})(\mu r)/I_{cg} + \omega_-$$

This relation looks very similar to the angular impulse equation that I showed you earlier in this chapter, and you can use it to approximate the friction-induced spin in specific collision problems.

Turn back to the equation for impulse, J, in the preceding section that includes both linear and angular effects. Here it is again for convenience:

$$J = -\mathbf{v}_r(e + 1)/[1/m_1 + 1/m_2 + \mathbf{n} \cdot (\mathbf{r}_1 \times \mathbf{n})/\mathbf{I}_1 + \mathbf{n} \cdot (\mathbf{r}_2 \times \mathbf{n})/\mathbf{I}_2]$$

This formula gives you the collision impulse in the normal direction. To see how friction fits in, you must keep in mind that friction acts tangentially to the contacting surfaces, that combining the friction force with the normal impact force yields a new effective line of action for the collision, and that the friction force (and impulse) is a function of the normal force (impulse) and coefficient of friction. Considering all these factors, the new equations to calculate the change in linear and angular velocities of two colliding objects are as follows:

$$\mathbf{v}_{1+} = \mathbf{v}_{1-} + [J\mathbf{n} + (\mu J)\mathbf{t}]/m_1$$
$$\mathbf{v}_{2+} = \mathbf{v}_{2-} + [-J\mathbf{n} + (\mu J)\mathbf{t}]/m_2$$
$$\omega_{1+} = \omega_{1-} + \{\mathbf{r}_1 \times [J\mathbf{n} + (\mu J)\mathbf{t}]\}/\mathbf{I}_{cg}$$
$$\omega_{2+} = \omega_{2-} + \{\mathbf{r}_2 \times (-J\mathbf{n} + (\mu J)\mathbf{t}]\}/\mathbf{I}_{cg}$$

In these equations, $\mathbf{t}$ is the unit tangent vector, which is tangent to the collision surfaces and at a right angle to the unit normal vector. You can calculate the tangent vector if you know the unit normal vector and the relative velocity vector in the same plane as the normal vector:

$$\mathbf{t} = (\mathbf{n} \times \mathbf{v}_r) \times \mathbf{n}$$
$$\mathbf{t} = \mathbf{t}/|\mathbf{t}|$$

For many problems that you'll face, you may be able to reasonably neglect friction in your collision response routines, since its effect may be small in comparison to the effect of the normal impulse itself. However, for some types of problems, friction is crucial. For example, the flight trajectory of a golf ball depends greatly on the spin imparted to it as a result of the club-ball collision. I'll discuss how spin affects trajectory in the next chapter, which covers projectile motion.

CHAPTER 6

Projectiles

This chapter is the first in a series of chapters that discuss specific real-world phenomena and systems, such as projectile motion and airplanes, with the idea of giving you a solid understanding of their real-life behavior. This understanding will help you to model these or similar systems accurately in your games. Instead of relying on purely idealized formulas, I'll present a wide variety of practical formulas and data that you can use. I've chosen the examples in this and the next several chapters to illustrate common forces and phenomena that exists in many systems, not just the ones I'll be discussing here. For example, while Chapter 8 on ships discusses buoyancy in detail, buoyancy is not limited to ships; any object immersed in a fluid experiences buoyant forces. The same applies for the topics discussed in this chapter and Chapters 7, 9, and 10.

Once you understand what's supposed to happen with these and similar systems, you'll be in a better position to interpret your simulation results to determine whether they make sense, that is, whether they are realistic enough. You'll also be better educated on what factors are most important for a given system such that you can make appropriate simplifying assumptions to help ease your effort. Basically, when designing and optimizing your code, you'll know where to cut things out without sacrificing realism. This gets into the subject of *parameter tuning*.

Over the next few chapters I want to give you enough of an understanding of certain physical phenomena that you can tune your models for the desired behavior. If you are modeling several similar objects in your simulation but want each one to behave slightly differently, then you have to tune the forces that get applied to each object to achieve the varying behavior. Since forces govern the behavior of objects in your simulations, I'll be focusing on force calculations with the intent of showing you how and why certain forces are what they are instead of simply using the idealized formulas that I showed you in Chapter 3. Parameter tuning isn't just limited to tuning your model's behavior; it also involves dealing with numerical issues, such as numerical stability in your integration algorithms. I'll discuss these issues more when I show you several simulation examples in Chapters 12 through 17.

I've devoted this entire chapter to projectile motion because so many physical problems that may find their way into your games fall into this category. Further, the forces governing projectile motion affect many other systems that aren't necessarily projectiles; for example, the drag force experienced by projectiles is similar to that experienced by airplanes, cars, or any other object moving through a fluid such as air or water.

A projectile is an object that is placed in motion by a force acting over a very short period of time, which you know from Chapter 5 is also called an impulse. After the projectile is set in motion by the initial impulse, during the launching phase, the projectile enters into the projectile motion phase, in which there is no longer a thrust or propulsive force acting on it. As you know already from the examples presented in Chapters 2 and 4, there are other forces that act on projectiles. (For the moment I'm not talking about self-propelled "projectiles" such as rockets, since, owing to their propulsive force, they don't follow what I'll refer to as classical projectile motion until after they've expended their fuel.)

In the simplest case, neglecting aerodynamic effects, the only force acting on a projectile other than the initial impulsive force is gravitation. For situations in which the projectile is near the earth's surface, the problem reduces to a constant acceleration problem. Assuming that the earth's surface is flat, that is, that its curvature is large in comparison to the range of the projectile, the following statements describe projectile motion:

- The trajectory is parabolic.
- The maximum range, for a given launch velocity, occurs when the launch angle is 45°.
- The velocity at impact is equal to the launch velocity when the launch point and impact point are at the same level.
- The vertical component of velocity is zero at the apex of the trajectory.
- The time required to reach the apex is equal to the time required to descend from the apex to the point of impact, assuming that the launch point and impact point are at the same level.
- The time required to descend from the apex to the point of impact equals the time required for an object to fall the same vertical distance when dropped straight down from a height equal to the height of the apex.

Simple Trajectories

There are four simple classes of projectile motion problems that I'll summarize:

- When the target and launch point are at the same level
- When the target is at a level higher than the launch point

- When the target is at a level lower than the launch point
- When the projectile is dropped from a moving system (such as an airplane) above the target

In the first type of problem the launch point and the target point are located on the same horizontal plane. Referring to Figure 6-1, v_0 is the initial velocity of the projectile at the time of launch, φ is the launch angle, R is the range of the projectile, and h is the height of the apex of the trajectory.

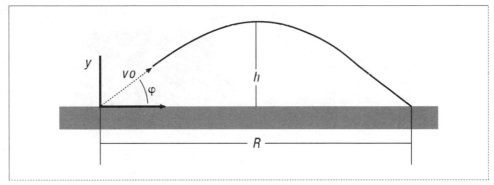

Figure 6-1. Target and Launch Point at the Same Level

To solve this type of problem, use the formulas shown in Table 6-1. Note that in these formulas, t represents any time instant after launch and T represents the total time from launch to impact.

Table 6-1. Formulas: Target and Launch Point at Same Level

To Calculate:	Use This Formula:
$x(t)$	$(v_0 \cos \varphi)t$
$y(t)$	$(v_0 \sin \varphi)t - (gt^2)/2$
$v_x(t)$	$v_0 \cos \varphi$
$v_y(t)$	$v_0 \sin \varphi - gt$
$v(t)$	$\sqrt{v_0^2 - 2gtv_0 \sin \varphi + g^2t^2}$
h	$(v_0^2 \sin^2 \varphi)/(2g)$
R	$v_0 T \cos \varphi$
T	$(2v_0 \sin \varphi)/g$

Remember to keep your units consistent when applying these formulas. If you are working in the English system, all your length and distance values should be in feet (ft), time should be in seconds (s), speed should be in feet per second (ft/s), and acceleration should be in feet per second squared (ft/s²). If you are using the SI (metric) system, length and distance values should be in meters (m), time should be in seconds (s), speed should be in meters per second (m/s), and acceleration should be in meters per second squared (m/s²). In the English system, g is 32.2 ft/s²; in the SI system, g is 9.8 m/s².

In the second type of problem the launch point is located on a lower horizontal plane than the target. Referring to Figure 6-2, the launch point's y-coordinate is lower than the target's y-coordinate.

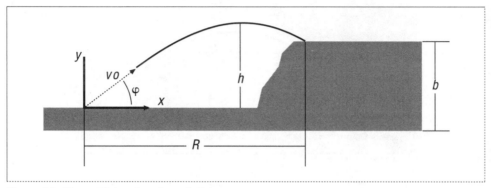

Figure 6-2. Target Higher than Launch Point

For this type of problem, use the formulas shown in Table 6-2. Notice that most of these formulas are the same as those shown in Table 6-1.

Table 6-2. Formulas Target Higher than Launch Point

To Calculate:	Use This Formula:
$x(t)$	$(v_0 \cos \varphi)t$
$y(t)$	$(v_0 \sin \varphi)t - (gt^2)/2$
$v_x(t)$	$v_0 \cos \varphi$
$v_y(t)$	$v_0 \sin \varphi - gt$
$v(t)$	$\sqrt{v_0^2 - 2gtv_0 \sin \varphi + g^2 t^2}$
h	$(v_0^2 \sin^2 \varphi)/(2g)$
R	$v_0 T \cos \varphi$
T	$(v_0 \sin \varphi)/g + \sqrt{[2(h-b)]/g}$

Actually, the only formula that has changed is that for T, which has been revised to account for the difference in elevation between the target and the launch point.

In the third type of problem the target is located on a plane lower than the launch point; the target's y-coordinate is lower than the launch point's y-coordinate (see Figure 6-3).

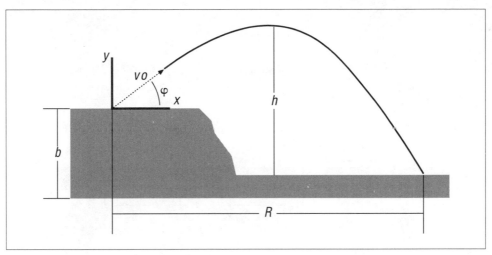

Figure 6-3. Target Lower than Launch Point

Table 6-3 shows the formulas to use for this type of problem. Here again, almost all of the formulas are the same as those shown in Table 6-1.

Table 6-3. Formulas: Target Lower than Launch Point

To Calculate:	Use This Formula:
$x(t)$	$(v_0 \cos \varphi)t$
$y(t)$	$(v_0 \sin \varphi)t - (gt^2)/2$
$v_x(t)$	$v_0 \cos \varphi$
$v_y(t)$	$v_0 \sin \varphi - gt$
$v(t)$	$\sqrt{v_0^2 - 2gtv_0 \sin\varphi + g^2t^2}$
h	$b + (v_0^2 \sin^2 \varphi)/(2g)$
R	$v_0 T \cos \varphi$
T	$(v_0 \sin \varphi)/g + \sqrt{(2h)/g}$

As in the second type of problem, the only formula that has changed is the formula for T, which has been revised to account for the difference in elevation between the target and the launch point (except this time the target is lower than the launch point).

Finally, the fourth type of problem involves dropping the projectile from a moving system, such as an airplane. In this case the initial velocity of the projectile is horizontal and equal to the speed of the vehicle dropping it. Figure 6-4 illustrates this type of problem.

Table 6-4 shows the formulas to use to solve this type of problem. Note here that when v_0 is zero, the problem reduces to a simple free-fall problem in which the projectile simply drops straight down.

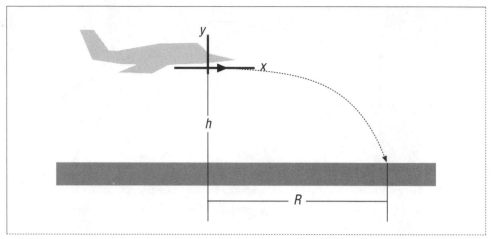

Figure 6-4. Projectile Dropped from a Moving System

Table 6-4. Formulas: Projectile Dropped from a Moving System

To Calculate:	Use This Formula:
$x(t)$	$v_0 t$
$y(t)$	$h - (gt^2)/2$
$v_x(t)$	v_0
$v_y(t)$	$-gt$
$v(t)$	$\sqrt{v_0^2 + g^2 t^2}$
h	$(gt^2)/2$
R	$v_0 T$
T	$\sqrt{(2h)/g}$

These formulas are useful if you're writing a game that does not require a more accurate treatment of projectile motion, that is, if you don't need or want to consider the other forces that can act on a projectile when in motion. If you are going for more accuracy, then you'll have to consider these other forces and treat the problem as we did in Chapter 4's example.

Drag

In Chapters 3 and 4 I showed you the idealized formulas for viscous fluid dynamic drag as well as how to implement drag in the equations of motion for a projectile. This was illustrated in the example program discussed in Chapter 4. Recall that the drag force is a vector just like any other force and that it acts on the line of action of the velocity vector but in a direction opposing velocity. While those formulas work in a game simulation, as I said before, they don't tell the whole story. Although we can't treat the subject of fluid dynamics in its entirety in this book, I do want to give you a better understanding of drag than just the simple idealized equation presented earlier.

It can be shown by analytical methods that the drag on an object moving through a fluid is proportional to its speed, size, and shape and the density and viscosity of the fluid through which it is moving. You can also come to these conclusions by drawing on your own real-life experience. For example, when waving your hand through the air, you feel very little resistance; however, if you put your hand out of a car window traveling at 60 mph, then you feel much greater resistance (drag force) on your hand. This is because drag is speed dependent. When you wave your hand under water, say, in a swimming pool, you'll feel a greater drag force on your hand than you do when waving it in the air. This is because water is more dense and viscous than air. As you wave your hand under water, you'll notice a significant difference in drag depending on the orientation of your hand. If your hand is such that your palm is in line with the direction of motion, that is, you are leading with your palm, then you'll feel a greater drag force than you would if your hand were turned 90 degrees as though you were executing a knife hand karate chop through the water. This tells you that drag is a function of the shape of the object. You get the idea.

To facilitate our discussion of fluid dynamic drag, let's look at the flow around a sphere moving through a fluid such as air or water. If the sphere is moving slowly through the fluid, the flow pattern around the sphere would look something like that shown in Figure 6-5.

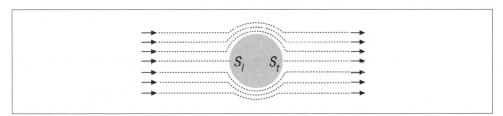

Figure 6-5. Flow Pattern Around a Slowly Moving Sphere

Bernoulli's equation, which relates pressure to velocity in fluid flow, says that as the fluid goes around the sphere and speeds up, the pressure in the fluid (locally) will go down. The equation, presented by Daniel Bernoulli in 1738, applies to frictionless incompressible fluid flow and looks like this*:

$$P/\gamma + z + V^2/(2g) = \text{constant}$$

where P is the pressure at a point in the fluid volume under consideration, γ is the specific weight of the fluid, z is the elevation of the point under consideration, V is the fluid velocity at that point, and g is the acceleration due to gravity. As you can see, if

---

* In a real fluid with friction, this equation will have extra terms that account for energy losses due to friction.

the expression on the left is to remain constant, and assuming that z is constant, then if velocity increases, pressure must decrease. Likewise, if pressure increases, then velocity must decrease.

Referring to Figure 6-5, the pressure will be greatest at the stagnation point, S_l, and will decrease around the leading side of the sphere and then start to increase again around the back of the sphere. In an ideal fluid with no friction, the pressure is fully recovered behind the sphere, and there is a trailing stagnation point, S_t, whose pressure is equal to the pressure at the leading stagnation point. Since the pressure fore and aft of the sphere is equal and opposite, there is no net drag force acting on the sphere.

The pressure on the top and bottom of the sphere will be lower than that at the stagnation points, since the fluid velocity is greater over the top and bottom. Since this is a case of symmetric flow around the sphere, there will be no net pressure difference between the top and bottom of the sphere.

In a real fluid there is friction, which affects the flow around the sphere such that the pressure is never fully recovered on the aft side of the sphere. As the fluid flows around the sphere, a thin layer sticks to the surface of the sphere due to friction. In this *boundary layer* the speed of the fluid varies from zero at the sphere surface to the ideal free stream velocity as illustrated in Figure 6-6.

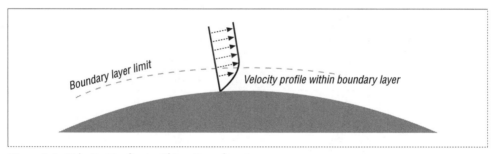

Figure 6-6. Velocity Gradient within a Boundary Layer

This velocity gradient represents a momentum transfer from the sphere to the fluid and gives rise to the frictional component of drag. Since a certain amount of fluid is *sticking* to the sphere, you can think of this as the energy required to accelerate the fluid and move it along with the sphere. (If the flow within this boundary layer is laminar, then the viscous shear stress between fluid "layers" gives rise to friction drag. When the flow is turbulent, the velocity gradient, and thus the transfer of momentum gives rise to friction drag.)

Moving further aft along the sphere, the boundary layer grows in thickness and will not be able to maintain its adherence to the sphere surface, and it will separate at some point. Beyond this *separation point*, the flow will be turbulent, and this is called the turbulent wake. In this region the fluid pressure is lower than that at the front of the sphere. This pressure differential gives rise to the pressure component of drag. Figure 6-7 shows how the flow might look.

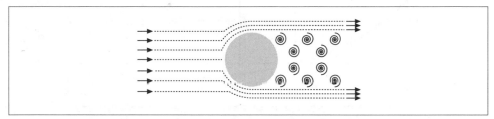

Figure 6-7. Flow Pattern Around a Sphere Showing Separation

For a slowly moving sphere the separation point will be approximately 80° from the leading edge.

Now, if you roughen the surface of the sphere, you'll affect the flow around it. As you would expect, this roughened sphere will have a higher friction drag component. However, more important, the flow will adhere to the sphere longer, and the separation point will be pushed further back to approximately 115°, as shown in Figure 6-8.

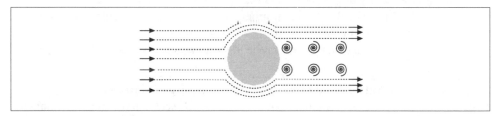

Figure 6-8. Flow Around a Roughened Sphere

This will reduce the size of the turbulent wake and the pressure differential, thus decreasing the pressure drag. It's paradoxical but true that, all other things being equal, a slightly roughened sphere will have less *total* drag than a smooth one. Have you ever wondered why golf balls have dimples? If so, there's your answer.

The total drag on the sphere depends very much on the nature of the flow around the sphere, that is, whether the flow is laminar or turbulent. This is best illustrated by looking at some experimental data. Figure 6-9 shows a typical curve of the total drag coefficient for a sphere plotted as a function of *Reynold's number*.

Reynold's number (commonly denoted N_r or R_n) is a dimensionless number that represents the speed of fluid flow around an object. It's a little more than just a speed measure, since Reynold's number includes a characteristic length for the object and the viscosity and density of the fluid. The formula for Reynold's number is

$$R_n = (vL)/\upsilon$$

or

$$R_n = (vL\rho)/\mu$$

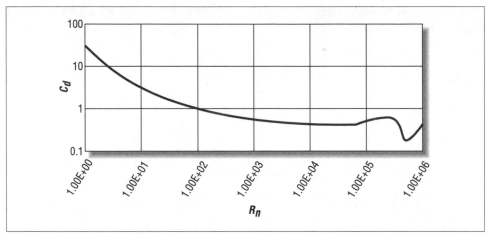

Figure 6-9. *Total Drag Coefficient for a Smooth Sphere Versus Reynold's Number**

where v is speed, L is a characteristic length of the object (diameter for a sphere), v is the kinematic viscosity of the fluid, ρ is the fluid mass density, and μ is the absolute viscosity of the fluid. For Reynold's number to work out as a dimensionless number, velocity, length, and kinematic viscosity must have units of ft/s, ft, and ft^2/s, respectively when working in the English system. In the SI system their units must be m/s, m, and m^2/s, respectively.

This number is useful for nondimensionalizing data measured from tests on an object of given size (such as a model) such that the data can be scaled to estimate the data for similar objects of different size. Here, "similar" means that the objects are geometrically similar, just different scales, and that the flow pattern around the objects is similar. For a sphere the characteristic length is diameter, so you can use drag data obtained from a small model sphere of a given diameter to estimate the drag for a larger sphere of a different diameter. A more useful application of this scaling technique is estimating the viscous drag on ship or airplane appendages on the basis of model test data obtained from wind tunnel or tow tank experiments.

Reynold's number is used as an indicator of the nature of fluid flow. A low Reynold's number generally indicates laminar flow, while a high Reynold's number generally indicates turbulent flow. Somewhere in between, there is a transition range where the flow makes the transition from laminar to turbulent flow. For carefully controlled experiments, this transition (*critical*) Reynold's number can consistently be determined. However, in general the ambient flow field around an object, that is, whether it has low or high turbulence, will affect when this transition occurs. Further, the transition Reynold's number is specific to the type of problem being investigated, for example,

---

* The curve shown here is intended to show the trend of C_d versus R_n for a smooth sphere. For more accurate drag coefficient data for spheres and other shapes, refer to any college-level fluid mechanics text, such as *Fluid Mechanics with Engineering Applications* by Daugherty, Franzini, and Finemore.

whether you're looking at flow within pipes, the flow around a ship, or the flow around an airplane, and so on.

The total drag coefficient, C_d, is calculated by measuring the total resistance, R_t, from tests and using the following formula:

$$C_d = R_t / (0.5 \rho v^2 A)$$

where A is a characteristic area that depends on the object being studied. For a sphere, A is typically the projected frontal area of the sphere, which is equal to the area of a circle of diameter equal to that of the sphere. By comparison, for ship hulls, A is typically taken as the underwater surface area of the hull. If you work out the units on the righthand side of this equation, you'll see that the drag coefficient is nondimensional, that is, it has no units.

Given the total drag coefficient, you can estimate the total resistance (drag) using the following formula:

$$R_t = (0.5 \rho v^2 A) C_d$$

This is a better equation to use than the ones given in Chapter 3, assuming that you have sufficient information available, namely, the total drag coefficient, density, velocity, and area. Note the dependence of total resistance on velocity squared. To get R_t in units of pounds (lb), you must have velocity in ft/s, area in ft^2, and density in slug/ft^3 (remember, C_d is dimensionless). In the SI system you'll get R_t in newtons (N) if you have velocity in m/s, area in m^2, and density in kg/m^3.

Turning back now to Figure 6-9, you can make a couple of observations. First you can see that the total drag coefficient decreases as Reynold's number increases. This is due to the formation of the separation point and its subsequent move aft on the sphere as Reynold's number increases and the relative reduction in pressure drag as discussed previously. At a Reynold's number of approximately 250,000 there is a dramatic reduction in drag. This is a result of the flow becoming fully turbulent with a corresponding reduction in pressure drag.

In the Cannon2 example in Chapter 4, I implemented the ideal formula for air drag on the projectile. In that case I used a constant value of drag coefficient that was arbitrarily defined. As I said earlier, it would be better to use the formula presented in this chapter for total drag along with the total drag coefficient data shown in Figure 6-9 to estimate the drag on the projectile. While this is more "accurate," it does complicate matters for you. Specifically, the drag coefficient is now a function of Reynold's number, which is a function of velocity. You'll have to set up a table of drag coefficients versus Reynold's number and interpolate this table given Reynold's number calculated at each time step. As an alternative, you can fit the drag coefficient data to a curve to derive a formula that you can use instead; however, the drag coefficient data may be such that you'll have to use a piecewise approach and derive curve fits for each segment of the drag coefficient curve. The sphere data presented herein is one such case. The data do not lend themselves nicely to a single polynomial curve fit over the full range of Reynold's number. In such cases you'll end up with a handful of formulas for drag coefficient with each formula valid over a limited range of Reynold's numbers.

While the Cannon2 example does have its limitations, it is useful to see the effects of drag on the trajectory of the projectile. The obvious effect is that the trajectory is no longer parabolic. You can see that the trajectory appears to drop off much more sharply when the projectile is making its descent after reaching its apex height.

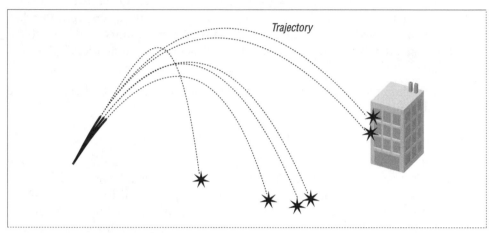

Figure 6-10. Cannon2 Example, Trajectories

Another important effect of drag on trajectory (this applies to objects in free fall as well) is the fact that drag will limit the maximum vertical velocity attainable. This limit is the so-called *terminal velocity*. Take an object in free fall for a moment. As the object accelerates toward the earth at the gravitation acceleration, its velocity increases. As velocity increases, so does drag, since drag is a function of velocity. At some speed the drag force retarding the object's motion will increase to a point at which it is equal to the gravitational force that's pulling the object toward the earth. In the absence of any other forces that may affect motion, the net acceleration on the object is zero, and it continues its descent at the constant terminal velocity.

Let me illustrate this further. Go back to the formula I derived for the y-component (vertical component) of velocity for the projectile modeled in the Cannon2 example. Here it is again so that you don't have to flip back to Chapter 4:

$$v_{y2} = (1/C_d)e^{(-C_d/m)t}(C_d v_{y1} + mg) - (mg)/C_d$$

It isn't obvious from looking at this equation, but the velocity component, v_{y2}, asymptotes to some constant value as time increases. To help visualize this, I've plotted this equation as shown in Figure 6-11.

As you can see, over time the velocity reaches a maximum absolute value of about -107.25 speed units. The negative velocities indicate that the velocity is in the negative

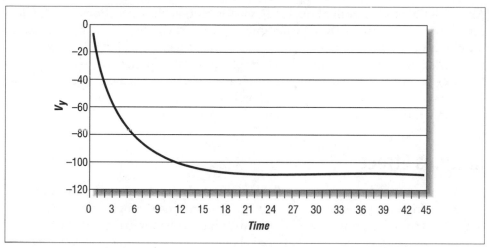

Figure 6-11. Terminal Velocity

y-direction, that is, the object is falling toward the earth in this case. (For this calculation I arbitrarily assumed a mass of 100, a drag coefficient of 30, and an initial velocity of zero.)

Assuming an initial velocity of zero and equating the formula for total resistance shown earlier to the weight of an object, you can derive the following formula for terminal velocity for an object in free fall:

$$v_t = \sqrt{(2mg)/(C_d \rho A)}$$

The trick in applying this formula is in determining the right value for the drag coefficient. Just for fun, let's assume a drag coefficient of 0.5 and calculate the terminal velocity for several different objects. This exercise will allow you to see the influence of the object's size on terminal velocity. Table 6-5 gives the terminal velocities for various objects in free fall using an air density of 2.37×10^{-3} slug/ft^3 (air at standard atmospheric pressure at 60°F). Using this equation with density in slug/ft^3 means that m must be in slugs, g in ft/s^2, and A in ft to get the terminal speed in ft/s. I went ahead and converted from ft/s to miles per hour (mph) to present the results in Table 6-5. The weight of each object shown in this table is simply its mass, m, times g.

Table 6-5. Terminal Velocities for Various Objects

Object	Weight (lb)	Area (ft²)	Terminal Velocity (mph)
Skydiver in free fall	180	9	125
Skydiver with open parachute	180	226	25
Baseball (2.88-in. diameter)	0.32	0.045	75
Golf ball (1.65-in. diameter)	0.10	0.015	72
Raindrop (0.16-in. diameter)	7.5×10^{-5}	1.39×10^{-4}	20

Although I've talked mostly about spheres in this section, the discussions on fluid flow generally apply to any object moving through a fluid. Of course, the more complex the object's geometry, the harder it is to analyze the drag forces on it. Other factors such as surface condition and whether or not the object is at the interface between two fluids (such a ship in the ocean) further complicate the analysis. In practice, scale model tests are particularly useful. In the bibliography I give several sources where you can find more practical drag data for objects other than spheres.

Magnus Effect

The *Magnus effect* (also known as the *Robbins* effect) is quite an interesting phenomenon. You know from the previous section that an object moving through a fluid encounters drag. What would happen if that object were spinning as it moved through the fluid. For example, consider the sphere that I talked about earlier and assume that while moving through a fluid such as air or water, it spins about an axis passing through its center of mass. What happens when the sphere spins is the interesting part: it actually generates lift! That's right—*lift*. From everyday experience, most people usually associate lift with a winglike shape such as an airplane wing or a hydrofoil. It is far less well known that cylinders and spheres can produce lift as well—that is, as long as they are spinning. I'll use the moving sphere to explain what's happening here.

From the previous section on drag, you know that for a fast-moving sphere there will be some point on the sphere where the flow separates, creating a turbulent wake behind the sphere. Recall that the pressure acting on the sphere within this turbulent wake is lower than the pressure acting on the leading surface of the sphere, and this pressure differential gives rise to the pressure drag component. When the sphere is spinning, say, clockwise about a horizontal axis passing through its center as shown in Figure 6-12, the fluid passing over the top of the sphere will be sped up, while the fluid passing under the sphere will be retarded.

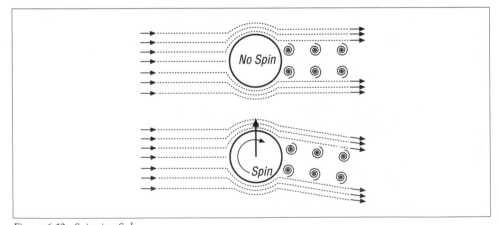

Figure 6-12. Spinning Sphere

Remember, because of friction, there is a thin boundary layer of fluid that attaches to the sphere's surface. At the sphere's surface the velocity of the fluid in the boundary layer is zero relative to the sphere. The velocity increases within the boundary layer as you move farther away from the sphere's surface. In the case of the spinning sphere there is now a difference in fluid pressure above and below the sphere due to the increase in velocity above the sphere and the decrease in velocity below the sphere. Further, the separation point on the top side of the sphere will be pushed farther back along the sphere. The result is an asymmetric flow pattern around the sphere with a net lift force (due to the pressure differential) perpendicular to the direction of flow. If the surface of the sphere is roughened a little, not only will frictional drag increase, but this lift effect will increase as well.

Don't let the term "lift" confuse you into thinking that this force always acts to lift, or elevate, the sphere. The effect of this lift force on the sphere's trajectory is very much tied to the axis of rotation about which the sphere is spinning as related to the direction in which the sphere is traveling, that is, its angular velocity.

The magnitude of the Magnus force is proportional to the speed of travel, the rate of spin, density of fluid, the size of the object, and the nature of the fluid flow. This force is not easy to calculate analytically, and as with many problems in fluid dynamics you must rely on experimental data to accurately estimate this force for a specific object under specific conditions. There are, however, some analytical techniques that will allow you approximate the Magnus force. Without going into the theoretical details, you can apply the *Kutta-Joukouski theroem* to estimate the lift force on rotating objects such as cylinders and spheres. The Kutta-Joukouski theorem is based on a frictionless idealization of fluid flow involving the concept of circulation around the object (such as a vortex around the object). You can find the details of this theory in any fluid dynamics text (I give some references in the bibliography), so I won't go into the details here. However, I will give you some results.

For a spinning circular cylinder moving through a fluid you can use this formula to estimate the Magnus lift force:

$$F_L = 2\pi\rho L v r^2 \omega$$

where v is speed of travel, L is the length of the cylinder, r is its radius, and ω is its angular velocity in radians per second (rad/s). If you have spin, n, in revolutions per second (rps), then $\omega = 2\pi n$. If you have spin, n, in revolutions per minute (rpm), then $\omega = (2\pi n)/60$.

For a spinning sphere moving through a fluid you can use this formula:

$$F_L = (2\pi\rho v r^4 \omega)/(2r)$$

where r is the radius of the sphere. Consistent units for these equations would yield lift force in pounds in the English system or newtons in the SI system. In the English system density, speed, length, and radius have units of slugs/ft^3, ft/s, and ft, respectively. In the SI system the appropriate units are for these quantities are kg/m^3, m/s, and m, respectively.

Keep in mind that these formulas only approximate the Magnus force; they'll get you in the ballpark, but they are not exact and could be off by up to 50% depending on the situation. These formulas assume that there is no slip between the fluid and the rotating surface of the object, there is no friction, surface roughness is not taken into account, and there is no boundary layer.

At any rate, these equations will allow you to approximate the Magnus effect for flying objects in your games, where you'll be able to model the relative differences between objects of different size that may be traveling at different speeds with different spin rates. You'll get the look right. If numerical accuracy is what you're looking for, then you'll have to turn to experimental data for your specific problem.

Similar to the drag data shown in the previous section, experimental lift data are generally presented in terms of lift coefficient. Using an equation similar to the drag equation, you can calculate the lift force with the following equation:

$$F_L = (0.5 \rho v^2 A) C_L$$

As usual, it's not as simple as this equation makes it appear. The trick is in determining the lift coefficient, C_L, which is a function of surface conditions, Reynold's number, velocity, and spin rate. Further, experiments show that the drag coefficient is also affected by spin.

For example, consider a golf ball struck perfectly (I wish) such that the ball spins about a horizontal axis perpendicular to its direction of travel while in flight. In this case the Magnus force will tend to lift the ball higher in the air, increasing its flight time and range. For a golf ball struck such that it initial velocity is 190 ft/s with a takeoff angle of 10 degrees the increase in range due to Magnus lift is on the order of 65 yards; thus, it's clear that this effect is significant. In fact, over the long history of the game of golf there has been an attempt to maximize this effect. In the late 1800s, when golf balls were still made with smooth surfaces, people observed that used balls with roughened surfaces flew even better than smooth balls. This observation prompted people to start making balls with rough surfaces so as to maximize the Magnus lift effect. The dimples that you see on modern golf balls are the result of many decades of experience and research and are thought to be optimum.

Typically, a golf ball takes off from the club with an initial velocity on the order of 250 ft/s, with a backspin on the order of 60 revolutions per second (rps). For these initial conditions the corresponding Magnus lift coefficient is within the range from 0.1 to 0.35. Depending on the spin rate, this lift coefficient can be as high as 0.45, and the lift force acting on the ball can be as much as 50% of the ball's weight.

If the golf ball is struck with a less than perfect stroke, the Magnus lift force may work against you. For example, if your swing is such that the ball leaves the club head spinning about an axis that is not horizontal, then the ball's trajectory will curve, resulting in a slice or a draw. If you top the ball such that the upper surface of the ball is spinning away from you, then the ball will tend to curve downward much more rapidly, significantly reducing the range of your shot.

As another example, consider a baseball that is pitched such that it is spinning with topspin about a horizontal axis perpendicular to its direction of travel. Here, the Magnus force will tend to cause the ball to curve in a downward direction, making it drop more rapidly than it would without spin. If the pitcher spins the ball such that the axis of rotation is not horizontal, then the ball will curve out of the vertical plane. Another trick that pitchers use is to give the ball backspin, making it appear (to the batter) to actually rise. This rising fast ball does not actually rise, but because of the Magnus lift force, it falls much less rapidly than it would without spin.

For a typical pitched speed and spin rate of 148 ft/s and 30 rps, respectively, the lift force can be up to 33% of the ball's weight. For a typical curve ball the lift coefficient is within the range of 0.1 to 0.2, and for fly balls it can be up to 0.4.

These are only two examples, however; you need not look far to find other examples of the Magnus force in action. Think about the behavior of cricket balls, soccer balls, tennis balls, or Ping-Pong balls when they spin in flight. Bullets fired from a gun with a rifling barrel also spin and are affected by this Magnus force. There have even been sailboats built with tall vertical rotating cylindrical "sails" that use the Magnus force for propulsion. I've also seen technical articles describing a propeller with spinning cylindrical blades instead of airfoil-type blades.

To further illustrate the Magnus effect, I have prepared a simple program that simulates a ball being thrown with varying amounts of backspin (or topspin). This example is based on the cannon example, so here again, the code should look familiar to you. In this example I've neglected drag, so the only forces that the ball will see are due to gravity and the Magnus effect. I did this to isolate the lift-generating effect of spin and to keep the equations of motion clearer.

Since most of the code for this example is identical, or very similar, to that in the previous cannon examples, I won't repeat it here. I will, however, show you the global variables used in this simulation along with a revised DoSimulation function that takes care of the equations of motion:

```
//-----------------------------------------------------------------------------//
// Global variables required for this simulation
//-----------------------------------------------------------------------------//
TVector     V1;      // Initial Velocity (given), m/s
TVector     V2;      // Velocity vector at time t, m/s
double      m;       // Projectile mass (given), kg
TVector     s1;      // Initial position (given), m
TVector     s2;      // The projectile's position (displacement) vector, m
double      time;    // The time from the instant the projectile
                     // is launched, s
double      tInc;    // The time increment to use when stepping
                     // through the simulation, s
double      g;       // acceleration due to gravity (given), m/s^2
double      spin;    // spin in rpm (given)
double      omega;   // spin in radians per second
double      radius;  // radius of projectile (given), m

#define     PI      3.14159f
#define     RHO     1.225f       // kg/m^3
```

```
//---------------------------------------------------------------------------//
int     DoSimulation(void)
//---------------------------------------------------------------------------//
{
    double     C = PI * RHO * RHO * radius * radius * radius * omega;
    double     t;

    // step to the next time in the simulation
    time+=tInc;
    t = time;

    // Calc. V2:
    V2.i = 1.0f/(1.0f-(t/m)*(t/m)*C*C) * (V1.i + C * V1.j * (t/m) -
            C * g * (t*t)/m);
    V2.j = V1.j + (t/m)*C*V2.i - g*t;

    // Calc. S2:
    s2.i = s1.i + V1.i * t + (1.0f/2.0f) * (C/m * V2.j) * (t*t);
    s2.j = s1.j + V1.j * t + (1.0f/2.0f) * ( ((C*V2.i) - m*g)/m ) * (t*t);

    // Check for collision with ground (xz-plane)
    if(s2.j <= 0)
        return 2;

    // Cut off the simulation if it's taking too long
    // This is so the program does not get stuck in the while loop
    if(time>60)
        return 3;

    return 0;
}
```

The heart of this simulation are lines that calculate v2 and s2, the instantaneous velocity and position of the projectile, respectively. The equations of motion here come from the 2D kinetic equations of motion including gravity, as discussed in Chapter 4, combined with the following formula (shown earlier) for estimating the Magnus lift on a spinning sphere:

$$F_{\mathrm{L}} = (2\pi^2 \rho v r^4 \omega)/(2r)$$

You can see the effect of spin on the projectile's trajectory by providing the sample program with different values for spin in revolutions per minute. The program converts this to radians per second and stores this value in the variable omega. A positive spin value indicates bottom spin such that the bottom of the sphere is spinning away from you; a negative spin indicates topspin, in which the top of the ball spins away from you. Bottom spin generates a positive lift force that will tend to extend the range of the projectile; topspin generates negative lift that will force the projectile toward the ground, shortening its range. (Note that this example assumes that the spin axis is horizontal and perpendicular to the plane of the screen.) Figure 6-13 illustrates this behavior.

Variable Mass

Earlier in this book I mentioned that some problems in dynamics involve variable mass. We'll look at variable mass here, since it applies to self-propelled projectiles such

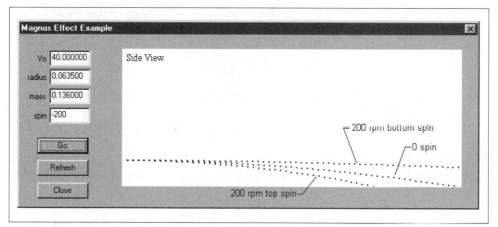

Figure 6-13. Magnus Effect Sample Program

as rockets. When a rocket is producing thrust to accelerate itself, it loses mass (fuel) at some rate. When all of the fuel is consumed (burnout), the rocket no longer produces thrust and has reached its maximum speed. After burnout you can treat the trajectory of the rocket just as you would a non-self-propelled projectile, as discussed earlier. However, while the rocket is producing thrust, you need to consider its mass change, since this will affect its motion.

In cases in which the mass change of the object under consideration is such that the mass being expelled or taken in has zero absolute velocity, like a ship consuming fuel, for example, you can set up the equations of motion as you normally would, where the sum of the forces equals the rate of change in momentum. However, in this case mass will be a function of time, and your equations of motion will look like this:

$$\sum F = ma = d/dt(mv) = m(dv/dt) + (dm/dt)v$$

You can proceed to solve them just as you would normally but keeping in mind the time dependence of mass.

A rocket, on the other hand, expels mass at some nonzero velocity, and you can't use the above approach to properly account for its mass change. In this case you need to consider the relative velocity between the expelled mass and the rocket itself. The linear equation of motion now looks like this:

$$\sum F = m\,dv/dt + dm/dt\,u$$

where u is the relative velocity between the expelled mass and the object (the rocket, in this case).

For a rocket traveling straight up, neglecting air resistance and the pressure at the exhaust nozzle, the only force acting on the rocket is due to gravity. But the rocket is expelling mass (burning fuel). How it expels this mass is not important here, since the forces involved there are internal to the rocket; we need only consider the external forces. Let the fuel burn rate be $-m'$. The equation of motion (in the vertical direction) for the rocket is as follows:

$$\sum F = m\, dv/dt + dm/dt\, u$$
$$-mg = m\, dv/dt - m'u$$

If you rearrange this so that it looks as though there's only an *ma* term on the right of the equation, you get

$$m'u - mg = m\, dv/dt = ma$$

Here you can see that the thrust that propels the rocket into the air is equal to $m'u$. Since the fuel burn rate is constant, the mass of the rocket at any instant in time is equal to

$$m = m_0 - m't$$

where m_0 is the initial mass and the burn rate, m', is in the form mass per unit time.

CHAPTER 7

Aircraft

If you are going to write a flight simulation game, one of the most important aspects of your game engine will be your flight model. Yes, your 3D graphics, user interface, story, avionics system simulation, and coding are all important, but what really defines the behavior of the aircraft that you are simulating is your flight model. Basically, this is your simplified version of the physics of aircraft flight, that is, your assumptions, your approximations, and all the formulas you'll use to calculate mass, inertia, and lift and drag forces and moments.

There are four major forces that act on an airplane in flight: gravity, thrust, lift, and drag. Gravity, of course, is the force that tends to pull the aircraft to the ground, while lift is the force generated by the wings (or lifting surfaces) of the aircraft to counteract gravity and enable it to stay aloft. The thrust force generated by the aircraft's propulsor (jet engine or propeller) increases the aircraft's velocity and enables the lifting surfaces to generate lift. Finally, drag counteracts the thrust force tending to impede the aircraft's motion. Figure 7-1 illustrates these forces.

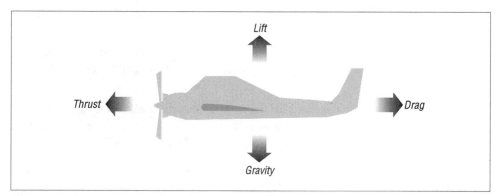

Figure 7-1. Forces on an Aircraft in Flight

I've already discussed the force due to gravity in earlier chapters so I won't address it again in this chapter except to say that when looking at all of the forces acting on an aircraft, the total of all lift forces must be greater than or equal to the gravitational force if the aircraft is to maintain flight.

To address the other three forces acting on an aircraft, I'll refer to a simplified, generic model of an airplane and use it as an illustrative example. There are far too many aircraft types and configurations to treat them all in this short chapter. Moreover, the subject of aerodynamics is too broad and complex. Therefore, the model that we'll look at will be of a typical subsonic configuration as shown in Figure 7-2.

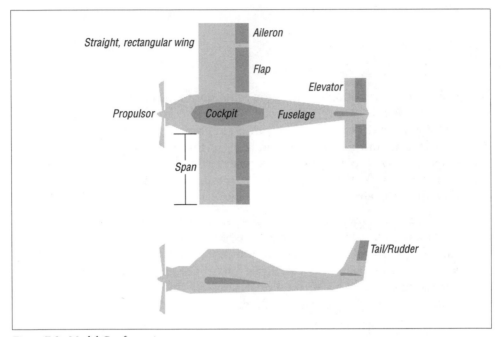

Figure 7-2. Model Configuration

In this configuration the main lifting surfaces (the large wings) are located forward on the aircraft, with relatively smaller lifting surfaces located toward the tail. This is the basic arrangement of most aircraft in existence today.

I'll have to make some further simplifying assumptions to make even this simplified model manageable. Further, I'll rely on empirical data and formulas for the calculation of lift and drag forces.

Geometry

Before getting into lift, drag, and thrust, I need to go over some basic geometry and terms to make sure we are speaking the same language. Familiarity with these terms will also help you quickly find what you are looking for when searching through the references that I'll provide later.

First, take another look at the arrangement of our model aircraft in Figure 7-2. The main body of the aircraft, the part usually occupied by cargo and people, is called the *fuselage*. The *wings* are the large rectangular lifting surfaces protruding from the fuselage near the forward end. The longer dimension of the wing is called its *span*, and its shorter dimension is called its chord length, or simply *chord*. The ratio of span squared to wing area is called the *aspect ratio*, and for rectangular wings this reduces to the ratio of span to chord.

In our model, the *ailerons* are located on the outboard ends of the wings. The *flaps* are also located on the wings inboard of the ailerons. The small winglike surfaces located near the tail are called *elevators*. And the vertical flap located on the aft end of the tail is the *rudder*. I'll talk more about what these *control surfaces* do later.

Taking a close look at a cross section of the wing as shown in Figure 7-3 helps to define a few more terms.

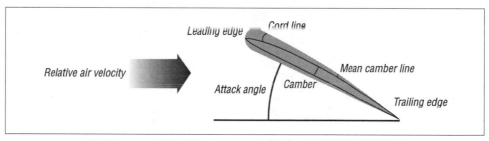

Figure 7-3. Airfoil Section

The airfoil shown in Figure 7-3 is a typical cambered airfoil. *Camber* represents the curvature of the airfoil. If you draw a straight line from the trailing edge to the leading edge, you end up with what's called the *chord line*. Now if you divide the airfoil into a number of cross sections, like slices in a loaf of bread, going from the trailing edge to the leading edge and then draw a curved line passing through the midpoint of each section's thickness, you end up with the *mean camber line*. The maximum difference between the mean camber line and the chord line is a measure of the camber of the airfoil. The angle measured between the direction of travel of the airfoil (the relative velocity vector of the airfoil as it passes through the air), and the chord line is called the absolute *angle of attack*.

When an aircraft is in flight, it may rotate about any axis. It is standard practice always to refer to an aircraft's rotations about three axes relative to the pilot. Thus, these axes are fixed to the aircraft, so to speak, irrespective of its actual orientation in three-dimensional space; they are the *pitch* axis, the *roll* axis, and the *yaw* axis.

The pitch axis runs transversely across the aircraft, that is, in the port-starboard direction.* Pitch rotation is when the nose of the aircraft is raised or lowered from the pilot's perspective. The roll axis runs longitudinally through the center of the aircraft. Roll motions (rotations) about this axis result in the wingtips being raised or lowered on either side of the pilot. Finally, the yaw axis is a vertical axis about which the nose of the aircraft rotates in the left-to-right (or right-to-left) direction with respect to the pilot. These rotations are illustrated in Figure 7-4.

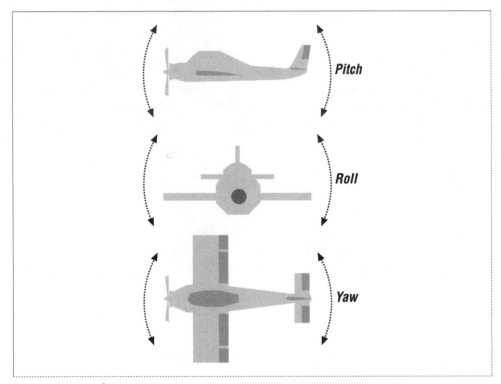

Figure 7-4. Aircraft Rotations

Lift and Drag

When an airfoil moves through a fluid such as air, lift is produced. The mechanisms by which this occurs are similar to those in the case of the Magnus lift force discussed in the previous chapter, in that Bernoulli's law is still in effect. However, this time, instead of rotation, it is the airfoil's shape and angle of attack that affect the flow of air so as to create lift.

Figure 7-5 shows an airfoil section moving through air at a speed V. V is the relative velocity between the foil and the undisturbed air ahead of the foil. As the air hits and

---

* Port is to the pilot's left and starboard is to the pilot's right when sitting in the cockpit facing forward.

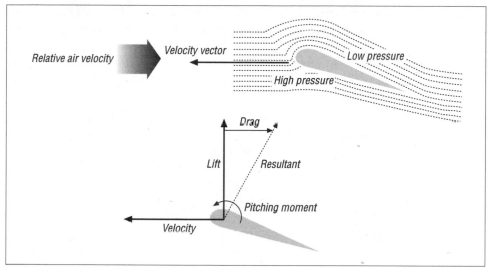

Figure 7-5. Airfoil Moving through Air

moves around the foil, it splits at the forward stagnation point located near the foil leading edge such that air flows both over and under the foil. The air that flows under the foil gets deflected downward, while the air that flows over the foil speeds up as it goes around the leading edge and over the surface of the foil. The air then flows smoothly off the trailing edge; this is the so-called Kutta condition. Ideally, the boundary layer remains "attached" to the foil without separating as in the case of the sphere discussed in the preceding chapter.

The relatively fast-moving air above the foil results in a region of low pressure above the foil (remember, Bernoulli's equation that shows pressure is inversely proportional to velocity in fluid flow). The air hitting and moving along the underside of the foil creates a region of relatively high pressure. The combined effect of this flow pattern is to create regions of relatively low and high pressure above and below the airfoil. It's this pressure differential that gives rise to the lift force. By definition the lift force is perpendicular to the line of flight, that is, the velocity vector.

Note that the airfoil does not have to be cambered to generate lift; a flat plate oriented at an angle of attack relative to the air flow will also generate lift. Likewise, an airfoil does not have to have an angle of attack. Cambered airfoils can generate lift at zero, even negative, angles of attack. Thus, in general, the total lift force on an airfoil is composed of two components: the lift due to camber and the lift due to attack angle.

Theoretically, the thickness of an airfoil does not contribute to lift. You can, after all, have a thin curved wing, as in the case of wings made of fabric such as those used for hang gliders. In practice, thickness is utilized for structural reasons. Further, thickness at the leading edge can help to delay stall (more on this in a moment).

The pressure differential between the upper and lower surfaces of the airfoil also gives rise to a drag force that acts in line with but opposing the velocity vector. The lift and drag forces are perpendicular to each other and lie in the plane defined by the velocity vector and the vector normal (perpendicular) to the airfoil chord line. These two force components, lift and drag, when combined yield the resultant force acting on the airfoil in flight. This is illustrated in Figure 7-5.

Both lift and drag are functions of air density, speed, viscosity, surface area, aspect ratio, and angle of attack. Traditionally, the lift and drag properties of a given foil design are expressed in terms of nondimensional coefficients:

$$C_L = L/[(1/2)\rho V^2 S]$$
$$C_D = D/[(1/2)\rho V^2 S]$$

where S is the wing planform area (span times chord for rectangular wings), L is the lift force, D is the drag force, V is the speed through the air, and ρ is air density. These coefficients are experimentally determined from wind tunnel tests of model airfoil designs at various angles of attack. The results of these tests are usually presented as graphs of lift and drag coefficient versus attack angle. Figure 7-6 illustrates some typical lift and drag charts for a wing section.

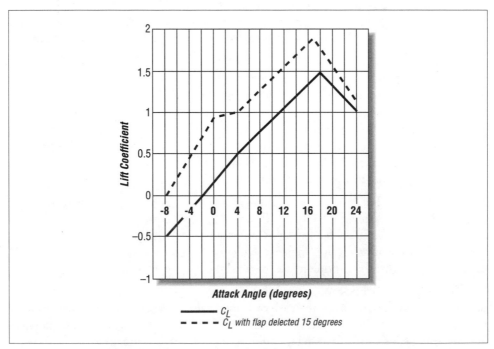

Figure 7-6. Typical C_L, C_D, and C_M versus Attack Angle

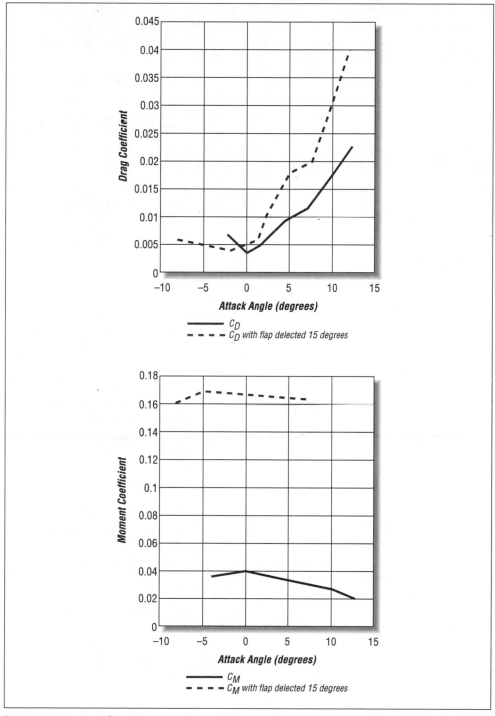

Figure 7-6. Continued

The most widely known family of foil section designs and test data are the NACA foil sections. *Theory of Wing Sections* by Ira H. Abbott and Albert E. Von Doenhoff contains a wealth of lift and drag data for practical airfoil designs (see the bibliography for a complete reference to this work).*

In practice, the flow of air around a wing is not strictly two-dimensional, that is, flowing uniformly over each parallel cross section of the wing, and there exists a spanwise flow of air along the wing. The flow is said to be three-dimensional. The more three-dimensional the flow, the less efficient the wing.[†] This effect is reduced on longer, high-aspect-ratio wings (and wings with end plates where the effective aspect ratio is increased); thus, high-aspect-ratio wings are comparatively more efficient.

To account for the effect of aspect ratio, wing sections of various aspect ratio for a given foil design are usually tested so as to produce a family of lift and drag curves versus attack angle. There are other geometrical factors that affect the flow around wings, and for a rigorous treatment of these I'll refer you to the *Theory of Wing Sections* and *Fluid-Dynamic Lift*.[‡]

Turning back to Figure 7-6, you'll notice that the drag coefficient increases sharply with attack angle. This is reasonable, as you would expect the wing to produce the most drag when oriented flat against or perpendicular to the flow of air.

A look at the lift coefficient curve, which initially increases linearly with attack angle, shows that at some attack angle the lift coefficient reaches a maximum value. This angle is called the *critical attack angle*. For angles beyond the critical, the lift coefficient drops off rapidly, and the airfoil (or wing) will *stall* and cease to produce lift. This is bad. When an aircraft stalls in the air, it will begin to drop rapidly until the pilot corrects the stall situation by, for example, reducing pitch and increasing thrust. When stall occurs, the air no longer flows smoothly over the trailing edge, and the corresponding high angle of attack results in flow separation, as illustrated in Figure 7-7. This loss in lift is also accompanied by an increase in drag.

Theoretically, the resultant force acting on an airfoil acts through a point located at one-fourth the chord length aft of the leading edge. This is called the *quarter-chord* point. In reality, the resultant force line of action will vary depending on attack angle, pressure distribution, and speed, among other factors. However, in practice, it is reasonable to assume that the line of action passes through the quarter-chord point for typical operational conditions. To account for the difference between the actual line of action of the resultant and the quarter-chord point, the pitching moment about the quarter-chord point must be considered. This pitching moment usually tends to tilt the leading

---

* *Theory of Wing Sections* includes standard foil section geometry and performance data, including the well-known NACA family of foil sections. The appendixes to *Theory of Wing Sections* have all the data you need to collect lift and drag coefficient data for various airfoil designs, including those with flaps.

[†] Lifting efficiency can be expressed in terms of lift-to-drag ratio. The higher the lift-to-drag ratio the more efficient the wing or foil section.

[‡] *Fluid-Dynamic Lift*, by Sighard F. Hoerner and Henry V. Borst, and *Fluid-Dynamic Drag*, by Sighard F. Hoerner, contain tons of practical charts, tables, and formulas for virtually every aspect of aircraft aerodynamics. They even include material that is appropriate for high-speed boats and automobiles.

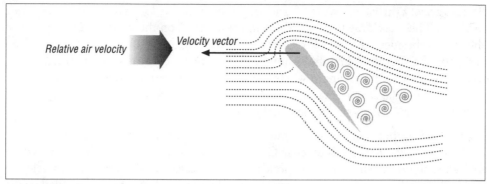

Figure 7-7. Stalled Airfoil

edge of the foil downward. In some cases this moment is relatively small in comparison to the other moments acting on the aircraft and may be neglected.* An exception may be when the foil has deflected flaps.

Flaps are control devices that are used to alter the shape of the foil so as to change its lift characteristics. Figure 7-6 also shows typical lift, drag, and moment coefficients for an airfoil fitted with a plain flap deflected downward at 15 degrees. Notice the significant increase in lift, drag, and pitch moment when the flap is deflected. *Theory of Wing Sections* also provides data for flapped airfoils for flap angles between −15 and 60 degrees.

Other Forces

The most notable force that I've yet to discuss is thrust—the propulsion force. Thrust provides forward motion, and without it, the aircraft's wings can't generate lift and the aircraft won't fly. Thrust, whether generated by a propeller or a jet engine, is usually expressed in pounds, and a common ratio that's used to compare the relative merits of aircraft powering is the thrust-to-weight ratio. The thrust-to-weight ratio is the maximum thrust deliverable by the propulsion plant divided by the aircraft's total weight. When the thrust-to-weight ratio is greater than 1, the aircraft is capable of overcoming gravity in a vertical climb. In this case the lift generated by the wings does not aid in maintaining (or increasing) altitude; however, lift is still being generated, which tends to pull the aircraft away from a vertical trajectory.

Thrust, whether produced by a propeller or a jet engine, is a function of air density. At high altitudes the air density (and oxygen content) is reduced, and thrust will decrease accordingly. At some point the engines will stall and cease to propel the aircraft higher. If you've ever been to an air show, you've probably seen this sort of stunt performed on purpose.

---

* Aircraft designers must always consider this pitching moment when designing the aircraft's structure, as this moment tends to want to twist the wings off the fuselage.

Besides gravity, thrust, and wing lift and drag, there are other forces that act on an aircraft in flight. These are drag forces (and lift in some cases) on the various components of the aircraft besides the wings. For example, the fuselage contributes to the overall drag acting on the aircraft. Additionally, anything sticking out of the fuselage will contribute to the overall drag. If they aren't wings, anything sticking out of the fuselage is typically called an appendage. Some examples of appendages are the aircraft landing gear, canopy, bombs, missiles, fuel pods, and air intakes.

Typically, drag data for fuselages and appendages are expressed in terms of a drag coefficient similar to that discussed in Chapter 6, where experimentally determined drag forces are nondimensionalized by projected frontal area (S), density (ρ), and velocity squared (V^2). This means that the experimentally measured drag force is divided by the quantity $(1/2)\rho V^2 S$ to get the dimensionless drag coefficient. Depending on the object under consideration, the drag coefficient data will be presented as a function of some important geometric parameter, such as attack angle in the case of airfoils or length-to-height ratio in the case of canopies. Here again, Hoerner's *Fluid Dynamic Drag* is an excellent source of practical data for all sorts of fuselage shapes and appendages.

For example, when an aircraft's landing gear is down, the wheels (as well as associated mechanical gear) contribute to the overall drag force on the aircraft. Hoerner reports drag coefficients based on frontal area of some small plane landing gear designs to be in the range of 0.25 to 0.55. By comparison, drag coefficients for typical external storage pods (such as for fuel), which are usually streamlined, can range from 0.06 to 0.26.

Another component of the total drag force acting on aircraft in flight is due to skin friction. Aircraft wings, fuselages, and appendages are not completely smooth. Weld seems, rivets and even paint cause surface imperfections that increase frictional drag. As in the case of the sphere data presented in Chapter 6, this frictional drag is dependent on the nature of the flow around the part of the aircraft under consideration, that is, whether the flow is laminar or turbulent. This implies that frictional drag coefficients for specific surfaces will generally be a function of Reynold's number.

In a rigorous analysis of a specific aircraft's flight, you would of course want to consider all these additional drag components. If you're interested in seeing the nitty-gritty details of such calculations, I suggest you take a look at Hoerner's *Fluid Dynamic Drag*, in which he gives a detailed example calculation of the total drag force on a fighter aircraft in his Chapter 14.

Control

The flaps located on the inboard trailing edge of the wing in our model are used to alter the chord and camber of the wing section to increase lift at a given speed. Flaps are used primarily to increase lift during slow-speed flight, such as when taking off or landing. When landing, flaps are typically deployed at a high downward angle (downward flap deflections are considered positive) on the order of 30 to 60 degrees. This increases both the lift and drag of the wings. When landing, this increase in drag also assists in slowing the aircraft to a suitable landing speed. When taking off, this increase in drag works against you in that it necessitates higher thrust to get up to speed; thus, flaps may not be deployed to as great an angle as when landing.

Ailerons control or induce roll motion by means of producing differential lift between the port and starboard wing sections. The basic aileron is nothing more than a pair of trailing edge flaps fitted to the tips of the wings. These flaps move opposite each other, one deflecting upward while the other deflects downward, to create a lift differential between the port and starboard wings. This lift differential, separated by the distance between the ailerons, creates a torque that rolls the aircraft. To roll the aircraft to the port side (the pilot's left), the starboard aileron would be deflected in a downward direction while the port aileron was deflected in an upward direction relative to the pilot. Likewise, the opposite deflections of the ailerons would induce a roll to the starboard side. In a real aircraft the ailerons are controlled by moving the flight stick to either the left or right.

Elevators, the tail "wings," are used to control the pitch of the aircraft. (Elevators can be flaps, as shown in Figure 7-2, or the entire tail wing can rotate, as on the Lockheed Martin F-16.) When the elevators are deflected such that their trailing edge goes downward with respect to the pilot, a nose-down pitch rotation will be induced; that is, the tail of the aircraft will tend to rise relative to its nose, and the aircraft will dive. In an actual aircraft this is achieved by pushing the flight stick forward. When elevators are deflected such that their tailing edge goes upward, a nose-up pitch rotation will be induced.

Elevators are very important for trimming (adjusting the pitch of) the aircraft. Generally, the center of gravity of the aircraft is located above the mean quarter-chord line of the aircraft wings such that the center of gravity is in line with the main lift force. However, as I explained earlier, the lift force does not always pass through the quarter-chord point. Further, the center of gravity of the aircraft may very well change during flight, for example, as fuel is burned off and when ordnance is released. By controlling the elevators, the pilot is able to adjust the attitude of the aircraft such that all of the forces balance and the aircraft flies at the desired orientation (pitch angle).

Finally, the rudder is used to control yaw. The pilot uses foot pedals to control the rudder; pushing the left (port) pedal yaws left, and pushing the right pedals yaws right (starboard). The rudder is useful for fine-tuning the alignment of the aircraft for approach on landing or when sighting up a target. Typically, large rudder action tends also to induce roll motion that must be compensated for by proper use of the ailerons.

In some cases the rudder consists of a flap on the trailing edge of the vertical tail; in other cases there is no rudder flap, and the entire vertical tail rotates. In both cases the vertical tail, which also provides directional stability, will usually have a symmetric airfoil shape; that is, its mean camber line will be coincident with its chord line. When the aircraft is flying straight and level, the tail will not generate lift, since it is symmetric and its attack angle will be zero. However, if the plane sideslips (yaws relative to its flight direction), then the tail will be at an angle of attack and will generate lift, tending to push the plane back to its original orientation.

Modeling

Although we've yet to cover a lot of the material required to implement a real-time flight simulator, I'd like to go ahead and outline some of the steps necessary to calculate the lift and drag forces on your model aircraft. Here are the steps:

1. Discretize the lifting surfaces into a number of smaller wing sections.
2. Collect geometric and foil performance data.
3. Calculate the relative air velocity over each wing section.
4. Calculate the attack angle for each wing section.
5. Determine the appropriate lift and drag coefficients, and calculate lift and drag forces.

The first step is relatively straightforward in that you need to divide the aircraft into smaller sections, each of which is approximately uniform in characteristics. Performing this step for the model shown in Figure 7-2, you might divide the wing into four sections: one for each wing section that's fitted with an aileron and one for each section that's fitted with a flap. You could also use two sections to model the elevators—one port and one starboard—and another section to model the tail/rudder. Finally, you could lump the entire fuselage together as one additional section or further subdivide it into smaller sections, depending on how detailed you want to get.

If you're going to model your aircraft as a rigid body, you'll have to account for all of the forces and moments acting on the aircraft while it is in flight. Since the aircraft is composed of a number of different components, each contributing to the total lift and drag, you'll have to break your calculations up into a number of smaller chunks and then sum all contributions to get the resultant lift and drag forces. You can then use these resultant forces along with thrust and gravity in the equations of motion for your aircraft. You can, of course, refine your model further by adding more components for such items as the cockpit canopy, landing gear, external fuel pods, and bombs. The level of detail to which you go depends on the degree of accuracy you're going for. If you are trying to mimic the flight performance of a specific aircraft, then you need to sharpen your pencil.

Once you have defined each section, you must prepare the appropriate geometric and performance data. For example, for the wings and other lifting surfaces you'll need to determine each section's initial incidence angle (its fixed pitch or attack angle relative to the aircraft reference system), span, chord length, aspect ratio, planform area, and quarter-chord location relative to the aircraft's center of gravity. You'll also have to prepare a table of lift and drag coefficients versus attack angle appropriate for the section under consideration. Since this data is usually presented in graphical form, you'll have to pull data from the charts to build your lookup table for use in your game. Finally, you'll need to calculate the unit normal vector perpendicular to the plane of each wing section. (You'll need this later when calculating angle of attack.)

These first two steps need be performed only once at the beginning of your game or simulation, since the data will remain constant (unless your plane changes shape or its center of gravity shifts during your simulation).

The third step involves calculating the relative velocity between the air and the each component so that you can calculate lift and drag forces. At first glance this might seem trivial, since the aircraft will be traveling at an air speed that will be known to you during your simulation. However, you must also remember that the aircraft is a rigid body, and in addition to the linear velocity of its center of gravity, you must also account for its rotational velocity.

Back in Chapter 2, I gave you a formula to calculate the relative velocity of any point on a rigid body that was undergoing both linear and rotational motion:

$$\mathbf{v}_R = \mathbf{v}_{cg} + (\boldsymbol{\omega} \times \mathbf{r})$$

This is the formula you'll need to calculate the relative velocity at each component in your model. In this case $\mathbf{v}_{cg}$ is the vector representing the air speed and flight direction of the aircraft, $\boldsymbol{\omega}$ is the angular velocity vector of the aircraft, and $\mathbf{r}$ is the distance vector from the aircraft center of gravity to the component under consideration.

When dealing with wings, once you have the relative velocity vector, you can proceed to calculate the attack angle for each wing section. The drag force vector will be parallel to the relative velocity vector, while the lift force vector will be perpendicular to the velocity vector. Angle of attack is then the angle between the lift force vector and the normal vector perpendicular to the plane of the wing section. This involves taking the dot product of these two vectors.

Once you have the attack angle, you can go to your coefficient of lift and drag versus attack angle tables to determine the lift and drag coefficients to use at this instant in your simulation. With these coefficients you can use the following formulas to estimate the magnitudes of lift and drag forces on the wing section under consideration:

$$\text{Lift} = C_L(1/2)\rho V^2 S$$
$$\text{Drag} = C_D(1/2)\rho V^2 S$$

The approach outlined here is a very simplified approach that only approximates the lift and drag characteristics. This approach does not account for spanwise flow effects, or the flow effects between adjacent wing sections. Nor does this approach account for air disturbances, such as downwash, that may affect the relative angle of attack for a wing section. Further, the air flow over each wing section is assumed to be steady and uniform.

As a simple example, consider wing panel 1, which is the starboard aileron wing section. Assume that the wing is set at an initial incidence angle of 3.5 degrees and that the plane is traveling at a speed of 75 knots in level flight at low altitude with a pitch angle of 4.5 degrees. This wing section has a chord length of 5.2 ft, and the span of this section is 6 ft. Using the lift and drag data presented in Figure 7-6, calculate the lift and drag on this wing section, assuming that the ailerons are not deflected and that the density of air 2.37×10^{-3} slug/ft^3.

The first step is to calculate the angle of attack, which is 8 degrees, based on the information provided. Now looking at Figure 7-6, you can find the airfoil lift and drag coefficients to be 0.92 and 0.013, respectively.

Next, you'll need to calculate the planform area of this section, which is simply its chord times its span. This yields 31.2 ft^2. Now you have enough information to calculate lift and drag as follows (don't forget to convert the speed in knots to ft/s; 1 knot = 1.688 ft/s):

$$\text{Lift} = C_L(1/2)\rho V^2 S$$
$$\text{Lift} = 0.92(1/2)(2.37 \times 10^{-3}\,\text{slug/ft}^3)[(75\,\text{kt})(1.688\,\text{ft/s/kt})]^2(31.2\,\text{ft}^2)$$
$$\text{Lift} = 542.2\,\text{lb}$$
$$\text{Drag} = C_D(1/2)\rho V^2 S$$
$$\text{Drag} = 0.013(1/2)(2.37 \times 10^{-3}\,\text{slug/ft}^3)[(75\,\text{kt})(1.688\,\text{ft/s/kt})]^2(31.2\,\text{ft}^2)$$
$$\text{Drag} = 8.0\,\text{lb}$$

In your simulation you'll have to perform a similar set of calculations for every component that you've defined. As you can see, using this sort of empirical data and formulas, although only approximate, lends itself to fairly easy calculations. The hard part is deciding what to model and finding the right data; after that the lift and drag calculations are pretty simple.

I've prepared an example program to show you how to model a simple airplane using the method shown here. The program is named FlightSim.exe and is a real-time, 3D flight simulator.* The small aircraft that is simulated resembles the one shown in Figure 7-2.

This program includes the following source files along with a text file (*Instructions.txt*) that explains the flight controls:

- *Physics.cpp* and *Physics.h*
- *D3dstuff.cpp* and *D3dstuff.h*
- *Mymath.h*
- *Winmain.cpp*

As I said, this program is a real-time simulation, and it treats the aircraft as a rigid body. We have yet to cover real-time simulations in this book, so a lot of the code may be confusing at this point. Don't worry, though; later in this book I'll cover all you need to know to fully understand this program. For now, however, I want you to focus on a few specific functions that implement the flight model. These functions are contained in the source file, *Physics.cpp*.

---

* I've used Microsoft's Direct3D for this program, so to run it, you'll have to make sure Direct3D is installed on your system.

The first function I want you to look at is CalcAirplaneMassProperties:

```
//---------------------------------------------------------------------------//
// This model uses a set of eight discrete elements to represent the
// airplane.  The elements are described below:
//
//              Element 1:  Outboard, Port (left) wing section fitted with ailerons
//              Element 2:  Inboard, Port wing section fitted with landing flaps
//              Element 3:  Inboard, Starboard (right) wing section fitted with
//                          landing flaps
//              Element 4:  Outboard, Starboard wing section fitted with ailerons
//              Element 5:  Port elevator fitted with flap
//              Element 6:  Starboard elevator fitted with flap
//              Element 7:  Vertical tail/rudder (no flap the whole thing rotates)
//              Element 8:  The fuselage
//
//   This function first sets up each element and then goes on to calculate
//   the combined weight, center of gravity, and inertia tensor for the plane.
//   Some other properties of each element are also calculated which you'll
//   need when calculating the lift and drag forces on the plane.
//---------------------------------------------------------------------------//
void      CalcAirplaneMassProperties(void)
{
    float       mass;
    Vector      vMoment;
    Vector      CG;
    int         i;
    float       Ixx, Iyy, Izz, Ixy, Ixz, Iyz;
    float       in, di;

    // Initialize the elements here
    // Initially, the coordinates of each element are referenced from
    // a design coordinates system located at the very tail end of the plane,
    // its baseline, and its centerline. Later, these coordinates will be
    // adjusted so that each element is referenced to the combined center of
    // gravity of the airplane.
    Element[0].fMass = 6.56f;
    Element[0].vDCoords = Vector(14.5f,12.0f,2.5f);
    Element[0].vLocalInertia = Vector(13.92f,10.50f,24.00f);
    Element[0].fIncidence = -3.5f;
    Element[0].fDihedral = 0.0f;
    Element[0].fArea = 31.2f;
    Element[0].iFlap = 0;

    Element[1].fMass = 7.31f;
    Element[1].vDCoords = Vector(14.5f,5.5f,2.5f);
    Element[1].vLocalInertia = Vector(21.95f,12.22f,33.67f);
    Element[1].fIncidence = -3.5f;
    Element[1].fDihedral = 0.0f;
    Element[1].fArea = 36.4f;
    Element[1].iFlap = 0;

    Element[2].fMass = 7.31f;
    Element[2].vDCoords = Vector(14.5f,-5.5f,2.5f);
    Element[2].vLocalInertia = Vector(21.95f,12.22f,33.67f);
    Element[2].fIncidence = -3.5f;
    Element[2].fDihedral = 0.0f;
    Element[2].fArea = 36.4f;
    Element[2].iFlap = 0;
```

```
Element[3].fMass = 6.56f;
Element[3].vDCoords = Vector(14.5f,-12.0f,2.5f);
Element[3].vLocalInertia = Vector(13.92f,10.50f,24.00f);
Element[3].fIncidence = -3.5f;
Element[3].fDihedral = 0.0f;
Element[3].fArea = 31.2f;
Element[3].iFlap = 0;

Element[4].fMass = 2.62f;
Element[4].vDCoords = Vector(3.03f,2.5f,3.0f);
Element[4].vLocalInertia = Vector(0.837f,0.385f,1.206f);
Element[4].fIncidence = 0.0f;
Element[4].fDihedral = 0.0f;
Element[4].fArea = 10.8f;
Element[4].iFlap = 0;

Element[5].fMass = 2.62f;
Element[5].vDCoords = Vector(3.03f,-2.5f,3.0f);
Element[5].vLocalInertia = Vector(0.837f,0.385f,1.206f);
Element[5].fIncidence = 0.0f;
Element[5].fDihedral = 0.0f;
Element[5].fArea = 10.8f;
Element[5].iFlap = 0;

Element[6].fMass = 2.93f;
Element[6].vDCoords = Vector(2.25f,0.0f,5.0f);
Element[6].vLocalInertia = Vector(1.262f,1.942f,0.718f);
Element[6].fIncidence = 0.0f;
Element[6].fDihedral = 90.0f;
Element[6].fArea = 12.0f;
Element[6].iFlap = 0;

Element[7].fMass = 31.8f;
Element[7].vDCoords = Vector(15.25f,0.0f,1.5f);
Element[7].vLocalInertia = Vector(66.30f,861.9f,861.9f);
Element[7].fIncidence = 0.0f;
Element[7].fDihedral = 0.0f;
Element[7].fArea = 84.0f;
Element[7].iFlap = 0;

// Calculate the vector normal (perpendicular) to each lifting surface.
// This is required when calculating the relative air velocity for
// lift and drag calculations.
for (i = 0; i< 8; i++)
{
    in = DegreesToRadians(Element[i].fIncidence);
    di = DegreesToRadians(Element[i].fDihedral);
    Element[i].vNormal = Vector((float)sin(in), (float)(cos(in)*sin(di)),
                                (float)(cos(in)*cos(di)));
    Element[i].vNormal.Normalize();
}

// Calculate total mass
mass = 0;
for (i = 0; i< 8; i++)
    mass += Element[i].fMass;

// Calculate combined center of gravity location
vMoment = Vector(0.0f, 0.0f, 0.0f);
for (i = 0; i< 8; i++)
```

```
    {
        vMoment += Element[i].fMass*Element[i].vDCoords;
    }
    CG = vMoment/mass;

    // Calculate coordinates of each element with respect to the combined CG
    for (i = 0; i< 8; i++)
    {
        Element[i].vCGCoords = Element[i].vDCoords - CG;
    }

    // Now calculate the moments and products of inertia for the
    // combined elements.
    // (This inertia matrix (tensor) is in body coordinates)
    Ixx = 0;      Iyy = 0;      Izz = 0;
    Ixy = 0;      Ixz = 0;      Iyz = 0;
    for (i = 0; i< 8; i++)
    {
        Ixx += Element[i].vLocalInertia.x + Element[i].fMass *
               (Element[i].vCGCoords.y*Element[i].vCGCoords.y +
               Element[i].vCGCoords.z*Element[i].vCGCoords.z);
        Iyy += Element[i].vLocalInertia.y + Element[i].fMass *
               (Element[i].vCGCoords.z*Element[i].vCGCoords.z +
               Element[i].vCGCoords.x*Element[i].vCGCoords.x);
        Izz += Element[i].vLocalInertia.z + Element[i].fMass *
               (Element[i].vCGCoords.x*Element[i].vCGCoords.x +
               Element[i].vCGCoords.y*Element[i].vCGCoords.y);
        Ixy += Element[i].fMass * (Element[i].vCGCoords.x *
               Element[i].vCGCoords.y);
        Ixz += Element[i].fMass * (Element[i].vCGCoords.x *
               Element[i].vCGCoords.z);
        Iyz += Element[i].fMass * (Element[i].vCGCoords.y *
               Element[i].vCGCoords.z);
    }

    // Finally, set up the airplane's mass and its inertia matrix and take the
    // inverse of the inertia matrix
    Airplane.fMass = mass;
    Airplane.mInertia.e11 = Ixx;
    Airplane.mInertia.e12 = -Ixy;
    Airplane.mInertia.e13 = -Ixz;
    Airplane.mInertia.e21 = -Ixy;
    Airplane.mInertia.e22 = Iyy;
    Airplane.mInertia.e23 = -Iyz;
    Airplane.mInertia.e31 = -Ixz;
    Airplane.mInertia.e32 = -Iyz;
    Airplane.mInertia.e33 = Izz;

    Airplane.mInertiaInverse = Airplane.mInertia.Inverse();
}
```

Among other things, this function essentially completes step 1 (and part of step 2) of our modeling method: discretize the airplane into a number of smaller pieces, each with its own mass and lift and drag properties. For this model I chose to use eight pieces, or elements, to describe the aircraft. My comments at the beginning of the function explain what each element represents.

The very first thing this function does is initialize the elements with the properties that I've defined to approximate the aircraft. Each element is given a mass, a set of *design coordinates* to its center of mass, a set of moments of inertia about each element's center of mass, an initial incidence angle, a planform area, and a *dihedral angle*.

The design coordinates are the coordinates of the element with respect to an origin located at the very tip of the aircraft's tail, on its centerline, and at its baseline. The *x*-axis of this system points toward the nose of the aircraft, and the *y*-axis points toward the port side. The *z*-axis points upward. You have to set up your elements in this design coordinate system first because you don't yet know the location of the whole aircraft's center of mass, which is the combined center of mass of all of the elements. Ultimately, you want each element referenced from the combined center of mass because it's the center of mass that you'll be tracking during the simulation. (Recall that we discussed this in Chapters 2 and 4.)

The dihedral angle is the angle about the *x*-axis at which the element is initially set. For our model, all of the elements have a zero dihedral angle, that is, they are horizontal, except for the tail rudder, which has a 90-degree dihedral, since it is oriented vertically.

After you set up the elements, the first calculation that this function performs is to find the unit normal vector to each element's surface based on the element's incidence and dihedral angles. You need this direction vector to help calculate the angle of attack between the air flow and the element.

The next calculation is the total mass calculation, which is simply the sum of all element masses. Immediately following that, the combined center of gravity location is determined using the technique I discussed in Chapter 1. The coordinates to the combined center of gravity are referenced to the design coordinate system. You need to subtract this coordinate from the design coordinate of each element to determine each element's coordinates relative to the combined center of gravity. After that you're all set, with the exception of the combined moment of inertia tensor, which I'll wait until Chapter 11 to discuss.

Step 2 of our modeling method says that you need to collect the airfoil performance data. For the example program I used a cambered airfoil with plain flaps to model the wings and elevators, and I used a symmetric airfoil without flaps to model the tail rudder. I didn't use flaps for the tail rudder, since I just made the whole thing rotate about a vertical axis to provide rudder action.

For the wings, I set up two functions to handle the lift and drag coefficients:

```
//----------------------------------------------------------------------------//
//   Given the attack angle and the status of the flaps, this function
//   returns the appropriate lift coefficient for a cambered airfoil with
//   a plain trailing edge flap (+/- 15 degree deflection).
//----------------------------------------------------------------------------//
float    LiftCoefficient(float angle, int flaps)
{
    float clf0[9] = {-0.54f, -0.2f, 0.2f, 0.57f, 0.92f, 1.21f, 1.43f, 1.4f,
                     1.0f};
```

```
    float clfd[9] = {0.0f, 0.45f, 0.85f, 1.02f, 1.39f, 1.65f, 1.75f, 1.38f,
                     1.17f};
    float clfu[9] = {-0.74f, -0.4f, 0.0f, 0.27f, 0.63f, 0.92f, 1.03f, 1.1f,
                     0.78f};
    float a[9]    = {-8.0f, -4.0f, 0.0f, 4.0f, 8.0f, 12.0f, 16.0f, 20.0f,
                     24.0f};
    float cl;
    int   i;
    cl = 0;
    for (i=0; i<8; i++)
    {
        if( (a[i] <= angle) && (a[i+1] > angle) )
        {
            switch(flaps)
            {
                case 0:// flaps not deflected
                    cl = clf0[i] - (a[i] - angle) * (clf0[i] - clf0[i+1]) /
                         (a[i] - a[i+1]);
                    break;
                case -1: // flaps down
                    cl = clfd[i] - (a[i] - angle) * (clfd[i] - clfd[i+1]) /
                         (a[i] - a[i+1]);
                    break;
                case 1: // flaps up
                    cl = clfu[i] - (a[i] - angle) * (clfu[i] - clfu[i+1]) /
                         (a[i] - a[i+1]);
                    break;
            }
            break;
        }
    }

    return cl;

}

//----------------------------------------------------------------------------//
//  Given the attack angle and the status of the flaps, this function
//  returns the appropriate drag coefficient for a cambered airfoil with
//  a plain trailing edge flap (+/- 15 degree deflection).
//----------------------------------------------------------------------------//
float    DragCoefficient(float angle, int flaps)
{
    float cdf0[9] = {0.01f, 0.0074f, 0.004f, 0.009f, 0.013f, 0.023f, 0.05f,
                     0.12f, 0.21f};
    float cdfd[9] = {0.0065f, 0.0043f, 0.0055f, 0.0153f, 0.0221f, 0.0391f, 0.1f,
                     0.195f, 0.3f};
    float cdfu[9] = {0.005f, 0.0043f, 0.0055f, 0.02601f, 0.03757f, 0.06647f,
                     0.13f, 0.18f, 0.25f};
    float a[9]    = {-8.0f, -4.0f, 0.0f, 4.0f, 8.0f, 12.0f, 16.0f, 20.0f,
                     24.0f};
    float cd;
    int   i;

    cd = 0.5;
    for (i=0; i<8; i++)
    {
        if( (a[i] <= angle) && (a[i+1] > angle) )
        {
            switch(flaps)
```

```
        {
            case 0:// flaps not deflected
                cd = cdf0[i] - (a[i] - angle) * (cdf0[i] - cdf0[i+1]) /
                    (a[i] - a[i+1]);
                break;
            case -1: // flaps down
                cd = cdfd[i] - (a[i] - angle) * (cdfd[i] - cdfd[i+1]) /
                    (a[i] - a[i+1]);
                break;
            case 1: // flaps up
                cd = cdfu[i] - (a[i] - angle) * (cdfu[i] - cdfu[i+1]) /
                    (a[i] - a[i+1]);
                break;
        }
        break;
    }
    }

    return cd;
}
```

Each of these functions takes the angle of attack as a parameter along with a flag used to indicate the state of the flaps, that is, whether the flaps are in neutral position, deflected downward, or deflected upward. Notice that the lift and drag coefficient data are given for a set of discrete attack angles; thus, linear interpolation is used to determine the coefficients for attack angles that fall between the discrete angles.

The functions for determining the tail rudder lift and drag coefficients are similar to those shown here for the wings, the only differences being the coefficients themselves and the fact that the tail rudder does not include flaps. Here are the functions:

```
//----------------------------------------------------------------------//
//  Given the attack angle this function returns the proper lift coefficient
//  for a symmetric (no camber) airfoil without flaps.
//----------------------------------------------------------------------//
float     RudderLiftCoefficient(float angle)
{
    float clf0[7] = {0.16f, 0.456f, 0.736f, 0.968f, 1.144f, 1.12f, 0.8f};
    float a[7]    = {0.0f, 4.0f, 8.0f, 12.0f, 16.0f, 20.0f, 24.0f};
    float cl;
    int       i;
    float     aa = (float) fabs(angle);

    cl = 0;
    for (i=0; i<8; i++)
    {
        if( (a[i] <= aa) && (a[i+1] > aa) )
        {
            cl = clf0[i] - (a[i] - aa) * (clf0[i] - clf0[i+1]) /
                (a[i] - a[i+1]);
            if (angle < 0) cl = -cl;
            break;
        }
    }
    return cl;
}
```

```
//-------------------------------------------------------------------//
//  Given the attack angle this function returns the proper drag coefficient
//  for a symmetric (no camber) airfoil without flaps.
//-------------------------------------------------------------------//
float      RudderDragCoefficient(float angle)
{
    float cdf0[7] = {0.0032f, 0.0072f, 0.0104f, 0.0184f, 0.04f, 0.096f, 0.168f};
    float a[7]    = {0.0f, 4.0f, 8.0f, 12.0f, 16.0f, 20.0f, 24.0f};
    float cd;
    int   i;
    float    aa = (float) fabs(angle);

    cd = 0.5;
    for (i=0; i<8; i++)
    {
        if( (a[i] <= aa) && (a[i+1] > aa) )
        {
            cd = cdf0[i] - (a[i] - aa) * (cdf0[i] - cdf0[i+1]) /
                (a[i] - a[i+1]);
            break;
        }
    }
    return cd;
}
```

With steps 1 and 2 out of the way, steps 3, 4, and 5 are handled in a single function called CalcAirplaneLoads:

```
//-------------------------------------------------------------------//
// This function calculates all of the forces and moments acting on the
// plane at any given time.
//-------------------------------------------------------------------//
void      CalcAirplaneLoads(void)
{
    Vector      Fb, Mb;

    // reset forces and moments:
    Airplane.vForces.x = 0.0f;
    Airplane.vForces.y = 0.0f;
    Airplane.vForces.z = 0.0f;

    Airplane.vMoments.x = 0.0f;
    Airplane.vMoments.y = 0.0f;
    Airplane.vMoments.z = 0.0f;

    Fb.x = 0.0f;     Mb.x = 0.0f;
    Fb.y = 0.0f;     Mb.y = 0.0f;
    Fb.z = 0.0f;     Mb.z = 0.0f;

    // Define the thrust vector, which acts through the plane's CG
    Thrust.x = 1.0f;
    Thrust.y = 0.0f;
    Thrust.z = 0.0f;
    Thrust *= ThrustForce;

    // Calculate forces and moments in body space:
    Vector      vLocalVelocity;
    float       fLocalSpeed;
    Vector      vDragVector;
    Vector      vLiftVector;
    float       fAttackAngle;
```

```
float      tmp;
Vector     vResultant;
int          i;
Vector     vtmp;

Stalling = false;

for(i=0; i<7; i++) // loop through the seven lifting elements
                   // skipping the fuselage
{
    if (i == 6) // The tail/rudder is a special case, since it can rotate;
    {             // therefore, you have to recalculate the normal vector
        float in, di;
        in = DegreesToRadians(Element[i].fIncidence); // incidence angle
        di = DegreesToRadians(Element[i].fDihedral); // dihedral angle
        Element[i].vNormal = Vector(    (float)sin(in),
                                        (float)(cos(in)*sin(di)),
                                        (float)(cos(in)*cos(di)));

        Element[i].vNormal.Normalize();
    }

    // Calculate local velocity at element
    // The local velocity includes the velocity due to linear
    // motion of the airplane,
    // plus the velocity at each element due to the
    // rotation of the airplane.

    // Here's the rotational part
    vtmp = Airplane.vAngularVelocity^Element[i].vCGCoords;

    vLocalVelocity = Airplane.vVelocityBody + vtmp;

    // Calculate local air speed
    fLocalSpeed = vLocalVelocity.Magnitude();

    // Find the direction in which drag will act.
    // Drag always acts inline with the relative
    // velocity but in the opposing direction
    if(fLocalSpeed > 1.)
        vDragVector = -vLocalVelocity/fLocalSpeed;

    // Find the direction in which lift will act.
    // Lift is always perpendicular to the drag vector
    vLiftVector = (vDragVector^Element[i].vNormal)^vDragVector;
    tmp = vLiftVector.Magnitude();
    vLiftVector.Normalize();

    // Find the angle of attack.
    // The attack angle is the angle between the lift vector and the
    // element normal vector. Note that the sine of the attack angle,
    // is equal to the cosine of the angle between the drag vector and
    // the normal vector.
    tmp = vDragVector*Element[i].vNormal;
    if(tmp > 1.) tmp = 1;
    if(tmp < -1) tmp = -1;
    fAttackAngle = RadiansToDegrees((float) asin(tmp));

    // Determine the resultant force (lift and drag) on the element.
    tmp = 0.5f * rho * fLocalSpeed*fLocalSpeed * Element[i].fArea;
    if (i == 6) // Tail/rudder
```

```
        {
            vResultant = (vLiftVector*RudderLiftCoefficient(fAttackAngle) +
                          vDragVector*RudderDragCoefficient(fAttackAngle))
                         * tmp;
        } else
            vResultant = (vLiftVector*LiftCoefficient(fAttackAngle,
                          Element[i].iFlap) +
                          vDragVector*DragCoefficient(fAttackAngle,
                          Element[i].iFlap) ) * tmp;
        // Check for stall.
        // We can easily determine when stalled by noting when the coefficient
        // of lift is zero. In reality stall warning devices give warnings well
        // before the lift goes to zero to give the pilot time to correct.
        if (i<=0)
        {
            if (LiftCoefficient(fAttackAngle, Element[i].iFlap) == 0)
                Stalling = true;
        }

        // Keep a running total of these resultant forces (total force)
        Fb += vResultant;

        // Calculate the moment about the CG of this element's force
        // and keep a running total of these moments (total moment)
        vtmp = Element[i].vCGCoords^vResultant;
        Mb += vtmp;
    }

    // Now add the thrust
    Fb += Thrust;

    // Convert forces from model space to earth space
    Airplane.vForces = QVRotate(Airplane.qOrientation, Fb);

    // Apply gravity (g is defined as -32.174 ft/s 2)
    Airplane.vForces.z += g * Airplane.fMass;

    Airplane.vMoments += Mb;
}
```

The first thing this function does is reset the variables that hold the total force and moment acting on the aircraft. Next, the thrust vector is set up. This is trivial in this example, since I'm assuming that the thrust vector always points in the plus *x*-axis direction (toward the nose) and passes through the aircraft center of gravity (so it does not create a moment).

After calculating the thrust vector, the function loops over the model elements to calculate the lift and drag forces on each element. I've skipped the fuselage in this model; however, if you want to account for its drag in your model, this is the place to add the drag calculation.

Going into the loop, the first thing the function does is check to see whether the current element is element number 6, the tail rudder. If it is, then the rudder's normal vector is recalculated on the basis of the current incidence angle. The incidence angle for the rudder is altered when you press the X or C key to apply rudder action.

The next calculation is to determine the relative velocity between the air and the element under consideration. As I stated earlier, this relative velocity consists of the linear velocity as the airplane moves through the air plus the velocity of each element due to the airplane's rotation. Once this vector has been obtained, you calculate the relative air speed by taking the magnitude of the relative velocity vector.

The next step is to determine the direction in which drag will act. Since drag opposes motion, it acts in line with but opposite to the relative velocity vector; thus, all you need to do is take the negative of the relative velocity vector and normalize the result (divide it by its magnitude) to obtain the drag direction vector. Since this vector was normalized, its length is equal to 1 (unity), so you can multiply it by the drag force that will be calculated later to get the drag force vector.

After obtaining the drag direction vector, this function uses it to determine the lift direction vector. The lift force vector is always perpendicular to the drag force vector, so to calculate its direction, you first take the cross product of the drag direction vector with the element normal vector and then cross the result with the drag direction vector again. Here again, the function normalizes the lift direction vector.

Now that the lift and drag direction vectors have been obtained, the function proceeds to calculate the angle of attack for the current element. The attack angle is the angle between the lift vector and the element normal. You can calculate the angle by taking the inverse cosine of the vector dot product of the lift direction vector with the element normal vector. Since the drag vector is perpendicular to the lift vector, you can get the same result by taking the inverse sine of the vector dot product of the drag direction vector with the element normal vector.

Now with all the lift and drag vector stuff out of the way, the function goes on to calculate the resultant force acting on the element. The resultant force vector is simply the vector sum of the lift and drag force vectors. Notice that this is where the lift and drag coefficient functions are called and where the empirical lift and drag formulas previously discussed are applied.

After calculating the resultant force, the function checks to see whether the calculated lift coefficient is zero. If the lift coefficient is zero, then the stall flag is set to warn us that the plane is in a stalled situation.

Finally, the resultant force is accumulated in the total force vector variable, and the moment is calculated by taking the cross product of the element coordinate vector with the resultant force. The resulting moment is accumulated in the total moment vector variable. After exiting the loop, the function adds the thrust vector to the total force.

So far, all of these forces and moments have been referenced in the body fixed coordinate system. The only thing left to do now is apply the gravity force, but this force acts in the negative y-axis direction in the earth fixed coordinate system. To apply the gravity force, the function must first rotate the body force vector from body space to earth space coordinates. I used a quaternion rotation technique in this example, which I'll discuss later on.

That's pretty much it for the flight model. The rest of the code in this example will be discussed later in this book where appropriate. About the only thing I won't get into detail on is the code to implement the Direct3D aspects of this program. I will give you some good references in the bibliography, though.

I encourage you to play with the flight model in this program. Go ahead and tweak element properties and watch to see what happens. Even though this is a rough model, the flight results look quite realistic.

CHAPTER 8

Ships

The purpose of this chapter is not to teach you how to design ships, but to explain by way of example some fundamental physical principles, such as buoyancy, stability, virtual mass, and resistance, that you may need to consider when writing physics-based games or simulations. The typical displacement-type ship lends itself well to illustrating these principles; however, many of these principles apply equally to other objects that are submerged or partially submerged in a fluid, such as submarines and air balloons. Remember, air is considered a fluid, too, when talking about buoyancy.

While surface ships, that is, ships that operate on the water's surface (at the air-water interface), are similar to fully submerged objects such as submarines or air balloons, in that they all experience buoyancy, there are some very distinct differences in their physical nature that I'll highlight in this chapter. These differences affect their behavior, so you need to be aware of them if you intend to simulate such objects accurately.

Since the examples in this chapter involve ships, I need to go over some terms and geometry so that we are speaking the same language. As I said, I'll discuss a typical displacement ship in this chapter. The term *displacement* in this context means that the ship is supported solely by buoyancy, that is, without dynamic or aerostatic lift such as you would see on a high-speed racing boat or a hovercraft. The word "displacement" itself refers to the volume of water that is displaced, that is, pushed out of the way by the ship as it sits floating in the water (more on this in the next section).

The *hull* of the ship is the watertight part of the ship that actually displaces the water. Everything in or on the ship is contained within the hull, which is partially submerged in the water. The length of the ship is the distance measured from the bow to the stern. In practice, there are several lengths that are used to denote the length of a ship, but here I'll refer to the *overall length* of the hull. The *bow* is the front of the ship, and the *stern* is the aft part. When you are on the ship facing the bow, the *port* side is to your left and the *starboard* side is to your right. The overall height of the hull is called the *depth*, and its width is called *beam*. When a ship is floating in the water, the distance from the water surface to the bottom of the hull is called the *draft*. Figure 8-1 illustrates these terms.

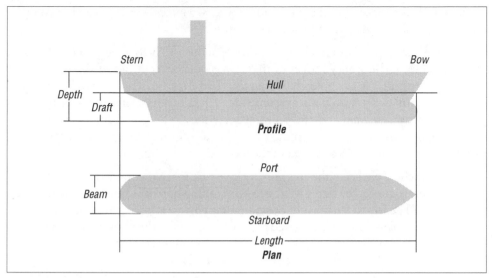

Figure 8-1. Ship Geometry

Flotation

The absolutely most important thing a ship must do is float. Not only that—it must float upright.

In Chapter 3 I introduced the concept of buoyancy and stated that the force on a submerged object due to buoyancy is a function of the submerged volume of the object. Archimedes' principle states that the weight of an object floating in a fluid is equal to the weight of the volume of fluid displaced by the object. This is an important principle. It says that a ship of a given weight must have sufficient volume to displace enough water, an amount equal to the weight of the ship, for it to float. Further, this principle provides a clever way of determining the weight of a ship: simply measure or calculate the amount of water displaced by the ship and you can calculate the weight of the ship. In the marine field, displacement is synonymous with the weight of the ship.

The buoyant force on any object can be calculated using the following formula:

$$F_B = \rho g \blacktriangledown$$

Here, $\blacktriangledown$ is the submerged volume of the object, ρ is the density of the fluid within which the object is submerged, and g is the acceleration due to gravity. Since buoyancy is a force, it has both magnitude and direction and always acts straight up through the center of buoyancy. The center of buoyancy is the geometric center of the submerged part of the object.

When a ship is floating in equilibrium on the surface of the water, its center of buoyancy must be located directly below the center of gravity of the ship. The weight of the ship, a force, acts straight down through the center of gravity opposing the force due to buoyancy. When the ship is in equilibrium, these two forces—weight and buoyancy—are equal in magnitude and opposite in direction.

Now, when the ship rolls, or pitches, the portion of the hull below the water is changed, and the center of buoyancy moves to the new geometric centroid of the underwater portion of the hull. For example, if the ship rolls to the starboard side, then the center of buoyancy shifts out toward the starboard side. When this happens, the lines of action of the weight of the ship and the buoyant force are no longer in line, which results in a moment (torque) that acts on the ship. This torque is equal to the perpendicular distance between the lines of action of the forces times the weight of the ship.

Now here's where we get to the floating upright part that I mentioned earlier. When a ship rolls, for example, you don't want it to keep rolling until it capsizes. No, you want it to return itself gently to the upright position after whatever force caused it to roll—the wind, for example—has been removed. In short, you want the ship to be stable. For a ship to be stable, the line of action of the buoyant force must cross the vessel's centerline at a point, called the *metacenter*, above the center of gravity. When this happens, the moment that is developed when the ship rolls tends to restore the ship to the upright position. If the metacenter is located below the center of gravity, then the moment that is developed would tend to capsize the ship. Figure 8-2 illustrates these two scenarios.

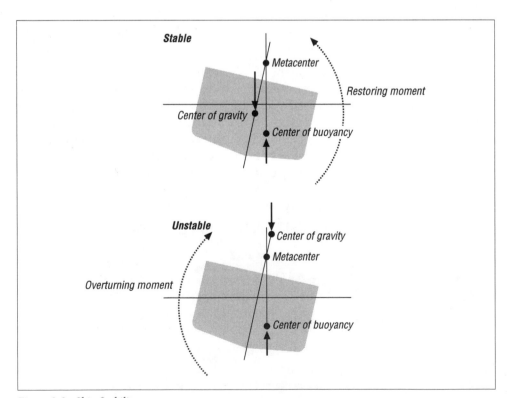

Figure 8-2. Ship Stability

If you're a sailor, then you know how important it is to keep the center of gravity of your boat low. This helps to increase the height of the metacenter above the center of gravity and thus helps with stability.

In the case of fully submerged objects, such as submarines or air balloons, the situation is different. The buoyant force still acts through the geometric centroid of the object, but for stability the center of buoyancy must be located above the center of gravity. This way, when the object rotates, the lines of action of the weight of the object and the buoyant force are separated and form a moment that tends to restore the object to its upright position. If it's the other way around, then the object would be unstable, like trying to balance one bowling ball on top of another. In this case the slightest disturbance would upset the balance, and the object would flip upside-down such that the center of gravity would be located below the center of buoyancy.

The tricky part to these calculations is determining the submerged volume and geometric centroid for all but the simplest of geometries. For example, ship hulls are generally complicated shapes with a lot of curvature, in many cases with recesses or appendages. Calculating the displaced volume for a ship requires the use of numerical integration techniques. I'll show you such a method in the next section.

Volume

There are various techniques and algorithms for calculating volume that arise from various fields of science and engineering. The techniques tend to be optimized for the particular task at hand and the nature or format of the geometry defining the object of which the volume is to be determined. For example, in the world of computer graphics, objects are typically represented by triangulated polyhedra, or polytopes, and there are various algorithms for calculating the volume of such polytopes by essentially constructing a number of tetrahedrons out of the surface triangles and calculating, and then summing, the volume of all of the tetrahedrons. (This is the technique that I'll show you in a moment.) Yet another volume calculation technique comes from the field of chemistry, in which the volume of certain molecules must be calculated. Here, techniques have been developed that are specifically optimized for calculating the volume of multiple interesting spheres.

The field of ship design, formally known as naval architecture, is no different. For ships the traditional technique of calculating volume involves integrating cross-sectional areas over the length of the ship hull. It is important to note, however, that while the implementation of these techniques are different, they are all essentially numerical integration techniques that involve discretizing the object under consideration into a number of smaller, simpler geometries whose volumes are easily calculated and then summing up all the volumes to get the total volume.

Let's look at a rather simple example of how to calculate the volume and center of volume for a triangulated cube. Figure 8-3 shows the cube under consideration.

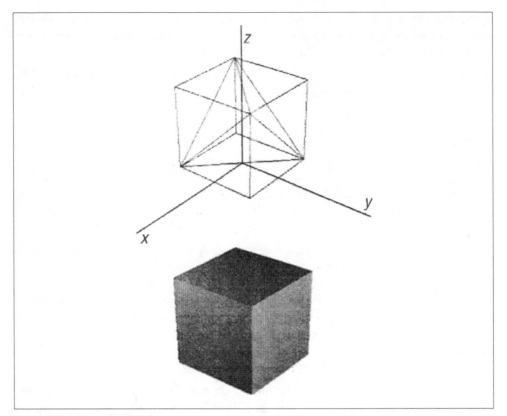

Figure 8-3. Triangulated Cube

The reason we're considering a cube is because its volume and centroid are readily verifiable by using simple hand calculations. Keep in mind, though, that the method I'm about to show you applies equally well to more complicated geometries as long as the object you are considering is a *simple, triangulated polyhedron*. This means that all of the following must be satisfied:

- All of the faces making up the object must be triangles.
- The object may not have any holes in it.
- The object must enclose a volume. This means that there can be no dangling faces or edges; each edge must connect two vertices, and each edge must be shared by exactly two faces.
- The object must satisfy *Euler's formula*, which states that the number of vertices minus the number of edges plus the number of faces must equal 2: No. of vertices − No. of edges + No. of faces = 2.

As I said earlier, the idea behind this method is to divide the object into a bunch of tetrahedrons, calculate the volume of each tetrahedron, and then sum all the tetrahedron volumes to obtain the total volume of the object. You can also use these tetrahedrons to determine the object's geometric center (center of volume) using a technique similar to that for finding the center of mass of a collection of masses. (I showed you how to do that in Chapter 1.) In this case you'll use the tetrahedron's volume instead of mass. Figure 8-4 illustrates how a tetrahedron is constructed from a triangular face.

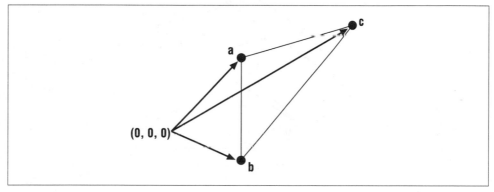

Figure 8-4. Tetrahedron

Here, the origin (0, 0, 0) is used along with the three vertices of the triangular face to define the four vertices of the tetrahedron. You can think of the edges of the tetrahedron that connect to the origin as vectors from the origin to each vertex of the face. Note that the vertices of the face are specified in counterclockwise order when viewing the face from the outside of the object.

To calculate the volume of such a tetrahedron, you can use the vector triple scalar product (see Appendix A for a code sample). Let vectors **a**, **b**, and **c** be the vectors shown in Figure 8-4; then the vector triple scalar product of these three vectors is

$$\mathbf{a} \cdot (\mathbf{b} \times \mathbf{c})$$

It just so happens that a handy physical interpretation of the triple scalar product is that it is equal to the volume of the *parallelepiped* formed by the three vectors as shown in Figure 8-5:*

More important for us is that the volume of the tetrahedron formed by these three vectors (as shown in Figure 8-4) is one sixth of the volume of the parallelepiped. Thus, the formula for calculating the volume of the tetrahedron is

$$[\mathbf{a} \cdot (\mathbf{b} \times \mathbf{c})]/6$$

Determining the tetrahedron's geometric center is relatively easy: you simply take the average of all four vertex coordinates. Note that even if one of the vertices is located at the origin, you still have to include it in the average. Referring to Figure 8-4 and using

---

* A parallelepiped is a solid that has three pairs of parallel sides. A box is a parallelepiped with perpendicular sides. A cube is also a parallelepiped but with all edges equal in length.

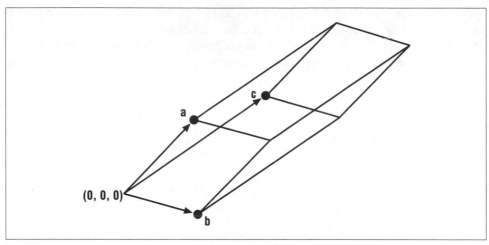

Figure 8-5. Parallelepiped

vector notation, the centroid, **d**, of the tetrahedron is

$$\mathbf{d} = (\mathbf{a} + \mathbf{b} + \mathbf{c})/4$$

This equation assumes that the fourth vertex is located at the origin with coordinates $(0, 0, 0)$; that's why you see only three vectors in the formula even though we are dividing by 4.

For this example I've prepared a simple class called `Body3D` that stores the object's vertex and face data and implements a method to read the object data from a file and another to actually calculate the object's volume and centroid:

```
#define     MAX_NUM_VERTICES      100
#define MAX_NUM_FACES             100

typedef struct VertexTag {
      float     x;  // x-coord of vertex
      float     y;  // y-coord of vertex
      float     z;  // z-coord of vertex

} TVertex;

typedef struct FaceTag {
      // vertices defining the face are in counterclockwise
      // order when looking at the face from outside the object

      int a; // 1st vertex (index of vertex in vertex list)
      int b; // 2nd vertex (index of vertex in vertex list)
      int c; // 3rd vertex (index of vertex in vertex list)

} TFace;

//---------------------------------------------------------------------//
// Body3D class that represents a simple, triangulated polyhedron
//---------------------------------------------------------------------//
class Body3D {
```

```
public:
        int        nFaces;    // number of triangular faces
        int        nVertices; // number of vertices
        TVertex    Vertex[MAX_NUM_VERTICES];  // vertex list
        TFace      Face[MAX_NUM_VERTICES];    // face list
        float      Volume;    // total volume
        Vector     Centroid;  // center of total volume

        Body3D(void);  // constructor

        void    ReadData(char *filename);  // reads vertex/face data
        void    CalculateProperties(void); // calculates Volume & Centroid
};
```

Each member of this class is readily identifiable from the comments in the code sample, so I won't elaborate on them. However, let me show you the two methods (the constructor is trivial, as it just sets everything to zero).

ReadData simply reads the object data in from a text file:

```
void    Body3D::ReadData(char *filename)
{
        FILE    *fptr;
        int      i;

        fptr = fopen(filename, "r");

        fscanf(fptr, "%d\n", &nVertices);
        for(i=0; i< nVertices; i++)
        {
                fscanf(     fptr,
                        "%f %f %f\n",
                        &(Vertex[i].x),
                        &(Vertex[i].y),
                        &(Vertex[i].z));
        }

        fscanf(fptr, "%d\n", &nFaces);
        for(i=0; i< nFaces; i++)
        {
                fscanf(     fptr,
                        "%d %d %d\n",
                        &(Face[i].a),
                        &(Face[i].b),
                        &(Face[i].c));     // counterclockwise order
        }

        fclose(fptr);
}
```

The first line of the file is an integer that represents the number of vertices to follow. The next set of lines are the actual vertices with the x-, y-, and z-coordinates (floats) for each vertex on a single line. After all the vertices are read in, another integer is read that represents the number of faces. The next set of lines contain the face data, where each line contains three numbers representing the vertex numbers (in counterclockwise order) that make up the face. Here's a sample object file defining the a cube that is 2 units tall, 2 units wide, and 2 units deep and located at the origin with its base on the *xy*-plane as shown in Figure 8-3:

```
8
-1.000000 -1.000000 0.000000
-1.000000 -1.000000 2.000000
1.000000 -1.000000 0.000000
1.000000 -1.000000 2.000000
-1.000000 1.000000 0.000000
1.000000 1.000000 0.000000
1.000000 1.000000 2.000000
-1.000000 1.000000 2.000000
12
2 3 1
2 1 0
4 5 2
4 2 0
6 3 2
6 2 5
6 7 1
6 1 3
6 5 4
6 4 7
1 7 4
1 4 0
```

The next method, `CalculateProperties`, is really the heart of this example. This method goes through the process of discretizing the object into a bunch of tetrahedrons to calculate the total volume and centroid, as I discussed earlier. I'll show the code here and then discuss it in detail:

```
void      Body3D::CalculateProperties(void)
{
      Vector      a;
      Vector      b;
      Vector      c;
      int         i;
      float       dv = 0;
      float       vol = 0;
      Vector      d;
      Vector      dmom;

      for(i=0; i<nFaces; i++)
      {
            a.x = Vertex[Face[i].a].x;
            a.y = Vertex[Face[i].a].y;
            a.z = Vertex[Face[i].a].z;

            b.x = Vertex[Face[i].b].x;
            b.y = Vertex[Face[i].b].y;
            b.z = Vertex[Face[i].b].z;

            c.x = Vertex[Face[i].c].x;
            c.y = Vertex[Face[i].c].y;
            c.z = Vertex[Face[i].c].z;

            dv = (TripleScalarProduct(a, b, c)) / 6.0f;
            vol += dv;
```

```
        d = ((a + b + c) / 4);
        dmom += (d * dv);
    }

    Volume = vol;
    Centroid = dmom / vol;
}
```

Note that this function defines a few local variables, a, b, and c, of type Vector to represent the vectors from the origin to each vertex of each face that will form a tetrahedron. Vector is defined in Appendix A. The integer variable i is just a counter. The float variables dv and vol are the volume of a single tetrahedron and the running total volume of the object, respectively. The Vector types d and dmom are the coordinates of a single tetrahedron and the running total first moment of volume of all the tetrahedrons, respectively.

After initializing all the local variables, the method iterates through the list of faces making up the object and constructs the vectors a, b, and c for the tetrahedron formed by the origin and the current face, Face[i]. Next, the triple scalar product of these three vectors is computed, and the result is divided by 6. This calculation yields the volume of the tetrahedron, dv, which gets added to the running total, vol. The method then goes on to calculate the center of the tetrahedron, d; multiplies it by the tetrahedron's volume, dv; and adds the result to dmom (the running total of first moments of volume). Finally, after iterating through all the faces, the total volume is vol and the centroid is the sum of first moments divided by the total volume, dmom/vol.

That's all there is to it. To test this class, I prepared a simple console application that instantiated Body3D, read the cube data in, and calculated the volume properties. Here's how my main function looks:

```
int main(int argc, char* argv[])
{
    Body3D      body = Body3D();
    float       volume = 0;
    int         i;
    Vector      centroid;

    // read the object data
    body.ReadData("cube.txt");

    // echo the data to the console
    printf("Number of vertices = %d\n", body.nVertices);
    for(i=0; i<body.nVertices; i++)
        printf(    "Vertex %d: x=%f y=%f z=%f\n",
                i,
                body.Vertex[i].x,
                body.Vertex[i].y,
                body.Vertex[i].z);

    printf("Number of faces = %d\n", body.nFaces);
    for(i=0; i<body.nFaces; i++)
        printf(    "Face %d: a=%d b=%d c=%d\n",
                i,
                body.Face[i].a,
                body.Face[i].b,
                body.Face[i].c);
```

```
        // calculate the volume and centroid
        body.CalculateProperties();

        // display the results to the console
        printf("\n");
        printf("Volume = %f\n", body.Volume);
        printf("\n");
        printf("Centroid:\n");
        printf("x=%f y=%f z=%f\n", body.Centroid.x, body.Centroid.y, body.Centroid.z);
        printf("\n");

        printf("Done.\n");

        return 0;
    }
```

If you rebuild this console application and run it, you should see that the volume of the cube is 8.0 units^3 with the centroid located at (0, 0, 1).

For a more interesting test, I prepared an object that resembles a generic boat hull (although not a very pretty one!) and ran it through the test program.

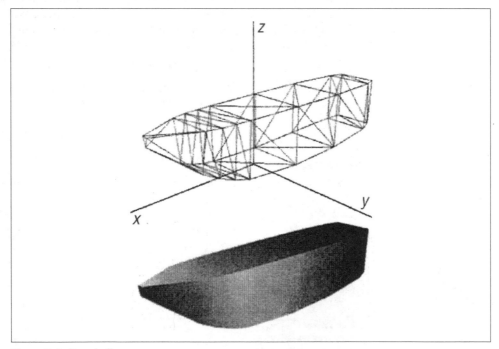

Figure 8-6. Boat hull

Figure 8-6 shows the hull object and the corresponding data file is as follows:

```
36
-5.500000 -0.693775 0.281525
```

```
-5.500000 -0.693775 2.000000
3.888562 0.000000 1.700000
3.888562 -0.100000 1.991344
-5.500000 0.693775 0.281525
3.888562 0.000000 1.700000
3.888562 0.100000 1.991344
-5.500000 0.693775 2.000000
1.000000 0.900000 0.105572
1.000000 0.950000 2.000000
1.000000 -0.950000 2.000000
1.000000 -0.900000 0.105572
1.500000 0.794000 0.219941
1.500000 0.900000 2.000000
1.500000 -0.900000 2.000000
1.500000 -0.793988 0.219941
2.000000 0.680000 0.387096
2.000000 0.870000 2.000000
2.000000 -0.870381 2.000000
2.000000 -0.680000 0.387096
2.500000 0.538000 0.633431
2.500000 0.747000 2.000000
2.500000 -0.747214 2.000000
2.500000 -0.538416 0.633431
-1.000000 -1.000000 0.000000
-1.000000 -1.000000 2.000000
-1.000000 1.000000 2.000000
-1.000000 1.000000 0.000000
-3.000000 -1.000000 0.070381
-3.000000 -1.000000 2.000000
-3.000000 1.000000 2.000000
-3.000000 1.000000 0.070381
-5.000000 -0.864029 0.211143
-5.000000 -0.864029 2.000000
-5.000000 0.864029 2.000000
-5.000000 0.864029 0.211143
68

2 3 22
2 22 23
20 5 23
5 2 23
6 3 2
6 2 5
6 21 3
3 21 22
6 5 20
6 20 21
1 7 4
1 4 0
34 35 4
34 4 7
34 7 1
34 1 33
32 33 1
32 1 0
4 35 0
0 35 32
13 12 8
13 8 9
```

```
13  9 14
14  9 10
15 14 10
15 10 11
 8 12 15
 8 15 11
17 16 12
17 12 13
17 13 18
18 13 14
19 18 14
19 14 15
12 16 19
12 19 15
21 20 16
21 16 17
21 17 22
22 17 18
23 22 18
23 18 19
16 20 23
16 23 19
11 10 25
11 25 24
 9 26 10
10 26 25
 9  8 27
 9 27 26
27  8 11
27 11 24
24 25 29
24 29 28
26 30 29
26 29 25
26 27 31
26 31 30
31 27 24
31 24 28
28 29 33
28 33 32
30 34 33
30 33 29
30 31 35
30 35 34
35 31 32
32 31 28
```

The results of this test yield a volume of 28.67 units^3 with its centroid located at $(-1.43, 0.00, 1.08)$.

I should point out that I did not include any error checking in these code samples so as to not complicate the purpose and simplicity of the method being demonstrated. As always, you should include error checking in your production work. Some things you'll want to do if you use this code include checks on the input data to make sure the object is a simple, triangulated polyhedron and catching any potential divide-by-zero errors in CalculateProperties.

Resistance

In Chapter 6 I discussed drag forces on objects moving through a fluid. Specifically, I discussed frictional and pressure drag. Ships moving on the water's surface experience these drag forces too; however, at the air-water interface, there are other drag components that you have to consider. If you were to write an equation breaking up the total resistance acting on a ship into its three main components, that equation would look something like this:

$$R_{total} = R_{friction} + R_{preassure} + R_{waves}$$

I'll describe each of these components and give you some empirical formulas in just a moment. First, however, I want to qualify the material to follow by saying that it is very general in nature and applicable only when little detail is known about the complete geometry of the particular ship under consideration. In the practice of ship design, these formulas would be used only in the very early stages of the design process to approximate resistance. That said, they are very useful for getting in the ballpark, so to speak, and are sometimes more important in performing parametric studies to see the effects of changes in major parameters.

The first resistance component is the frictional drag on the underwater surface of the hull as it moves through the water. This is the same as the frictional drag that I discussed in Chapter 6. However, for ships there is a convenient set of empirical formulas that you can use to calculate this force:

$$R_f = (1/2)\rho V^2 S C_f$$

In this formula, ρ is the density of water, V is the speed of the ship, S is the surface area of the underwater portion of the hull, and C_f is the coefficient of frictional resistance. You can use this empirical formula to calculate C_f:

$$C_f = 0.075/(\log 10 R_n - 2)^2$$

Here, R_n is the Reynolds number, as defined in Chapter 6, based on the length of the ship's hull. This formula was adopted in 1957 by the International Towing Tank Conference (ITTC) and is widely used in the field of naval architecture for estimating frictional resistance coefficients for ships.

To apply the formula for R_f, you'll also have to know the surface area of the underwater portion of the hull, S. You can directly calculate this area using numerical integration techniques, similar to those for calculating volume, or you can use yet another empirical formula:

$$S = C_{ws}\sqrt{\blacktriangledown L}$$

In this formula, $\blacktriangledown$ is the displaced volume, L the length of the ship, and C_{ws} is the wetted surface coefficient. This coefficient is a function of the ship's shape, its beam-to-draft ratio, and statistically it ranges from 2.6 to 2.9 for typical displacement hull forms.

The pressure drag experienced by a ship is the same as that experienced by projectiles as discussed in Chapter 6. Remember, this drag is due to the viscous effects causing a region of relatively low pressure behind the ship. Quantifying this force is difficult for ships of arbitrary geometry. Computational fluid dynamics algorithms can be used to approximate this force, but this requires detailed knowledge of the hull geometry and a whole lot of time-consuming computations. An alternative is to rely on scale model test data in which results from the model test are extrapolated to approximate drag on the full-size ship.

Just like pressure drag, wave drag is difficult to compute, and model testing is usually relied on in practice. Wave drag is due to the energy transfer, or momentum transfer, from the ship to the fluid; in other words, it is a function of the work done by the ship on the surrounding fluid to generate the waves. The visible presence of wave resistance is seen as the large bow wave that builds up at the front of the ship as well as the wave system that originates at the stern of the ship as it moves through the water. These waves affect the pressure distribution around the ship and thus affect the pressure drag, which makes it difficult to separate the wave drag component from pressure drag in performing an analysis.

When scale model tests are performed, pressure drag and wave drag are usually lumped together in what's known as residual resistance. Analogous to the coefficient of frictional drag, you can determine a coefficient of residual resistance, such that

$$R_r = R_{pressure} + R_{wave} = (1/2)\rho V^2 S C_r$$

Here, R_r is the total residual resistance, and C_r is the coefficient of residual resistance.

There are many resistance estimation methods available that allow you to estimate the coefficient of residual resistance for a ship; however, they are usually presented for specific ship types. For example, one method might give empirical formulas for C_r for destroyer-type ships, while another might give formulas for C_r for large oil tankers. The trick, of course, is to choose a method appropriate for the type of ship you are analyzing.* Generally, C_r increases as the displacement and speed of the ship increase. A typical range for C_r for large displacement hulls is from $1.0e^{-3}$ to $3.0e^{-3}$.

While these three resistance components—friction, pressure and wave—are the most important for typical displacement-type ships, they aren't the only ones. Since a ship operates at the air-water interface, a large part of its structure is above the water surface, exposed to the air. This means that the ship will also experience air resistance. You can approximate this air resistance using the following formula:

$$R_{air} = (1/2)\rho V^2 A_p C_{air}$$

Here, C_{air} is the coefficient of air resistance, ρ is the density of air, V is the speed of the ship, and A_p is the projected transverse (profile) area of the ship. C_{air} typically ranges from 0.6 to 1.1 depending on the type of ship. Tankers and large cargo ships tend to be

---

* These methods are quite involved, and there are far too many to discuss here, so I've included some references in the bibliography for you.

near the upper end of the range, while combatant ships tend to be near the lower end. In lieu of enough information to calculate the projected transverse area of the ship, you can approximate it by

$$A_p = B^2/2$$

where B is the beam (width) of the ship.

Ships experience other forms of resistance as well depending on their age, the sea conditions, and their type of service. For example, when a ship has been operating in seawater for a long time without having its hull cleaned, it will build up a layer of marine growth that will increase its frictional resistance. If a ship were to operate in shallow water or a restricted channel, its resistance might be increased owing to restricted flow effects, which cause the ship to sink deeper in the water. If the sea conditions are very rough, with heavy winds and large waves, then the ship will experience greater resistance as it encounters these sea conditions. For some ships with lots of appendages sticking out of the hull underwater, its resistance can be increased by 10% to 15% above its bare-hull resistance. All of these components are very specific to the situation under consideration and must be treated on a case-by-case basis.

Virtual Mass

The concept of *virtual mass* is important in calculating the acceleration of a ship in a real-time simulator. Virtual mass is equal to the mass of the ship plus the mass of the water that is accelerated with the ship.

Back in Chapter 6 I told you about the viscous boundary layer, and I said that the relative velocity (relative to the moving body) of the fluid particles near the moving body's surface is zero at the body surface and increases to the free stream velocity as distance from the body surface increases. Essentially, some of the fluid sticks to the body as it moves and is accelerated with the body. Since the velocity of the fluid varies within the boundary layer, so does the acceleration. The *added mass*, the mass of water that gets accelerated, is a weighted integration of the entire mass of fluid that is affected by the body's acceleration.

For a ship the viscous boundary layer can be quite thick, up to several feet near the end of the ship depending on its length, and the mass of water that gets accelerated is significant. Therefore, when doing any sort of analysis that involves the acceleration of the ship, you need to consider added mass too. The calculation of added mass is beyond the scope of this book. I should also point out that, unlike mass, added mass is a tensor, that is, it depends on the direction of acceleration. Further, added mass applies to both linear and angular motion.

Added mass is typically expressed in terms of an added mass coefficient, which equals the added mass divided by the mass of the ship. Calculations for added mass are well beyond the scope of this book. Some methods integrate over the actual hull surface, while others approximate the hull as an ellipsoid with proportions matching the ship's.

Using this approximation, the ellipsoid's length corresponds to the ship's length, while its width corresponds to the ship's beam. For longitudinal motion, that is, linear motion along an axis parallel to the ship's length, the added mass coefficient varies nearly linearly from zero at a beam-to-length ratio of zero (the ship is infinitely thin) up one half at a beam-to-length ratio of 1 (a sphere).

When the added mass coefficient is expressed as a percentage of the ship's mass, virtual mass can be calculated as $m_v = m(1 + x_a)$, where m is mass and x_a is the added mass coefficient, for example, 0.2 for 20%. For typical displacement ship proportions the longitudinal added mass ranges from about 4% to 15% of the mass of the ship. Conservative estimates generally use 20%.

CHAPTER 9

Hovercraft

Hovercraft, or air cushion vehicles (ACVs), have made their way into a video game or two recently. Their appeal seems to stem from their futuristic aura, high speed, and levitating ability, which lets them go anywhere. If you slap a couple of large-caliber guns on one of these craft and throw in a couple of bad guys, you then have yourself the makings of an exciting round of shoot-'em-up bumper cars. In real life, hovercraft have been around since the 1950s and have been used in combat, search and rescue, cargo transport, ferrying, and recreational roles. They come in all shapes and sizes, but they all work pretty much the same, with the basic idea of getting the craft up off of the land or water to reduce its drag. In this chapter I'll explain the basics of how hovercraft work and discuss the main forces you'll want to consider if you try to simulate them in your games.

How They Work

I was fortunate enough to work on several hovercraft designs when I was a junior naval architect at Textron Marine Systems.* While some of the craft that I worked on turned out to be quite complicated systems, owing to military requirements, the basic principle of how hovercraft work is quite simple.

The first hovercraft designs pumped air through an annular nozzle around the periphery of the craft (see the top diagram in Figure 9-1). Large fans are used to feed the air through the nozzle under the craft. This jet of air creates a region of relatively high pressure over the area underneath the craft, which results in a net lifting force. The lifting force must equal the weight of the craft if the craft is to attain hovering flight. This sort of lifting is known as *aerostatic lift*. The hover height is limited by the amount of power available and the lifting fan's ability to pump enough air through the nozzle; the higher the hover height, the greater the power demand.

---

* Textron is located in New Orleans, Louisiana. When I was there, I worked on several hovercraft, one of which is the U.S. Navy's LCAC, which is used by the Marines for amphibious operations.

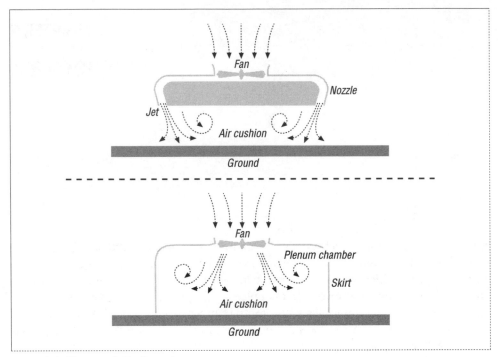

Figure 9-1. Hovercraft Configurations

This approach proved impractical because hover heights were very limited and made the clearance between the hard structure of the craft and the ground (or water) too small to overcome all but the smallest obstacles. The solution to this problem was to fit a flexible *skirt* around the craft to contain the air cushion in what's called the *plenum chamber* (see the bottom diagram in Figure 9-1). This approach extended the clearance between the ground and the hard structure of the craft significantly even though the gap between the bottom of the skirt and the ground was very small. This is the basic configuration of most hovercraft in operation today, although there are all sorts of skirt designs. Some of these skirts are simple curtains, while others are sophisticated pressurized bag and finger arrangements. The result is that hovercraft fitted with skirts can clear relatively large obstacles without damage to their hard structure; the skirt simply distorts and conforms to the terrain over which the craft operates.

The actual calculation of the aerostatic lift force is fairly complicated because the pressure distribution within the air cushion is nonuniform and because you must also take into account the performance of the lift fan system. There are theories available to treat both the annular jet and plenum chamber configurations, but they are beyond the scope of this book. Besides, for a game simulation, what's important is that you realize that the lift force must equal the weight of the craft in order for it to maintain equilibrium in hovering flight.

Ideally, the ability of hovercraft to eliminate contact with the ground (or water) over which it operates means that it can travel relatively fast, since it no longer experiences contact drag forces. Notice I said "ideally." In reality, hovercraft often pitch and roll, causing parts of the skirt to drag, and any obstacle that comes into contact with the skirt will cause more drag. At any rate, while eliminating ground contact is good for speed, it's not so good for maneuverability.

Hovercraft are notoriously difficult to control, since they glide across the ground. They tend to continue on their original trajectory even after you try to turn them. Currently, several means are employed in various configurations for directional control. Some hovercraft use vertical tail rudders much like an airplane, while others actually vector their propulsion thrust. Still others use bow thrusters, which offer very good control. All of these means are fairly easy to model in a simulation; they are all simply forces acting on the craft at some distance from its center of gravity so as to create a yawing moment. The 2D simulation that I'll walk you through in Chapter 12 shows how to handle bow thrusters. You can handle vertical tail rudders as I showed you in Chapter 7.

Resistance

Let's take a look now at the some of the drag forces acting on a hovercraft during flight. To do this, I'll handle operation over land separately from operation over water, since there are some specific differences in the drag forces experienced by the hovercraft.

When operating over smooth land, the total drag acting against the hovercraft is aerodynamic in nature. This assumes that drag induced by dragging the skirt or hitting obstacles is ignored. The three components of aerodynamic drag are

- Skin friction and viscous pressure drag on the body of the craft
- Induced drag when the craft is pitched
- Momentum drag

In equation form, the total drag is as follows:

$$R_{total} = R_{viscous} + R_{induced} + R_{momentum}$$

The first of these components, the viscous drag on the body of the craft, is the same sort of drag as is experienced by projectiles when flying through the air, as explained in Chapter 6. This drag is estimated using the by now familiar formula:

$$R_{viscous} = (1/2)\rho V^2 S_p C_d$$

Here, ρ is the mass density of air, V is the speed of the hovercraft, S_p is the projected frontal area of the craft normal to the direction of V, and C_d is the drag coefficient. Typical values of C_d for craft in operation today range from 0.25 to 0.4.

The next drag component, the induced drag, is a result of the craft assuming a pitched attitude when moving. When the bow of the craft pitches upward by an angle τ, there will be a component of the aerostatic lift vector that acts in a direction opposing V. This component is approximately equal to the weight of the craft times the tangent of the pitch angle:

$$R_{\text{induced}} \approx W(\tan \tau)$$

Finally, momentum drag results from the destruction of horizontal momentum of air, relative to the craft, entering the lift fan intake. This component is difficult to compute unless you know the properties of the entire lifting system such that the mass flow rate of air into the fan is known. Given the mass flow rate, R_{momentum} is equal to the mass flow rate times the velocity of the craft:

$$R_{\text{momentum}} = (dm_{\text{fan}}/dt)V$$

Mass flow rate is expressed in units such as slugs/s, which when multiplied by velocity in ft/s yields pounds.

In addition to these three drag components, hovercraft will experience other forms of resistance when operating over water. These additional components are *wave* drag and what's called *wetted* drag. The equation for total drag can thus be revised for operation over water as follows:

$$R_{\text{total}} = R_{\text{viscous}} + R_{\text{induced}} + R_{\text{momentum}} + R_{\text{wave}} + R_{\text{wetted}}$$

When a hovercraft operates over water, its air cushion creates a depression in the water surface due the cushion pressure (see Figure 9-2). At zero to low speeds the weight of this displaced volume of water is equal to the weight of the craft just as if the craft were floating in the water supported by buoyancy. As the craft starts to move forward, it tends to pitch upward by the bow. When that happens, the surface of the water in the depressed region is approximately parallel to the bottom of the craft. As speed increases, the depression is reduced, and the pitch angle tends to decrease.

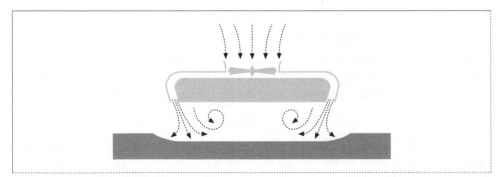

Figure 9-2. Hovercraft over Water

Wave drag is a result of this depression and is equal to the horizontal components of pressure forces acting on the water surface in the depressed region. As it turns out, for small pitch angles and at low speeds, wave drag is on the same order of magnitude as the induced drag:

$$R_{wave} \approx W(\tan \tau)$$

Since wave drag is proportional to the size of the depression, it tends to be highest at low speeds and is reduced at higher operational speeds. If you were to plot the wave drag curve as a function of speed for a typical hovercraft, you'd find that it is not a straight line or even a parabolic curve but has a hump in the curve at the lower speed range as illustrated in Figure 9-3.

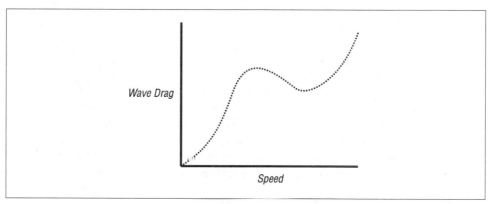

Figure 9-3. Wave Drag

There are several theoretical treatments of wave drag in the literature that aim to predict the speed at which this hump occurs along with its magnitude. These theories indicated that the hump depends on the planform geometry of the hovercraft, and it tends to occur at speeds in the range of $\sqrt{gL}/2$ to $\sqrt{gL}$, where g is the acceleration due to gravity and L is the length of the air cushion. In practice, the characteristics of a particular hovercraft's wave drag are usually best determined through scale model testing.

The so-called wetted drag is a function of several things:

- The fact that parts of the hull and skirt tend to hit the water surface during flight
- The impact of spray on the hull and skirt
- The increase in weight as the hovercraft gets wet and sometimes takes on water.

Wetted drag is difficult to predict, and in practice, model tests are relied on to determine its magnitude for a particular design. It's important to note, however, that this tends to be a significant drag component, sometimes accounting for as much as 30% of the total drag force.

CHAPTER 10

Cars

In this chapter I want to discuss certain aspects of the physics behind automobile motion. As in the previous four chapters, the purpose of this chapter is to explain, by example, certain physical phenomena. I also want to give you a basic understanding of the mechanics involved in automobile motion in case you want to simulate one in your games. In keeping with the theme of this book, I'll be talking about mechanics in the sense of rigid body motion and not in the sense of how an internal combustion engine works, how power is transferred through the transmission system to the wheels, and so on. Those are all internal to the car as a rigid body, and I'll focus on the external forces. I will, however, discuss how the torque applied to the drive wheel is translated to a force that pushes the car along.

Resistance

When a car drives down a road, it experiences two main components of resistance that try to slow it down. The first component is aerodynamic drag, and the second is called *rolling resistance*. The total resistance felt by the car is the sum of these two components:

$$R_{total} = R_{air} + R_{rolling}$$

The aerodynamic drag is primarily skin friction and pressure drag similar to that experienced by projectiles discussed in Chapter 6 and the planes, boats, and hovercraft discussed in Chapters 7, 8, and 9. Here again, you can use the familiar drag formula of the form

$$R_{air} = (1/2)\rho V^2 S_p C_d$$

Here, ρ is the mass density of air, V is the speed of the car, S_p is the projected frontal area of the car normal to the direction of V, and C_d is the drag coefficient. Typical ranges of drag coefficients for different types of vehicles are 0.29 to 0.4 for sports cars, 0.43 to 0.5 for pickup trucks, 0.6 to 0.9 for tractor-trailers, and 0.4 to 0.5 for the average economy car. Drag coefficient is a function of the shape of the vehicle, that is, the degree of boxiness or streamline. Streamlined body styles have lower drag coefficients; for example, the Chevy Corvette has a low drag coefficient of 0.29, while the typical tractor-trailer without fairings has a high drag coefficient of up to 0.9. You can use these coefficients in your simulations to tune the behavior of different types and shapes of vehicles.

When a tire rolls on a road, it experiences what's known as rolling resistance, which tends to retard its motion. Rolling resistance is not frictional resistance but instead has to do with the deformation of the tire while it is rolling. It's a difficult quantity to calculate theoretically, since it is a function of a number of complicated factors, such as tire and road deformation, the pressure over the contact area of the tire, the elastic properties of the tire and road materials, the roughness of the tire and road surfaces, and tire pressure, to name a few, so instead you'll have to rely on an empirical formula. The formula to use is as follows:

$$R_{\text{rolling}} = C_r w$$

This gives you the rolling resistance per tire, where w is the weight supported by the tire and C_r is the *coefficient of rolling resistance*. C_r is simply the ratio of the rolling resistance force to the weight supported by the tire. Luckily for you, tire manufacturers generally provide the coefficient of rolling resistance for their tires under design conditions. Typical car tires have a C_r of about 0.015, while truck tires fall within the range of 0.006 to 0.01. If you assume that a car has four identical tires, then you can estimate the total rolling resistance for the car by substituting the total car weight for w in the above equation.

Power

Now that you know how to calculate the total resistance on your car, you can easily calculate the power required to overcome the resistance at a given speed. Power is a measure of the amount of *work* done by a force, or torque, over time. Mechanical work done by a force is equal to the force times the distance an object moves under the action of that force. It is expressed in units such as foot-pounds. Since power is a measure of work done over time, its units are, for example, foot-pounds per second. Power in the context of car engine output is usually expressed in units of *horsepower*, where 1 horsepower equals 550 ft-lb/s.

To calculate the horsepower required to overcome total resistance at a give speed, you simply use this formula:

$$P = (R_{\text{total}} V)/550$$

Here, P is power in units of horsepower, and R_{total} is the total resistance corresponding to the car's speed, V. Note that in this equation R_{total} must be in pounds and V must be in units of ft/s.

Now this is not the engine output power required to reach the speed V for your car; it is the required power delivered by the drive wheel to reach the speed V. The installed engine power will be higher for several reasons. First, there will be mechanical losses associated with delivering the power from the engine through the transmission and drive train to the tire. The power will actually reach the tire in the form of torque, which, given the radius of the tire, will create a force F_w that will overcome the total resistance. This force is calculated as follows:

$$F_w = T_w/r$$

Here, F_w is the force delivered by the tire to the road to push the car along, T_w is the torque on the tire, and r is the radius of the tire. The second reason why the installed engine power will be greater is because some engine power will be transferred to other systems in the car. For example, power is required to charge the battery and to run the air conditioner.

Stopping Distance

Under normal conditions stopping distance is a function of the braking system and how hard the driver applies the brakes; the harder the brakes are applied, the shorter the stopping distance. That's not the case when the tires start to skid. Under skidding conditions, stopping distance is a function of the frictional force that develops between the tires and the road and the inclination of the roadway. If the car is traveling uphill, then the skidding distance will be shorter because gravity helps to slow the car, while it will tend to accelerate the car and increase the skidding distance when the car is traveling downhill.

There's a simple formula that considers these factors that you can use to calculate skidding distance:

$$d_s = V^2/[2g(\mu \cos \varphi + \sin \varphi)]$$

Here, d_s is the skidding distance, g is the acceleration due to gravity, μ is the coefficient of friction between the tires and road, V is the initial speed of the car, and φ is the inclination of the roadway, where a positive angle means uphill and a negative angle means downhill. Note that this equation does not take into account any aerodynamic drag that will help to slow the car down.

The coefficient of friction will vary depending on the condition of the tires and the surface of the road, but for rubber on pavement the dynamic friction coefficient is typically around 0.4, while the static coefficient is around 0.55.

When calculating the actual frictional force between the tire and road, say in a real-time simulation, you'll use the same formula that I showed you in Chapter 4:

$$F_f = \mu W$$

Here, F_f is the friction force applied to each tire, assuming that they are not rolling, and W is the weight supported by each tire. If you assume that all tires are identical, then you can use the total weight of the car in the formula above to determine the total friction force applied to all tires.

Roadway Banking

When you turn the steering wheel of a car, the front wheels exert a side force such that the car starts to turn. In terms of Euler angles, this would be yaw, although Euler angles aren't usually used in talking about turning cars. Even if the car's speed is constant, it experiences acceleration due to the fact that its velocity vector has changed direction. Remember, acceleration is the time rate of change in velocity, which has both magnitude and direction.

For a car to maintain its curved path, there must be a *centripetal* force ("center-seeking" in Greek) that acts on the car. This force can result from either the side friction between the tires and the road or the roadway bank, which is called *superelevation*, or both. When riding in a turning car, you feel an apparent *centrifugal* acceleration or force directed away from the center of the turn. This acceleration is really a result of inertia, the tendency of your body and the car to continue on its original path, and is not a real force acting on the car or your body. The real force is the centripetal force, and without it your car would continue on its straight path and not along the curve.

If a car is trying to turn too quickly, the side friction between the tires and road might not be enough to hold the car in the turn. This is why roads are banked around turns. The superelevation helps to keep the car in the turn because as the car is inclined, a force component develops that acts toward the center of curvature of the turn (see Figure 10-1).

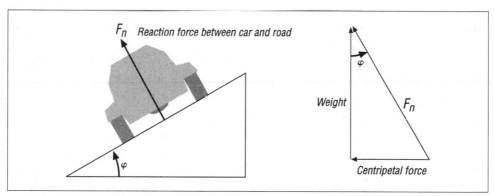

Figure 10-1. Superelevation

There's a simple formula that relates the superelevation angle of a roadway to the speed of the car and the coefficient of friction between the tires and road:

$$\tan \varphi = V_t^2/(gr) - \mu$$

Here φ is the superelevation angle as shown in Figure 10-1, V_t is the tangential component of velocity of the car going around the turn, g is the acceleration due to gravity, r is the radius of the curve, and μ is the coefficient of friction between the tires and the road. If you know φ, r, and μ, then you can calculate the speed at which the car will begin to slip out of the turn and off the road.

CHAPTER 11
Real-Time Simulations

This chapter is the first in a series of chapters designed to give you a thorough introduction to the subject of real-time simulation. I say "introduction" because the subject is too vast and complex to treat adequately in a few chapters; however, I say "thorough" because I'll do more than talk about real-time simulations. In fact, I'll walk you through the development of two simple simulations, one in two dimensions and the other in three dimensions.

What I hope to do is give you enough of an understanding of this subject that you can pursue it further with confidence. What I mean is that I want you to have a solid understanding of the fundamentals before jumping in to use someone else's physics engine or venturing out to write your own.

In the context of this book, a real-time simulation is a process whereby you calculate the state of the object (or objects) you're trying to represent on the fly. You don't rely on pre-scripted motion sequences to animate your object; instead, you rely on your physics model, the equations of motion, and your differential equation solver to take care of the motion of your object as the simulation progresses.

This sort of simulation can be used to model rigid bodies such as the airplane in our FlightSim example or flexible bodies such as cloth and human figures. Perhaps one of the most fundamental aspects of implementing a real-time rigid body simulator is solving the equations of motion using numerical integration techniques. Because of this, I'll spend this entire chapter explaining the numerical integration techniques that you'll use later in the 2D and 3D simulators that we'll develop.

If you refer back to Chapter 4 for a moment, where I outlined a generic procedure for solving kinetics problems, you'll see that we've covered a lot of ground so far. The preceding chapters showed you how to estimate mass properties, develop the governing equations of motion, and accurately model forces and torques. This chapter will show you how to solve the equations of motion to determine acceleration, velocity, and displacement.

Integrating the Equations of Motion

By now you should have a thorough understanding of the dynamic equations of motion for particles and rigid bodies. If not, you might want to go back and review Chapters 1 through 4 before reading this one. The next aspect of dealing with the equations of motion is actually solving them in your simulation. The equations of motion that we've been discussing can be classified as ordinary differential equations. In Chapters 2 and 4 you were able to solve these differential equations explicitly, since you were dealing with simple functions for acceleration, velocity, and displacement. This won't be the case for your simulations. As you've seen already in previous chapters, force and moment calculations for your system can get pretty complicated and may even rely on tabulated empirical data, which will prevent you from writing simple mathematical functions that can be easily integrated. This means that you have to use numerical integration techniques to approximately integrate the equations of motion. I say "approximately" because solutions based on numerical integration won't be exact and will have a certain amount of error depending on the chosen method.

I'm going to start with a rather informal explanation of how we'll apply numerical integration because it will be easier to grasp. Later I'll get into some of the formal mathematics. Take a look at the differential equation of linear motion for a particle (or rigid body's center of mass):

$$F = m \, dv/dt$$

In the simple examples of the earlier chapters of this book, I rewrote this equation in the following form so that it could be integrated explicitly:

$$dv/dt = F/m$$
$$dv = (F/m) \, dt$$

One way to interpret this equation is that an infinitesimally small change in velocity, dv, is equal to (F/m) times an infinitesimally small change in time. In earlier examples I integrated explicitly by taking the definite integral of the left side of this equation with respect to velocity and the right side with respect to time. In numerical integration you have to take finite steps in time; thus, dt goes from being infinitely small to some discrete time increment, Δt, and you end up with a discrete change in velocity, Δv:

$$\Delta v = (F/m) \, \Delta t$$

It is important to notice here that this does not give a formula for instantaneous velocity; it only gives you an approximation of the change in velocity. Thus, to approximate the actual velocity of your particle (or rigid body), you have to know what its velocity was before the time change Δt. At the start of your simulation, at time zero, you have to know the starting velocity of your particle. This is an initial condition and is required to uniquely define your particle's velocity as you step through time using this equation:*

$$v_{t+\Delta t} = v_t + (F/m)\,\Delta t$$

where the initial condition is

$$v_{t=0} = v_0$$

Here, v_t is velocity at some time t, $v_{t+\Delta t}$ is velocity at some time plus the time step, Δt is the time step, and v_0 is the initial velocity at time zero.

You can integrate the linear equation of motion one more time to approximate your particle's displacement (or position). Once you've determined the new velocity value, at time $t + \Delta t$, you can approximate displacement using

$$s_{t+\Delta t} = s_t + \Delta t (v_{t+\Delta t})$$

where the initial condition on displacement is

$$s_{t=0} = s_0$$

The integration technique discussed here is known as Euler's method, and it is the most basic integration method. While Euler's method is easy to grasp and fairly straightforward to implement, it isn't necessarily the most accurate method.

You can reason that the smaller you make your time step, that is, as Δt approaches dt, the closer you'll get to the exact solution. However, there are computational problems associated with using very small time steps. Specifically, you'll need a huge number of calculations at very small Δt's, and since your calculations won't be exact (depending on numerical precision, you'll be rounding off and truncating numbers), you'll end up with a buildup of round-off error. This means that there is a practical limit as to how small a time step you can take. Fortunately, there are several numerical integration techniques at your disposal that are designed to increase accuracy for reasonable step sizes.

Even though I used the linear equation of motion for a particle, this integration technique (and the ones I'll show you later) applies equally well to the angular equations of motion.

Euler's Method

The preceding explanation of Euler's method was, as I said, informal. To treat Euler's method in a more mathematically rigorous way, it's helpful to have a look at the Taylor series expansion of a general function, $y(x)$. Taylor's theorem lets you approximate the value of a function at some point by knowing something about that function and its derivatives at some other point. This approximation is expressed as an infinite polynomial series of the form

$$y(x + \Delta x) = y(x) + (\Delta x)y'(x) + [(\Delta x)^2/2!]y''(x) + [(\Delta x)^3/3!]y'''(x) + \cdots$$

* In mathematics this sort of problem is termed an *initial value problem*.

where y is some function of x, $(x + \Delta x)$ is the new value of x at which you want to approximate y, y' is the first derivative of y, y'' is the second derivative of y, and so on.

In the case of the equation of motion discussed in the preceding section, the function that you are trying to approximate is the velocity as function of time. Thus, you can write $v(t)$ instead of $y(x)$, which yields the Taylor expansion:

$$v(t + \Delta t) = v(t) + (\Delta t)v'(t) + [(\Delta t)^2/2!]v''(t) + [(\Delta t)^3/3!]v'''(t) + \cdots$$

Note here that $v'(t)$ is equal to dv/dt, which equals F/m in the example equation of motion discussed in the preceding section. Note also that you know the value of v at time t. What you want to find is the value of v at time $t + \Delta t$ knowing v at time t and its derivative at time t. As a first approximation, and since you don't know anything about v's second, third, or higher derivatives, you can truncate the polynomial series after the term $(\Delta t)\, v'(t)$, which yields

$$v(t + \Delta t) = v(t) + (\Delta t)v'(t)$$

This is the Euler integration formula that you saw in the preceding section. Since Euler's formula goes out only to the term that includes the first derivative, the rest of the series that was left off is the *truncation error*. These terms that were left off are called higher-order terms, and getting rid of them results in a first-order approximation. The rationale behind this approximation is that the further you go in the series, the smaller the terms and the less influence they have on the approximation. Since Δt is presumed to be a small number, Δt^2 is even smaller, Δt^3 even smaller, and so on, and since these Δt terms appear in the numerators, each successively higher-order term gets smaller and smaller. In this case the first truncated term, $[(\Delta t)^2/2!]v''(t)$, dominates the truncation error, and this method is said to have an error of *order $(\Delta t)^2$*.

Geometrically, Euler's method approximates a new value, at the current step, for the function under consideration by extrapolating in the direction of the derivative of the function at the previous step. This is illustrated in Figure 11-1.

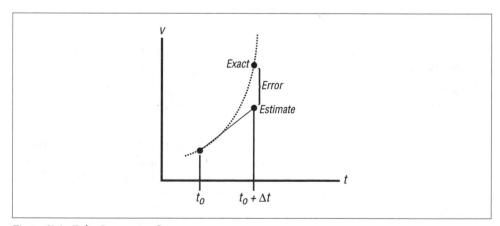

Figure 11-1. Euler Integration Step

Figure 11-1 illustrates the truncation error and shows that Euler's method will result in a polygonal approximation of the smooth function under consideration. Clearly, if you decrease the step size, you increase the number of polygonal segments and better approximate the function. As I said before, though, this isn't always efficient to do, since the number of computations in your simulation will increase, and round-off error will accumulate more rapidly.

To illustrate Euler's method in practice, let's examine the linear equation of motion for the ship example of Chapter 4:

$$T - (Cv) = ma$$

where T is the propeller's thrust, C is a drag coefficient, v is the ship's velocity, m its mass, and a its acceleration.

Figure 11-2 shows the Euler integration solution superimposed over the exact solution derived in Chapter 4 for the ship's speed over time.

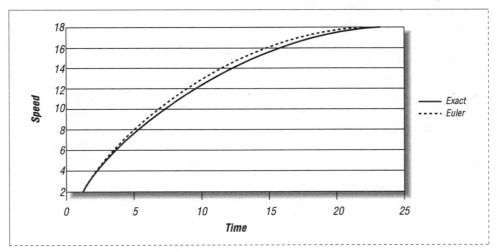

Figure 11-2. Euler Integration Comparison

Zooming in on this graph allows you to see the error in the Euler approximation. This is shown in Figure 11-3.

Table 11-1 shows the numerical values of speed versus time for the range shown in Figure 11-3. Also shown in Table 11-1 is the percent difference, the error, between the exact solution and the Euler solution at each time step.

As you can see, the truncation error in this example isn't too bad. It could be better, though, and I'll show you some more accurate methods in a moment. Before that, however, you should notice that in this example Euler's method is also stable, that is, it converges well with the exact solution as shown in Figure 11-4, where I've carried the time range out farther.

Table 11-1. Exact Solution Versus Euler Solution

Time (s)	Velocity, Exact (ft/s)	Velocity, Euler (ft/s)	Error
6.5	9.559084	9.733158	1.82 %
7	10.06829	10.2465	1.77 %
7.5	10.55267	10.73418	1.72 %
8	11.01342	11.19747	1.67 %
8.5	11.4517	11.63759	1.62 %

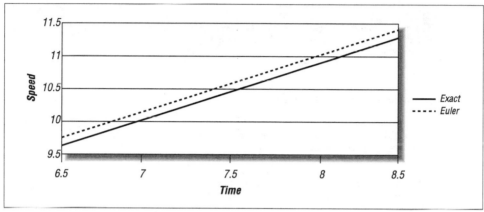

Figure 11-3. Euler Error

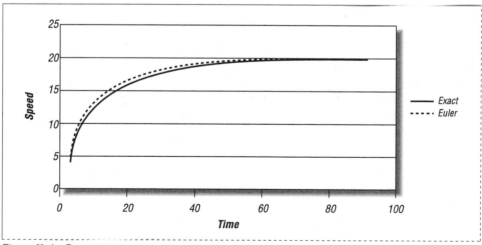

Figure 11-4. Convergence

Here's a code snippet that implements Euler's method for this example:

```
// Global Variables
float     T;      // thrust
float     C;      // drag coefficient
float     V;      // velocity
float     M;      // mass
float     S;      // displacement
 .
 .
 .
// This function progresses the simulation by dt seconds using
// Euler's basic method
void StepSimulation(float dt)
{
      float     F;      // total force
      float     A;      // acceleration
      float     Vnew;   // new velocity at time t + dt
      float     Snew;   // new position at time t + dt

      // Calculate the total force
      F = (T - (C * V));

      // Calculate the acceleration
      A = F / M;

      // Calculate the new velocity at time t + dt
      // where V is the velocity at time t
      Vnew = V + A * dt;

      // Calculate the new displacement at time t + dt
      // where S is the displacement at time t
      Snew = S + Vnew * dt;

      // Update old velocity and displacement with the new ones
      V = Vnew;
      S = Snew;
}
```

Although Euler's method is stable in this example, it isn't always so, depending on the problem you're trying to solve. This is something that you must keep in mind when implementing any numerical integration scheme. What I mean here by "stable" is that in this case the Euler solution converges with the exact. If it weren't stable, it would diverge from the exact solution, and the error would grow as you stepped through time. Instability can also manifest itself in the form of the numerical solution oscillating above and below the exact solution and never quite converging on it.

Often, your choice of step size affects stability when smaller step sizes tend to eliminate or minimize instability and larger step sizes aggravate the problem. If you're working with a particularly unwieldy function, you might find that you have to decrease your step size substantially to achieve stability. This, however, increases the number of computations you need to make. One way around this difficulty is to employ what's called an adaptive step size method, in which you change your step size on the fly depending on the magnitude of a predicted amount of truncation error from one step to the next. If the truncation error is too large, then you back up a step, decrease your step size, and try again.

One way to implement this for Euler's method is to first take a step size, Δt, to obtain an estimate at time $t + \Delta t$, and then take two steps (starting from time t again) of size $\Delta t / 2$ to obtain another estimate at time $t + \Delta t$. Since we've been talking about velocity in the examples so far, let's call the first estimate v_1 and the second estimate v_2.* A measure of the truncation error is then

$$e_t = |v_1 - v_2|$$

If it is desired to keep the truncation error within a specified limit, e_{to}, then you can use the following formula to find out what your step size should be to maintain the desired accuracy:

$$h_{new} = h_{old}(e_{to}/e_t)^{(1/2)}$$

Here, h_{old} is the old time step and h_{new} is the new one that you should use to maintain the desired accuracy. You'll have to make this check for each time step, and if you find that the error warrants a smaller time step, then you'll have to back up a step and repeat it with the new time step.

Here's a revised StepSimulation function that implements this adaptive step size technique, checking the truncation error on the velocity integration:

```
// New global variable
float     eto;     // truncation error tolerance

// This function progresses the simulation by dt seconds using
// Euler's basic method with an adaptive step size
void StepSimulation(float dt)
{
    float     F;      // total force
    float     A;      // acceleration
    float     Vnew;   // new velocity at time t + dt
    float     Snew;   // new position at time t + dt
    float     V1, V2; // temporary velocity variables
    float     dtnew;  // new time step
    float     et;     // truncation error

    // Take one step of size dt to estimate the new velocity
    F = (T - (C * V));
    A = F / M;
    V1 = V + A * dt;

    // Take two steps of size dt/2 to estimate the new velocity
    F = (T - (C * V));
    A = F / M;
    V2 = V + A * (dt/2);

    F = (T - (C * V2));
    A = F / M;
    V2 = V2 + A * (dt/2);

    // Estimate the truncation error
    et = absf(V1 - V2);
```

---

* Even though I'm talking about velocity and time here, these techniques apply to any function, for example, displacement versus time.

```
        // Estimate a new step size
        dtnew = dt * SQRT(eto/et);

        if (dtnew < dt)
        { // take at step at the new smaller step size
              F = (T - (C * V));
              A = F / M;
              Vnew = V + A * dtnew;
              Snew = S + Vnew * dtnew;
        } else
        { // original step size is okay
              Vnew = V1;
              Snew = S + Vnew * dt;
        }

        // Update old velocity and displacement with the new ones
        V = Vnew;
        S = Snew;
    }
```

Other Methods

At this point you might be wondering why you can't simply use more terms in the Taylor series to reduce the truncation error of Euler's method. In fact, this is the basis for several integration methods that offer greater accuracy than Euler's basic method for a given step size. Part of the difficulty associated with picking up more terms in the Taylor's series expansion is in being able to determine the second, third, fourth, and higher derivatives of the function you're trying to integrate. The way around this problem is to perform additional Taylor series expansions to approximate the derivatives of the function under consideration and then substitute those values back into your original expansion.

Taking this approach to include one more Taylor term beyond the basic Euler method yields a so-called *improved Euler method* that has a reduced truncation error, on the order of $(\Delta t)^3$ instead of $(\Delta t)^2$. The formulas for this method are as follows:

$$k_1 = (\Delta x)y'(x, y)$$
$$k_2 = (\Delta x)y'(x + \Delta x, y + k_1)$$
$$y(x + \Delta x) = y(x) + 1/2(k_1 + k_2)$$

Here y is a function of x, y' is the derivative as a function of x and possibly of y, and Δx the step size.

To make this clearer for you, I'll show these formulas in terms of the ship example equation of motion of Chapter 4, the same example that I discussed in the preceding section. In this case velocity is approximated by the following formulas:

$$k_1 = \Delta t[1/m(T - Cv_t)]$$
$$k_2 = \Delta t\{1/m[T - C(v_t + k_1)]\}$$
$$v_{t+\Delta t} = v_t + 1/2(k_1 + k_2)$$

where v_t is the velocity at time t, and $v_{t+\Delta t}$ is the new velocity at time $t + \Delta t$.

Here is the revised StepSimulation function showing how to implement this method in code:

```
// This function progresses the simulation by dt seconds using
// the "improved" Euler method
void StepSimulation(float dt)
{
    float    F;      // total force
    float    A;      // acceleration
    float    Vnew;   // new velocity at time t + dt
    float    Snew;   // new position at time t + dt
    float    k1, k2;

    F = (T - (C * V));
    A = F/M;
    k1 = dt * A;

    F = (T - (C * (V + k1)));
    A = F/M;
    k2 = dt * A;

    // Calculate the new velocity at time t + dt
    // where V is the velocity at time t
    Vnew = V + (k1 + k2) / 2;

    // Calculate the new displacement at time t + dt
    // where S is the displacement at time t
    Snew = S + Vnew * dt;

    // Update old velocity and displacement with the new ones
    V = Vnew;
    S = Snew;
}
```

This procedure of taking on more Taylor terms can be carried out even further. The popular Runge-Kutta method takes such an approach to reduce the truncation error to the order of $(\Delta t)^5$. The integration formulas for this method are as follows:

$$k_1 = (\Delta x)y'(x, y)$$
$$k_2 = (\Delta x)y'(x + \Delta x/2, y + k_1/2)$$
$$k_3 = (\Delta x)y'(x + \Delta x/2, y + k_2/2)$$
$$k_4 = (\Delta x)y'(x + \Delta x, y + k_3)$$
$$y(x + \Delta x) = y(x) + 1/6[k_1 + 2(k_2) + 2(k_3) + k_4]$$

Applying these formulas to our ship example yields

$$k_1 = \Delta t[1/m(T - Cv_t)]$$
$$k_2 = \Delta t\{1/m[T - C(v_t + k_1/2)]\}$$
$$k_3 = \Delta t\{1/m[T - C(v_t + k_2/2)]\}$$
$$k_4 = \Delta t\{1/m[(T - C(v_t + k_3)]\}$$
$$v_{t+\Delta t} = v_t + 1/6[(k_1 + 2(k_2) + 2(k_3) + k_4]$$

For our example the Runge-Kutta method is implemented as follows:

```
// This function progresses the simulation by dt seconds using
// the Runge-Kutta method
void StepSimulation(float dt)
{
    float    F;      // total force
    float    A;      // acceleration
    float    Vnew;   // new velocity at time t + dt
    float    Snew;   // new position at time t + dt
    float    k1, k2, k3, k4;

    F = (T - (C * V));
    A = F/M;
    k1 = dt * A;

    F = (T - (C * (V + k1/2)));
    A = F/M;
    k2 = dt * A;

    F = (T - (C * (V + k2/2)));
    A = F/M;
    k3 = dt * A;

    F = (T - (C * (V + k3)));
    A = F/M;
    k4 = dt * A;

    // Calculate the new velocity at time t + dt
    // where V is the velocity at time t
    Vnew = V + (k1 + 2*k2 + 2*k3 + k4) / 6;

    // Calculate the new displacement at time t + dt
    // where S is the displacement at time t
    Snew = S + Vnew * dt;

    // Update old velocity and displacement with the new ones
    V = Vnew;
    S = Snew;
}
```

To show you how accuracy is improved over the basic Euler method, I've superimposed integration results for the ship example using these two methods over those shown in Figures 11-2 and 11-3. Figures 11-5 and 11-6 show the results, where Figure 11-6 is a zoomed view of 11-5.

As you can see from these figures, it's difficult to discern the curves for the improved Euler and Runge-Kutta methods from the exact solution because they fall almost right on top of each other. These results clearly show the improvement in accuracy over the basic Euler method, whose curve is distinct from the other three. Over the interval from 6.5 to 8.5 seconds, the average truncation error is 1.72%, 0.03%, and 3.6×10^{-6} % for Euler's method, the improved Euler method, and the Runge-Kutta method, respectively. It obvious, on the basis of these results, that for this problem the Runge-Kutta method yields substantially better results for a given step size than the other two methods. Of course, you pay for this accuracy, since you have several more computations per step in the Runge-Kutta method.

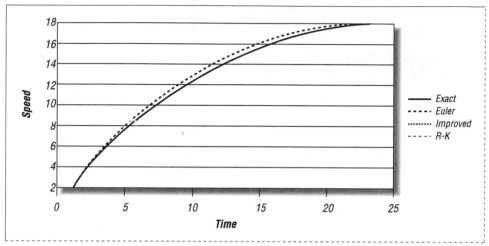

Figure 11-5. Method Comparison

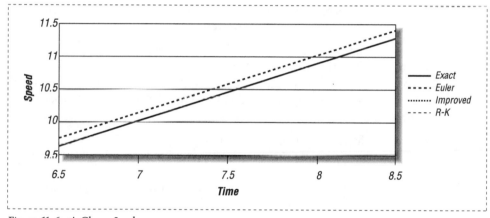

Figure 11-6. A Closer Look

These methods aren't the only ones at your disposal; however, they are the most common. Other methods attempt to improve computational efficiency even further; that is, they are designed to minimize truncation error while still allowing you to take relatively large step sizes so as to reduce the number of steps you have to take in your integration. I cite some pretty good references for further reading on this subject in the bibliography.

CHAPTER 12

2D Rigid Body Simulator

Now it's time to put all of what you've learned so far to work and implement an actual real-time simulator. I chose to model two vehicles in this example so that in the next chapter I can show you how to handle collision response between these two vehicles when they run into each other. For now, though, I'll keep it simple to clearly illustrate the material that you studied in the earlier chapters.

Although the source code for this example is available on O'Reilly's web site, I'm going to include just about all of it in this chapter. For the most part I'll concentrate on the code that implements the physics part of the simulator, and I'll refer you to O'Reilly's web site for the rest of the code that implements rendering the simulation using Microsoft's Direct3D technology.

There are four main elements to this simulation:

Model
>   The model refers to your idealization of the thing, in this case a hovercraft, that you are trying to simulate.

Integrator
>   The integrator refers to the method by which you integrate the differential equations of motion.

User Input
>   User input refers to how you'll allow the user to interact with your simulation.

Rendering
>   Finally, rendering refers to how you'll allow the user to view your simulation.

In this simulation the world coordinate system has its x-axis pointing into the screen, its y-axis pointing to the left of your screen, and its z-axis pointing upward. Even though this is a 2D example, in which all motion is confined to the xy-plane, you still need a z-axis about which the hovercraft will rotate. Also, the local, or body-fixed, coordinate system has its x-axis pointing toward the front of the hovercraft, its y-axis pointing to the port side, and its z-axis pointing upward.

Model

The vehicles that are modeled in this simulation are a couple of generic hovercraft operating over smooth land. The two vehicles are identical and have the properties shown in Table 12-1.

Table 12-1. Hovercraft Properties

Property	Value
Length	70 ft
Width	50 ft
Average projected area of entire vehicle	1500 ft²
Center of drag location	2.5 ft aft of the CG
Weight	10 tons (20,000 lb)
Mass	621.6 slugs
Center of gravity (CG) location	35 ft aft of the bow on the centerline (assumed to be in the center of the craft)
Mass moment of inertia[a]	383,320 lb-ft-s²
Max thrust (air propeller)	2000 lb
Propeller location	30 ft aft of the CG on centerline
Bow thrusters	one to port and one to starboard, each 30 ft forward of the CG and 25 ft off the centerline to either side
Bow thruster thrust	500 lb
Top speed	40 kt (67.51 ft/s)

[a] Remember, in two dimensions the moment of inertia term is a scalar. In this case it's the moment of inertia for rotation about the local z-axis passing through the center of gravity.

Each craft is fitted with a single air screw propeller that provides forward (or reverse) thrust located toward the aft end of the craft. For controllability each craft is fitted with two bow thrusters, one to port and the other to starboard, each capable of delivering 500 lb of thrust to either side. These bow thrusters are used to steer the hovercraft.

I've used a simplified drag model in which the only drag component is due to aerodynamic drag on the entire craft. For these calculations I've assumed a mean projected area of 1500 ft and a drag coefficient of 0.25. A more rigorous model would consider the actual projected area of the craft as a function of the direction of relative velocity, as in the flight simulator example discussed in Chapter 7, as well as the frictional drag between the bottom of the craft's skirt and the ground. I've also assumed that the center of drag is 2.5 ft aft of the center of gravity so as to give a little directional stability, that is, to counteract rotation. This serves the same function as the vertical tail fins on aircraft.

In code, the first thing you need to do to represent these vehicles is define a rigid body structure that contains all of the information you'll need to track the vehicles and calculate the forces and moments acting on them. Here's how I did it:

```
typedef struct _RigidBody {

    float      fMass;      // total mass (constant)
    float      fInertia;   // mass moment of inertia in body coordinates
    float      fInertiaInverse;    // inverse of mass moment of inertia
    Vector     vPosition;          // position in earth coordinates
    Vector     vVelocity;          // velocity in earth coordinates
    Vector     vVelocityBody;      // velocity in body coordinates
    Vector     vAngularVelocity;   // angular velocity in
                                   // body coordinates

    float      fSpeed;             // speed (magnitude of the velocity)
    float      fOrientation;       // orientation
    Vector     vForces;            // total force on body
    Vector     vMoment;            // total moment (torque) on body
                                   // (2D: about z-axis only)

    Vector     CD;                 // location of the center of
                                   // drag relative to the center
                                   // of gravity
    Vector     CT;                 // location of center of thrust
                                   // relative to the center of gravity
    Vector     CPT;                // location of the port bow thruster
                                   // relative to the center of gravity
    Vector     CST;                // location of the starboard bow
                                   // thruster relative to the center
                                   // of gravity
    float      ProjectedArea;      // mean projected area
                                   // (for drag calcs.)
    float      ThrustForce;        // magnitude of the thrust force
    Vector     PThrust, SThrust;   // bow thruster vectors

    float      fWidth;             // bounding dimensions
    float      fLength;

} RigidBody2D, *pRigidBody2D;
```

This structure contains all the information you'll need to track the state of each craft.

The next step in defining the model is to write an initialization function to initialize the states of these hovercraft when the program first starts up. Here's what that function looks like:

```
void      InitializeHovercraft(pRigidBody2D body)
{
    // Set initial position
    body->vPosition.x = 0.0f;
    body->vPosition.y = 0.0f;
    body->vPosition.z = 0.0f;        // set all z's to zero b/c this is 2D
    // Set initial velocity
    body->vVelocity.x = 0.0f;
    body->vVelocity.y = 0.0f;
    body->vVelocity.z = 0.0f;      // set all z's to zero b/c this is 2D
body->fSpeed = 0.0f;

    // Set initial angular velocity
    body->vAngularVelocity.x = 0.0f;      // will always be zero in 2D
    body->vAngularVelocity.y = 0.0f;      // will always be zero in 2D
    body->vAngularVelocity.z = 0.0f;      // in 2D only this component
                                          // with be used
```

```
    // Set the initial thrust, forces, and moments
    body->vForces.x = 0.0f;
    body->vForces.y = 0.0f;
    body->vForces.z = 0.0f;         // set all z's to zero
    body->vMoment.x = 0.0f;         // will always be zero in 2D
    body->vMoment.y = 0.0f;         // will always be zero in 2D
    body->vMoment.z = 0.0f;         // in 2D only this component
                                    // with be used

    // Zero the velocity in body space coordinates
    body->vVelocityBody.x = 0.0f;
    body->vVelocityBody.y = 0.0f;
    body->vVelocityBody.z = 0.0f;

    // Set the initial orientation
    body->fOrientation = 0.0;

    // Now define the mass properties
    body->fMass = 621.6;
    body->fInertia = 383320;
    body->fInertiaInverse = 1.0f / body->fInertia;

    // coordinates of the body center of drag
    body->CD.x = -2.5f;             body->CD.y = 0.0f;

    // coordinates of the propeller thrust vector
    body->CT.x =   30.0f;       body->CT.y = 0.0f;

    // coordinates of the port bow thruster
    body->CPT.x = 30.0f;        body->CPT.y = 25.0f;

    // coordinates of the starboard bow thruster
    body->CST.x = 30.0f;        body->CST.y = -25.0f;

    body->ProjectedArea = 1500.0f;  // mean projected area
    body->ThrustForce = 0;          // initial thrust force

    body->fWidth = 50;    // width of the body (measured along y-axis)
    body->fLength = 70;   // length of the body (measured along x-axis)
}
```

You'll notice here that the Vector class that I've used is actually a *triple*, that is, it has three components: x, y, and z. Since this is a 2D example, the z-components will always be zero, except in the case of the angular velocity vector, in which only the z-component will be used (since rotation occurs only about the z-axis). The class that I've used in this example is discussed in Appendix A, so I won't give the source code here. The reason I didn't write a separate 2D vector class, one with only x- and y-components, is because I'll be extending this code to 3D later and wanted to get you used to using the 3D vector class. Besides, it's pretty easy to create a 2D vector class from the 3D class by simply stripping out the z-component.

Notice that this function takes as a parameter a pointer to a RigidBody structure. This way, you can call this same function to initialize each hovercraft, and then later, if you want to make some changes to a particular hovercraft's initial state, you can do so by changing only the property of interest. For example, here's how I initialized the two hovercraft in this example:

```
void    Initialize(void)
{
    InitializeHovercraft(&Hovercraft1);
    InitializeHovercraft(&Hovercraft2);

    Hovercraft2.vPosition.y = -50;
    Hovercraft2.vPosition.x = 1500;
    Hovercraft2.fOrientation = 180;
}
```

Here, `Hovercraft1` and `Hovercraft2` are defined as global variables:

```
RigidBody2D      Hovercraft1, Hovercraft2;    // our two hovercraft rigid
bodies
```

You can see here that I didn't want to start the program with both hovercraft occupying the same position, one on top of the other. Instead, I set Hovercraft2 some distance away from the first and then rotated it 180 degrees so that it faces the first hovercraft.

This `Initialize` function is called at the very start of the program. I found it convenient to make the call right after the application's main window is created and shown, in this case in the standard Windows API `InitInstance` function as shown here:

```
BOOL InitInstance(HINSTANCE hInstance, int nCmdShow)
{
    hInst = hInstance;
    nShowCmd = nCmdShow;

    hTheMainWindow = CreateWindow(szAppName,
                        szTitle,
                        WS_OVERLAPPEDWINDOW |
                        WS_CLIPCHILDREN | WS_CLIPSIBLINGS,
                        0, 0, 640, 480,
                        NULL, NULL, hInst, NULL);

    if (!CreateD3DRMObject())
        return (FALSE);

    if (!CreateD3DRMClipperObject(hTheMainWindow))
        return (FALSE);

    if (!CreateViewPort(hTheMainWindow))
        return (FALSE);

    ShowWindow(hTheMainWindow, nCmdShow);
    UpdateWindow(hTheMainWindow);

    Initialize();

    return (TRUE);
}
```

Now that everything is initialized, you need to develop a function to calculate the forces and moments that will act on the hovercraft throughout the simulation. Without such a function, the hovercraft will just sit there and do nothing, so obviously, this function is crucial. Let me also say that while most of the code that I'll show you in this chapter can be reused without much modification for your own rigid body simulations, the same is not true of this function. You'll need a function to calculate forces and moments for whatever you're simulating, but the body of the function will likely be very different depending on what you are modeling and how you have idealized your physical model. That said, here's the function that I've developed for the hovercraft:

```
void       CalcLoads(pRigidBody2D body)
{
    Vector      Fb;                      // stores the sum of forces
    Vector      Mb;                      // stores the sum of moments
    Vector      Thrust;                  // thrust vector

    // reset forces and moments:
    body->vForces.x = 0.0f;
    body->vForces.y = 0.0f;
    body->vForces.z = 0.0f;              // always zero in 2D

    body->vMoment.x = 0.0f;              // always zero in 2D
    body->vMoment.y = 0.0f;              // always zero in 2D
    body->vMoment.z = 0.0f;

    Fb.x = 0.0f;
    Fb.y = 0.0f;
    Fb.z = 0.0f;

    Mb.x = 0.0f;
    Mb.y = 0.0f;
    Mb.z = 0.0f;

    // Define the thrust vector, which acts through the craft's CG
    Thrust.x = 1.0f;
    Thrust.y = 0.0f;
    Thrust.z = 0.0f;   // zero in 2D
    Thrust *= body->ThrustForce;

    // Calculate forces and moments in body space:
    Vector      vLocalVelocity;
    float       fLocalSpeed;
    Vector      vDragVector;
    float       tmp;
    Vector      vResultant;
    Vector      vtmp;

    // Calculate the aerodynamic drag force:
    // Calculate local velocity:
    // The local velocity includes the velocity due to
    // linear motion of the craft,
    // plus the velocity at each element due to the rotation
    // of the craft.
    vtmp = body->vAngularVelocity^body->CD; // rotational part
    vLocalVelocity = body->vVelocityBody + vtmp;

    // Calculate local air speed
    fLocalSpeed = vLocalVelocity.Magnitude();

    // Find the direction in which drag will act.
    // Drag always acts inline with the relative velocity
    // but in the opposing direction
    if(fLocalSpeed > tol)
    {
        vLocalVelocity.Normalize();
        vDragVector = -vLocalVelocity;
```

```
        // Determine the resultant force on the element.
        tmp = 0.5f * rho * fLocalSpeed*fLocalSpeed *
                body->ProjectedArea;
        vResultant = vDragVector * LINEARDRAGCOEFFICIENT * tmp;
        // Keep a running total of these resultant
        // forces (total force)
        Fb += vResultant;

        // Calculate the moment about the CG of this
        // element's force
        // and keep a running total of these moments (total moment)
        vtmp = body->CD^vResultant;
        Mb += vtmp;
    }

    // Calculate the port and starboard bow thruster forces:
    // Keep a running total of these resultant forces (total force)
    Fb += body->PThrust;

    // Calculate the moment about the CG of this element's force
    // and keep a running total of these moments (total moment)
    vtmp = body->CPT^body->PThrust;
    Mb += vtmp;

    // Keep a running total of these resultant forces (total force)
    Fb += body->SThrust;

    // Calculate the moment about the CG of this element's force
    // and keep a running total of these moments (total moment)
    vtmp = body->CST^body->SThrust;
    Mb += vtmp;

    // Now add the propulsion thrust
    Fb += Thrust; // no moment, since line of action is through CG

    // Convert forces from model space to earth space
    body->vForces = VRotate2D(body->fOrientation, Fb);

    body->vMoment += Mb;
}
```

Since the two hovercraft are identical, this same function is used to calculate the loads on each by passing this function a pointer to the RigidBody structure for the hovercraft under consideration.

The first thing that CalcLoads does is initialize the force and moment variables that will contain the total of all forces and moments acting on the craft at any instant in time.

The function then goes on to define a vector representing the propeller thrust. In this case the thrust vector acts in the positive (local) x-direction and has a magnitude defined by ThrustForce, which is set by the user via the keyboard interface. (I'll get to that later.) Note that if ThrustForce is negative, then the thrust will actually be a reversing thrust instead of a forward thrust.

After defining the thrust vector, this function goes on to calculate the aerodynamic drag acting on the hovercraft. These calculations are very similar to those discussed in Chapter 7. The first thing to do is determine the relative velocity at the center of drag, considering both linear and angular motion. You'll need the magnitude of the relative velocity vector when calculating the magnitude of the drag force, and you'll need the direction of the relative velocity vector to determine the direction of the drag force, since it always opposes the velocity vector. Once the drag force has been determined, the function adds it to the running total of forces and then calculates the moment about the center of gravity of the drag force and adds that moment to the running total of moments. Note that the drag coefficient, LINEARDRAGCOEFFICIENT, is defined as follows:

```
#define LINEARDRAGCOEFFICIENT        0.25f
```

With the drag calculation complete, the function proceeds to calculate the forces and moments due to the bow thrusters, which may be active or inactive at any given time.

Next, the propeller thrust force is added to the running total of forces. Remember, since the propeller thrust force acts through the center of gravity, there is no moment to worry about.

Finally, the total force is converted from local coordinates to world coordinates via a vector rotation given the orientation of the hovercraft, and the total forces and moments are stored in the RigidBody structure for the given hovercraft. These values are stored so that they are available when it comes time to integrate the equations of motion at each time step throughout the simulation.

Integration

Now that the code to define, initialize, and calculate loads on the rigid bodies is complete, you need to develop the code to actually integrate the equations of motion so that the simulation can progress through time. The first thing you need to do is decide on the integration scheme that you want to use, as discussed in Chapter 11. For this example I've chosen the *improved Euler* method. To that end, I've developed the function UpdateBody that takes as parameters a pointer to a RigidBody and the time step to take (in seconds):

```
void      UpdateBody(pRigidBody2D craft, float dtime)
{
          Vector Ae;
          float Aa;
          RigidBody2D    body;
          Vector         k1, k2;
          float          k1a, k2a;
          float          dt = dtime;

          // make a copy of the hovercraft's state
          memcpy(&body, craft, sizeof(RigidBody2D));

          // calculate the k1 terms for both linear and angular velocity
          CalcLoads(&body);
          Ae = body.vForces / body.fMass;
          k1 = Ae * dt;

          Aa = body.vMoment.z / body.fInertia;
          k1a = Aa * dt;
```

```
// add the k1 terms to the respective initial velocities
body.vVelocity += k1;
body.vAngularVelocity.z += k1a;

// calculate new loads and the k2 terms
CalcLoads(&body);
Ae = body.vForces / body.fMass;
k2 = Ae * dt;

Aa = body.vMoment.z / body.fInertia;
k2a = Aa * dt;

// now calculate the hovercraft's new velocities at time t + dt
craft->vVelocity += (k1 + k2) / 2.0f;
craft->vAngularVelocity.z += (k1a + k2a) / 2.0f;

// calculate the new position
craft->vPosition += craft->vVelocity * dt;
craft->fSpeed = craft->vVelocity.Magnitude();

// calculate the new orientation
craft->fOrientation +=
            RadiansToDegrees(craft->vAngularVelocity.z * dt);

craft->vVelocityBody =
            VRotate2D(-craft->fOrientation, craft->vVelocity);
}
```

By passing this function a pointer to a `RigidBody`, we can reuse this same function regardless of the particular body that is under consideration. Further, passing the time step allows us to vary the size of the time step as we see fit. I'll do just that in the next chapter when I show you how to handle collision response.

The first thing that `UpdateBody` does is to make a temporary copy of the current state of the rigid body under consideration. This has to be done because in the improved Euler method you have to take the intermediate step of adding the $k1$ terms to the initial velocities before completing the integration, and you don't want to corrupt the initial velocity values of the rigid body, since you'll need them to finish the integration step.

The next thing to do is calculate the loads (forces and moments) acting on the rigid body by passing a pointer to the temporary copy to the `CalcLoads` function. With the loads calculated, the function proceeds to calculate the $k1$ terms for both linear and angular velocity. These $k1$ terms are then added to the initial velocities, which are then used during another call to `CalcLoads`. The $k2$ terms are calculated after this second call to `CalcLoads`.

Now that the $k1$ and $k2$ terms have been calculated, the new velocities are calculated by using the improved Euler formula. Next, the function integrates the new velocities, using Euler's method, to determine the new position and orientation of the rigid body.

The last thing that `UpdateBody` does is calculate the rigid body's velocity in local coordinates by applying a vector rotation of the world space velocity by the body's new orientation. You need the velocity in local coordinates when calculating drag in the `CalcLoads` function, and this is a convenient place to calculate it.

Since there are two rigid bodies—the two hovercraft—in this simulation, UpdateBody must be called twice, once for each hovercraft. I do this in the StepSimulation function:

```
void StepSimulation(float dt)
{
    UpdateBody(&Hovercraft1, dt);
    UpdateBody(&Hovercraft2, dt);
}
```

StepSimulation is trivial in this simulation, since there are only two rigid bodies and there's no collision response mechanism in the simulation yet. If you had several rigid bodies in your own simulation, you could set up an array of RigidBody structures and then loop through your array in StepSimulation to update each rigid body.

StepSimulation is called once per game loop cycle. In this example I set up another function call NullEvent that gets called every time through the main window message loop as shown here:

```
int APIENTRY WinMain(HINSTANCE hInstance,
                     HINSTANCE hPrevInstance,
                     LPSTR lpCmdLine,
                     int nCmdShow)
{
.
.
.

    OldTime = timeGetTime();
    NewTime = OldTime;
    // Main message loop:
    while (1) {

        while(PeekMessage(&msg, NULL, 0, 0, PM_REMOVE)) {
            if (msg.message == WM_QUIT) {
                return msg.wParam;
            }
            TranslateMessage(&msg);
            DispatchMessage(&msg);
        }

        NullEvent();

    }
.
.
.
}
```

When NullEvent calls StepSimulation, it passes the size of the time step in as the *dt* parameter. You don't have to do it this way. I chose to because I was experimenting with having the time step calculated in real time as the difference in time between the last call to StepSimulation and the current time as shown here:

```
void      NullEvent(void)
{
.
.
.
```

```
NewTime = timeGetTime();
dt = (float) (NewTime - OldTime)/1000;
OldTime = NewTime;

if (dt > 0.016) dt = 0.016;
if (dt < 0.001f) dt = 0.001f;

StepSimulation(dt);

  .
  .
  .

}
```

This approach progresses the simulation in realistically scaled time. The problem is that if the program spends too much doing something else during one cycle, then the next time step may be too large relative to the last time step, and the motion of the rigid body will be less smooth, not to mention that too large a time step could result in inaccuracies and instability during integration. As you can see, I put in a little check to prevent the time step from getting too large. I also put in a check to keep the time increment from falling below 1 millisecond (ms). timeGetTime has a documented accuracy resolution of 1 ms, but I found that it would sometimes return values less than that. So I put the 1-ms check in there to keep things consistent and to make sure we're within the stated accuracy of timeGetTime.

As an alternative, you can fix the time step in your simulations so that each step is the same as the last, regardless of any delay encountered in your game loop. You'll have to experiment here to determine a good step size. If you choose one that's too small, your simulation will seem to move in slow motion. Conversely, if the step is too large, your simulation will seem as though it's in fast-forward mode, and of course, you'll increase the likelihood of numerical problems.

Flight Controls

If you were to run the program as we have it so far, you would find that even though our model and integrator are in place, the hovercraft would still sit there and do nothing. That is, of course, because there is no control mechanism built in yet. The user input code that I'll show you next is your way to interact with the hovercraft and control their behavior. Specifically, I'll associate certain keys on the keyboard with certain forces that will be applied to the model. I've already mentioned what those forces are: the propeller's thrust and the bow thrusters' thrust. In this way you don't directly push or turn the hovercraft; you can only apply forces and let the integrator take care of how the hovercraft will behave under the action of those forces.

The flight controls in this example are pretty simple. For hovercraft 1, the up arrow key increments the propeller thrust by 100-lb increments up to a maximum of 2000 lb; the down arrow key decrements the propeller thrust by 100-lb increments down to a minimum of −2000 lb (for reversing); the left arrow key applies the starboard bow thruster to yaw (turn) the craft to port (the left); and the right arrow key applies the port bow thruster to yaw the craft to starboard. For hovercraft 2, the W, Z, A, and S keys perform the same functions, respectively.

I've prepared several functions to handle the propeller and bow thrusters that should be called whenever the user is pressing the flight control keys. The first two functions handle the propeller:

```
void        IncThrust(int craft)
{
        if(craft == 1)
        {
                Hovercraft1.ThrustForce += _DTHRUST;
                if(Hovercraft1.ThrustForce > _MAXTHRUST)
                        Hovercraft1.ThrustForce = _MAXTHRUST;
        } else {
                Hovercraft2.ThrustForce += _DTHRUST;
                if(Hovercraft2.ThrustForce > _MAXTHRUST)
                        Hovercraft2.ThrustForce = _MAXTHRUST;
        }
}

void        DecThrust(int craft)
{

        if(craft == 1)
        {
                Hovercraft1.ThrustForce -= _DTHRUST;
                if(Hovercraft1.ThrustForce < -_MAXTHRUST)
                        Hovercraft1.ThrustForce = -_MAXTHRUST;
        } else {
                Hovercraft2.ThrustForce -= _DTHRUST;
                if(Hovercraft2.ThrustForce < -_MAXTHRUST)
                        Hovercraft2.ThrustForce = -_MAXTHRUST;
        }
}
```

IncThrust simply increases the thrust by _DTHRUST checking to make sure it does not exceed _MAXTHRUST. I've defined _DTHRUST and _MAXTHRUST as follows:

```
#define     _DTHRUST      100.0f
#define     _MAXTHRUST    2000.0f
```

DecThrust, on the other hand, decreases the thrust by _DTHRUST, checking to make sure it does not fall below -_MAXTHRUST. Both of these functions take as a parameter an integer identifying the hovercraft, Hovercraft1 or Hovercraft2, to which the changes are to be applied.

The next few functions handle the bow thrusters:

```
void        PortThruster(int craft)
{
        if(craft == 1)
                Hovercraft1.PThrust.y = -500.0f;
        else
                Hovercraft2.PThrust.y = -500.0f;
}
```

```
void        STBDThruster(int craft)
{
        if(craft == 1)
                Hovercraft1.SThrust.y = 500.0f;
        else
                Hovercraft2.SThrust.y = 500.0f;
}

void        ZeroThrusters(int craft)
{
        if(craft == 1)
        {
                Hovercraft1.PThrust.x = 0.0f;
                Hovercraft1.PThrust.y = 0.0f;
                Hovercraft1.PThrust.z = 0.0f;

                Hovercraft1.SThrust.x = 0.0f;
                Hovercraft1.SThrust.y = 0.0f;
                Hovercraft1.SThrust.z = 0.0f;
        } else {
                Hovercraft2.PThrust.x = 0.0f;
                Hovercraft2.PThrust.y = 0.0f;
                Hovercraft2.PThrust.z = 0.0f;

                Hovercraft2.SThrust.x = 0.0f;
                Hovercraft2.SThrust.y = 0.0f;
                Hovercraft2.SThrust.z = 0.0f;
        }
}
```

PortThruster simply sets the thrust of the port bow thruster to −500, which is 500 lb toward the starboard to turn the craft to starboard. The minus 500 means that the port thrust vector points in the negative (local) y-direction. Similarly, STBDThruster sets the thrust of the starboard bow thruster to 500 lb, which turns the craft to port. In this case the starboard thrust vector points in the positive (local) y-direction. ZeroThrusters simply turns off the port and starboard bow thrusters. All three of these functions take an integer parameter identifying the craft to which the changes will apply.

As I said, these functions should be called when the user is pressing the flight control keys. Further, they need to be called before the StepSimulation function is called so that they can be included in the current time step's forces and moments calculations. Since I put the StepSimulation call in my NullEvent function, it makes sense to handle the flight controls in that function as well. Here's how I did it:

```
void        NullEvent(void)
{
.
.
.

        // figure out which flight control keys are down
        ZeroThrusters(1);

        if (IsKeyDown(VK_UP))
                IncThrust(1);
```

```
    if (IsKeyDown(VK_DOWN))
        DecThrust(1);

    if (IsKeyDown(VK_RIGHT))
    {
        ZeroThrusters(1);
        PortThruster(1);
    }

    if (IsKeyDown(VK_LEFT))
    {
        ZeroThrusters(1);
        STBDThruster(1);
    }

    ZeroThrusters(2);

    if (IsKeyDown(0x57)) // W key
        IncThrust(2);

    if (IsKeyDown(0x5A)) // Z key
        DecThrust(2);

    if (IsKeyDown(0x53)) // S key
    {
        ZeroThrusters(2);
        PortThruster(2);
    }

    if (IsKeyDown(0x41)) // A key
    {
        ZeroThrusters(2);
        STBDThruster(2);
    }

    NewTime = timeGetTime();
    dt = (float) (NewTime - OldTime)/1000;
    OldTime = NewTime;

    if (dt > 0.016) dt = 0.016;
    if (dt < 0.001f) dt = 0.001f;
    StepSimulation(dt);

        .
        .
        .
}
```

Before StepSimulation is called, each of the flight control keys for each hovercraft is checked to see whether it is being pressed. If so, then the appropriate thrust or thruster function is called.

The function IsKeyDown that checks whether a certain key is pressed looks like this:

```
BOOL IsKeyDown(short KeyCode)
{
    SHORT   retval;

    retval = GetAsyncKeyState(KeyCode);
```

```
        if (HIBYTE(retval))
                return TRUE;

        return FALSE;
    }
```

I used this function because it is possible that more than one key will be pressed at any given time, and I wanted to handle them all simultaneously instead of one at a time in the standard window message processing function.

The addition of flight control code pretty much completes the physics part of the simulation. So far, you have the model, the integrator, and the user input or flight control elements completed. All that remains is setting up the application's main window and actually drawing something to look at that represents what you're simulating.

Rendering

Setting up the main window and drawing something interesting to look at aren't really related to physics; however, for completeness I'll briefly present the code that I used in this example to set up the main window and render the simulation using Direct3D.*

Starting with the main window, I used standard Windows API code to initialize the application, create and update the main window, and handle window messages and user input. I assume that you're are familiar with Windows API programming, so I won't go into a detailed explanation of the code.

I've already shown you part of the WinMain function; here's the whole thing:

```
int APIENTRY WinMain(HINSTANCE hInstance, HINSTANCE hPrevInstance, LPSTR
lpCmdLine, int nCmdShow)
{
    MSG msg;
    HANDLE hAccelTable;

    if (!hPrevInstance) {
        // Perform instance initialization:
        if (!InitApplication(hInstance)) {
            return (FALSE);
        }
    }

    // Perform application initialization:
    if (!InitInstance(hInstance, nCmdShow)) {
        return (FALSE);

    }

    hAccelTable = LoadAccelerators (hInstance, szAppName);

    OldTime = timeGetTime();
    NewTime = OldTime;
```

---

* If you aren't already familiar with programming Direct3D, you should check out the book entitled *The Awesome Power of Direct3D/DirectX* by Peter J. Kovack. Simply put, it's very useful.

```
    // Main message loop:
    while (1) {

        while(PeekMessage(&msg, NULL, 0, 0, PM_REMOVE)) {
            if (msg.message == WM_QUIT) {
                return msg.wParam;
            }
            TranslateMessage(&msg);
            DispatchMessage(&msg);
        }

        NullEvent();
    }

    return (msg.wParam);
}
```

WinMain makes calls to InitInstance and InitApplication. I've already shown you InitInstance, so here's InitApplication:

```
BOOL InitApplication(HINSTANCE hInstance)
{
    WNDCLASS   wc;
    HWND       hwnd;

    hwnd = FindWindow (szAppName, NULL);
    if (hwnd) {
        if (IsIconic(hwnd)) {
            ShowWindow(hwnd, SW_RESTORE);
        }
        SetForegroundWindow (hwnd);

        return FALSE;
    }

    wc.style         = CS_HREDRAW | CS_VREDRAW | CS_DBLCLKS;
    wc.lpfnWndProc   = (WNDPROC)WndProc;
    wc.cbClsExtra    = 0;
    wc.cbWndExtra    = 0;
    wc.hInstance     = hInstance;
    wc.hIcon         = NULL;
    wc.hCursor       = LoadCursor(NULL, IDC_ARROW);
    wc.hbrBackground = (HBRUSH)GetStockObject(BLACK_BRUSH);

    wc.lpszMenuName  = NULL;
    wc.lpszClassName = szAppName;

    return RegisterClass(&wc);
}
```

So far, this API code creates a window class for the main window, registers that class, creates and displays a 640 × 480 window, creates a couple of Direct3D objects that are needed to render into a Direct3D view port (these calls are in InitInstance), and starts the main program loop calling NullEvent each time.

The only other API function that's needed is the window message processing function, WndProc:

```
LRESULT CALLBACK WndProc(HWND hWnd,
                         UINT message,
                         WPARAM wParam,
                         LPARAM lParam)
{

    int          wmId, wmEvent;
    BOOL         validmenu = FALSE;
    int          selection =0;
    PAINTSTRUCT  ps;
    HDC          pDC;
    WPARAM       key;

    switch (message) {
        case WM_ACTIVATE:
            if (SUCCEEDED(D3D.Device->QueryInterface(
                        IID_IDirect3DRMWinDevice,
                        (void **) &WinDev)))
            {
                    if (FAILED(WinDev->HandleActivate(wParam)))
                        WinDev->Release();
            }

            break;

        case WM_DESTROY:
            CleanUp();
            PostQuitMessage(0);
            break;

        case WM_KEYDOWN:
            key = (int) wParam;

            if (key == 0x31) // 1
                SetCamera1();

            if (key == 0x32) // 2
                SetCamera2();

            if (key == 0x33) // 3
                SetCamera3();

            if (key == 0x34) // 4
                SetCamera4();

            if (key == 0x35) // 5
                SetCamera5();

            if (key == 0x36) // 6
                SetCamera6();

            break;

        case WM_PAINT:
                pDC = BeginPaint(hTheMainWindow, (LPPAINTSTRUCT) &ps);

                if (SUCCEEDED(D3D.Device->QueryInterface(
                            IID_IDirect3DRMWinDevice,
                            (void **) &WinDev)))
```

```
            {
                if (FAILED(WinDev->HandlePaint(ps.hdc)))
                    WinDev->Release();
            }

            EndPaint(hTheMainWindow, (LPPAINTSTRUCT) &ps);
            return (0);
        break;
        default:
            return (DefWindowProc(hWnd, message, wParam, lParam));
    }
    return (0);
}
```

In response to `WM_ACTIVATE`, this function acquires a IDirect3DRMWinDevice that's needed for using Direct3D retained mode.

In response to `WM_KEYDOWN`, this function switches to one of the six cameras that I've set up to view the simulation from different perspectives. Camera 1 is a view from the cockpit of hovercraft 1, camera 2 is a view from outside and just behind hovercraft 1, and camera 3 is a view from directly above looking down on hovercraft 1. Cameras 4, 5, and 6 are similar to cameras 1, 2, and 3 except that they are relative to hovercraft 2.

The response to `WM_PAINT` handles painting the scene to the main window. Finally, the response to `WM_DESTROY` cleans up all the Direct3D stuff and quits the application.

Before showing you the Direct3D code that I used, I need to show you yet another version of my `NullEvent` function:

```
void        NullEvent(void)
{
    Vector     vz, vx;
    char       buf[256];
    char       s[256];
    // figure out which flight control keys are down
    ZeroThrusters(1);

    if (IsKeyDown(VK_UP))
        IncThrust(1);

    if (IsKeyDown(VK_DOWN))
        DecThrust(1);

    if (IsKeyDown(VK_RIGHT))
    {
        ZeroThrusters(1);
        PortThruster(1);
    }

    if (IsKeyDown(VK_LEFT))
    {
        ZeroThrusters(1);
        STBDThruster(1);
    }

    ZeroThrusters(2);
```

```
if (IsKeyDown(0x57)) // W key
    IncThrust(2);

if (IsKeyDown(0x5A)) // Z key
    DecThrust(2);

if (IsKeyDown(0x53)) // S key
{
    ZeroThrusters(2);
    PortThruster(2);
}

if (IsKeyDown(0x41)) // A key
 {
    ZeroThrusters(2);
    STBDThruster(2);
}

NewTime = timeGetTime();
dt = (float) (NewTime - OldTime)/1000;
OldTime = NewTime;

if (dt > 0.016) dt = 0.016;
if (dt < 0.001f) dt = 0.001f;

StepSimulation(dt);

if(FrameCounter >= RENDER_FRAME_COUNT)
{
    SetCameraPosition(-Hovercraft1.vPosition.y,
                       Hovercraft1.vPosition.z,
                       Hovercraft1.vPosition.x);

    vz = GetBodyZAxisVector();   // pointing up in
                                 // our coordinate system
    vx = GetBodyXAxisVector(1); // pointing forward in
                                 // our coordinate system

    SetCameraOrientation(-vx.y, vx.z, vx.x,
                          -vz.y, vz.z, vz.x);

    SetCameraPosition2(-Hovercraft2.vPosition.y,
                        Hovercraft2.vPosition.z,
                        Hovercraft2.vPosition.x);

    vz = GetBodyZAxisVector(); // pointing up in
                               // our coordinate system
    vx = GetBodyXAxisVector(2); // pointing forward in
                                // our coordinate system

    SetCameraOrientation2(-vx.y, vx.z, vx.x,
                           -vz.y, vz.z, vz.x);

    Render();

    sprintf( buf, "Craft 1 (blue): T= %.0f ; ",
            Hovercraft1.ThrustForce);
    strcpy(s, buf);
    sprintf( buf, "S= %.0f ",
```

```
                    Hovercraft1.fSpeed/1.688); // divide by 1.688
                                               // to convert ft/s to knots
            strcat(s, buf);

            sprintf( buf,
                "       Craft 2 (red): T= %.0f ; ",
                Hovercraft2.ThrustForce);
            strcat(s, buf);
            sprintf( buf,
                "S= %.0f ",
                Hovercraft2.fSpeed/1.688);
                // divide by 1.688 to convert ft/s to knots

            strcat(s, buf);

            SetWindowText(hTheMainWindow, s);
        } else
            FrameCounter++;
    }
```

The code that you have not seen yet appears just after the call to StepSimulation. There are several things going on here.

First, I put in a frame counter check such that the rendering code is not executed as often as the physics code. This technique allows you to advance the physics simulation at a smaller time step without the overhead of updating the display at each time step. For this simulation I have RENDER_FRAME_COUNT set to 300 as follows:

```
#define    RENDER_FRAME_COUNT    300
```

This means that the physics simulation will take 300 time steps for every screen update. 300 works here, but it's not a practical number for production simulations. This simulation has only two bodies in it and, so far, no collision detection, so the physics calculations are fairly minimal. You'll have to tune this value to get the desired frame rate or physics-update-to-screen-update ratio for your specific simulations.

Next, the camera positions have to be updated to reflect to new location of each hovercraft. That's pretty easy to do, but you have to take note that the coordinate system used by Direct3D is not the same as the one used in the simulation. Direct3D uses a left-handed coordinate system with the x-axis pointing to the right, the y-axis pointing upward, and the z-axis pointing into the screen. Thus, Direct3D's x-axis is our negative y-axis, its y-axis is our z-axis, and its z-axis is our x-axis.

In addition to setting the proper location for each camera, you also have to make sure its orientation is correct. To do that, Direct3D requires a couple of vectors, one defining the frame's new z-axis and the other defining its new y-axis. To make things easier, I've prepared a couple of functions to get the correct x- and z-axis vectors for each hovercraft so that they can be used for Direct3D's z- and y-axis vectors, respectively, when setting the camera orientation to align with the orientation of each hovercraft. You'll want to do this, for example, when looking out of camera 1, which is a cockpit view from hovercraft 1; as the hovercraft rotates, you'll want the scene that you are viewing to reflect that rotation as if you were sitting in the hovercraft.

```
Vector     GetBodyZAxisVector(void)
{
    Vector     v;

    v.x = 0.0f;
    v.y = 0.0f;
    v.z = 1.0f;

    return v;
}

Vector     GetBodyXAxisVector(int     craft)
{
    Vector v;

    v.x = 1.0f;
    v.y = 0.0f;
    v.z = 0.0f;

    if(craft == 1)
        return VRotate2D(Hovercraft1.fOrientation, v);
    else
        return VRotate2D(Hovercraft2.fOrientation, v);
}
```

Getting back to the `NullEvent` function, after the cameras are positioned, the scene is actually rendered to the main window by calling the `Render` function. Once that's done, the window caption is changed to show a few statistics for each hovercraft, namely, each hovercraft's thrust setting in pounds and its speed in knots.

The rest of the code required for this simulation is related to rendering using Direct3D and has nothing directly to do with physics, so I have not included that code here. However, you can obtain the full source code for this example from O'Reilly's web site at *www.oreilly.com*.

CHAPTER 13

Implementing Collision Response

In this chapter I'll show you how to add a little excitement to the hovercraft example discussed in Chapter 12. Specifically, I'll show you how to add collision response so that the hovercraft can crash into each other and bounce off like a couple of bumper cars. This is an important element for many types of games, so it's important that you understand the code that I'll present here. Now would be a good time to go back and review Chapter 5 to refresh your memory on the fundamentals of rigid body collision response, since I'll use the principles and formulas discussed there to develop the collision response algorithms for the hovercraft simulation.

To start simply, I'll first show you how to implement collision response as if the hovercraft were a couple of particles—or a couple of spheres, to be more accurate. This approach uses only linear impulse and does not include angular effects, so the results will be somewhat unrealistic for these hovercraft. However, this approach is applicable to other types of problems that you might be interested in, such as billiard ball collisions.

After we get the linear impulse approach implemented, I'll go back and show you what you need to do to capture angular effects. This will make the simulation much more realistic. When the hovercraft crash into each other, not only will they bounce off of each other, but they will also spin, depending on the nature of the collision.

To get this stuff to work, I'll have to add a couple of new functions and make some significant changes to the StepSimulation function discussed in the preceding chapter. There's not a whole lot of new code, but it is a little more complicated, so I'll go through each new piece of code step by step to explain what's going on.

I also want to emphasize that the objective of this chapter is to show you how to implement basic collision *response*, which is a distinct subject, separate from collision *detection*. While collision detection is a necessary part of any collision response algorithm, collision detection is more of a computational geometry problem than a physics problem. Here, I will focus on physics—collision response—and will implement only the bare necessities in way of collision detection in order to get the simulation to work. If you're interested in more in-depth discussion on collision detection, I'll refer you to the computational geometry technical literature, where there is a wealth of information to be found.

Linear Collision Response

In this section I'll show you how to implement simple collision response assuming that the two hovercraft are particles (or spheres). I'm going to implement only bare minimum collision detection in this simulation; however, regardless of the level of sophistication of your collision detection routines, there are very specific pieces of information that must be collected from your collision detection routine(s) for your physics-based collision response routines to work.

To revise the hovercraft example of the previous chapter to include simple collision response, you'll have to modify the StepSimulation function and add a few more functions: CheckForCollision and ApplyImpulse. Let's take a good look at these functions now.

Before showing you CheckForCollision, I want to explain what your collision detection function must do. First, it must let you know whether or not a collision is occurring between the hovercraft. Second, it must let you know whether the hovercraft are penetrating each other. Third, if the hovercraft are colliding, it must tell you what the collision normal vector is and what the relative velocity is between the colliding hovercraft.

To determine whether or not there is a collision, you need to consider two factors:

- Whether or not the objects are close enough, within numerical tolerances, to be considered in colliding contact
- What the relative normal velocity is between the objects

If the objects aren't close to each other, they obviously have not collided. If they are within your tolerance for contact, then they may be colliding, and if they are touching and overlapping such that they are moving inside each other, they are penetrating, as illustrated in Figure 13-1. If your collision detection routine finds that the two objects

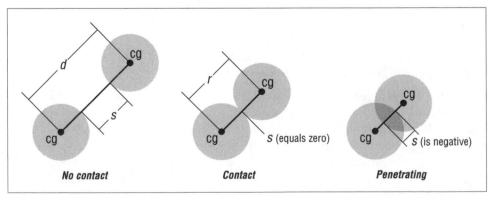

Figure 13-1. Collision Nomenclature

are indeed close enough to be in colliding contact, then you have to do another check on the relative normal velocity to see whether they are moving away from each other or toward each other. A collision occurs when the objects are in contact and the contact points are moving toward each other.

Penetration is important because if your objects overlap during the simulation, the results won't look realistic—you'll have one hovercraft moving inside the other as they did in the preceding chapter. What you have to do is detect this penetration condition and then back up your simulation, reduce the time step, and try again. You keep doing this until they are no longer penetrating or they are within tolerance to be considered colliding.

You need to determine the normal velocity vector of the collision to calculate the collision impulse that will be used to simulate their response to the collision. For simple cases, determining this normal vector is fairly straightforward. In the case of particles or spheres the collision normal is simply along the line that connects the centers of gravity of each colliding object; this is *central impact*, as discussed in Chapter 5. This is the situation you have here, since you are considering each hovercraft as a particle or sphere.

Now take a look at the function I've prepared for this simulation to check for collisions:

```
int     CheckForCollision (pRigidBody2D body1, pRigidBody2D body2)
{
    Vector    d;
    float     r;
    int       retval = 0;
    float     s;
    Vector    v1, v2;
    float     Vrn;

    r = body1->fLength/2 + body2->fLength/2;
    d = body1->vPosition - body2->vPosition;
    s = d.Magnitude() - r;

    d.Normalize();
    vCollisionNormal = d;

    v1 = body1->vVelocity;
    v2 = body2->vVelocity;
    vRelativeVelocity = v1 - v2;

    Vrn = vRelativeVelocity * vCollisionNormal;
    if((fabs(s) <= ctol) && (Vrn < 0.0))
    {
        retval = 1; // collision
    } else      if(s < -ctol)
    {
        retval = -1; // interpenetrating
    } else
        retval = 0; // no collision
    return retval;
}
```

This function uses a simple bounding circle check to determine whether or not the hovercraft are colliding. The first thing it does is calculate the distance, r, that represents the absolute minimum separation between these hovercraft when they are in contact.

I'm assuming that the bounding circle for each hovercraft has a diameter equal to the craft's length.

Next, the distance separating the hovercraft at the time this function is called is determined and stored in the variable d. Since I'm assuming that these hovercraft are particles, determining d is simply a matter of calculating the distance between the coordinates of the center of gravity of each craft. Using vectors, this is simply the position vector of one craft minus the position vector of the other.

Once the function has d and r, it needs to determine the actual amount of space, s, separating the hovercrafts' bounding circles. After this separation is determined, the function normalizes the vector d. Since the vector d is along the line that separates the centers of gravity of the hovercraft, normalizing it yields the collision normal vector that we need for our collision response calculations. The collision normal vector is saved in the global variable vCollisionNormal.

After calculating the collision normal, this function goes on to determine the relative velocity between the hovercraft. In vector form, this is simply the difference between the velocity vectors of each craft. Note that the velocity vectors that are used here must be in global coordinates, not body-fixed (local) coordinates. Since what's really needed to determine whether a collision is made is the relative *normal* velocity, the function proceeds to take the vector dot product of the relative velocity and the collision normal vectors, saving the result in the variable Vrn.

At this point, all of the calculations are complete, and the only thing left to do is make the appropriate checks to determine whether there is a collision, a penetration, or no collision at all.

The first check is to see whether the hovercraft are colliding. This is determined by comparing the absolute value of the separation between the hovercraft, s, with a distance tolerance, ctol. If the absolute value of s is less than ctol, a collision might be occurring. The second requirement is that the relative normal velocity be negative, which implies that the points of impact on the hovercraft are moving toward each other. If there is a collision, the function returns a 1 to indicate that collision response is necessary.

If the hovercraft are found not to be colliding, then a second check is performed to see whether they have moved so close together that they are penetrating each other. In this case, if s is less than -ctol, the hovercraft are penetrating and the function returns a -1. If the hovercraft are not colliding and not penetrating, then the function simply returns a 0, indicating that no further action is required.

Take a look now at the other new function, ApplyImpulse:

```
void        ApplyImpulse(pRigidBody2D body1, pRigidBody2D body2)
{
        float j;

        j =   (-(1+fCr) * (vRelativeVelocity*vCollisionNormal)) /
              ( (vCollisionNormal*vCollisionNormal) *
                (1/body1->fMass + 1/body2->fMass) );
```

```
        body1->vVelocity += (j * vCollisionNormal) / body1->fMass;
        body2->vVelocity -= (j * vCollisionNormal) / body2->fMass;
    }
```

This is a simple but crucial function for collision response. What it does is calculate the linear collision impulse as a function of the colliding hovercrafts' relative normal velocity, masses, and coefficient of restitution, using the formula that I showed you in Chapter 5. Further, it applies this impulse to each hovercraft, effectively changing their velocities in response to the collision. Note that the impulse is applied to one hovercraft, and then the negative impulse is applied to the other.

With those two new functions complete, it's now time to revise StepSimulation to handle collision detection and response as the simulation steps through time. Here's what the new StepSimulation function looks like:

```
void    StepSimulation(float dt)
{
    float       dtime = dt;
    bool        tryAgain = true;
    int             check=0;
    RigidBody2D     craft1Copy, craft2Copy;
    bool        didPen = false;
    int             count = 0;

    while(tryAgain && dtime > tol)
    {
        tryAgain = false;
        memcpy(&craft1Copy, &Hovercraft1, sizeof(RigidBody2D));
        memcpy(&craft2Copy, &Hovercraft2, sizeof(RigidBody2D));

        UpdateBody(&craft1Copy, dtime);
        UpdateBody(&craft2Copy, dtime);

        CollisionBody1 = 0;
        CollisionBody2 - 0;
        check = CheckForCollision(&craft1Copy, &craft2Copy);

        if(check == PENETRATING)
        {
            dtime = dtime/2;
            tryAgain = true;
            didPen = true;
        } else if(check == COLLISION)
        {
            if(CollisionBody1 != 0 && CollisionBody2 != 0)
                ApplyImpulse(CollisionBody1, CollisionBody2);
        }
    }
    if(!didPen)
    {
        memcpy(&Hovercraft1, &craft1Copy, sizeof(RigidBody2D));
        memcpy(&Hovercraft2, &craft2Copy, sizeof(RigidBody2D));
    }
}
```

Obviously, this version is more complicated than the original version. There's one main reason for this: penetration could occur because the hovercraft can move far enough within a single time step to become overlapped. Visually, this situation is unappealing and looks unrealistic, so you need to try to prevent it.

The first thing this function does is go into a `while` loop:

```
while(tryAgain && dtime > tol)
{
        .
        .
        .
}
```

This loop is used to back up the simulation if penetration has occurred on the initial time step. What happens is this: the function first tries to update the hovercraft and then checks to see whether there is a collision. If there is a collision, then it gets handled by applying the impulse. If there is penetration, however, then you know the time step was too big, and you have to try again. When this occurs, `tryAgain` is set to `true`, the time step is cut in half, and another attempt is made. The function stays in this loop as long as there is penetration or until the time step has been reduced to a size small enough to force an exit from the loop. The purpose of this looping is to find the largest step size, less than or equal to `dt`, that can be taken and still avoid penetration. You want either a collision or no collision.

Looking inside this `while` loop reveals what's going on. First, `tryAgain` is set to `false`, optimistically assuming that there will be no penetration, and copies are made of the states of the hovercraft reflecting the last successful call to `StepSimulation`.

Next, the usual call to `UpdateBody` is made for each copy of the hovercraft. Then a call to the collision detection function, `CheckForCollision`, is made to see whether `Hovercraft1` is colliding with or penetrating `Hovercraft2`. If there is penetration, then `tryAgain` is set to true, `dtime` is cut in half, `didPen` is set to true, and the function takes another lap through the `while` loop. `didPen` is a flag that lets us know that a penetration condition did occur.

If there was a collision, the function handles it by applying the appropriate impulse:

```
if(CollisionBody1 != 0 && CollisionBody2 != 0)
    ApplyImpulse(CollisionBody1, CollisionBody2);
```

After getting through the `while` loop, the updated hovercraft states are saved, and `StepSimulation` is complete.

The last bit of code you need to add includes a few new global variables and defines:

```
#define LINEARDRAGCOEFFICIENT    0.25f
#define     COEFFICIENTOFRESTITUTION    0.5f
#define     COLLISIONTOLERANCE          2.0f

Vector    vCollisionNormal;    // the collision normal
Vector    vRelativeVelocity;   // the world space relative velocity of the
                               //  two bodies at the point of collision
float     fCr = COEFFICIENTOFRESTITUTION;        // the coefficient of
restitution
float        const    ctol = COLLISIONTOLERANCE;  // the collision
(distance) tolerance
```

The only one I haven't mentioned so far, although you've seen it in `ApplyImpulse`, is `fCr`, the coefficient of restitution. Here, I have it set to 0.5, which means that the collisions are halfway between perfectly elastic and perfectly inelastic. (Refer back to my earlier discussions on coefficients of restitution in Chapter 5 if you've forgotten these terms.) This is one of those parameters that you'll have to tune to get the desired behavior.

While I'm on the subject of tuning, I should mention that you'll also have to play with the linear drag coefficient that is used to calculate the drag force on the hovercraft. While this coefficient is used to simulate fluid dynamic drag, it also plays an important role in terms of numerical stability. You need some damping in your simulation so that your integrator does not blow up, that is, diverge away from the theoretical solution to the governing equations of motion. When that happens, your simulator can become quite unrealistic and unpredictable. In Chapter 17, when I show you how to simulate cloth, the importance of damping will become quite clear.

That's pretty much it as far as implementing basic collision response. If you run this example, you'll be able to drive the hovercraft into each other and bounce off accordingly. You can play around with the mass of each hovercraft and the coefficient of restitution to see how the craft behave when one is more massive than the other or when the collision is somewhere in between perfectly elastic and perfectly inelastic.

You might notice that the collision response in this example sometimes looks a little strange. Keep in mind that this is because this collision response algorithm, so far, assumes that the hovercraft are round when in fact they are rectangular. This approach will work just fine for round objects such as billiard balls, but to get the level of realism required for nonround rigid bodies, you need to include angular effects. I'll show you that in the next section.

Angular Effects

Including angular effects will yield more realistic collision response for these rigid bodies, the hovercraft. To get this to work, you'll have to make several changes to `ApplyImpulse` and `CheckForCollision`; `StepSimulation` will remain unchanged. The more extensive changes are in `CheckForCollision`, so I'll discuss that one first.

The new version of `CheckForCollision` will do more than a simple bounding circle check. Here, each hovercraft will be represented by a polygon with four edges and four vertices, and the types of contact that will be checked for are vertex-vertex and vertex-edge contact (see Figure 13-2).*

In addition to the tasks discussed in the preceding section, this new version of `Check-ForCollision` must also determine the exact point of contact between the hovercraft. This is a very important distinction between this new version and the last. You need to

---

* Note that this function does not handle multiple contact points.

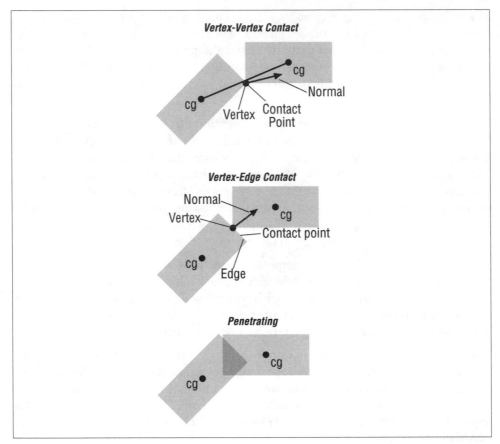

Figure 13-2. Types of Collision

know the point of contact because to affect the angular velocity, you need to apply the impulse at the point of contact. In the preceding section the normal to the contact point always passed through the center of gravity of the hovercraft because we assumed that they were spheres, and that's not the case here.

This now brings up the challenge of finding the collision normal. There are two cases to consider here. In edge-vertex collisions the normal is always perpendicular to the edge that is involved in the collision. In vertex-vertex collisions, however, the normal is ambiguous, so what I've done is resort to taking the normal parallel to the line connecting the centers of gravity of the hovercraft.

All of these considerations make CheckForCollisions a little more involved than it was in the previous section. The following code listing shows what I mean:

```
int     CheckForCollision(pRigidBody2D body1, pRigidBody2D body2)
{
    Vector  d;
    float   r;
    int     retval = 0;
```

```
float       s;
Vector      vList1[4], vList2[4];
float       wd, lg;
int         i,j;
bool        haveNodeNode = false;
bool        interpenetrating = false;
bool        haveNodeEdge = false;
Vector      v1, v2, u;
Vector      edge, p, proj;
float       dist, dot;
float       Vrn;

// First check to see if the bounding circles are colliding
r = body1->fLength/2 + body2->fLength/2;
d = body1->vPosition - body2->vPosition;
s = d.Magnitude() - r;

if(s <= ctol)
{    // We have a possible collision, check further
     // build vertex lists for each hovercraft
     wd = body1->fWidth;
     lg = body1->fLength;
     vList1[0].y = wd/2;          vList1[0].x = lg/2;
     vList1[1].y = -wd/2;         vList1[1].x = lg/2;
     vList1[2].y = -wd/2;         vList1[2].x = -lg/2;
     vList1[3].y = wd/2;          vList1[3].x = -lg/2;

     for(i=0; i<4; i++)
     {
          VRotate2D(body1->fOrientation, vList1[i]);
          vList1[i] = vList1[i] + body1->vPosition;
     }
     wd = body2->fWidth;
     lg = body2->fLength;
     vList2[0].y = wd/2;          vList2[0].x = lg/2;
     vList2[1].y = -wd/2;         vList2[1].x = lg/2;
     vList2[2].y = -wd/2;         vList2[2].x = -lg/2;
     vList2[3].y - wd/2;          vList2[3].x = -lg/2;

     for(i=0; i<4; i++)
     {
          VRotate2D(body2->fOrientation, vList2[i]);
          vList2[i] = vList2[i] + body2->vPosition;
     }

     // Check for vertex-vertex collision
     for(i=0; i<4 && !haveNodeNode; i++)
     {
          for(j=0; j<4 && !haveNodeNode; j++)
          {

               vCollisionPoint = vList1[i];
               body1->vCollisionPoint = vCollisionPoint -
                                        body1->vPosition;

               body2->vCollisionPoint = vCollisionPoint -
                                        body2->vPosition;

               vCollisionNormal = body1->vPosition -
                                  body2->vPosition;
```

```
                vCollisionNormal.Normalize();

                v1 = body1->vVelocityBody +
                    (body1->vAngularVelocity^body1->vCollisionPoint);

                v2 = body2->vVelocityBody +
                    (body2->vAngularVelocity^body2->vCollisionPoint);

                v1 = VRotate2D(body1->fOrientation, v1);
                v2 = VRotate2D(body2->fOrientation, v2);

                vRelativeVelocity = v1 - v2;
                Vrn = vRelativeVelocity * vCollisionNormal;

                if( ArePointsEqual(vList1[i],
                                   vList2[j]) &&
                    (Vrn < 0.0) )
                      haveNodeNode = true;

            }
        }

        // Check for vertex-edge collision
        if(!haveNodeNode)
        {
            for(i=0; i<4 && !haveNodeEdge; i++)
            {
                for(j=0; j<3 && !haveNodeEdge; j++)
                {
                    if(j==3)
                        edge = vList2[0] - vList2[j];
                    else
                        edge = vList2[j+1] - vList2[j];
                    u = edge;
                    u.Normalize();

                    p = vList1[i] - vList2[j];
                    proj = (p * u) * u;

                    d = p^u;
                    dist = d.Magnitude();

                    vCollisionPoint = vList1[i];
                    body1->vCollisionPoint = vCollisionPoint -
                                             body1->vPosition;

                    body2->vCollisionPoint = vCollisionPoint -
                                             body2->vPosition;

                    vCollisionNormal = ((u^p)^u);
                    vCollisionNormal.Normalize();

                    v1 = body1->vVelocityBody +
                        (body1->vAngularVelocity ^
                         body1->vCollisionPoint);

                    v2 = body2->vVelocityBody +
                        (body2->vAngularVelocity ^
                         body2->vCollisionPoint);
```

```
                v1 = VRotate2D(body1->fOrientation, v1);
                v2 = VRotate2D(body2->fOrientation, v2);

                vRelativeVelocity = (v1 - v2);
                Vrn = vRelativeVelocity * vCollisionNormal;

                if( (proj.Magnitude() > 0.0f) &&
                    (proj.Magnitude() <= edge.Magnitude()) &&
                    (dist <= ctol) &&
                    (Vrn < 0.0) )
                        haveNodeEdge = true;
            }
        }
    }

    // Check for penetration
    if(!haveNodeNode && !haveNodeEdge)
    {
        for(i=0; i<4 && !interpenetrating; i++)
        {
            for(j=0; j<4 && !interpenetrating; j++)
            {
                if(j==3)
                    edge = vList2[0] - vList2[j];
                else
                    edge = vList2[j+1] - vList2[j];
                p = vList1[i] - vList2[j];
                dot = p * edge;
                if(dot < 0)
                {
                    interpenetrating = true;
                }
            }
        }
    }

    if(interpenetrating)
    {
            retval = -1;
    } else if(haveNodeNode || haveNodeEdge)
    {
            retval = 1;
    } else
            retval = 0;

} else
{
    retval = 0;
}

    return retval;
}
```

The first thing that CheckForCollision does is perform a quick bounding circle check to see whether there is a possible collision. If no collision is detected, the function simply exists returning 0. This is the same bounding circle check that was performed in the earlier version:

```
r = body1->fLength/2 + body2->fLength/2;
d = body1->vPosition - body2->vPosition;
s = d.Magnitude() - r;

if(s <= ctol)
{
    .
    .
    .
} else
    retval = 0;
}
```

If the bounding circle check indicates the possibility of a collision, then `CheckForColli-sion` proceeds by setting up a couple of polygons, represented by vertex lists, for each hovercraft:

```
wd = body1->fWidth;
lg = body1->fLength;
vList1[0].y = wd/2;          vList1[0].x = lg/2;
vList1[1].y = -wd/2;         vList1[1].x = lg/2;
vList1[2].y = -wd/2;         vList1[2].x = -lg/2;
vList1[3].y = wd/2;          vList1[3].x = -lg/2;

for(i=0; i<4; i++)
{
    VRotate2D(body1->fOrientation, vList1[i]);
    vList1[i] = vList1[i] + body1->vPosition;
}

wd = body2->fWidth;
lg = body2->fLength;
vList2[0].y = wd/2;          vList2[0].x = lg/2;
vList2[1].y = -wd/2;         vList2[1].x = lg/2;
vList2[2].y = -wd/2;         vList2[2].x = -lg/2;
vList2[3].y = wd/2;          vList2[3].x = -lg/2;
for(i=0; i<4; i++)
{
    VRotate2D(body2->fOrientation, vList2[i]);
    vList2[i] = vList2[i] + body2->vPosition;
}
```

The vertex lists are initialized in unrotated body-fixed (local) coordinates based on the length and width of the hovercraft. The vertices are then rotated to reflect the orientation of each hovercraft. After that, the position of each hovercraft is added to each vertex to convert from local coordinates to global coordinates.

Checking first for vertex-vertex collisions, the function iterates through each vertex in one list, comparing it with each vertex in the other list to see whether the points are coincident:

```
// Check for vertex-vertex collision
for(i=0; i<4 && !haveNodeNode; i++)
{
    for(j=0; j<4 && !haveNodeNode; j++)
    {
```

```
        vCollisionPoint = vList1[i];
        body1->vCollisionPoint = vCollisionPoint -
                                 body1->vPosition;

        body2->vCollisionPoint = vCollisionPoint -
                                 body2->vPosition;

        vCollisionNormal = body1->vPosition -
                           body2->vPosition;

        vCollisionNormal.Normalize();

        v1 = body1->vVelocityBody +
             (body1->vAngularVelocity^body1->vCollisionPoint);

        v2 = body2->vVelocityBody +
             (body2->vAngularVelocity^body2->vCollisionPoint);

        v1 = VRotate2D(body1->fOrientation, v1);
        v2 = VRotate2D(body2->fOrientation, v2);

        vRelativeVelocity = v1 - v2;
        Vrn = vRelativeVelocity * vCollisionNormal;

        if( ArePointsEqual(vList1[i],
                           vList2[j]) &&
            (Vrn < 0.0) )
             haveNodeNode = true;


        }
    }
```

This comparison makes a call to another new function, `ArePointsEqual`:

```
    if( ArePointsEqual(vList1[i],
                       vList2[j]) &&
        (Vrn < 0.0) )
         haveNodeNode = true;
```

`ArePointsEqual` simply checks to see whether the points are within a specified distance from each other as shown here:

```
    bool    ArePointsEqual(Vector p1, Vector p2)
    {
        // Points are equal if each component is within ctol of each other
        if( (fabs(p1.x - p2.x) <= 0.1) &&
            (fabs(p1.y - p2.y) <= 0.1) &&
            (fabs(p1.z - p2.z) <= 0.1) )
            return true;
        else
            return false;
    }
```

Within the nested for loops of the vertex-vertex check, a number of important calculations are performed to determine the collision normal vector and relative velocity that are required for collision response.

First, the collision point is calculated, which is simply the coordinates of a vertex that is involved in the collision. Note that this point will be in global coordinates, so it will have to be converted to local coordinates for each hovercraft to be useful for collision response. Here is how that's done:

```
vCollisionPoint = vList1[i];
body1->vCollisionPoint = vCollisionPoint -
                         body1->vPosition;

body2->vCollisionPoint = vCollisionPoint -
                         body2->vPosition;
```

The second calculation is aimed at determining the collision normal vector, which for vertex-vertex collisions I've assumed is along the line connecting the centers of gravity of each hovercraft. The calculation is the same as that shown in the earlier version of CheckForCollision:

```
vCollisionNormal = body1->vPosition -
                   body2->vPosition;

vCollisionNormal.Normalize();
```

The third and final calculation is aimed at determining the relative velocity between the points of impact. This is an important distinction from the earlier version, since the velocities of the points of impact on each body are functions of the linear and angular velocities of the hovercraft:

```
v1 = body1->vVelocityBody +
     (body1->vAngularVelocity^body1->vCollisionPoint);

v2 = body2->vVelocityBody +
     (body2->vAngularVelocity^body2->vCollisionPoint);

v1 = VRotate2D(body1->fOrientation, v1);
v2 = VRotate2D(body2->fOrientation, v2);

vRelativeVelocity = v1 - v2;
Vrn = vRelativeVelocity * vCollisionNormal;
```

Here, v1 and v2 represent the velocities of the points of collision relative to each hovercraft in local coordinates, which are then converted to global coordinates. Once the relative velocity is obtained, vRelativeVelocity, the relative normal velocity, Vrn, is obtained by taking the dot product of the relative velocity with the collision normal vector.

If there is no vertex-vertex collision, CheckForCollision proceeds to check for vertex-edge collisions:

```
// Check for vertex-edge collision
if(!haveNodeNode)
{
    for(i=0; i<4 && !haveNodeEdge; i++)
    {
        for(j=0; j<3 && !haveNodeEdge; j++)
        {
            if(j==3)
                edge = vList2[0] - vList2[j];
            else
```

```
            edge = vList2[j+1] - vList2[j];
u = edge;
u.Normalize();

p = vList1[i] - vList2[j];
proj = (p * u) * u;

d = p^u;
dist = d.Magnitude();

vCollisionPoint = vList1[i];
body1->vCollisionPoint = vCollisionPoint -
                            body1->vPosition;

body2->vCollisionPoint = vCollisionPoint -
                            body2->vPosition;

vCollisionNormal = ((u^p)^u);
vCollisionNormal.Normalize();

v1 = body1->vVelocityBody +
     (body1->vAngularVelocity ^
       body1->vCollisionPoint);

v2 = body2->vVelocityBody +
     (body2->vAngularVelocity ^
       body2->vCollisionPoint);

v1 = VRotate2D(body1->fOrientation, v1);
v2 = VRotate2D(body2->fOrientation, v2);

vRelativeVelocity = (v1 - v2);
Vrn = vRelativeVelocity * vCollisionNormal;

if( (proj.Magnitude() > 0.0f) &&
    (proj.Magnitude() <= edge.Magnitude()) &&
    (dist <= ctol) &&
    (Vrn < 0.0) )
      haveNodeEdge = true;
        }
      }
    }
```

Here, the nested for loops check each vertex in one list to see whether it is in contact with each edge built from the vertices in the other list. After the edge under consideration is built, a copy of it is saved and normalized to represent a unit vector pointing along the edge:

```
if(j==3)
     edge = vList2[0] - vList2[j];
else
     edge = vList2[j+1] - vList2[j];
u = edge;
u.Normalize();
```

Variable u represents that unit vector, and it will be used in subsequent calculations. The next set of calculations determines the location of the projection of the vertex under consideration onto the edge under consideration, as well as the minimum distance from the vertex to the edge:

```
p = vList1[i] - vList2[j];
proj = (p * u) * u;

d = p^u;
dist = d.Magnitude();
```

Variable p is a vector from the first vertex on the edge to the vertex under consideration, and proj is the distance from the first edge vertex, along the edge, to the point upon which the vertex projects. dist is the minimum distance from the vertex to the edge. Figure 13-3 illustrates this geometry.

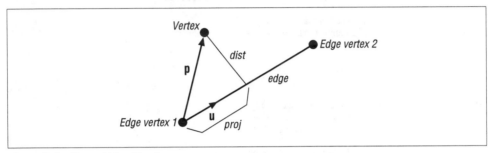

Figure 13-3. Vertex-Edge Check

If there is a collision, the global location of the point of impact is equal to the vertex under consideration, which must be converted to local coordinates for each hovercraft as shown here:

```
vCollisionPoint = vList1[i];
body1->vCollisionPoint = vCollisionPoint -
                         body1->vPosition;

body2->vCollisionPoint = vCollisionPoint -
                         body2->vPosition;
```

Since in this type of collision, the collision normal vector is perpendicular to the edge, you can determine it by taking the result of the cross product of u and p and crossing it with u as follows:

```
vCollisionNormal = ((u^p)^u);
vCollisionNormal.Normalize();
```

These calculations give you a unit length vector in the plane of vectors u and p and perpendicular to the edge.

Next, the relative velocity between the points of impact on each hovercraft is determined, just as in the vertex-vertex collision check:

```
v1 = body1->vVelocityBody +
     (body1->vAngularVelocity ^
      body1->vCollisionPoint);
```

```
v2 = body2->vVelocityBody +
    (body2->vAngularVelocity ^
     body2->vCollisionPoint);

v1 = VRotate2D(body1->fOrientation, v1);
v2 = VRotate2D(body2->fOrientation, v2);

vRelativeVelocity = (v1 - v2);
Vrn = vRelativeVelocity * vCollisionNormal;
```

In determining whether or not the vertex under consideration is in fact colliding with an edge, you have to check to see whether the distance from the vertex is within your collision tolerance, and you also have to make sure the vertex actually projects onto the edge (that is, it does not project beyond the endpoints of the edge). Additionally, you need to make sure the relative normal velocity indicates that the points of contact are moving toward each other. Here's how this check looks:

```
if( (proj.Magnitude() > 0.0f) &&
    (proj.Magnitude() <= edge.Magnitude()) &&
    (dist <= ctol) &&
    (Vrn < 0.0) )
    haveNodeEdge = true;
```

After `CheckForCollision` checks for vertex-vertex and vertex-edge collisions, it goes on to check for penetration:

```
if(!haveNodeNode && !haveNodeEdge)
{
    for(i=0; i<4 && !interpenetrating; i++)
    {
        for(j=0; j<4 && !interpenetrating; j++)
        {
            if(j==3)
                edge = vList2[0] - vList2[j];
            else
                edge = vList2[j+1] - vList2[j];

            p = vList1[i] - vList2[j];
            dot = p * edge;
            if(dot < 0)
            {
                interpenetrating = true;
            }
        }
    }
}
```

This check is a standard point-in-polygon check using the vector dot product to determine whether any vertex of one polygon lies within the bounds of the other polygon. After this check, the function simply returns the appropriate result. Here again, 0 indicates no collision or penetration, 1 indicates a collision, and -1 indicates penetration.

With `CheckForCollision` out of the way, turn your attention to `ApplyImpulse`, which also has to be revised to include angular effects. Specifically, you need to use the impulse formula that includes angular as well as linear effects (see Chapter 5), and you also have to apply the impulse to the hovercrafts' angular velocities in addition to their linear velocities. Here's how the new ApplyImpulse function looks:

```
void    ApplyImpulse(pRigidBody2D body1, pRigidBody2D body2)
{
    float j;

    j = (-(1+fCr) * (vRelativeVelocity*vCollisionNormal)) /
        ( (1/body1->fMass + 1/body2->fMass) +
        (vCollisionNormal * (((body1->vCollisionPoint ^
         vCollisionNormal)/body1->fInertia)^body1->vCollisionPoint)) +
        (vCollisionNormal * (((body2->vCollisionPoint ^
         vCollisionNormal)/body2->fInertia)^body2->vCollisionPoint))
        );

    body1->vVelocity += (j * vCollisionNormal) / body1->fMass;
    body1->vAngularVelocity += (body1->vCollisionPoint ^
                               (j * vCollisionNormal)) /
                               body1->fInertia;

    body2->vVelocity -= (j * vCollisionNormal) / body2->fMass;
    body2->vAngularVelocity -= (body2->vCollisionPoint ^
                               (j * vCollisionNormal)) /
                               body2->fInertia;
}
```

Remember, the impulse is applied to one hovercraft while its negative is applied to the other.

That does it for this new version of the hovercraft simulation. If you run the program now, you'll see that you can crash the hovercraft into each other and they will bounce and rotate accordingly. This makes for a much more realistic simulation than the simple linear collision response approach of the preceding section. Here again, you can play with the mass of each hovercraft and the coefficient of restitution to see how these parameters affect the collision response between the hovercraft.

CHAPTER 14

Rigid Body Rotation

Before showing you how to implement a 3D simulator, as I'll do in the next chapter, I need to discuss the issue of expressing orientation, or rotation, in three dimensions. In two dimensions it's quite easy to express the orientation of a rigid body; you need only a single scalar to represent the body's rotation about a single axis. In three dimensions, however, there are three primary coordinate axes, and a rigid body may rotate about each of them. Moreover, a rigid body in three dimensions may rotate about any arbitrary axis, not necessarily one of the coordinate axes.

In two dimensions we say that a rigid body has only one rotational degree of freedom, whereas in three dimensions we say that a rigid body has three rotational degrees of freedom. This might lead you to infer that in three dimensions you need to have three scalar quantities to represent a body's rotation. Indeed, this is a minimum requirement, and you've already seen a set of angles that represent the orientation of a rigid body in 3D—the three Euler angles that I talked about in Chapter 7: roll, pitch, and yaw.

These three angles—roll, pitch, and yaw—are very intuitive and easy to visualize. For example, in an airplane the nose pitches up or down, the plane rolls (or banks) left or right, and the yaw (or heading) changes to the left or right. Unfortunately, there's a problem with using these three Euler angles in rigid body simulations. The problem is a numerical one that occurs when the pitch angle reaches plus or minus 90 degrees ($\pi/2$). When this happens, roll and yaw become ambiguous. Worse yet, the angular equations of motion written in terms of Euler angles contain terms involving the cosine of the pitch angle in the denominator, which means that when the pitch angle is plus or minus 90 degrees, the equations become singular (there is division by zero). If this happens in your simulation, the results would be unpredictable, to say the least. Given this problem with Euler angles, you must use some other means of keeping track of orientation in your simulation. I'll discuss two such means in this chapter: rotation matrices and quaternions.

Virtually every computer graphics book that I've read contains a chapter or section on using rotation matrices. Far fewer discuss quaternions, but if you're familiar with quaternions, it's probably in the same context as rotation matrices, that is, how they are used to rotate 3D points, objects, scenes, points of view, and so on. In a simulation, however, you need to get a little more out of rotation matrices or quaternions and will use them in a different context that what you might be used to. Specifically, you need to keep track of a body's orientation in space and, moreover, the change in orientation over time. So it's in this light that I'll discuss rotation matrices and quaternions in the remainder of this chapter. I'll try to be as concise as possible so as not to cloud the water with the proofs and derivations that you can find in the texts I refer to in the bibliography.

Rotation Matrices

A rotation matrix is a 3×3 matrix that, when multiplied by a point, or vector, results in the rotation of that point about some axis, yielding a new set of coordinates. You can rotate points about axes in one coordinate system, or you can use rotation matrices to convert points from one coordinate system to another, where one is rotated relative to the other.

Rotating a vector by a rotation matrix is typically written as follows: If $\mathbf{v}$ is a vector and $\mathbf{R}$ is a rotation matrix, then $\mathbf{v}'$ is $\mathbf{v}$ rotated by $\mathbf{R}$ according to the following formula:

$$\mathbf{v}' = \mathbf{R}\mathbf{v}$$

Multiple rotation matrices reflecting multiple sequential rotations can be combined into a single rotation matrix using usual matrix multiplication. If the rotation matrices are expressed in terms of fixed, global coordinates, then they are combined as follows:

$$\mathbf{R}_c = \mathbf{R}_2\mathbf{R}_1$$

Here, $\mathbf{R}_c$ is the combined rotation matrix reflecting a rotation first by $\mathbf{R}_1$ and then by $\mathbf{R}_2$. If the rotation matrices are expressed in terms of rotating, body-fixed coordinates, then they are combined in the reverse order as follows:

$$\mathbf{R}_c = \mathbf{R}_1\mathbf{R}_2$$

I won't go into the proof of this relation, but the reason it's different, depending on how you have defined your rotation matrices, is that rotation matrices that are defined in fixed coordinates are unaffected by the rotation itself, since the coordinate axes stay fixed. On the other hand, if the rotation matrices are defined relative to a coordinate system that is rotating because of sequential application of rotation matrices, then all rotation matrices after the first will be affected, since they were first defined relative to the original state of the coordinate system, before the first rotation matrix was applied. This means that before the subsequent rotation matrices can be correctly applied, they must be corrected to reflect the new system as affected by the previous rotation. In other words, you have to rotate $\mathbf{R}_2$ by $\mathbf{R}_1$ to get a new $\mathbf{R}_2$ before applying it. All this happens to work out in such a way that you reverse the order of multiplication of rotation matrices when they are defined in a rotating coordinate system.

I'm sure that you've seen how rotation matrices are put together to reflect rotations about the three coordinate axes. However, I'll show you these matrices here just in case.

Figure 14-1 shows a right-handed coordinate system that illustrates the directions of positive rotation about each coordinate axis.

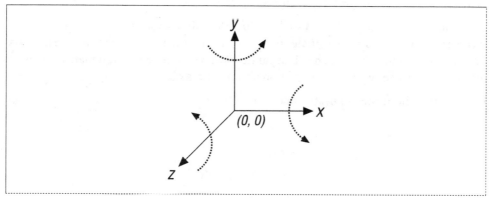

Figure 14-1. Right-Handed Coordinate System

Let's consider rotation around the z-axis where the point shown in Figure 14-2 is rotated through an angle θ.

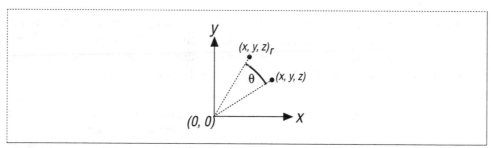

Figure 14-2. Rotation Around the z-axis

The coordinates of the point before the rotation are (x, y, z), and after the rotation the coordinates are (x_r, y_r, z_r). The rotated coordinates are related to the original coordinates and the rotation angle by the following:

$$x_r = x \cos\theta + y \sin\theta$$
$$y_r = -x \sin\theta + y \cos\theta$$
$$z_r = z$$

Notice that since the point is rotating about the z-axis, its z-coordinate remains unchanged. To write this in vector matrix notation, $\mathbf{v}' = \mathbf{R}\mathbf{v}$, let $\mathbf{v} = [x\,y\,z]$ and let $\mathbf{R}$ be the matrix

$$\begin{vmatrix} \cos(\theta_z) & -\sin(\theta_z) & 0 \\ \sin(\theta_z) & \cos(\theta_z) & 0 \\ 0 & 0 & 1 \end{vmatrix}$$

Here, $\mathbf{v'}$ will be the new, rotated vector, $\mathbf{v'} = [x_r\ y_r\ z_r]$.

Rotation about the x- and y-axes is similar to rotation about the z-axis; however, in those cases the x- and y-coordinates remain constant during rotations about each axis. Looking at rotation about each axis separately will yield three rotation matrices similar to the one I just showed you for rotation about the z-axis.

For rotation about the x-axis, the matrix is

$$\begin{vmatrix} 1 & 0 & 0 \\ 0 & \cos(\theta_x) & -\sin(\theta_x) \\ 0 & \sin(\theta_x) & \cos(\theta_x) \end{vmatrix}$$

And for rotation about the y-axis, the matrix is

$$\begin{vmatrix} \cos(\theta_y) & 0 & \sin(\theta_y) \\ 0 & 1 & 0 \\ -\sin(\theta_y) & 0 & \cos(\theta_y) \end{vmatrix}$$

These are the rotation matrices that you typically see in computer graphics texts in the context of matrix transforms, such as translation, scaling, and rotation. You can combine all three of these matrices into a single rotation matrix to represent combinations of rotations about each coordinate axis, using matrix multiplication as I mentioned earlier.

In rigid body simulations you can use a rotation matrix to represent the orientation of a rigid body. Another way to think of it is that the rotation matrix, when applied to the unrotated rigid body aligned with the fixed global coordinate system, will rotate the rigid body's coordinates so as to resemble the body's current orientation at any given time. This leads me to another important consideration when using rotation matrices to keep track of orientation in rigid body simulations: the fact that the rotation matrix will be a function of time.

Once you set up your initial rotation matrix for the rigid body, you'll never directly calculate it again from orientation angles; instead, the forces and moments applied to the rigid body will change the body's angular velocity, likewise causing small changes in orientation at each time step throughout the simulation. Thus, you can see that you must have a means of relating the rotation matrix to angular velocity so that you can update the orientation accordingly. The formula you need is as follows:

$$d\mathbf{R}/dt = \Omega\mathbf{R}$$

Here, Ω is a skew symmetric matrix built from the angular velocity vector components as follows:

$$\Omega = \begin{vmatrix} 0 & -\omega_z & \omega_y \\ \omega_z & 0 & -\omega_x \\ -\omega_y & \omega_x & 0 \end{vmatrix}$$

Notwithstanding a rigorous proof of this relation, it's easy to see its beauty, which is that you can differentiate the rotation matrix by simply matrix multiplying by the angular velocity (in the form of Ω). In a simulation you'll know your initial rotation matrix, and you'll calculate the angular velocity at each time step; thus, you can easily progress, or integrate, the rotation matrix.

You should be able to see here that since you'll explicitly calculate the rotation matrix only once and will update with a matrix multiplication, you won't have to use computationally expensive trigonometric functions during each time step. Further, you avoid the singularity problem that I mentioned in the introduction to this chapter.

It should also be obvious that you gain these benefits at some price. First, you have to deal with nine parameters in the rotation matrix (each element in the 3 × 3 rotation matrix) to represent three angular degrees of freedom. Second, to do that, you need to impose constraints on the rotation matrix; specifically, you need to enforce the constraint that the matrix be orthogonal with a determinant of 1 such that it satisfies the following (each column in the matrix represents a unit vector and they are all at right angles to each other)*:

$$\mathbf{R}^T\mathbf{R} = \mathbf{I}$$

Here, $\mathbf{R}^T$ is the transpose of $\mathbf{R}$, and $\mathbf{I}$ is the identity matrix. Owing to numerical errors such as round-off and truncation, you'll have to enforce this constraint very often in your simulation. Otherwise, your rotation matrix will do more than rotate your objects; it might scale or translate them too.

Instead of dealing with nine parameters and trying to constrain six degrees of freedom so that only the three you want can be represented, you could take an alternative approach that lets you keep the advantages that rotation matrices offer, but at a cheaper price. That alternative is the subject of the next section: quaternions.

Quaternions

Quaternions are somewhat of a mathematical oddity. They were developed over 100 years ago by William Hamilton through his work in complex (imaginary) math but have found very little practical use. A quaternion is a quantity, somewhat like a vector

---

* Two vectors are orthogonal if their dot product is zero.

but made up of four components. It is typically written in the form

$$\mathbf{q} = q_0 + q_x\mathbf{i} + q_y\mathbf{j} + q_z\mathbf{k}$$

A quaternion is really a four-dimensional quantity in complex space and, unfortunately, does not lend itself to visualization. Don't worry, though; our use of quaternions to represent orientation in three dimensions does allow us to attach a physical meaning to them, as you'll see in a moment.

Of particular interest to us is what's known as a unit quaternion that satisfies the following:

$$q_0^2 + q_x^2 + q_y^2 + q_z^2 = 1$$

This is analogous to a normalized, or unit, vector.

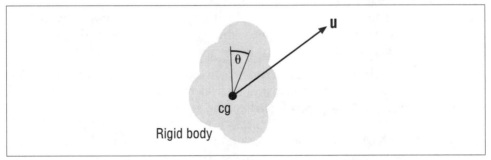

Figure 14-3. Quaternion Rotation

You can also write a quaternion in the form $\mathbf{q} = [q_0, \mathbf{v}]$, where $\mathbf{v}$ is the vector, $q_x\mathbf{i} + q_y\mathbf{j} + q_z\mathbf{k}$, and q_0 is a scalar. In the context of rotation, $\mathbf{v}$ represents the direction in which the axis of rotation points. For a given rotation, θ, about an arbitrary axis represented by the unit vector $\mathbf{u}$, the representative quaternion can be written as follows:

$$\mathbf{q} = [\cos(\theta/2), \sin(\theta/2)\mathbf{u}]$$

This is illustrated in Figure 14-3 for an arbitrary rigid body rotating about an axis passing through its center of gravity. Here, the unit vector $\mathbf{u}$ is the vector $\mathbf{v}$ normalized to unit length.

You can readily see that quaternions, when used to represent rotation or orientation, require you to deal with only four parameters instead of nine, subject to the easily satisfied constraint that the quaternion be a unit quaternion. In my opinion this makes quaternions the preferred choice over rotation matrices to represent orientation in rigid body simulations. In fact, this is the approach I take in the next chapter.

The use of quaternions to represent orientation is similar to how you would use rotation matrices. First, you set up a quaternion that represents the initial orientation of the rigid body at time zero. (This is the only time you'll calculate the quaternion explicitly.) Then you update the orientation to reflect the new orientation at a given instant in time, using the angular velocities that are calculated for that instant. The differential equation relating an orientation quaternion to angular velocity is very similar to that for rotation matrices and is as follows:

$$d\mathbf{q}/dt = (1/2)\boldsymbol{\omega}\mathbf{q}$$

Here, the angular velocity is written in quaternions form as $[0, \boldsymbol{\omega}]$ and is expressed in fixed, global coordinates. If $\boldsymbol{\omega}$ is expressed in rotating, body-fixed coordinates, then you need to use this equation:

$$d\mathbf{q}/dt = (1/2)\mathbf{q}\boldsymbol{\omega}$$

As can be done with rotation matrices, you can use quaternion to rotate points, or vectors. If $\mathbf{v}$ is a vector, then $\mathbf{v}'$ is the rotated vector subject to the quaternion $\mathbf{q}$:

$$\mathbf{v}' = \mathbf{q}\mathbf{v}\mathbf{q}^*$$

Here, $\mathbf{q}^*$ is the conjugate of the quaternion $\mathbf{q}$, defined as

$$\mathbf{q}^* = q_0 - q_x\mathbf{i} - q_y\mathbf{j} - q_z\mathbf{k}$$

You can also use the above formula to convert vectors from one coordinate system to another, where one is rotated relative to the other. You might have to do this, for example, in your simulations when you are converting forces defined in fixed, global coordinates to rotating, body-fixed coordinates so that you can apply the forces to the body. Or you might have to convert a body's velocity defined in global coordinates to body coordinates so that you can use the velocity in force calculations.

As with vectors and matrices, quaternions have their own rules for the various operations that you'll need, such as multiplication, addition, and subtraction. To make it easy on you, I've included sample code in Appendix C that implements all of the quaternion operations you'll need.

CHAPTER 15

3D Rigid Body Simulator

In this chapter I'll show you how to make the leap from 2D to 3D by implementing a rigid body simulation of an airplane. Specifically, this is a simulation of the hypothetical airplane model that I discussed extensively in Chapter 7. Recall that this airplane is of typical configuration with its large wings forward, its elevators aft, a single vertical tail, and plain flaps fitted on the wings.

Here again, the source code for this example is available on O'Reilly's web site, but I'll still include most of it in this chapter. As with the 2D simulator of Chapters 12 and 13, I'll concentrate on the code that implements the physics part of the simulator, and I'll refer you to O'Reilly's web site for the rest of the code that implements rendering using Microsoft's Direct3D technology.

Even though this is a 3D simulation, its implementation is very similar to the 2D hovercraft simulation that I showed you earlier. When I started talking about that 2D simulation, I mentioned that I was going to use a 3D vector class to represent the vectors even though they were 2D, to make the transition to 3D easier. Well, as it turns out, since I've done that, there's very little obvious difference—with the exception of the model, of course—between the code in the 2D simulation and the code in the 3D one that we'll be discussing here. Thus, you'll be familiar with a lot of the code presented herein after having already gone through Chapter 12.

As in 2D, there are four main elements to this 3D simulation: the model, integrator, user input, and rendering. Remember, the model refers to your idealization of the thing—an airplane, in this case—that you are trying to simulate, while the integrator refers to the method by which you integrate the differential equations of motion. These two elements take care of most of the physics of the simulation. The user input and rendering elements refer to how you'll allow the user to interact with and view your simulation. Here again, I'll use keyboard input for control and, as before, I'll use Direct3D for rendering.

In this simulation the world coordinate system has its x-axis pointing into the screen, its y-axis pointing to the left of your screen, and the z-axis pointing upward. Also, the local, or body-fixed, coordinate system has its x-axis pointing toward the front of the airplane, its *y*-axis pointing to the port side, and its *z*-axis pointing upward. Since this is a 3D simulation of an airplane, once you get it running, you'll be able to fly in any direction, looping, banking, diving, and, climbing, or performing any other aerobatic maneuver you desire.

Model

One of the most important aspects of this simulation is the flight model. I spent all of Chapter 7 discussing the physics behind this flight model, so I won't repeat the discussion here, except to refresh your memory on the pertinent source code. If you have not already read Chapter 7, then I suggest you go back now and take a look at it, at least the section entitled "Modeling."

To implement the flight model, you first need to prepare a rigid body structure to encapsulate all of the data required to completely define the state of the rigid body at any instant during the simulation. I've defined a structure called RigidBody for this purpose:

```
typedef struct _RigidBody {

    float       fMass;              // total mass
    Matrix3x3   mInertia;          // mass moment of inertia
                                   // in body coordinates

    Matrix3x3   mInertiaInverse;   // inverse of mass moment of inertia
    Vector      vPosition;         // position in earth coordinates
    Vector      vVelocity;         // velocity in earth coordinates
    Vector      vVelocityBody;     // velocity in body coordinates
    Vector      vAngularVelocity;  // angular velocity in body coordinates
    Vector      vEulerAngles;      // Euler angles in body coordinates
    float       fSpeed;            // speed (magnitude of the velocity)
    Quaternion  qOrientation;      // orientation in earth coordinates
    Vector      vForces;           // total force on body
    Vector      vMoments;          // total moment (torque) on body
} RigidBody, *pRigidBody;
```

You'll notice that it is very similar to the RigidBody2D structure that I used in the 2D hovercraft simulation. One significant difference, however, is that in the 2D case, orientation was a single float value, and now in 3D it's a quaternion of type Quaternion. I discussed the use of quaternions for tracking rigid body orientation in the preceding chapter, and Appendix C contains a complete definition of the Quaternion class.

The next step in defining the flight model is to prepare an initialization function to initialize the airplane at the start of the simulation. For this purpose I've prepared a function called InitializeAirplane:

```
RigidBody  Airplane;      // global variable representing the airplane
.
.
.

void       InitializeAirplane(void)
{
    float iRoll, iPitch, iYaw;
```

```
// Set initial position
Airplane.vPosition.x = -5000.0f;
Airplane.vPosition.y = 0.0f;
Airplane.vPosition.z = 2000.0f;

// Set initial velocity
Airplane.vVelocity.x = 60.0f;
Airplane.vVelocity.y = 0.0f;
Airplane.vVelocity.z = 0.0f;
Airplane.fSpeed = 60.0f;

// Set initial angular velocity
Airplane.vAngularVelocity.x = 0.0f;
Airplane.vAngularVelocity.y = 0.0f;
Airplane.vAngularVelocity.z = 0.0f;

// Set the initial thrust, forces, and moments
Airplane.vForces.x = 500.0f;
Airplane.vForces.y = 0.0f;
Airplane.vForces.z = 0.0f;
ThrustForce = 500.0;

Airplane.vMoments.x = 0.0f;
Airplane.vMoments.y = 0.0f;
Airplane.vMoments.z = 0.0f;

// Zero the velocity in body space coordinates
Airplane.vVelocityBody.x = 0.0f;
Airplane.vVelocityBody.y = 0.0f;
Airplane.vVelocityBody.z = 0.0f;

// Set these to false at first,
//you can control later using the keyboard
Stalling = false;
Flaps = false;

// Set the initial orientation
iRoll = 0.0f;
iPitch = 0.0f;
iYaw = 0.0f;
Airplane.qOrientation = MakeQFromEulerAngles(iRoll, iPitch, iYaw);

// Now go ahead and calculate the plane's mass properties
CalcAirplaneMassProperties();
}
```

This function sets the initial location, speed, attitude, and thrust for the airplane and goes on to calculate its mass properties by making a call to CalcAirplaneMassProperties. You've already seen this function in Chapter 7, where I discussed it in detail. I won't show the whole thing again here, but I do want to point out a portion of the code that is distinctly different from what you do in a 2D simulation, and that's the calculation of the moment of inertia tensor:

```
void     CalcAirplaneMassProperties(void)
{
     .
     .
     .
```

```
// Now calculate the moments and products of inertia for the
// combined elements.
// (This inertia matrix (tensor) is in body coordinates)
Ixx = 0;     Iyy = 0;     Izz = 0;
Ixy = 0;     Ixz = 0;     Iyz = 0;
for (i = 0; i< 8; i++)
{
    Ixx += Element[i].vLocalInertia.x + Element[i].fMass *
           (Element[i].vCGCoords.y*Element[i].vCGCoords.y +
           Element[i].vCGCoords.z*Element[i].vCGCoords.z);
    Iyy += Element[i].vLocalInertia.y + Element[i].fMass *
           (Element[i].vCGCoords.z*Element[i].vCGCoords.z +
           Element[i].vCGCoords.x*Element[i].vCGCoords.x);
    Izz += Element[i].vLocalInertia.z + Element[i].fMass *
           (Element[i].vCGCoords.x*Element[i].vCGCoords.x +
           Element[i].vCGCoords.y*Element[i].vCGCoords.y);
    Ixy += Element[i].fMass * (Element[i].vCGCoords.x *
           Element[i].vCGCoords.y);
    Ixz += Element[i].fMass * (Element[i].vCGCoords.x *
           Element[i].vCGCoords.z);
    Iyz += Element[i].fMass * (Element[i].vCGCoords.y *
           Element[i].vCGCoords.z);
}

// Finally, set up the airplane's mass and its inertia matrix and take
// the inverse of the inertia matrix
Airplane.fMass = mass;
Airplane.mInertia.e11 = Ixx;
Airplane.mInertia.e12 = -Ixy;
Airplane.mInertia.e13 = -Ixz;
Airplane.mInertia.e21 = -Ixy;
Airplane.mInertia.e22 = Iyy;
Airplane.mInertia.e23 = -Iyz;
Airplane.mInertia.e31 = -Ixz;
Airplane.mInertia.e32 = -Iyz;
Airplane.mInertia.e33 = Izz;

Airplane.mInertiaInverse = Airplane.mInertia.Inverse();
}
```

Recall that the airplane is modeled by a number of elements, each representing a different part of the airplane's structure—for example, the tail rudder, elevators, wings, and fuselage. The code highlighted here takes the mass properties of each element and combines them using the techniques discussed in Chapter 11 to come up with the combined inertia tensor for the entire aircraft. The important distinction between these calculations in a 3D simulation and the 2D simulation is that here the inertia is a tensor, and in 2D it is a single scalar.

InitializeAirplane is called at the very start of the program. I found it convenient to make the call right after the application's main window is created and shown, in this case in the standard Windows API InitInstance function as shown here:

```
BOOL InitInstance(HINSTANCE hInstance, int nCmdShow)
{
    hInst = hInstance;
    nShowCmd = nCmdShow;
```

```
hTheMainWindow = CreateWindow(szAppName,
                              szTitle,
                              WS_OVERLAPPEDWINDOW |
                              WS_CLIPCHILDREN | WS_CLIPSIBLINGS,
                              0, 0, 640, 480,
                              NULL, NULL, hInst, NULL);

if (!CreateD3DRMObject())
    return (FALSE);

if (!CreateD3DRMClipperObject(hTheMainWindow))
    return (FALSE);

if (!CreateViewPort(hTheMainWindow))
    return (FALSE);

ShowWindow(hTheMainWindow, nCmdShow);
UpdateWindow(hTheMainWindow);

InitializeAirplane();

return (TRUE);
}
```

The final part of the flight model has to do with calculating the forces and moments that act on the airplane at any given instant in time during the simulation. As in the 2D hovercraft simulation, without this sort of function, the airplane will do nothing. For this purpose I've defined a function called CalcAirplaneLoads, which is called at every step through the simulation. This function relies on a few other functions, namely, LiftCoefficient, DragCoefficient, RudderLiftCoefficient, and RudderDragCoefficient. All of these functions are shown and discussed in detail in the section of Chapter 7 entitled "Modeling."

For the most part, the code contained in CalcAirplaneLoads is similar to the code you saw in the CalcLoads function of the hovercraft simulation. CalcAirplanLoads is a little more involved, since the airplane is modeled by a number of elements that contribute to the total lift and drag on the airplane. There's also another difference, which I've highlight here:

```
void      CalcAirplaneLoads(void)
{
    .
    .
    .


    // Convert forces from model space to earth space
    Airplane.vForces = QVRotate(Airplane.qOrientation, Fb);

    // Apply gravity (g is defined as -32.174 ft/s^2)
    Airplane.vForces.z += g * Airplane.fMass;

    .
    .
    .
}
```

Just about all of the forces acting on the airplane are first calculated in body-fixed coordinates and then converted to earth coordinates before the gravity force is applied.

The coordinate conversion is effected through the use of the function QVRotate, which rotates the force vector based on the airplane's current orientation represented by a quaternion.*

Integration

Now that the code to define, initialize, and calculate loads on the airplane is complete, you need to develop the code to actually integrate the equations of motion so that the simulation can progress through time. The first thing you need to do is decide on the integration scheme that you want to use. In this example I decided to go with the basic Euler method. I've already discussed some better methods in Chapter 11 and indeed implemented one of those methods in the 2D simulation of Chapters 12 and 13. I'm going with Euler's method here because it's simple, and I didn't want to make the code here overly complex, burying some key code that I need to point out to you. That said, I've prepared a function called StepSimulation that handles all of the integration necessary to actually propagate the simulation.

```
void      StepSimulation(float dt)
{
    // Take care of translation first:
    // (If this body were a particle, this is all you would need to do.)

        Vector Ae;

        // calculate all of the forces and moments on the airplane:
        CalcAirplaneLoads();

        // calculate the acceleration of the airplane in earth space:
        Ae = Airplane.vForces / Airplane.fMass;

        // calculate the velocity of the airplane in earth space:
        Airplane.vVelocity += Ae * dt;

        // calculate the position of the airplane in earth space:
        Airplane.vPosition += Airplane.vVelocity * dt;

    // Now handle the rotations:
        float            mag;

        // calculate the angular velocity of the airplane in body space:
        Airplane.vAngularVelocity += Airplane.mInertiaInverse *
                            (Airplane.vMoments -
                            (Airplane.vAngularVelocity^
                            (Airplane.mInertia *
                              Airplane.vAngularVelocity)))
                            * dt;

        // calculate the new rotation quaternion:
        Airplane.qOrientation += (Airplane.qOrientation *
                            Airplane.vAngularVelocity) *
                            (0.5f * dt);
```

---

* QVRotate is defined in Appendix C.

```
// now normalize the orientation quaternion:
mag = Airplane.qOrientation.Magnitude();
if (mag != 0)
    Airplane.qOrientation /= mag;

// calculate the velocity in body space:
// (we'll need this to calculate lift and drag forces)
Airplane.vVelocityBody = QVRotate(~Airplane.qOrientation,
                                  Airplane.vVelocity);

// calculate the air speed:
Airplane.fSpeed = Airplane.vVelocity.Magnitude();

// get the Euler angles for our information
Vector u;

u = MakeEulerAnglesFromQ(Airplane.qOrientation);
Airplane.vEulerAngles.x = u.x;        // roll
Airplane.vEulerAngles.y = u.y;        // pitch
Airplane.vEulerAngles.z = u.z;        // yaw
```

```
}
```

The very first thing that StepSimulation does is call CalcAirplaneLoads to calculate the loads acting on the airplane at the current instant in time. StepSimulation then goes on to calculate the linear acceleration of the airplane based on current loads. Next, the function goes on to integrate, using Euler's method, once to calculate the airplane's linear velocity and then a second time to calculate the airplane's position. As I've commented in the code, if you were simulating a particle, then this is all you would have to do. However, since this is not a particle, you need to handle angular motion.

The first step in handling angular motion is to calculate the new angular velocity at this time step, using Euler integration, based on the previously calculated moments acting on the airplane and its mass properties. This is done in body coordinates by using the equation of motion that I discussed previously:

$$\sum \mathbf{M}_{cg} = d\mathbf{H}_{cg}/dt = \mathbf{I}(d\boldsymbol{\omega}/dt) + [\boldsymbol{\omega} \times (\mathbf{I}\boldsymbol{\omega})]$$

The next step is to integrate again to update the airplane's orientation, which is expressed as a quaternion. Here, you need to use the differential equation relating an orientation quaternion to angular velocity that I showed you in the preceding chapter:

$$d\mathbf{q}/dt = (1/2)\boldsymbol{\omega}\mathbf{q}$$

Next to enforce the constraint that this orientation quaternion be a unit quaternion, the function normalizes the orientation quaternion.

Since the linear velocity was previously calculated in global coordinates (the fixed coordinate system), and since CalcAirplaneLoads needs the velocity in the body-fixed (rotating) coordinates system, the function rotates the velocity vector, storing the body-fixed vector in the vVelocityBody member of the RigidBody structure. This is done here as a matter of convenience and uses the quaternion rotation function QVRotate to rotate the vector on the basis of the airplane's current orientation. Notice here that the conjugate of the orientation quaternion is used, since we're now rotating from global coordinates to body coordinates.

As another convenience, the air speed is calculated, which is simply the magnitude of the linear velocity vector. This is used to report the air speed in the main window title bar.

Finally, the three Euler angles—roll, pitch, and yaw—are extracted from the orientation quaternion so that they can also be reported in the main window title bar. The function to use here is `MakeEulerAnglesFromQ`, which is defined in Appendix C.

`StepSimulation` is called once per game loop cycle. In this example I set up another function called `NullEvent` that gets called every time through the main window message loop as shown here:

```
int APIENTRY WinMain(HINSTANCE hInstance,
                     HINSTANCE hPrevInstance,
                     LPSTR lpCmdLine,
                     int nCmdShow)
{
.
.
.

    OldTime = timeGetTime();
    NewTime = OldTime;
    // Main message loop:
    while (1) {

        while(PeekMessage(&msg, NULL, 0, 0, PM_REMOVE)) {
            if (msg.message == WM_QUIT) {
                return msg.wParam;
            }
            TranslateMessage(&msg);
            DispatchMessage(&msg);
        }

        NullEvent();

    }
.
.
.
}
```

When `NullEvent` calls `StepSimulation`, it passes the size of the time step in as the `dt` parameter. As with the hovercraft example, you don't have to do it this way. I chose to because I was experimenting with having the time step calculated in real time as the difference in time between the last call to `StepSimulation` and the current time as shown here:

```
void      NullEvent(void)
{
.
.
.
```

```
NewTime = timeGetTime();
dt - (float) (NewTime - OldTime)/1000;
OldTime = NewTime;

if (dt > (0.016f)) dt = (0.016f);
if (dt < 0.001f) dt = 0.001f;

StepSimulation(dt);
    .
    .
    .
    .
}
```

Here again, I bracket the time step with the upper limit governed by numerical stability and the lower limit by the timer accuracy. You'll have to tune these limits for your simulations on the basis of your integration technique and chosen timer.

Flight Controls

At this point, the simulation still won't work right because you have not implemented the flight controls. The flight controls allow you to interact with the airplane's various controls surfaces to actually fly the plane. I'll use the keyboard as the main input device for the flight controls. Remember, in a physics-based simulation such as this one, you don't directly control the motion of the airplane; you control only how various forces are applied to the airplane, which then, by integration over time, affect the motion of the airplane.

For this simulation the flight stick is simulated by the arrow keys. The down arrow pulls back on the stick, raising the nose; the up arrow pushes the stick forward, causing the nose to dive; the left arrow rolls the plane to the left (port side); and the right arrow rolls the plane to the right (starboard side). The X key applies left rudder action to cause the nose of the plane to yaw toward the left, and the C key applies right rudder action to cause the nose to yaw toward the right. Thrust is controlled by the A and Z keys. The A key increments the propeller thrust by 100 lb, and the Z key decrements the thrust by 100 lb. The minimum thrust is zero, and the maximum available thrust is 3000 lb. The F key activates the landing flaps to increase lift at low speed, and the D key deactivates the landing flaps.

Pitch is affected by deflecting the flaps on the aft elevators; for example, to pitch the nose up, the aft elevator flaps are deflected upward, that is, the trailing edge of the elevator is raised with respect to the leading edge. Roll is affected in this simulation by applying the flaps differentially; for example, to roll right, the right flap deflects upward and the left flap deflects downward. Yaw is affected by deflecting the vertical tail rudder; for example, to yaw left, the trailing edge of the tail rudder is deflected toward the left.

I've prepared several functions to handle the flight controls that should be called whenever the user is pressing one of the flight control keys. There are two functions for the propeller thrust:

```
void      IncThrust(void)
{
     ThrustForce += _DTHRUST;
     if(ThrustForce > _MAXTHRUST)
          ThrustForce = _MAXTHRUST;


}

void      DecThrust(void)
{
     ThrustForce -= _DTHRUST;
     if(ThrustForce < 0)
          ThrustForce = 0;
}
```

IncThrust simply increases the thrust by _DTHRUST checking to make sure it does not exceed _MAXTHRUST. I've defined _DTHRUST and _MAXTHRUST as follows:

```
#define      _DTHRUST      100.0f
#define      _MAXTHRUST    3000.0f
```

DecThrust, on the other hand, decreases the thrust by _DTHRUST, checking to make sure it does not fall below zero.

To control yaw, I've prepared three functions that manipulate the rudder:

```
void      LeftRudder(void)
{
     Element[6].fIncidence = 16;
}

void      RightRudder(void)
{
     Element[6].fIncidence = -16;
}

void      ZeroRudder(void)
{
     Element[6].fIncidence = 0;
}
```

LeftRudder changes the incidence angle of Element[6], the vertical tail rudder, to 16 degrees; RightRudder changes the incidence angle to −16 degrees. ZeroRudder centers the rudder at zero degrees.

The ailerons, or flaps, are manipulated by these functions to control roll:

```
void      RollLeft(void)
{
     Element[0].iFlap = 1;
     Element[3].iFlap = -1;
}

void      RollRight(void)
```

```
{
    Element[0].iFlap = -1;
    Element[3].iFlap = 1;
}

void    ZeroAilerons(void)
{
    Element[0].iFlap = 0;
    Element[3].iFlap = 0;
}
```

RollLeft deflects the port aileron, located on the port wing section (Element[0]), upward and deflects the starboard aileron, located on the starboard wing section (Element[3]), downward. RollRight does just the opposite, and ZeroAilerons resets the flaps back to their undeflected positions.

I've defined yet another set of functions to control the aft elevators so as to control pitch:

```
void    PitchUp(void)
{
    Element[4].iFlap = 1;
    Element[5].iFlap = 1;
}

void    PitchDown(void)
{
    Element[4].iFlap = -1;
    Element[5].iFlap = -1;
}

void    ZeroElevators(void)
{
    Element[4].iFlap = 0;
    Element[5].iFlap = 0;
}
```

Element[4] and Element[5] are the elevators. PitchUp deflects their flaps upward, and PitchDown deflects their flaps downward. ZeroElevators resets their flaps back to their undeflected positions.

Finally, there are two more functions to control the landing flaps:

```
void    FlapsDown(void)
{
    Element[1].iFlap = -1;
    Element[2].iFlap = -1;
    Flaps = true;
}

void    ZeroFlaps(void)
{
    Element[1].iFlap = 0;
    Element[2].iFlap = 0;
    Flaps = false;
}
```

The landing flaps are fitted on the inboard wings sections, port and starboard, which are Element[1] and Element[2], respectively. FlapsDown deflects the flaps downward, and ZeroFlaps resets them back to their undeflected position.

As I said, these functions should be called when the user is pressing the flight control keys. Further, they need to be called before StepSimulation is called so that they can be included in the current time step's forces and moments calculations. Since I put the StepSimulation call in my NullEvent function, it makes sense to handle the flight controls in that function as well. Here's how I did it:

```
void      NullEvent(void)
{
.
.
.

      ZeroRudder();
      ZeroAilerons();
      ZeroElevators();

      // pitch down
      if (IsKeyDown(VK_UP))
            PitchDown();

      // pitch up
      if (IsKeyDown(VK_DOWN))
            PitchUp();

      // roll left
      if (IsKeyDown(VK_LEFT))
            RollLeft();

      // roll right
      if (IsKeyDown(VK_RIGHT))
            RollRight();

      // Increase thrust
      if (IsKeyDown(0x41)) // A
            IncThrust();

      // Decrease thrust
      if (IsKeyDown(0x5A)) // Z
            DecThrust();

      // yaw left
      if (IsKeyDown(0x58)) // x
            LeftRudder();

      // yaw right
      if (IsKeyDown(0x43)) // c
            RightRudder();

      // landing flaps down
      if (IsKeyDown(0x46)) //f
            FlapsDown();

      // landing flaps up
      if (IsKeyDown(0x44)) // d
            ZeroFlaps();

      NewTime = timeGetTime();
      dt = (float) (NewTime - OldTime)/1000;
      OldTime = NewTime;
```

```
        if (dt > (0.016f)) dt = (0.016f);
        if (dt < 0.001f) dt = 0.001f;

        StepSimulation(dt);

        .
        .
        .
}
```

Before `StepSimulation` is called, each of the flight control keys is checked to see whether it is being pressed. If so, then the appropriate function is called.

The function `IsKeyDown` that checks whether a certain key is pressed looks like this:

```
BOOL IsKeyDown(short KeyCode)
{

    SHORT  retval;

    retval = GetAsyncKeyState(KeyCode);

    if (HIBYTE(retval))
            return TRUE;

    return FALSE;
}
```

I used this function because it is possible that more than one key will be pressed at any given time, and I wanted to handle them all simultaneously instead of one at a time in the standard window message processing function.

The addition of flight control code pretty much completes the physics part of the simulation. So far, you have the model, the integrator, and the user input or flight control elements completed. All that remains is setting up the application's main window and actually drawing something to look at that represents what you're simulating.

Rendering

Setting up the main window and drawing something interesting to look at isn't really related to physics. However, for completeness I'll briefly present the code that I used in this example to set up the main window and render the simulation using Direct3D.*

Starting with the main window, I used standard Windows API code to initialize the application, create and update the main window, and handle window messages and user input. I assume that you're are familiar with Windows API programming, so I won't go into detailed explanation of the code.

---

* If you aren't already familiar with programming Direct3D, you should check out the book entitled *The Awesome Power of Direct3D/DirectX* by Peter J. Kovack. Simply put, it's very useful.

I've already shown you part of the `WinMain` function, but here's the whole thing:

```c
int APIENTRY WinMain(HINSTANCE hInstance, HINSTANCE hPrevInstance, LPSTR
lpCmdLine, int nCmdShow)
{
    MSG msg;
    HANDLE hAccelTable;

    if (!hPrevInstance) {
        // Perform instance initialization:
        if (!InitApplication(hInstance)) {
            return (FALSE);
        }
    }

    // Perform application initialization:
    if (!InitInstance(hInstance, nCmdShow)) {
        return (FALSE);
    }

    hAccelTable = LoadAccelerators (hInstance, szAppName);

    OldTime = timeGetTime();
    NewTime = OldTime;
    // Main message loop:
    while (1) {

        while(PeekMessage(&msg, NULL, 0, 0, PM_REMOVE)) {
            if (msg.message == WM_QUIT) {
                return msg.wParam;
            }
            TranslateMessage(&msg);
            DispatchMessage(&msg);
        }

        NullEvent();
    }

    return (msg.wParam);
}
```

`WinMain` makes calls to `InitInstance` and `InitApplication`. I've already shown you `InitInstance`, so here's `InitApplication`:

```c
BOOL InitApplication(HINSTANCE hInstance)
{
    WNDCLASS wc;
    HWND     hwnd;

    hwnd = FindWindow (szAppName, NULL);
    if (hwnd) {
        if (IsIconic(hwnd)) {
            ShowWindow(hwnd, SW_RESTORE);
        }
        SetForegroundWindow (hwnd);

        return FALSE;
    }
```

```
wc.style          = CS_HREDRAW | CS_VREDRAW | CS_DBLCLKS;
wc.lpfnWndProc    = (WNDPROC)WndProc;
wc.cbClsExtra     = 0;
wc.cbWndExtra     = 0;
wc.hInstance      = hInstance;
wc.hIcon          = NULL;
wc.hCursor        = LoadCursor(NULL, IDC_ARROW);
wc.hbrBackground  = (HBRUSH)GetStockObject(BLACK_BRUSH);

wc.lpszMenuName = NULL;
wc.lpszClassName = szAppName;

return RegisterClass(&wc);
}
```

So far this API code creates a window class for the main window, registers that class, creates and displays a 640 × 480 window, creates a couple of Direct3D objects that are needed to render into a Direct3D view port (these calls are in InitInstance), and starts the main program loop, calling NullEvent each time.

The only other API function that's needed is the window message processing function, WndProc:

```
LRESULT CALLBACK WndProc(HWND hWnd,
                         UINT message,
                         WPARAM wParam,
                         LPARAM lParam)
{
    int           wmId, wmEvent;
    BOOL          validmenu = FALSE;
    int           selection = 0;
    PAINTSTRUCT   ps;
    HDC           pDC;
    WPARAM        key;

    switch (message) {
        case WM_ACTIVATE:
            if (SUCCEEDED(D3D.Device->QueryInterface(
                        IID_IDirect3DRMWinDevice,
                        (void **) &WinDev)))
            {
                    if (FAILED(WinDev->HandleActivate(wParam)))
                        WinDev->Release();
            }

            break;

        case WM_DESTROY:
            CleanUp();
            PostQuitMessage(0);
            break;

        case WM_KEYDOWN:
            key = (int) wParam;

            if (key == 0x31) // 1 key
                SetCamera1();
```

```
                if (key == 0x32) // 2 key
                    SetCamera2();

                if (key == 0x33) // 3 key
                    SetCamera3();

            break;

        case WM_PAINT:
                pDC = BeginPaint(hTheMainWindow, (LPPAINTSTRUCT) &ps);

                if (SUCCEEDED(D3D.Device->QueryInterface(
                            IID_IDirect3DRMWinDevice,
                            (void **) &WinDev)))
                {
                    if (FAILED(WinDev->HandlePaint(ps.hdc)))
                        WinDev->Release();
                }

                EndPaint(hTheMainWindow, (LPPAINTSTRUCT) &ps);
                return (0);
            break;

        default:
                return (DefWindowProc(hWnd, message, wParam, lParam));
    }
    return (0);
}
```

In response to WM_ACTIVATE, this function acquires a IDirect3DRMWinDevice that's needed for using Direct3D retained mode.

In response to WM_KEYDOWN, this function switches to one of the three cameras that I've set up to view the simulation from different perspectives. Camera 1 is a view from the cockpit of the airplane, camera 2 is a view from outside and just behind plane, and camera 3 is a view from the global origin that always looks at the airplane and follows its movement.

The response to WM_PAINT handles painting the scene to the main window. Finally, the response to WM_DESTROY cleans up all the Direct3D stuff and quits the application.

Now I need to show you yet another version of my NullEvent function:

```
void    NullEvent(void)
{
    Vector  vz, vx;
    char    buf[256];
    char    s[256];

    ZeroRudder();
    ZeroAilerons();
    ZeroElevators();

    // pitch down
    if (IsKeyDown(VK_UP))
        PitchDown();
```

```
    // pitch up
    if (IsKeyDown(VK_DOWN))
        PitchUp();

    // roll left
    if (IsKeyDown(VK_LEFT))
        RollLeft();

    // roll right
    if (IsKeyDown(VK_RIGHT))
        RollRight();

    // Increase thrust
    if (IsKeyDown(0x41)) // A
        IncThrust();

    // Decrease thrust
    if (IsKeyDown(0x5A)) // Z
        DecThrust();

    // yaw left
    if (IsKeyDown(0x58)) // x
        LeftRudder();

    // yaw right
    if (IsKeyDown(0x43)) // c
        RightRudder();

    // landing flaps down
    if (IsKeyDown(0x46)) //f
        FlapsDown();

    // landing flaps up
    if (IsKeyDown(0x44)) // d
        ZeroFlaps();

    NewTime = timeGetTime();
    dt = (float) (NewTime - OldTime)/1000;
    OldTime = NewTime;

    if (dt > (0.016f)) dt = (0.016f);
    if (dt < 0.001f) dt = 0.001f;

    StepSimulation(dt);

if(FrameCounter >= RENDER_FRAME_COUNT)
{
    // Direct3D x = - our y
    // Direct3D y = our z
    // Direct3D z = our x
    SetCameraPosition( -Airplane.vPosition.y,
                        Airplane.vPosition.z,
                        Airplane.vPosition.x);

    vz = GetBodyZAxisVector(); // pointing up in our coordinate system
    vx = GetBodyXAxisVector(); // pointing forward
                               // in our coordinate system

    SetCameraOrientation(-vx.y, vx.z, vx.x, -vz.y, vz.z, vz.x);
    Render();
```

```
            OldTime = NewTime;

            // Report stats in window title
            sprintf( buf, "Roll= %.2f ; ", Airplane.vEulerAngles.x);
            strcpy(s, buf);
            // take negative here, since pilots like to see
            //positive pitch as nose up:
            sprintf( buf, "Pitch= %.2f ; ", -Airplane.vEulerAngles.y);
            strcat(s, buf);
            sprintf( buf, "Yaw= %.2f , ", Airplane.vEulerAngles.z);
            strcat(s, buf);
            sprintf( buf, "Alt= %.0f ; ", Airplane.vPosition.z);
            strcat(s, buf);
            sprintf( buf, "T= %.0f ; ", ThrustForce);
            strcat(s, buf);
            sprintf( buf, "S= %.0f ", Airplane.fSpeed/1.688); // divide by 1.688
                                                              // to convert
                                                              // ft/s to knots
            strcat(s, buf);
            if(Flaps)
                 strcat(s, "; Flaps");

            if(Stalling)
            {
                 strcat(s, "; Stall!");
                 Beep(10000, 250);
            }

            SetWindowText(hTheMainWindow, s);
        } else
            FrameCounter++;
    }
```

The code that you have not seen yet appears just after the call to StepSimulation. There
are several things going on here.

First, the camera positions have to be updated to reflect to new location of the plane.
That's pretty easy to do, but remember from the 2D hovercraft example that you have to
take note that the coordinate system used by Direct3D is not the same as the one used in
the simulation. Direct3D uses a left-handed coordinate system with the x-axis pointing
to the right, the y-axis pointing upward, and the z-axis pointing into the screen. Thus,
Direct3D's x-axis is our negative y-axis, its y-axis is our z-axis, and its z-axis is our
x-axis.

In addition to setting the proper location for each camera, you also have to make sure
its orientation is correct. To do that, Direct3D requires a couple of vectors, one defining
the frame's new z-axis and the other defining its new y-axis. To make things easier, I've
prepared a couple of functions to get the correct x- and z-axis vectors for the airplane
so that they can be used for Direct3D's z- and y-axis vectors, respectively, when setting
the camera orientation to align with the orientation of airplane. You'll want to do this,
for example, when looking out of camera 1, which is a cockpit view; as the plane rolls,
pitches, or yaws, you'll want the scene that you are viewing to reflect that movement as
if you were sitting in the airplane:

```
Vector      GetBodyZAxisVector(void)
{

    Vector      v;

    v.x = 0.0f;
    v.y = 0.0f;
    v.z = 1.0f;

    return QVRotate(Airplane.qOrientation, v);
}

Vector      GetBodyXAxisVector(void)
{
    Vector v;

    v.x = 1.0f;
    v.y = 0.0f;
    v.z = 0.0f;

    return QVRotate(Airplane.qOrientation, v);

}
```

Getting back to the `NullEvent` function, after the cameras are positioned, the scene is actually rendered to the main window by calling the `Render` function. Once that's done, the window caption is changed to show a few statistics, namely, the three Euler angles, propeller thrust, and air speed. Further, if the landing flaps are down, then the word "flaps" will appear in the title bar, and if a stall condition is encountered, the word "stall" will appear.

Notice here that I'm using the same technique that I applied in the 2D hovercraft example of advancing the physics simulation more often than the display. Again, you'll have to adjust the physics update to display update for you own specific simulations.

The rest of the code required for this simulation is related to rendering using Direct3D and has nothing directly to do with physics, so I have not included that code here. However, you can obtain the full source code for this example from O'Reilly's web site at *www.oreilly.com*.

CHAPTER 16

Multiple Bodies in 3D

In this chapter I'll show you how to handle multiple rigid bodies along with collision response in three dimensions. The example that I'll show you here is a simulation of a car crashing into a couple of test blocks. Figure 16-1 is a snapshot of the simulation just after impact.

This example is set up to automatically cycle through three different crash scenarios corresponding to different block arrangements.* You can view the simulation from different camera angles by pressing the keyboard buttons 1, 2, and 3 corresponding to views from the car's center of gravity, from outside and behind the car, and from outside on the left side of the car, respectively.

This example uses a lot of the same code as the flight simulation example presented in the previous chapter, so I won't repeat the shared code here. Instead, I'll highlight the specific sections of code that are unique to this example. The procedure for handling this simulation is very similar to the simulations that I've already discussed; the steps are as follows:

- Set up a rigid body structure to store the state information for each object.
- Setup an array of rigid bodies.
- Initialize the objects.
- Calculate the forces on each object at each time step.
- Integrate to update each object's velocity and position.
- Handle any collisions.

In the next several sections I'll address each of these steps. After that I'll discuss tuning the simulation. I'll also discuss the limitations of this simulation and recommend some improvements.

---

* I want to remind you that the source and executable files for all the examples discussed in this book are available on the O'Reilly web site.

Figure 16-1. Impact Simulation

Model

The purpose of this simulation is not to show you how to model specific objects in detail, like the flight simulation of the last chapter, so I'm going to use simple models in this example. What I want to emphasize here is how to handle multiple objects, and I don't want to clutter that issue with complex initialization and force calculations. Later, in your own simulations, you can develop highly detailed models of the specific object(s) that you're trying to simulate using the techniques that I've discussed earlier in this book combined with those presented in this chapter.

Initialization

Let's start by taking a look at the `RigidBody` structure that will be used to keep track of the state of each object in the simulation:

```
//----------------------------------------------------------------------------
//
// Rigid body structure
//----------------------------------------------------------------------------
//
typedef struct _RigidBody {
```

```
float           fMass;              // total mass (constant)
Matrix3x3       mInertia;           // mass moment of inertia
                                    // in body coordinates
Matrix3x3       mInertiaInverse;    // inverse of mass
                                    // moment of inertia matrix

Vector          vPosition;          // position in earth coordinates
Vector          vVelocity;          // velocity in earth coordinates
Vector          vVelocityBody;      // velocity in body coordinates
Vector          vAcceleration;      // acceleration of cg
                                    // in earth space
Vector          vAngularAcceleration; // angular acceleration
                                    // in body coordinates
Vector          vAngularVelocity;   // angular velocity in
                                    // body coordinates
Vector          vEulerAngles;       // Euler angles in body coordinates
float           fSpeed;             // speed
Quaternion      qOrientation;       // orientation in earth coordinates

Vector          vForces;            // total force on body
Vector          vMoments;           // total moment (torque) on body

Matrix3x3       mIeInverse;         // inverse of moment of
                                    // inertia in earth coordinates

float           fRadius;
Vector          vVertexList[8];

} RigidBody, *pRigidBody;
```

For the most part, this structure is identical to the one shown in Chapter 15's flight simulation example but with a few additions. Since we'll be handling collisions in the simulation, I've added fRadius and vVertexList[8] to the structure. fRadius stores the radius of the minimum bounding sphere for the object, which is used in an initial bounding sphere collision check, and vVertexList[8] is a list of vertices that will be used to represent the body's *hard points*, that is, the points that will be used for collision detection.

I've also added vAcceleration and vAngularAcceleration to store the object's linear and angular acceleration, respectively. We'll need these values to handle the contact forces between the objects and the ground when they are sitting on the ground but not colliding with it. I'll talk more about this in a moment.

Now that you have the structure defined, you can go ahead and set up an array of rigid bodies as follows:

```
#define         NUMBODIES                                           3
RigidBody       Bodies[NUMBODIES];
```

At the start of the simulation you need to initialize all the objects. In this example I've set up a function called InitializeObjects for this purpose:

```
//----------------------------------------------------------------------------//
// This function sets the initial state of the objects
//----------------------------------------------------------------------------//
void    InitializeObjects(int      configuration)
```

```
{
    float   iRoll, iPitch, iYaw;
    int     i;
    float   Ixx, Iyy, Izz;
    float   s;

    // Initialize the car:
    // Set initial position
    Bodies[0].vPosition.x = -50.0f;
    Bodies[0].vPosition.y = 0.0f;
    Bodies[0].vPosition.z = CARHEIGHT/2.0f;

    // Set initial velocity
    switch(configuration)
    {
        case 0: s = 110.0f; break; // ft/s
        case 1: s = 120.0f; break; // ft/s
        case 2: s = 115.0f; break; // ft/s
    }
    Bodies[0].vVelocity.x = s;
    Bodies[0].vVelocity.y = 0.0f;
    Bodies[0].vVelocity.z = 0.0f;
    Bodies[0].fSpeed = s;

    // Set initial angular velocity
    Bodies[0].vAngularVelocity.x = 0.0f;
    Bodies[0].vAngularVelocity.y = 0.0f;
    Bodies[0].vAngularVelocity.z = 0.0f;

    Bodies[0].vAngularAcceleration.x = 0.0f;
    Bodies[0].vAngularAcceleration.y = 0.0f;
    Bodies[0].vAngularAcceleration.z = 0.0f;

    Bodies[0].vAcceleration.x = 0.0f;
    Bodies[0].vAcceleration.y = 0.0f;
    Bodies[0].vAcceleration.z = 0.0f;

    // Set the initial thrust, forces, and moments
    Bodies[0].vForces.x = 0.0f;
    Bodies[0].vForces.y = 0.0f;
    Bodies[0].vForces.z = 0.0f;
    ThrustForce = 0.0;

    Bodies[0].vMoments.x = 0.0f;
    Bodies[0].vMoments.y = 0.0f;
    Bodies[0].vMoments.z = 0.0f;

    // Zero the velocity in body space coordinates
    Bodies[0].vVelocityBody.x = 0.0f;
    Bodies[0].vVelocityBody.y = 0.0f;
    Bodies[0].vVelocityBody.z = 0.0f;

    // Set the initial orientation
    iRoll = 0.0f;
    iPitch = 0.0f;
    iYaw = 0.0f;
    Bodies[0].qOrientation = MakeQFromEulerAngles(iRoll, iPitch, iYaw);

    // Set the mass properties
    Bodies[0].fMass = 2000.0f/(-g);
```

```
Ixx = Bodies[0].fMass/12.0f *
    (CARWIDTH*CARWIDTH + CARHEIGHT*CARHEIGHT);
Iyy = Bodies[0].fMass/12.0f *
    (CARHEIGHT*CARHEIGHT + CARLENGTH*CARLENGTH);
Izz = Bodies[0].fMass/12.0f *
    (CARWIDTH*CARWIDTH + CARLENGTH*CARLENGTH);

Bodies[0].mInertia.e11 = Ixx;
Bodies[0].mInertia.e12 = 0;
Bodies[0].mInertia.e13 = 0;
Bodies[0].mInertia.e21 = 0;
Bodies[0].mInertia.e22 = Iyy;
Bodies[0].mInertia.e23 = 0;
Bodies[0].mInertia.e31 = 0;
Bodies[0].mInertia.e32 = 0;
Bodies[0].mInertia.e33 = Izz;

Bodies[0].mInertiaInverse = Bodies[0].mInertia.Inverse();

Bodies[0].fRadius = CARLENGTH/2; // for bounding sphere check

// bounding verteces relative to CG (assumed centered here for now)
Bodies[0].vVertexList[0].x = CARLENGTH/2.0f;
Bodies[0].vVertexList[0].y = CARWIDTH/2.0f;
Bodies[0].vVertexList[0].z = -CARHEIGHT/2.0f;

Bodies[0].vVertexList[1].x = CARLENGTH/2.0f;
Bodies[0].vVertexList[1].y = CARWIDTH/2.0f;
Bodies[0].vVertexList[1].z = CARHEIGHT/2.0f;

Bodies[0].vVertexList[2].x = CARLENGTH/2.0f;
Bodies[0].vVertexList[2].y = -CARWIDTH/2.0f;
Bodies[0].vVertexList[2].z = CARHEIGHT/2.0f;

Bodies[0].vVertexList[3].x = CARLENGTH/2.0f;
Bodies[0].vVertexList[3].y = -CARWIDTH/2.0f;
Bodies[0].vVertexList[3].z = -CARHEIGHT/2.0f;

Bodies[0].vVertexList[4].x = -CARLENGTH/2.0f;
Bodies[0].vVertexList[4].y = CARWIDTH/2.0f;
Bodies[0].vVertexList[4].z = -CARHEIGHT/2.0f;

Bodies[0].vVertexList[5].x = -CARLENGTH/2.0f;
Bodies[0].vVertexList[5].y = CARWIDTH/2.0f;
Bodies[0].vVertexList[5].z = CARHEIGHT/2.0f;

Bodies[0].vVertexList[6].x = -CARLENGTH/2.0f;
Bodies[0].vVertexList[6].y = -CARWIDTH/2.0f;
Bodies[0].vVertexList[6].z = CARHEIGHT/2.0f;

Bodies[0].vVertexList[7].x = -CARLENGTH/2.0f;
Bodies[0].vVertexList[7].y = -CARWIDTH/2.0f;
Bodies[0].vVertexList[7].z = -CARHEIGHT/2.0f;

ThrustForce = 0.0f;

// Initialize the blocks

for(i=1; i<NUMBODIES; i++)
```

```
{
    // Set initial position
    switch(configuration)
    {
        case 2:
            if(i==1)
            {
                Bodies[i].vPosition.x = BLOCKSIZE*4;
                Bodies[i].vPosition.y = -(BLOCKSIZE/2.0f+1.0f);
                Bodies[i].vPosition.z = BLOCKSIZE/2.0f;
            } else {
                Bodies[i].vPosition.x = 0.0f;
                Bodies[i].vPosition.y = 0.0f;
                Bodies[i].vPosition.z = BLOCKSIZE/2.0f;
            }
            break;

        case 1:
            if(i==1)
            {
                Bodies[i].vPosition.x = BLOCKSIZE*4;
                Bodies[i].vPosition.y = -(BLOCKSIZE/2.0f+1.0f);
                Bodies[i].vPosition.z = BLOCKSIZE/2.0f;
            } else {
                Bodies[i].vPosition.x = 0.0f;
                Bodies[i].vPosition.y = BLOCKSIZE/2.0f+1.0f;
                Bodies[i].vPosition.z = BLOCKSIZE/2.0f;
            }
            break;

        case 0:
            if(i==1)
            {
                Bodies[i].vPosition.x = BLOCKSIZE+1.0f;
                Bodies[i].vPosition.y = BLOCKSIZE/2.0f+1.0f;
                Bodies[i].vPosition.z = BLOCKSIZE/2.0f;
            } else {
                Bodies[i].vPosition.x = 0.0f;
                Bodies[i].vPosition.y = BLOCKSIZE/2.0f+1.0f;
                Bodies[i].vPosition.z = BLOCKSIZE/2.0f;
            }
            break;
    }

    // Set initial velocity
    Bodies[i].vVelocity.x = 0.0f;
    Bodies[i].vVelocity.y = 0.0f;
    Bodies[i].vVelocity.z = 0.0f;
    Bodies[i].fSpeed = 0.0f;

    // Set initial angular velocity
    Bodies[i].vAngularVelocity.x = 0.0f;
    Bodies[i].vAngularVelocity.y = 0.0f;
    Bodies[i].vAngularVelocity.z = 0.0f;

    Bodies[i].vAngularAcceleration.x = 0.0f;
    Bodies[i].vAngularAcceleration.y = 0.0f;
    Bodies[i].vAngularAcceleration.z = 0.0f;

    Bodies[i].vAcceleration.x = 0.0f;
    Bodies[i].vAcceleration.y = 0.0f;
    Bodies[i].vAcceleration.z = 0.0f;
```

```
// Set the initial thrust, forces and moments
Bodies[i].vForces.x = 0.0f;
Bodies[i].vForces.y = 0.0f;
Bodies[i].vForces.z = 0.0f;

Bodies[i].vMoments.x = 0.0f;
Bodies[i].vMoments.y = 0.0f;
Bodies[i].vMoments.z = 0.0f;

// Zero the velocity in body space coordinates
Bodies[i].vVelocityBody.x = 0.0f;
Bodies[i].vVelocityBody.y = 0.0f;
Bodies[i].vVelocityBody.z = 0.0f;

// Set the initial orientation
iRoll = 0.0f;
iPitch = 0.0f;
if(configuration == 2)
    iYaw = 45.0f;
else
    iYaw = 0.0f;
Bodies[i].qOrientation = MakeQFromEulerAngles(iRoll,
                                             iPitch,
                                             iYaw);

// Set the mass properties
Bodies[i].fMass = 500.0f/(-g);
Ixx = Iyy = Izz = Bodies[i].fMass/12.0f *
                (BLOCKSIZE*BLOCKSIZE + BLOCKSIZE*BLOCKSIZE);

Bodies[i].mInertia.e11 = Ixx;
Bodies[i].mInertia.e12 = 0;
Bodies[i].mInertia.e13 = 0;
Bodies[i].mInertia.e21 = 0;
Bodies[i].mInertia.e22 = Iyy;
Bodies[i].mInertia.e23 = 0;
Bodies[i].mInertia.e31 = 0;
Bodies[i].mInertia.e32 = 0;
Bodies[i].mInertia.e33 = Izz;

Bodies[i].mInertiaInverse = Bodies[i].mInertia.Inverse();

Bodies[i].fRadius = BLOCKSIZE/2; // for bounding sphere check

// bounding verteces relative to CG (assumed centered)
Bodies[i].vVertexList[0].x = BLOCKSIZE/2.0f;
Bodies[i].vVertexList[0].y = BLOCKSIZE/2.0f;
Bodies[i].vVertexList[0].z = -BLOCKSIZE/2.0f;

Bodies[i].vVertexList[1].x = BLOCKSIZE/2.0f;
Bodies[i].vVertexList[1].y = BLOCKSIZE/2.0f;
Bodies[i].vVertexList[1].z = BLOCKSIZE/2.0f;

Bodies[i].vVertexList[2].x = BLOCKSIZE/2.0f;
Bodies[i].vVertexList[2].y = -BLOCKSIZE/2.0f;
Bodies[i].vVertexList[2].z = BLOCKSIZE/2.0f;

Bodies[i].vVertexList[3].x = BLOCKSIZE/2.0f;
Bodies[i].vVertexList[3].y = -BLOCKSIZE/2.0f;
Bodies[i].vVertexList[3].z = -BLOCKSIZE/2.0f;
```

```
        Bodies[i].vVertexList[4].x = -BLOCKSIZE/2.0f;
        Bodies[i].vVertexList[4].y = BLOCKSIZE/2.0f;
        Bodies[i].vVertexList[4].z = -BLOCKSIZE/2.0f;

        Bodies[i].vVertexList[5].x = -BLOCKSIZE/2.0f;
        Bodies[i].vVertexList[5].y = BLOCKSIZE/2.0f;
        Bodies[i].vVertexList[5].z = BLOCKSIZE/2.0f;

        Bodies[i].vVertexList[6].x = -BLOCKSIZE/2.0f;
        Bodies[i].vVertexList[6].y = -BLOCKSIZE/2.0f;
        Bodies[i].vVertexList[6].z = BLOCKSIZE/2.0f;

        Bodies[i].vVertexList[7].x = -BLOCKSIZE/2.0f;
        Bodies[i].vVertexList[7].y = -BLOCKSIZE/2.0f;
        Bodies[i].vVertexList[7].z = -BLOCKSIZE/2.0f;
    }

}
```

This is a long function, but it's really quite simple. All it does is initialize each parameter in the `RigidBody` structure for each body, where body [0] is the car.

The `configuration` parameter that's passed into the function is used to control which of the three different crash scenarios is initialized.

I would also like to point out that I'm assuming that each object's moment of inertia, including the car's, can be approximated as a rectangular cylinder (a box). Therefore, you can use the inertia formulas for a rectangular cylinder that I gave you back in Chapter 1.

Forces and Moments

As I said earlier, I'm using a simplified approach to handling the forces that act the objects in this simulation. There are four basic loads that I consider:

- Thrust (for the car only)
- Aerodynamic drag (linear and angular)
- Gravity
- Contact with the ground plane

All of these loads are taken care of in the function `CalcObjectForces`:

```
//------------------------------------------------------------------------------
//
// This function calculates all of the forces and moments acting on the objects at
// any given time.
//------------------------------------------------------------------------------
//
void    CalcObjectForces(void)
{
    Vector      Fb, Mb;
    Vector      vDragVector;
    Vector      vAngularDragVector;
    int         i, j;
    Vector      ContactForce;
    Vector      pt;
    int         check = NOCOLLISION;
```

```
pCollision  pCollisionData; // used for contact forces here
Vector      FrictionForce;
Vector      fDir;

for(i=0; i<NUMBODIES; i++)
{
    // reset forces and moments:
    Bodies[i].vForces.x = 0.0f;
    Bodies[i].vForces.y = 0.0f;
    Bodies[i].vForces.z = 0.0f;

    Bodies[i].vMoments.x = 0.0f;
    Bodies[i].vMoments.y = 0.0f;
    Bodies[i].vMoments.z = 0.0f;

    Fb.x = 0.0f;        Mb.x = 0.0f;
    Fb.y = 0.0f;        Mb.y = 0.0f;
    Fb.z = 0.0f;        Mb.z = 0.0f;

    // Define the thrust vector, which acts through the CG
    if(i==0)
    {
        Thrust.x = 1.0f;
        Thrust.y = 0.0f;
        Thrust.z = 0.0f;
        Thrust *= ThrustForce;
        Fb += Thrust;
    }

    // Do drag force
    vDragVector = -Bodies[i].vVelocityBody;
    vDragVector.Normalize();
    Fb += vDragVector * (Bodies[i].fSpeed * Bodies[i].fSpeed * rho *
        LINEARDRAGCOEFFICIENT * Bodies[i].fRadius *
        Bodies[i].fRadius);

    vAngularDragVector = -Bodies[i].vAngularVelocity;
    vAngularDragVector.Normalize();
    Mb += vAngularDragVector *
        (Bodies[i].vAngularVelocity.Magnitude() *
        Bodies[i].vAngularVelocity.Magnitude() * rho *
        ANGULARDRAGCOEFFICIENT * Bodies[i].fRadius *
        Bodies[i].fRadius);

    // Convert forces from model space to earth space
    Bodies[i].vForces = QVRotate(Bodies[i].qOrientation, Fb);

    // Apply gravity
    Bodies[i].vForces.z += GRAVITY * Bodies[i].fMass;

    // Save the moments
    Bodies[i].vMoments += Mb;

    // Handle contacts with ground plane
    Bodies[i].vAcceleration = Bodies[i].vForces / Bodies[i].fMass;
    Bodies[i].vAngularAcceleration = Bodies[i].mInertiaInverse *
                                (Bodies[i].vMoments -
                                (Bodies[i].vAngularVelocity ^
                                (Bodies[i].mInertia *
                                 Bodies[i].vAngularVelocity)));
```

```
pCollisionData = Collisions;
NumCollisions = 0;
check = CheckGroundPlaneContacts(pCollisionData, i);
if(check == CONTACT)
{// have contact....
    for(j=0; j<NumCollisions; j++)
    {
        ContactForce = (Bodies[i].fMass/NumCollisions * (
                        -Collisions[j].vRelativeAcceleration *
                        Collisions[j].vCollisionNormal)) *
                        Collisions[j].vCollisionNormal;
        FrictionForce = (ContactForce.Magnitude() *
                        FRICTIONCOEFFICIENT) *
                        Collisions[j].vCollisionTangent;
        Bodies[i].vForces += ContactForce;
        Bodies[i].vForces += FrictionForce;
        ContactForce = QVRotate(~Bodies[i].qOrientation,
                                ContactForce);
        FrictionForce = QVRotate(~Bodies[i].qOrientation,
                                FrictionForce);
        pt = Collisions[j].vCollisionPoint -
            Bodies[i].vPosition;
        Bodies[i].vMoments += pt ^ ContactForce;
        Bodies[i].vMoments += pt ^ FrictionForce;
    }
}
}
}
```

For the most part, the calculations within this function should look familiar to you, that is, with the exception of contact forces. Also, you'll notice that here, the function initially enters a loop to cycle through all the objects in the rigid body array so that loads are calculated for all of the objects in the simulation with a single call to CalcObjectForces.

Upon entering the loop, this function first applies the thrust force to the car object only. This thrust force is assumed to act through the object's center of gravity and therefore does not create a moment. Next, the linear and angular drag forces are calculated. Once these loads have been determined, the function converts the accumulated forces to world coordinates and applies the force due to gravity. All of these calculations so far are very similar, although simplified, to those shown in the previous simulation.

The last part of this function takes care of contact forces between the objects and the ground plane.

Contact

Contact forces are forces that exist between objects that are in physical contact but are not colliding. You've already seen that objects are considered colliding when they are in contact and the relative velocity between contacting points is such that the points are moving toward each other. In resting contact, the contacting points are indeed touching; however, they are not moving toward each other. Instead, they are accelerating toward each other, and there exists a force that keeps the objects from penetrating each other. This force is an action-reaction, or equal and opposite, force that acts on each body with identical magnitude but applied in the opposite directions.

In this simulation, since the objects are initially sitting on the ground, contact forces must exist between the objects and the ground to counter the gravitational pull on the objects that would tend to pull them down through the ground plane. When the objects are sitting still on the ground, the only force acting them is that due to gravity, where the magnitude of this force is equal to the objects' mass times the acceleration due to gravity. Thus, the contact force that opposes the objects' penetration through the ground plane must be equal in magnitude to the force due to gravity but opposite in direction. In this way, the two forces cancel each other out, and the objects sit there on the ground plane.

In reality, calculating contact forces is a difficult proposition because of several complicating factors: there could be any number of contacting points located at various points relative to the object's center of gravity that share the contact loads, though not necessarily equally; and the body may be accelerating due to other factors in addition to gravity, such as angular acceleration. There are methods that have been developed to handle contact forces, and I give several references in the Bibliography that deal with the subject. Some methods handle contact using temporary springs inserted at the contact points (penalty methods), while others assume that they can be handled by using impulses (impulse methods) in a manner similar to how we handle collisions; still other methods use analytical approaches to deal with contact. I'll show you a simplified, approximate approach in this simulation that really does not fit nicely in any of these categories.

Here's how this method works: first you determine which points are actually making contact; then you determine whether or not they are in resting contact; then you must determine the acceleration of each point; finally, assuming a mass of each point as though the object is an assembly connected point masses, you can determine the required contact force.

Determining which points are close enough to be considered in contact involves the same sort of calculation that you must perform to determine whether two objects are colliding. I've set up a function called CheckGroundPlaneContacts that is nearly identical to the function I use to check for collisions; the purpose of this one is to check for possible contact between the object and the ground plane. In fact the two functions are so similar that you could actually just use a single function with some slight modifications to indicate whether you are checking for contact or collisions. I kept them separate here for clarity. Here's the code for CheckGroundPlaneContacts:

```
int       CheckGroundPlaneContacts(pCollision CollisionData, int body1)
{
    int       i;
    Vector    v1[8];
    Vector    tmp;
    Vector    u, v;
    float     d;
    Vector    f[4];
    Vector    vel1;
    Vector    pt1;
    Vector    Vr;
    float     Vrn;
```

```
Vector      n;
int         status = NOCOLLISION;
Vector      Ar;
float       Arn;

//rotate bounding vertices and covert to global coordinates
for(i=0; i<8; i++)
{
    tmp = Bodies[body1].vVertexList[i];
    v1[i] = QVRotate(Bodies[body1].qOrientation, tmp);
    v1[i] += Bodies[body1].vPosition;
}

//check each vertex of body1 against the ground plane
for(i=0; i<8; i++)
{
    u.x = 1.0f;
    u.y = 0.0f;
    u.z = 0.0f;
    v.x = 0.0f;
    v.y = 1.0f;
    v.z = 0.0f;
    tmp.x = 0.0f;
    tmp.y = 0.0f;
    tmp.z = 0.0f;
    d = CalcDistanceFromPointToPlane(v1[i], u, v, tmp);
    if(d < COLLISIONTOLERANCE)
    {
        // Calculate relative velocity
        pt1 = v1[i] - Bodies[body1].vPosition;

        vel1 = Bodies[body1].vVelocityBody +
               (Bodies[body1].vAngularVelocity^pt1);

        vel1 = QVRotate(Bodies[body1].qOrientation, vel1);

        n = u^v;
        n.Normalize();

        Vr = vel1;
        Vrn = Vr * n;

        if(fabs(Vrn) <= VELOCITYTOLERANCE) // at rest
        {
            // Now check the relative acceleration
            Ar = Bodies[body1].vAcceleration +
                (Bodies[body1].vAngularVelocity
                  ^ (Bodies[body1].vAngularVelocity^pt1)) +
                (Bodies[body1].vAngularAcceleration ^ pt1);

            Arn = Ar * n;

            if(Arn <= 0.0f)
            {
                // We have a contact, fill the data
                // structure and return
                assert(NumCollisions < (NUMBODIES*8));
                if(NumCollisions < (NUMBODIES*8))
                {
                    CollisionData->body1 = body1;
```

```
                              CollisionData->body2 = -1;
                              CollisionData->vCollisionNormal = n;
                              CollisionData->vCollisionPoint = v1[i];
                              CollisionData->vRelativeVelocity = Vr;
                              CollisionData->vRelativeAcceleration = Ar;
                              CollisionData->vCollisionTangent = -(Vr-
                                                          ((Vr*n)*n));
                              // note the negative of the tangent vector
                              // indicates that it opposes the tangential
                              // velocity; this is so we can handle
                              // friction later
                              CollisionData->vCollisionTangent.Normalize();
                              CollisionData++;
                              NumCollisions++;
                              status = CONTACT;
                          }
                      }
                  }
              }
          }

          return status;
      }
```

Since I'm representing each object with a collection of hard points for collisions and contact that were initialized in body fixed coordinates, the first thing that this function must do is rotate these points to reflect the current orientation of the object and then convert them to world coordinates.

Next comes the part where each vertex, or hard point, is checked against the ground plane to see whether it is close enough to be considered in contact. This is accomplished via the call to CalcDistanceFromPointToPlane. v1 is the point that is being checked, and the vectors u, v, and tmp describe the ground plane. u and v are axis-aligned vectors in the plane of the ground, and tmp is any point on the ground plane, which in this case is the origin. CalcDistanceFromPointToPlane is a short function that simply returns the closest distance (perpendicular to the plane) from the point to the plane. Here's what it looks like:

```
      float       CalcDistanceFromPointToPlane(Vector pt, Vector u, Vector v,
      Vector ptOnPlane)
      {
          Vector n = u^v;
          Vector PQ = pt - ptOnPlane;

          n.Normalize();

          return PQ*n;
      }
```

As you can see, it first determines the ground plane's normal vector by taking the cross product of vectors u and v and then normalizing the result. Next, a vector is constructed from any point on the plane, in this case tmp, to the point under consideration. Finally, this vector is dotted with the normal vector to find the projected distance, perpendicular to the plane, from the point to the plane and returns the result.

If the distance returned from CalcDistanceFromPointToPlane is within the collision tolerance, then CheckGroundPlaneContacts goes on to perform two crucial checks to determine
whether the point is in resting contact:

Relative Velocity

  The relative velocity must be zero or within some minimum velocity threshold.

Relative Acceleration

  The relative acceleration must be such that the object is accelerating toward the
  ground plane.

If either of these checks fails, then there is no resting contact. If the relative velocity is
such that the object is moving toward the ground, then this is a collision and will be
handled later. If the relative velocity or acceleration is such that the object is moving or
accelerating away from the ground, then there is neither a collision nor resting contact,
and no action is required.

I've already shown you how to calculate relative velocity and acceleration of a point on
a rigid body, so I won't go into it again here, except to remind you that you must not
forget to consider both linear velocity and acceleration along with angular velocity and
acceleration when performing such calculations for any point on the rigid body object.

If the check was such that the point is indeed in contact, then you need to save the
contact data in the collision data structure. I've used the same data structure to handle
collision data and contact data, so don't let the name of the structure confuse you.
Furthermore, I've set up an array of such structures so that multiple collision and
contact points can be accounted for. Here's what the data structure looks like, along
with the global array that I've set up:

```
typedef struct      _Collision {
    int                 body1; // index to body 1 (-1 used to indicate
                               // the ground plane)
    int                 body2; // index to body 2 (-1 used to indicate
                               // ground plane)
    Vector              vCollisionNormal; // normal vector outward from
                                          // face of body2
    Vector              vCollisionPoint; // contact point in global
                                         // coordinates
    Vector              vRelativeVelocity;// relative velocity
    Vector              vRelativeAcceleration; // relative acceleration
    Vector              vCollisionTangent; // tangent vector opposing
                                           // relative velocity tangent
                                           // to contacting plane
}           Collision, *pCollision;

Collision           Collisions[NUMBODIES*8];
int                 NumCollisions = 0;
```

The elements in the Collision data structure are commented to indicate the purpose
of each one. Since there are eight hard points defined for each object, there can be a
total of NUMBODIES * 8 possible or collisions or contacts at any given time. This sets the
size of the collisions array. NumCollisions is used to keep track of the current number
of collisions or contacts at any given time.

Getting back now to `CalcObjectForces`, you can see down toward the bottom where the contact check and calculations are made. This is the part of `CalcObjectForces` after gravity is applied and the sum of moments is stored in the object's data structure. Here's that bit of code again for convenience:

```
        .
        .
        .
// Handle contacts with ground plane
Bodies[i].vAcceleration = Bodies[i].vForces / Bodies[i].fMass;
Bodies[i].vAngularAcceleration = Bodies[i].mInertiaInverse *
                            (Bodies[i].vMoments -
                            (Bodies[i].vAngularVelocity ^
                            (Bodies[i].mInertia *
                            Bodies[i].vAngularVelocity)));

pCollisionData = Collisions;
NumCollisions = 0;
check = CheckGroundPlaneContacts(pCollisionData, i);
if(check == CONTACT)
{// have contact....
    for(j=0; j<NumCollisions; j++)
    {
        ContactForce = (Bodies[i].fMass/NumCollisions * (
                        -Collisions[j].vRelativeAcceleration *
                        Collisions[j].vCollisionNormal)) *
                        Collisions[j].vCollisionNormal;
        FrictionForce = (ContactForce.Magnitude() *
                        FRICTIONCOEFFICIENT) *
                        Collisions[j].vCollisionTangent;
        Bodies[i].vForces += ContactForce;
        Bodies[i].vForces += FrictionForce;
        ContactForce = QVRotate(~Bodies[i].qOrientation,
                        ContactForce);
        FrictionForce = QVRotate(~Bodies[i].qOrientation,
                        FrictionForce);
        pt = Collisions[j].vCollisionPoint -
             Bodies[i].vPosition;
        Bodies[i].vMoments += pt^ContactForce;
        Bodies[i].vMoments += pt^FrictionForce;
    }
}
        .
        .
        .
```

Before making any checks at all, the object's acceleration, both linear and angular, is calculated and stored. This is the same calculation that you've seen already in the `StepSimulation` function of the flight simulation example and that you will see again later in this example. After the call is made to `CheckGroundPlaneContacts`, if the value returned in the variable `check` indicates a contact, then the contact forces are calculated for each contact stored in the `Collisions` array.

`ContactForce` is the normal force of contact between the point and the plane and is equal to the mass of the contacting particle times the acceleration of that particle. Here I'm assuming that the object is made up of a collection of equal-sized particles located at each of the hard points that were defined earlier. I'm also considering friction here, which acts tangential to the contact plane. FrictionForce is the force due to friction and is equal to the magnitude of the normal force times the coefficient of friction times the collision tangent of unit length. This gives us a friction force that opposes the tangential velocity of the contacting point. Note that the collision tangent was already negated in function CheckGroundPlaneContacts such that it opposes the tangential velocity of the contacting point. Also note that this is a simplified friction model in that it assumes that the friction is kinetic and ignores the static case.

Once these two forces have been determined, they are applied to the body in the usual manner; that is, the forces are accumulated in the object's data structure, and any resulting moments are accounted for.

Integration

Turning now to integrating the equations of motion, I want to show you the StepSimulation function for this example. For the most part, it's similar to the StepSimulation functions shown in the previous examples; however, here I've added a loop to cycle through all the objects in the rigid body array. Here's the new function:

```
//---------------------------------------------------------------------------------
//
// Using Euler's method
//---------------------------------------------------------------------------------
//
void    StepSimulation(float dtime)
{
    Vector   Ae;
    int      i;
    float    dt = dtime;

    // Calculate all of the forces and moments on all objects
    CalcObjectForces();

    // Integrate
    for(i=0; i<NUMBODIES; i++)
    {
        // calculate acceleration earth space:
        Ae = Bodies[i].vForces / Bodies[i].fMass;
        Bodies[i].vAcceleration = Ae;

        // calculate velocity in earth space:
        Bodies[i].vVelocity += Ae * dt;

        // calculate position in earth space:
        Bodies[i].vPosition += Bodies[i].vVelocity * dt;

        // Now handle the rotations:
        float          mag;
```

```
            Bodies[i].vAngularAcceleration = Bodies[i].mInertiaInverse *
                                             (Bodies[i].vMoments -
                                             (Bodies[i].vAngularVelocity^
                                             (Bodies[i].mInertia *
                                              Bodies[i].vAngularVelocity)));

            Bodies[i].vAngularVelocity += Bodies[i].vAngularAcceleration *
                                          dt;

            // calculate the new rotation quaternion:
            Bodies[i].qOrientation += (Bodies[i].qOrientation *
                                       Bodies[i].vAngularVelocity) *
                                      (0.5f * dt);

            // now normalize the orientation quaternion:
            mag = Bodies[i].qOrientation.Magnitude();
            if (mag != 0)
                Bodies[i].qOrientation /= mag;

            // calculate the velocity in body space:
            Bodies[i].vVelocityBody = QVRotate(~Bodies[i].qOrientation,
                                               Bodies[i].vVelocity);

            // calculate speed:
            Bodies[i].fSpeed = Bodies[i].vVelocity.Magnitude();

            // get the Euler angles for our information
            Vector u;

            u = MakeEulerAnglesFromQ(Bodies[i].qOrientation);
            Bodies[i].vEulerAngles.x = u.x;      // roll
            Bodies[i].vEulerAngles.y = u.y;      // pitch
            Bodies[i].vEulerAngles.z = u.z;      // yaw
      }

      // Handle Collisions
      if(CheckForCollisions() == COLLISION)
            ResolveCollisions();
}
```

I'm using Euler's method here for simplicity, not because it's necessarily the best choice in terms of numerical stability. The first thing that StepSimulation does is make a call to CalcObjectForces to update the forces and moments acting on each object. Then the function enters a loop to cycle through all the objects and integrate so as to update each object's velocity, position, and orientation. All of this integration code is taken directly from the flight simulation example, so it should be familiar to you.

After all of the object loads have been updated and the integration is complete, the last thing that StepSimulation does is handle any collisions by making a call to CheckFor-Collisions and then ResolveCollisions if appropriate, that is, if there were indeed any collisions. Remember, these are collisions that are being checked for; contact forces have already been accounted for and included in the force and moment computations before integration of the equations of motion.

Collision Response

As you know already, there are two parts to handling collisions: collision detection and response. As I said earlier, collision detection, while not exactly physics, is very important in terms of being able to respond to collisions in your simulations. One of the difficult aspects of collision detection for your game simulations will be balancing speed and accuracy. You have no doubt come across very accurate collision detection routines in various computational geometry sources; however, you'll probably find that such methods would be too slow for your games, or perhaps they get to a level of detail that your simulations don't require. At any rate, whatever collision detection scheme you use, it needs to give you some specific pieces of information about the collision. These pieces of information are the ones that I've included in the `Collision` data structure that I showed you earlier, in the section discussing contact forces.

While the method of collision detection that I've used in this simulation is not perfect — it's not super accurate and does not catch penetration—it is simple and serves its purpose here, which is to show you how to handle collision response in three dimensions. I won't go into the collision detection code in detail here, since it's similar to the method I showed you in Chapter 13 and you can find the source code on O'Reilly's web site; however, I will outline the procedure I use so that you will at least know where the collision data are coming from.

Basically, I first make a bounding sphere check to check for possible collisions between objects. If this check passes, indicating a potential collision, I go on to check each hard point on one body with each bounding box face on the other body. If the check indicates that the hard point is within the collision tolerance, then I go on to calculate the relative velocities between the potentially colliding points to see whether they are indeed moving toward each other. If they are, then we have a collision, and the appropriate collision data are stored, which include the array indices of the two colliding bodies, the collision normal and tangent vectors, the actual point of collision in earth coordinates, and the relative velocity between colliding points. The data for each collision get stored in the same collision data array I used earlier to handle contacts so that they can be iterated through when handling the response to each collision. Note, however, that the collision data overwrite any contact data previously stored in the array, since the contact data are no longer needed (at least not until the next time forces are calculated, at which point new contact data will be generated).

Now, to handle collision response, you need to cycle through each collision data structure and calculate and then apply the appropriate impulse, since we are using impulse-based response as discussed in Chapters 5 and 13. The function I've set up to handle collision response is called `ResolveCollisions`:

```
void ResolveCollisions(void)
{
    int     i;
    Vector  pt1, pt2;
    float   j;
```

```
float    fCr = COEFFICIENTOFRESTITUTION;
int      b1, b2;
float    Vrt;
float    mu = FRICTIONCOEFFICIENT;

for(i=0;   i<NumCollisions; i++)
{
    b1 = Collisions[i].body1;
    b2 = Collisions[i].body2;

    if(b2 != -1) // not ground plane
    {
        pt1 = Collisions[i].vCollisionPoint - Bodies[b1].vPosition;
        pt2 = Collisions[i].vCollisionPoint - Bodies[b2].vPosition;

        // calculate impulse
        j = (-(1+fCr) * (Collisions[i].vRelativeVelocity *
            Collisions[i].vCollisionNormal)) /
            ( (1/Bodies[b1].fMass + 1/Bodies[b2].fMass) +
            (Collisions[i].vCollisionNormal * ( ( (pt1 ^
            Collisions[i].vCollisionNormal) *
            Bodies[b1].mInertiaInverse )^pt1) ) +
            (Collisions[i].vCollisionNormal * ( ( (pt2 ^
            Collisions[i].vCollisionNormal) *
            Bodies[b2].mInertiaInverse )^pt2) ) );

        Vrt = Collisions[i].vRelativeVelocity *
            Collisions[i].vCollisionTangent;

        if(fabs(Vrt) > 0.0) {
            Bodies[b1].vVelocity += ( (j *
                    Collisions[i].vCollisionNormal) + ((mu * j)
                    * Collisions[i].vCollisionTangent) ) /
                    Bodies[b1].fMass;

            Bodies[b1].vAngularVelocity += (pt1 ^((j *
                    Collisions[i].vCollisionNormal) + ((mu * j)
                    * Collisions[i].vCollisionTangent))) *
                    Bodies[b1].mInertiaInverse;

            Bodies[b2].vVelocity -= ((j *
                    Collisions[i].vCollisionNormal) + ((mu * j)
                    * Collisions[i].vCollisionTangent)) /
                    Bodies[b2].fMass;

            Bodies[b2].vAngularVelocity -= (pt2 ^((j *
                    Collisions[i].vCollisionNormal) + ((mu * j)
                    * Collisions[i].vCollisionTangent))) *
                    Bodies[b2].mInertiaInverse;

    } else {
        // apply impulse
        Bodies[b1].vVelocity += (j *
                Collisions[i].vCollisionNormal) /
                Bodies[b1].fMass;

        Bodies[b1].vAngularVelocity += (pt1 ^(j *
                Collisions[i].vCollisionNormal)) *
                Bodies[b1].mInertiaInverse;
```

```
                    Bodies[b2].vVelocity -= (j *
                            Collisions[i].vCollisionNormal) /
                            Bodies[b2].fMass;

                    Bodies[b2].vAngularVelocity -= (pt2 ^(j *
                            Collisions[i].vCollisionNormal)) *
                            Bodies[b2].mInertiaInverse;

            }
        } else { // ground plane
            fCr = COEFFICIENTOFRESTITUTIONGROUND;
            pt1 = Collisions[i].vCollisionPoint - Bodies[b1].vPosition;

            // calculate impulse
            j = (-(1+fCr) * (Collisions[i].vRelativeVelocity *
                Collisions[i].vCollisionNormal)) /
                ( (1/Bodies[b1].fMass) +
                (Collisions[i].vCollisionNormal * ( ( (pt1^
                 Collisions[i].vCollisionNormal) *
                 Bodies[b1].mInertiaInverse ) ^pt1)));

            Vrt = Collisions[i].vRelativeVelocity *
                Collisions[i].vCollisionTangent;
            if(fabs(Vrt) > 0.0) {
                Bodies[b1].vVelocity += ( (j *
                        Collisions[i].vCollisionNormal) + ((mu * j) *
                        Collisions[i].vCollisionTangent) ) /
                        Bodies[b1].fMass;

                Bodies[b1].vAngularVelocity += (pt1 ^((j *
                        Collisions[i].vCollisionNormal) + ((mu * j) *
                        Collisions[i].vCollisionTangent))) *
                        Bodies[b1].mInertiaInverse;

            } else {
                // apply impulse
                Bodies[b1].vVelocity += (j *
                        Collisions[i].vCollisionNormal) /
                        Bodies[b1].fMass;

                Bodies[b1].vAngularVelocity += (pt1 ^(j *
                        Collisions[i].vCollisionNormal)) *
                        Bodies[b1].mInertiaInverse;
            }
        }
    }
}
```

This function looks more complicated that it really is because I have two sections in there to separately handle collisions between objects and collisions between objects and the ground plane.

Upon entering this function, a loop is entered to cycle through each collision that is stored in the global collision data array. Since all the information for each collision has been precalculated and stored in this array, all this function has to do is calculate the appropriate impulse and apply it to each colliding object.

In the case of two colliding objects, the function first calculates the impulse and then determines whether or not the magnitude of the relative tangential velocity is greater than zero. If it is, then the formulas for applying impulse with friction are used when updating each object's linear and angular velocities; otherwise, the formulas that don't account for friction are used. Both sets of formulas are presented in Chapter 5, and you might want to go back and refresh your memory if you've forgotten the differences between the two sets.

In the case of an object colliding with the ground, I take the same approach by first calculating impulse and then checking the tangential relative velocity and update the object accordingly. There is one notable difference in the way I calculate the impulse and update the objects that are colliding with the ground. First, when calculating impulse, I assume that the ground plane is infinitely massive with infinite inertia such that the terms for `Bodies[b2]` that include mass or inertia in the denominator go to zero and drop out of the impulse equation. Second, since the ground plane is static, there's no need to update its velocities, and that's why you see only calculations to update `Bodies[b1]`. Note that my collision detection scheme assumes that when an object collides with the ground, the ground is always `body2`, which is set to `-1` in the `Collisions` data array.

All these calculations are performed for each set of collision data stored in the `Collisions` data array up to the index `NumCollisions-1`, inclusive. After each one is handled, the function returns and the simulation progresses to the next time step.

Tuning

I must admit that the first time I tried to run this simulation after setting everything up, it didn't work—that is to say, the results were less that realistic. The main reason for this was because of my initially assumed parameters, such as coefficient of restitution for collision response, coefficients of drag, and time step size, among others. I had to go through and tune each of these parameters to get the simulation to work correctly. As I discussed earlier in this book, parameter tuning is an important part of simulation development. You'll often find that you need to balance realism and accuracy for numerical stability and speed. Of course, depending on your application, one or more of these issues may take precedence over the others.

In this simulation I was not too concerned about speed, and since I didn't implement penetration in my collision detection routines, I was not very concerned about penetration. These factors led me to small time step sizes and large collision tolerances. At the same time, since I implemented Euler's method instead of the improved Euler method or Runge-Kutta method, I found that I had to increase my drag coefficients to provide enough damping for numerical stability.

To make it easy on myself, I included all the important parameters that were the subject of tuning as global defines. Here they are:

```
#define     GRAVITY                     -32.174f
#define     LINEARDRAGCOEFFICIENT       5.0f
#define     ANGULARDRAGCOEFFICIENT      1200.0f
#define     COLLISIONTOLERANCE          0.9f
```

```
#define    COEFFICIENTOFRESTITUTION         0.5f
#define    COEFFICIENTOFRESTITUTIONGROUND   0.025f
#define    VELOCITYTOLERANCE                0.05f
#define    FRICTIONCOEFFICIENT              0.9f
```

You can modify each of these on your own if you would like to see how the simulation is affected. You probably won't have to change them too much to get things to go astray in the simulation. For example, if you change the collision tolerance to something too small, then it's likely that you will see objects pass through each other owing to penetration's not being accounted for. Also, if you increase the coefficients of restitution and decrease the drag factors, you're likely to see things bounce around wildly owing to numerical instability.

There are some things that I recommend you try in order to improve the simulation. First, implement a better collision detection system. By "better," I don't necessarily mean that you must check each vertex on a polyhedron with each face on other polyhedrons or do triangle-triangle intersections. I mean implementing the penetration check, as I showed you in Chapter 13, or adding some more hard points to each object (the ones that are not shaped like boxes) to use during collision detection. In the bibliography I give several references that discuss collision detection in detail.

The next thing I'd recommend is that you implement is the improved Euler method that I showed you in Chapter 11, instead of Euler's method. This will help with numerical stability and perhaps allow you get away with larger step sizes.

Finally, the last thing I'd recommend is that you fine-tune the force calculations to suit the system that you are trying to model. You can use techniques similar to those I showed in the previous examples—for example, the flight simulation, in which I showed you how to accurately calculate mass properties using an assembly of point masses and showed you how to accurately deal with lift and drag forces.

CHAPTER 17

Particle Systems

This chapter is somewhat of a departure from the rigid body simulations that I've been discussing in that here, I'll show you how to implement a simulation of a flexible object. Specifically, the example presented in this chapter will be a simulation of a cloth flag, attached to a flagpole, waving in the wind. Figure 17-1 shows a snapshot of the simulation.

Figure 17-1. Cloth Simulation

The aim of this example is not to show you how to handle cloth specifically, but rather to show you what you can do with collections of particles and springs instead of rigid bodies. Particle systems can be used to simulate a wide variety of things such as cloth, smoke, and fire. What's nice about using particles is that they are much simpler to handle than rigid bodies, in that you don't have to deal with rotation and the angular equations of motion. Not only does this simplify force calculations and integration, but collision response also becomes easier, since you need only deal with linear impulse.

When you first run this simulation, you'll be facing the flag, as shown in Figure 17-1, and it will be waving in a moderate wind. You can use keys 1 through 6 to control the strength of the wind, 1 being low and 6 being high. Press the 0 key for no wind, and watch as the flag drapes down under its own weight. If you press the R key, the flag will be released from the pole and fall to the ground. If the wind setting is 0, then it will fall straight down; otherwise, it will be carried away by the wind. You can navigate through the simulation using the arrow keys, where the up and down arrows move the camera forward and back, respectively, and the left and right arrows turn the camera to the left and right, respectively.

Here again, you can find the executable and source files for this simulation on O'Reilly's web site. Much of the code for this simulation is identical, or very similar, to code that you've seen in the past several examples, and I won't repeat that code here. Instead, I will show you the code that is unique to this example.

Model

To simulate the flag in this example, I'm using a collection of particles that are initially arranged in a gridlike pattern and then connected by several springs. The springs act as structural elements that resist loads and hold the particles together. Figure 17-2, is a wire frame view of the flag that shows the gridlike arrangement of particles and connecting springs.

Each line in the wire frame flag represents a spring-damper element, while the nodes where these springs intersect represent the particles. The springs are modeled by using the spring-damper formulas that I showed you back in Chapter 3. The (initially) horizontal and vertical springs provide the basic structure for the flag, and the diagonal springs are there to resist shear forces and lend further strength to the cloth. Without these shear springs, the cloth would be quite stretchy. Note that there are no particles located at the intersection of the diagonal springs.

To handle the particles, I've set up an array of Particle structures to hold the state information for each particle during the simulation. Actually, I made the array multidimensional, since it's easier to visualize the grid position of each particle when setting up the connecting springs. Here's the code for the Particle structure and global array:

```
typedef    struct _Particle {
    float      fMass;
    float      fInvMass;
```

Figure 17-2. Particle-Spring System

```
        Vector      vPosition;
        Vector      vVelocity;
        Vector      vAcceleration;
        Vector      vForces;
        BOOL        bLocked;
    } Particle, *pParticle;
    // NUMROWS is the number of spaces between the rows of particles
    // NUMCOLUMNS is the number of spaces between the columns of particles

    Particle                Particles[NUMROWS+1][NUMCOLUMNS+1];
```

Each element in the Particle structure is fairly self-explanatory and should already be familiar to you. Essentially, these parameters include the mass properties of the particle along with its position, velocity, acceleration, and total force acting on it at any given instant in time.

The only parameter that might not be obvious is bLocked. This parameter is used to indicate whether or not the particle is fixed, that is, whether or not it will be allowed to move under the influence of force. If bLocked is true, then the particle is locked and skipped when the equations of motion are integrated. In this simulation I initially lock the upper and lower left particles to attach them to the flagpole. When you press the R key to release the flag, the bLocked parameter for these two particles gets reset to false, and they are allowed to move.

To handle the springs, I've set up another structure along with a global array to hold all the spring data during the simulation:

```
typedef struct _ParticleRef {
    int     r;          // row index
    int     c;          // column index
} ParticleRef;

typedef    struct    _Spring {
    ParticleRef  p1;        // reference to connected particle #1
    ParticleRef  p2;        // reference to connected particle #2
    float        k;         // tensile spring constant
    float        d;         // damping factor
    float        L;         // rest length of spring
} Spring, *pSpring;

#define NUMSTRUCTURALSPRINGS (NUMCOLUMNS*(NUMROWS+1) +
                              NUMROWS*(NUMCOLUMNS+1) +
                              NUMCOLUMNS*NUMROWS*2)

Spring                        StructuralSprings[NUMSTRUCTURALSPRINGS];
```

Elements p1 and p2 in the Spring data structure are references to particles in the grid. They are of type ParticleRef, shown above, that holds the row and column position (zero-based array indices) of the particle in the Particles array. The other three parameters, k, d, and L, hold information describing the spring that will be used in calculating the spring force between each connected particle pair; k, d, and L are the spring constant, damping factor, and unstretched (or compressed) length of the spring, respectively.

Since the geometry of the flag will change continuously throughout the simulation, you must rebuild its vertex and face data on the basis of the particle states at each time step. To keep track of the flag geometry, I set up two additional global arrays to hold vertex and face data that will be used in constructing the 3D object using Direct3D. Here are those arrays:

```
unsigned int      ClothFaces[NUMFACES*3*2];
float             ClothVertices[NUMVERTICES*3*2];
```

Each face is actually a triangle consisting, of course, of three nodes. Note here this it appears as though I have twice the number of faces and nodes required to represent the flag (see the *2 in the array size calculation). I had to do this because I'm using Direct3D retained mode, which automatically performs back face culling. Thus, I actually construct two sides of the flag so that it will be visible from either side. Had I used immediate mode, or perhaps OpenGL, instead, I would have turned off back face culling.

To set up the start of the simulation, I've prepared a function called Initialize that fills all the data structures for the particles, springs, and cloth geometry:

```
#define      MASSPERFACE   (CLOTHMASS/(float) NUMFACES)
#define      CSTEP         ((float) CLOTHWIDTH / (float) NUMCOLUMNS)
#define      RSTEP         ((float) CLOTHHEIGHT / (float) NUMROWS)
```

```
void      Initialize(void)
{
    int             r, c;
    float           f;
    unsigned int    *faceVertex;
    float           *vertices;
    Vector          L;
    int             count;
    int             n;

    for(r=0; r<=NUMROWS; r++)
    {
        for(c=0; c<=NUMCOLUMNS; c++)
        {
            // calc mass of this particle
            if((r == 0) && (c == 0))
                f = 1;
            else if((r == NUMROWS) && (c == 0))
                f = 2;
            else if((r == 0) && (c == NUMCOLUMNS))
                f = 2;
            else if((r == NUMROWS) && (c == NUMCOLUMNS))
                f = 1;
            else if(((r == 0) || (r == NUMROWS)) && ((c != 0) &&
                    (c != NUMCOLUMNS)))
                f = 3;
            else
                f = 6;

            Particles[r][c].fMass = (f * MASSPERFACE) / 3;
            Particles[r][c].fInvMass = 1 / Particles[r][c].fMass;

            // set initial position of this particle
            Particles[r][c].vPosition.x = c * CSTEP;
            Particles[r][c].vPosition.y = (CLOTHHEIGHT - (r * RSTEP)) +
                                           YOFFSET;
            Particles[r][c].vPosition.z = 0.0f;

            // set initial velocity and forces to zero
            Particles[r][c].vVelocity.x = 0.0f;
            Particles[r][c].vVelocity.y = 0.0f;
            Particles[r][c].vVelocity.z = 0.0f;

            Particles[r][c].vAcceleration.x = 0.0f;
            Particles[r][c].vAcceleration.y = 0.0f;
            Particles[r][c].vAcceleration.z = 0.0f;

            Particles[r][c].vForces.x = 0.0f;
            Particles[r][c].vForces.y = 0.0f;
            Particles[r][c].vForces.z = 0.0f;
            if((c == 0) && (r == 0 || r == NUMROWS))
                Particles[r][c].bLocked = TRUE;
            else
                Particles[r][c].bLocked = FALSE;

        }
    }

    vertices = ClothVertices;
    for(r=0; r<=NUMROWS; r++)
```

```
{
    for(c=0; c<=NUMCOLUMNS; c++)
    {
        // setup vertices
        *vertices = Particles[r][c].vPosition.x; vertices++;
        *vertices = Particles[r][c].vPosition.y; vertices++;
        *vertices = Particles[r][c].vPosition.z; vertices++;
    }
}
for(r=0; r<=NUMROWS; r++)
{
    for(c=0; c<=NUMCOLUMNS; c++)
    {
        // setup vertices
        *vertices = Particles[r][c].vPosition.x; vertices++;
        *vertices = Particles[r][c].vPosition.y; vertices++;
        *vertices = Particles[r][c].vPosition.z; vertices++;
    }
}

faceVertex = ClothFaces;
for(r=0; r<NUMROWS; r++)
{
    for(c=0; c<=NUMCOLUMNS; c++)
    {
        // setup faces
        if(c == 0)
        {
            *faceVertex = ((NUMCOLUMNS+1)*r) + c;
            faceVertex++; // vertex 1

            *faceVertex = ((NUMCOLUMNS+1)*r) + (c+1);
            faceVertex++; // vertex 2

            *faceVertex = ((NUMCOLUMNS+1)*r) + (NUMCOLUMNS+1) + c;
            faceVertex++; // vertex 3
        } else if(c == NUMCOLUMNS) {
            *faceVertex = ((NUMCOLUMNS+1)*r) + c;
            faceVertex++; // vertex 1

            *faceVertex = ((NUMCOLUMNS+1)*r) + (NUMCOLUMNS+1) + c;
            faceVertex++; // vertex 2

            *faceVertex = ((NUMCOLUMNS+1)*r) + (NUMCOLUMNS+1) +
                          (c-1);
            faceVertex++; // vertex 3
        } else {
            *faceVertex = ((NUMCOLUMNS+1)*r) + c;
            faceVertex++; // vertex 1

            *faceVertex = ((NUMCOLUMNS+1)*r) + (NUMCOLUMNS+1) + c;
            faceVertex++; // vertex 2

            *faceVertex = ((NUMCOLUMNS+1)*r) + (NUMCOLUMNS+1) +
                            (c-1);
            faceVertex++; // vertex 3

            *faceVertex = ((NUMCOLUMNS+1)*r) + c;
            faceVertex++; // vertex 1
```

```
                    *faceVertex = ((NUMCOLUMNS+1)*r) + (c+1);
                    faceVertex++; // vertex 2

                    *faceVertex = ((NUMCOLUMNS+1)*r) + (NUMCOLUMNS+1) + c;
                    faceVertex++; // vertex 3


            }
        }
    }

    for(r=0; r<NUMROWS; r++)
    {
        for(c=0; c<=NUMCOLUMNS; c++)
        {
            // setup faces
            if(c == 0)
            {
                    *faceVertex = NUMVERTICES + ((NUMCOLUMNS+1)*r) +
                                  (NUMCOLUMNS+1) + c;
                    faceVertex++; // vertex 3

                    *faceVertex = NUMVERTICES + ((NUMCOLUMNS+1)*r) +
                                  (c+1);
                    faceVertex++; // vertex 2

                    *faceVertex = NUMVERTICES + ((NUMCOLUMNS+1)*r) + c;
                    faceVertex++; // vertex 1
            } else if(c == NUMCOLUMNS) {
                    *faceVertex = NUMVERTICES + ((NUMCOLUMNS+1)*r) +
                                  (NUMCOLUMNS+1) + (c-1);
                    faceVertex++; // vertex 3

                    *faceVertex = NUMVERTICES + ((NUMCOLUMNS+1)*r) +
                                  (NUMCOLUMNS+1) + c;
                    faceVertex++; // vertex 2

                    *faceVertex = NUMVERTICES + ((NUMCOLUMNS+1)*r) + c;
                    faceVertex++; // vertex 1

            } else {
                    *faceVertex = NUMVERTICES + ((NUMCOLUMNS+1)*r) +
                                  (NUMCOLUMNS+1) + (c-1);
                    faceVertex++; // vertex 3

                    *faceVertex = NUMVERTICES + ((NUMCOLUMNS+1)*r) +
                                  (NUMCOLUMNS+1) + c;
                    faceVertex++; // vertex 2

                    *faceVertex = NUMVERTICES + ((NUMCOLUMNS+1)*r) + c;
                    faceVertex++; // vertex 1

                    *faceVertex = NUMVERTICES + ((NUMCOLUMNS+1)*r) +
                                  (NUMCOLUMNS+1) + c;
                    faceVertex++; // vertex 3

                    *faceVertex = NUMVERTICES + ((NUMCOLUMNS+1)*r) +
                                  (c+1);
                    faceVertex++; // vertex 2
```

```
                         *faceVertex = NUMVERTICES + ((NUMCOLUMNS+1)*r) + c;
                         faceVertex++; // vertex 1

            }
        }
    }

    // Create a D3D object to represent the cloth
    CreateCloth("test.bmp", ClothFaces, NUMFACES*2, ClothVertices,
                NUMVERTICES*2, FALSE);
    // setup the structural springs
    // connect springs between each adjacent vertex
    count = 0;
    n = NUMSTRUCTURALSPRINGS;
    for(r=0; r<=NUMROWS; r++)
    {
        for(c=0; c<=NUMCOLUMNS; c++)
        {
            if(c<NUMCOLUMNS)
            {
                StructuralSprings[count].p1.r = r;
                StructuralSprings[count].p1.c = c;
                StructuralSprings[count].p2.r = r;
                StructuralSprings[count].p2.c = c+1;
                StructuralSprings[count].k = SPRINGTENSIONCONSTANT;
                StructuralSprings[count].d = SPRINGDAMPINGCONSTANT;
                L = Particles[r][c].vPosition -
                    Particles[r][c+1].vPosition;
                StructuralSprings[count].L = L.Magnitude();
                count++;
            }
            if(r<NUMROWS)
            {
                StructuralSprings[count].p1.r = r;
                StructuralSprings[count].p1.c = c;
                StructuralSprings[count].p2.r = r+1;
                StructuralSprings[count].p2.c = c;
                StructuralSprings[count].k = SPRINGTENSIONCONSTANT;
                StructuralSprings[count].d = SPRINGDAMPINGCONSTANT;
                L = Particles[r][c].vPosition -
                    Particles[r+1][c].vPosition;
                StructuralSprings[count].L = L.Magnitude();
                count++;
            }
            if(r<NUMROWS && c<NUMCOLUMNS)
            {
                StructuralSprings[count].p1.r = r;
                StructuralSprings[count].p1.c = c;
                StructuralSprings[count].p2.r = r+1;
                StructuralSprings[count].p2.c = c+1;
                StructuralSprings[count].k = SPRINGSHEARCONSTANT;
                StructuralSprings[count].d = SPRINGDAMPINGCONSTANT;
                L = Particles[r][c].vPosition -
                    Particles[r+1][c+1].vPosition;
                StructuralSprings[count].L = L.Magnitude();
                count++;
            }
            if(c>0 && r<NUMROWS)
            {
                StructuralSprings[count].p1.r = r;
                StructuralSprings[count].p1.c = c;
```

```
                    StructuralSprings[count].p2.r = r+1;
                    StructuralSprings[count].p2.c = c-1;
                    StructuralSprings[count].k = SPRINGSHEARCONSTANT;
                    StructuralSprings[count].d = SPRINGDAMPINGCONSTANT;
                    L = Particles[r][c].vPosition -
                        Particles[r+1][c-1].vPosition;
                    StructuralSprings[count].L = L.Magnitude();
                    count++;
                }
            }
        }

        WindVector.x = 10.0;
        WindVector.y = 0.0;
        WindVector.z = 1.0;


    }
```

The first set of nested for loops you see in this function iterate through the entire list of particles and fill their data structures. The position of each particle is calculated so as to arrange them in a grid, as I explained earlier. Each particle is assigned a mass calculated as one third the sum of masses of each face that shares that particle.

The next series of loops, up to the call to CreateCloth, set up the flag's face and vertex data, which will be passed to Direct3D. CreateCloth actually constructs the flag object using Direct3D. Since it is Direct3D-specific code I won't show it here, but you can get it from the O'Reilly web site.

The last set of nested loops sets up the springs that give the flag its structure. This is a somewhat trivial operation in this case, as most of the spring data are fixed, and determining the indices to each particle is made easy by the fact that the Particles array is multidimensional, corresponding to the rows and columns in the grid.

The very last thing that gets initialized is the vector, WindVector, that is used to represent the direction of the wind. WindVector is a global variable declared as follows:

```
Vector                  WindVector;
float                   WindForceFactor = WINDFACTOR;
```

I've also shown here the variable WindForceFactor that gets multiplied by WindVector when determining the wind force acting on the flag.

In the model I've put together here, there are several other forces, in addition to the wind force, that act on the particles making up the flag. You already know that the springs will exert forces on the particles to provide structure for the flag. Further, I've modeled in gravity as well as viscous drag. All of these forces are taken care of in the function CalcForces:

```
// I'm using Direct3D's coordinate system in this example, where the z-
// axis points into the screen, the x-axis points to the right, and the y-
// axis points upward.

void    CalcForces(Particle particles[NUMROWS+1][NUMCOLUMNS+1])
```

```
{
    int        r, c, i, r1, c1, r2, c2;
    Vector     dragVector;
    Vector     f1, f2, d, v;
    float      L;

    // zero all forces
    for(r=0; r<=NUMROWS; r++)
    {
        for(c=0; c<=NUMCOLUMNS; c++)
        {
            particles[r][c].vForces.x = 0;
            particles[r][c].vForces.y = 0;
            particles[r][c].vForces.z = 0;
        }
    }

    // process gravity and drag forces
    for(r=0; r<=NUMROWS; r++)
    {
        for(c=0; c<=NUMCOLUMNS; c++)
        {

            if(particles[r][c].bLocked == FALSE)
            {
                // gravity
                particles[r][c].vForces.y += (float) (GRAVITY *
                                                particles[r][c].fMass);

                // viscous drag
                dragVector = -particles[r][c].vVelocity;
                dragVector.Normalize();
                particles[r][c].vForces += dragVector *
                            (particles[r][c].vVelocity.Magnitude() *
                             particles[r][c].vVelocity.Magnitude())
                            * DRAGCOEFFICIENT;
                // wind
                SetWindVector(tb_Rnd(0, 10), 0, tb_Rnd(0, 1));
                WindVector.Normalize();
                particles[r][c].vForces += WindVector *
                            tb_Rnd(0, WindForceFactor);

            }
        }
    }

    // Process spring forces
    for(i = 0; i<NUMSTRUCTURALSPRINGS; i++)
    {
        r1 = StructuralSprings[i].p1.r;
        c1 = StructuralSprings[i].p1.c;
        r2 = StructuralSprings[i].p2.r;
        c2 = StructuralSprings[i].p2.c;

        d = particles[r1][c1].vPosition - particles[r2][c2].vPosition;
        v = particles[r1][c1].vVelocity - particles[r2][c2].vVelocity;
        L = StructuralSprings[i].L;

        f1 = -(StructuralSprings[i].k * (d.Magnitude() - L) +
            StructuralSprings[i].d * ( (v * d) / d.Magnitude() )) *
            ( d / d.Magnitude() );
        f2 = -f1;
```

```
        if(particles[r1][c1].bLocked == FALSE)
            particles[r1][c1].vForces += f1;

        if(particles[r2][c2].bLocked == FALSE)
            particles[r2][c2].vForces += f2;
    }
}
```

The first thing this function does is zero the forces acting on each particle. Next, the function goes on to calculate the gravity, viscous drag, and wind force acting on each particle. These calculations are all very similar to those you've seen in the previous examples. Note, however, that I've included a little randomness in the wind force calculation. I did this to ensure that that flag is perturbed enough out of the vertical plane that it's initialized in so as to flutter more realistically.

The last loop in this function handles all the spring forces acting on each particle. Since all the spring data are set up during initialization, it's a simple matter of extracting the data for each spring and applying the spring-damper force to the attached particles using the spring-damper force formulas that I gave you in Chapter 3.

Notice that within all these calculations, checks are made to see whether any given particle is locked. If it is locked, forces don't get applied to it, so it remains static.

Integration

For this example I again use Euler's method because of its simplicity. As with the previous examples, I've set up a function called StepSimulation that handles integration of the equations of motion. In this particular case the function is quite simple:

```
void        StepSimulation(float dt)
{
    Vector      Ae;
    int         r, c;
    int         check = 0;

    // Calculate all of the forces
    CalcForces(Particles);

    // Integrate
    for(r=0; r<=NUMROWS; r++)
    {
        for(c=0; c<=NUMCOLUMNS; c++)
        {
            Ae = Particles[r][c].vForces * Particles[r][c].fInvMass;
            Particles[r][c].vAcceleration = Ae;
            Particles[r][c].vVelocity += Ae * dt;
            Particles[r][c].vPosition += Particles[r][c].vVelocity *
                                            dt;
        }
    }
    // Check for collisions
    check = CheckForCollisions(Particles);
```

```
    if(check == COLLISION)
        ResolveCollisions(Particles);

    // Update the D3D cloth object's geometry
    UpdateClothGeometry();
}
```

Since we're dealing only with particles here and not rigid bodies, the equations of motion are limited to linear motion. After making the call to CalcForces, the function cycles through all of the particles and updates each one's position, velocity, and acceleration.

After that, a call to CheckForCollisions is made to see whether any of the particles has collided with the flagpole or the ground plane. If so, then a call to ResolveCollisions is made to apply the appropriate impulse to any particle involved in a collision.

Finally, UpdateClothGeometry is called to provide Direct3D the new face and vertex information, based on the updated particles, for the flag object.

Collision Response

In this example I check for collisions between the particles and the flagpole and the particles and the ground plane. If you set the wind to zero, the flag will drape down against the flagpole. If you release the locked particles (by pressing the R key), the flag will drop to the ground and either sit there or be blown away, depending on the wind setting.

Since there are a number of particles making up the flag object, you have to be able to account for multiple collisions. In this case the maximum number of possible collisions is equal to the number of particles (assuming that a particle cannot collide with the flagpole and ground at the same time). To store the collision data, I've set up a Collision structure along with a global array of these structures:

```
typedef struct      _Collision {
    ParticleRef         p1;
    Vector              n;
}    Collision, *pCollision;

Collision               Collisions[NUMVERTICES];
```

The first parameter in the Collision structure, p1, is simply a reference to the particle that is involved in the collision. The second parameter, n, is the collision normal vector that will be used to calculate the linear impulse.

Whenever the call to CheckForCollisions is made, the array elements in the Collisions array are filled with collision data. Any unfilled elements will have their p1 set to -1 to indicate the absence of collision data.

After all of the collisions, if any, have been identified, a call to ResolveCollisions is made. Here's what that function looks like:

```
void      ResolveCollisions(Particle p[NUMROWS+1][NUMCOLUMNS+1])
{
    int      i;
    int      r, c;
    Vector   Vn, Vt;

    for(i=0; i<NUMVERTICES; i++)
    {
        if(Collisions[i].p1.r !- -1)
        {
            r = Collisions[i].p1.r;
            c = Collisions[i].p1.c;
            Vn = (Collisions[i].n * p[r][c].vVelocity) *
                 Collisions[i].n;
            Vt = p[r][c].vVelocity - Vn;
            p[r][c].vVelocity = (-(KRESTITUTION+1) * Vn) +
                                (FRICTIONFACTOR*Vt);
        }
    }
}
```

As you can see, the function is quite short, owing to the fact that we're dealing with particles colliding with nonmovable objects; that is, I'm assuming that the flagpole and ground are infinitely massive relative to each particle. In this case, all we really need to do is calculate the normal component of the colliding particle's velocity, reverse it, and scale it by the coefficient of restitution to get the particle's normal velocity after impact. Next, you can determine the tangential component of velocity and scale it by a friction factor to simulate sliding friction. Adding these new normal and tangential velocity components yields the new velocity of the particle at the instant just after collision.

Tuning

Just as in the previous example, I've placed all the important, controlling parameters in a set of global defines so that I can tune the simulation. Here are those defines:

```
#define      GRAVITY                  -32.174
#define      SPRINGTENSIONCONSTANT    500.0f
#define      SPRINGSHEARCONSTANT      300.0f
#define      SPRINGDAMPINGCONSTANT    2.0f
#define      YOFFSET                  120.0f
#define      DRAGCOEFFICIENT          0.01f
#define      WINDFACTOR               100
#define      FLAGPOLEHEIGHT           200
#define      FLAGPOLERADIUS           10
#define      COLLISIONTOLERANCE       0.05f
#define      KRESTITUTION             0.25f
#define      FRICTIONFACTOR           0.5f
```

In spite of using Euler's method instead of, say, the improved Euler method, I found this simulation to be quite robust as long as the springs were tuned properly. For this example I fixed the step size to 16 milliseconds and set the physics update-to-display update rate at 10 to 1.

As you can see, I've defined two different spring constants to represent the main structural springs and the shear springs. I did this so that I could tune the shear springs independent of the tension springs to see how they affect the overall behavior of the flag. If you play around with these numbers, you'll see that if the shear spring constant is set very low, then the flag appears very rubbery. On the other hand, if you set this constant to a very high number, the flag appears quite inelastic in that it does not stretch so much under the wind load.

You have to be careful, though, when increasing these spring constants. If you set either of these spring constants too high in an effort to eliminate any stretchiness, you'll end up with what are called *stiff* equations, and you're likely to run into numerical instability. Damping can help you a little here. In fact, you should always include a little damping, whether it's viscous damping or spring damping, to help alleviate instability.

If you want to see the effect of damping, change the spring damping constant to a lower number. What you'll find is that the particles making up the cloth jump around and oscillate quite unrealistically. This is especially evident if you release the flag and let it fall to the ground, where the particles start colliding with the ground.

Speaking of collisions, you'll probably want to try implementing the penetration check that I showed you back in Chapter 13. I was not too concerned about penetration here, since the particles could collide only with the flagpole and the ground; however, if you are going to implement a system in which your cloth model may collide with arbitrarily shaped objects, you should handle penetration.

Vector Operations

This appendix implements a class called `Vector` that encapsulates all of the vector operations that you need when writing 2D or 3D rigid body simulations. Although, `Vector` represents 3D vectors, you can easily reduce it to handle 2D vectors by eliminating all of the z-terms or simply constraining the z-terms to zero where appropriate in your implementation.

Vector Class

The `Vector` class is defined with three components, x, y, and z, along with several methods and operators that implement basic vector operations. The class has two constructors, one of which initializes the vector components to zero and the other of which initializes the vector components to those passed to the constructor.

```
//---------------------------------------------------------------------------
// Vector Class and vector functions
//---------------------------------------------------------------------------
class Vector {
public:
    float x;
    float y;
    float z;

    Vector(void);
    Vector(float xi, float yi, float zi);

    float Magnitude(void);
    void  Normalize(void);
    void  Reverse(void);

    Vector& operator+=(Vector u);
    Vector& operator-=(Vector u);
    Vector& operator*=(float s);
    Vector& operator/=(float s);

    Vector operator-(void);

};
```

```
// Constructor
inline Vector::Vector(void)
{
    x = 0;
    y = 0;
    z = 0;
}

// Constructor
inline Vector::Vector(float xi, float yi, float zi)
{
    x = xi;
    y = yi;
    z = zi;
}
```

Magnitude

The `Magnitude` method simply calculates the scalar magnitude of the vector according to the formula

$$|\mathbf{v}| = \sqrt{x^2 + y^2 + z^2}$$

This is for a zero-based vector in which the components are specified relative to the origin. The magnitude of a vector is equal to its length, as illustrated in Figure A-1.

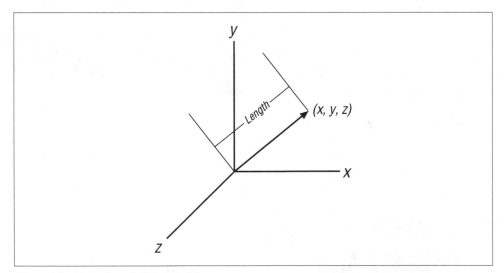

Figure A-1. Vector Length (Magnitude)

Here's the code that calculates the vector magnitude for our `Vector` class:

```
inline    float Vector::Magnitude(void)
{
    return (float) sqrt(x*x + y*y + z*z);
}
```

Note that you can calculate the components of a vector if you know its length and direction angles. *Direction angles* are the angles between each coordinate axis and the vector, as shown in Figure A-2.

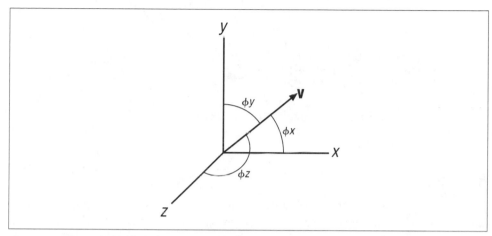

Figure A-2. Direction Angles

The components of the vector shown in this figure are as follows:

$$v_x = |\mathbf{v}| \cos \varphi_x$$
$$v_y = |\mathbf{v}| \cos \varphi_y$$
$$v_z = |\mathbf{v}| \cos \varphi_z$$

The cosines of the direction angles seen in these equations are known as *direction cosines*. The sum of the squares of the direction cosines is always equal to 1:

$$\cos^2 \varphi_x + \cos^2 \varphi_y + \cos^2 \varphi_z = 1$$

Normalize

The `Normalize` method normalizes the vector, or converts it to a unit vector satisfying the following equation:

$$|\mathbf{v}| = \sqrt{x^2 + y^2 + z^2} = 1$$

In other words, the length of the normalized vector is 1 unit. If $\mathbf{v}$ is a nonunit vector with components x, y, and z, then the unit vector $\mathbf{u}$ can be calculated from $\mathbf{v}$ as follows:

$$\mathbf{u} = \mathbf{v}/|\mathbf{v}| = (x/|\mathbf{v}|)\mathbf{I} + (y/|\mathbf{v}|)\mathbf{j} + (z/|\mathbf{v}|)\mathbf{k}$$

Here, $|\mathbf{v}|$ is simply the magnitude, or length, of vector $\mathbf{v}$ as described earlier.

Here's the code that converts our `Vector` class vector to a unit vector:

```
inline    void  Vector::Normalize(void)
{
    float m = (float) sqrt(x*x + y*y + z*z);
    if(m <= tol) m = 1;
    x /= m;
    y /= m;
    z /= m;

    if (fabs(x) < tol) x = 0.0f;
    if (fabs(y) < tol) y = 0.0f;
    if (fabs(z) < tol) z = 0.0f;
}
```

In this function `tol` is a float type tolerance, for example,

```
float    const tol = 0.0001f;
```

Reverse

The `Reverse` method reverses the direction of the vector, which is accomplished by simply taking the negative of each component. After calling `Reverse`, the vector will point in a direction opposite to the direction in which it was pointing before `Reverse` was called.

```
inline    void Vector::Reverse(void)
{
    x = -x;
    y = -y;
    z = -z;
}
```

This operation is illustrated in Figure A-3.

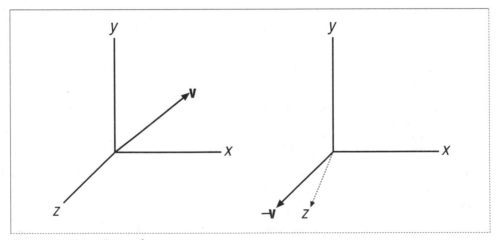

Figure A-3. Vector Reversal

Vector Addition: The += Operator

This summation operator is used for vector addition, whereby the passed vector is added to the current vector component by component. Graphically, vectors are added in tip-to-tail fashion as illustrated in Figure A-4.

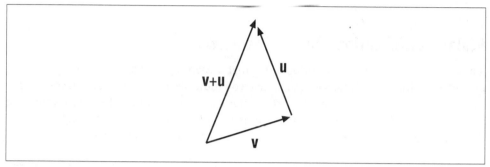

Figure A-4. Vector Addition

Here's the code that adds the vector **u** to our Vector class vector:

```
inline Vector& Vector::operator+=(Vector u)
{
    x += u.x;
    y += u.y;
    z += u.z;
    return *this;
}
```

Vector Subtraction: The −= Operator

This subtraction operator is used to subtract the passed vector from the current one, which is performed on a component-by-component basis. Vector subtraction is very similar to vector addition except that you take the reverse of the second vector and add it to the first as illustrated in Figure A-5.

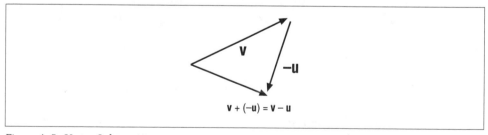

Figure A-5. Vector Subtraction

Here's the code that subtracts vector **u** from our Vector class vector:

```
inline     Vector& Vector::operator-=(Vector u)
{
    x -= u.x;
    y -= u.y;
    z -= u.z;
    return *this;
}
```

Scalar Multiplication: The *= Operator

This is the scalar multiplication operator that's used to multiply a vector by a scalar, effectively scaling the vector's length. When you multiply a vector by a scalar, you simply multiply each vector component by the scalar quantity to obtain the new vector. The new vector points in the same direction as the unscaled one, but its length will be different (unless the scale factor is 1). This is illustrated in Figure A-6.

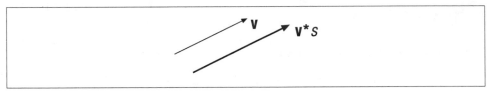

Figure A-6. Scalar Multiplication

Here's the code that scales our Vector class vector:

```
inline     Vector& Vector::operator*=(float s)
{
    x *=s;
    y *=s;
    z *=s;
    return *this;
}
```

Scalar Division: The /= Operator

This scalar division operator is similar to the scalar multiplication operator except that each vector component is divided by the passed scalar quantity.

```
inline     Vector& Vector::operator/=(float s)
{
    x /=s;
    y /=s;
    z /=s;
    return *this;
}
```

Conjugate: The — Operator

The conjugate operator simply takes the negative of each vector component and can be used when subtracting one vector from another or for reversing the direction of the vector. Applying the conjugate operator is the same as reversing a vector, as discussed earlier.

```
inline    Vector Vector::operator-(void)
{
    return Vector(-x, -y, -z);
}
```

Vector Functions and Operators

The functions and overloaded operators that follow are useful in performing operations with two vectors, or with a vector and a scalar, where the vector is based on the Vector class.

Vector Addition: The + Operator

This addition operator adds vector **v** to vector **u** according to the formula

$$\mathbf{u} + \mathbf{v} = (u_x + v_x)\mathbf{i} + (u_y + v_y)\mathbf{j} + (u_z + v_z)\mathbf{k}$$

Here's the code:

```
inline    Vector operator+(Vector u, Vector v)
{
    return Vector(u.x + v.x, u.y + v.y, u.z + v.z);
}
```

Vector Subtraction: The — Operator

This subtraction operator subtracts vector **v** from vector **u** according to the formula

$$\mathbf{u} - \mathbf{v} = (u_x - v_x)\mathbf{i} + (u_y - v_y)\mathbf{j} + (u_z - v_z)\mathbf{k}$$

Here's the code:

```
inline    Vector operator-(Vector u, Vector v)
{
    return Vector(u.x - v.x, u.y - v.y, u.z - v.z);
}
```

Vector Cross Product: The ˆ Operator

This cross product operator takes the vector cross product between vectors **u** and **v**, **u** × **v**, and returns a vector perpendicular to both **u** and **v** according to the formula

$$\mathbf{u} \times \mathbf{v} = (u_y{}^*v_z - u_z{}^*v_y)\mathbf{i} + (-u_x{}^*v_z + u_z{}^*v_x)\mathbf{j} + (u_x{}^*v_y - u_y{}^*v_x)\mathbf{k}$$

The resulting vector is perpendicular to the plane that contains vectors **u** and **v**. The direction in which this resulting vector points can be determined by the righthand rule. If you place the two vectors, **u** and **v**, tail to tail as shown in Figure A-7 and curl your fingers (of your right hand) in the direction from **u** to **v**, your thumb will point in the direction of the resulting vector.

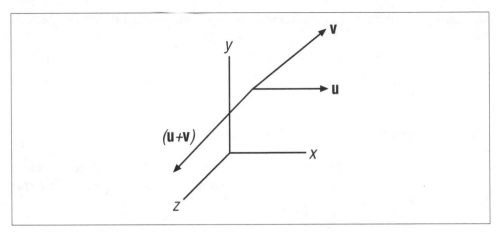

Figure A-7. Vector Cross Product

In this case the resulting vector points out of the page along the z-axis, since the vectors **u** and **v** lie in the plane formed by the x- and y-axes.

If two vectors are parallel, then their cross product will be zero. This is useful when you need to determine whether or not two vector are indeed parallel.

The cross product operation is distributive; however, it is not commutative:

$$\mathbf{u} \times \mathbf{v} \neq \mathbf{v} \times \mathbf{u}$$

$$\mathbf{u} \times \mathbf{v} = -(\mathbf{v} \times \mathbf{u})$$

$$s(\mathbf{u} \times \mathbf{v}) = (s)(\mathbf{u}) \times \mathbf{v} = \mathbf{u} \times (s)(\mathbf{v})$$

$$\mathbf{u} \times (\mathbf{v} + \mathbf{p}) = (\mathbf{u} \times \mathbf{v}) + (\mathbf{u} \times \mathbf{p})$$

Here's the code that takes the cross product of vectors **u** and **v**:

```
inline    Vector operator^(Vector u, Vector v)
{
      return Vector(    u.y*v.z - u.z*v.y,
                       -u.x*v.z + u.z*v.x,
                        u.x*v.y - u.y*v.x );
}
```

Vector cross products are handy when you need to find normal (perpendicular) vectors. For example, when performing collision detection, you often need to find the vector normal to the face of a polygon. You can construct two vectors in the plane of the polygon using the polygon's vertices and then take the cross product of these two vectors to get normal vector.

Vector Dot Product: The * Operator

This operator takes the vector dot product between the vectors **u** and **v**, according to the formula

$$\mathbf{u} \cdot \mathbf{v} = (u_x * v_x) + (u_y * v_y) + (u_z * v_z)$$

The dot product represents the projection of the vector **u** onto the vector **v** as illustrated in Figure A-8.

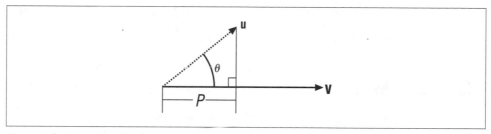

Figure A-8. Vector Dot Product

In this figure, P is the result of the dot product, and it is a scalar. You can also calculate the dot product if you the know the angle between the vectors:

$$P = \mathbf{u} \cdot \mathbf{v} = |\mathbf{u}|\,|\mathbf{v}|\cos\theta$$

Here's the code that takes the dot product of **u** and **v**:

```
// Vector dot product
inline    float operator*(Vector u, Vector v)
{
    return (u.x*v.x + u.y*v.y + u.z*v.z);
}
```

Vector dot products are handy when you need to find the magnitude of a vector projected onto another one. Going back to collision detection as an example, you often have to determine the closest distance from a point, which may be a polygon vertex on one body (body 1), to a polygon face on another body (body 2). If you construct a vector from the face under consideration on body 2, using any of its vertices, to the point under consideration from body 1, then you can find the closest distance of that point from the plane of body 2's face by taking the dot product of that point with the normal vector to the plane. (If the normal vector is not of unit length, you'll have to divide the result by the magnitude of the normal vector.)

Scalar Multiplication: The * Operator

This operator multiplies the vector **u** by the scalar s on a component-by-component basis. There are two versions of this overloaded operator depending on the order in which the vector and scalar are encountered:

```
inline    Vector operator*(float s, Vector u)
{
    return Vector(u.x*s, u.y*s, u.z*s);
}

inline    Vector operator*(Vector u, float s)
{
    return Vector(u.x*s, u.y*s, u.z*s);
}
```

Scalar Division: The / Operator

This operator divides the vector **u** by the scalar s on a component-by-component basis:

```
inline    Vector operator/(Vector u, float s)
{
    return Vector(u.x/s, u.y/s, u.z/s);
}
```

Triple Scalar Product

This function takes the triple scalar product of the vectors **u**, **v**, and **w** according to the formula

$$s = \mathbf{u} \cdot (\mathbf{v} \times \mathbf{w})$$

Here, the result, s, is a scalar. The code is as follows:

```
inline    float TripleScalarProduct(Vector u, Vector v, Vector w)
{
    return float(    (u.x * (v.y*w.z - v.z*w.y)) +
                     (u.y * (-v.x*w.z + v.z*w.x)) +
                     (u.z * (v.x*w.y - v.y*w.x)) );
}
```

Matrix Operations

This appendix implements a class called Matrix3x3 that encapsulates all of the operations you need to handle 3×3 (nine-element) matrices when writing 3D rigid body simulations.

Matrix3x3 Class

The Matrix3x3 class is defined with nine elements, e_{ij}, where i represents the ith row and j represents the jth column. For example, e_{21} refers to the element on the second row in the first column. Here's how all of the elements are arranged:

$$\mathbf{M} = \begin{vmatrix} e_{11} & e_{12} & e_{13} \\ e_{21} & e_{22} & e_{23} \\ e_{31} & e_{32} & e_{33} \end{vmatrix}$$

The class has two constructors, one of which initializes the matrix elements to zero and the other of which initializes the elements to those passed to the constructor:

```
class Matrix3x3 {
public:
    // elements eij: i -> row, j -> column
    float      e11, e12, e13, e21, e22, e23, e31, e32, e33;
    Matrix3x3(void);
    Matrix3x3(float r1c1, float r1c2, float r1c3,
              float r2c1, float r2c2, float r2c3,
              float r3c1, float r3c2, float r3c3 );

    float       det(void);
    Matrix3x3   Transpose(void);
    Matrix3x3   Inverse(void);

    Matrix3x3& operator+=(Matrix3x3 m);
    Matrix3x3& operator-=(Matrix3x3 m);
    Matrix3x3& operator*=(float s);
    Matrix3x3& operator/=(float s);
};
```

```
// Constructor
inline      Matrix3x3::Matrix3x3(void)
{
    e11 = 0;
    e12 = 0;
    e13 = 0;
    e21 = 0;
    e22 = 0;
    e23 = 0;
    e31 = 0;
    e32 = 0;
    e33 = 0;
}

// Constructor
inline      Matrix3x3::Matrix3x3(float r1c1, float r1c2, float r1c3,
                                 float r2c1, float r2c2, float r2c3,
                                 float r3c1, float r3c2, float r3c3 )

{
    e11 = r1c1;
    e12 = r1c2;
    e13 = r1c3;
    e21 = r2c1;
    e22 = r2c2;
    e23 = r2c3;
    e31 = r3c1;
    e32 = r3c2;
    e33 = r3c3;
}
```

Determinant

The method, det, returns the determinant of the matrix. The determinant of a 2×2 matrix,

$$\mathbf{m} = \begin{vmatrix} e_{11} & e_{12} \\ e_{21} & e_{22} \end{vmatrix}$$

is as follows:

$$\det[m] = e_{11}e_{22} - e_{21}e_{12}$$

The determinant of a 3×3 matrix is found by first expanding the matrix by minors, and then resolving the determinants of the 2×2 minors. Here's how you expand a 3×3 matrix by minors:

$$\mathbf{M} = e_{11}\begin{vmatrix} e_{22} & e_{23} \\ e_{32} & e_{33} \end{vmatrix} - e_{12}\begin{vmatrix} e_{21} & e_{23} \\ e_{31} & e_{33} \end{vmatrix} + e_{13}\begin{vmatrix} e_{21} & e_{22} \\ e_{31} & e_{32} \end{vmatrix}$$

Here's how this all looks in code:

```
inline      float      Matrix3x3::det(void)
{
    return      e11*e22*e33 -
                e11*e32*e23 +
                e21*e32*e13 -
```

```
        e21*e12*e33 +
        e31*e12*e23 -
        e31*e22*e13;
    }
```

Transpose

The method, Transpose, transposes the matrix by swapping rows with columns, that is, the elements in the first row become the elements in the first column and so on for the second and third rows and columns. The following relations are true for transpose operations:

$$(\mathbf{M}^t)^t = \mathbf{M}$$
$$(s\mathbf{M})^t = s(\mathbf{M}^t)$$
$$(\mathbf{MN})^t = \mathbf{N}^t\mathbf{M}^t$$
$$(\mathbf{M} + \mathbf{N})^t = \mathbf{M}^t + \mathbf{N}^t$$
$$\det[\mathbf{M}^t] = \det[\mathbf{M}]$$

Here, $\mathbf{M}$ and $\mathbf{N}$ are matrices, t is the transpose operator, and s is a scalar.

Here's the Transpose method for our Matrix3x3 class:

```
inline    Matrix3x3    Matrix3x3::Transpose(void)
{
    return Matrix3x3(e11,e21,e31,e12,e22,e32,e13,e23,e33);
}
```

Inverse

The method Inverse computes the inverse matrix such that the following relation is satisfied:

$$\mathbf{M}\mathbf{M}^{-1} = \mathbf{M}^{-1}\mathbf{M} = \mathbf{I}$$

Here, $\mathbf{M}^{-1}$ is the inverse of matrix $\mathbf{M}$, and $\mathbf{I}$ is the identity matrix. For a 3×3 matrix, the inverse is found as follows:

$$\mathbf{M}^{-1} = 1/\det[\mathbf{M}] \begin{vmatrix} E_{11} & E_{12} & E_{13} \\ E_{21} & E_{22} & E_{23} \\ E_{31} & E_{32} & E_{33} \end{vmatrix}$$

Here, E_{ij} represents the cofactor of element e_{ij}, which can be found by taking the determinant of the minor of each element. Only square matrices, those with the same number of rows as columns, can be inverted. Note, however, that not all square matrices can be inverted. A matrix can be inverted only if its determinant is nonzero.

The follow relation applies to matrix inversion:

$$(\mathbf{MN})^{-1} = \mathbf{N}^{-1}\mathbf{M}^{-1}$$

Here's how matrix inversion looks in code for our `Matrix3x3` class:

```
inline     Matrix3x3     Matrix3x3::Inverse(void)
{
    float     d = e11*e22*e33 -
                  e11*e32*e23 +
                  e21*e32*e13 -
                  e21*e12*e33 +
                  e31*e12*e23 -
                  e31*e22*e13;

    if (d == 0) d = 1;

    return     Matrix3x3(  (e22*e33-e23*e32)/d,
                          -(e12*e33-e13*e32)/d,
                           (e12*e23-e13*e22)/d,
                          -(e21*e33-e23*e31)/d,
                           (e11*e33-e13*e31)/d,
                          -(e11*e23-e13*e21)/d,
                           (e21*e32-e22*e31)/d,
                          -(e11*e32-e12*e31)/d,
                           (e11*e22-e12*e21)/d );
}
```

Matrix Addition: The += Operator

This operator simply adds the passed matrix to the current one on an element-by-element basis. For two matrices to be added, they must be of the same *order*, that is, they must have the same number of rows and columns.

```
inline     Matrix3x3& Matrix3x3::operator+=(Matrix3x3 m)
{
    e11 += m.e11;
    e12 += m.e12;
    e13 += m.e13;
    e21 += m.e21;
    e22 += m.e22;
    e23 += m.e23;
    e31 += m.e31;
    e32 += m.e32;
    e33 += m.e33;
    return *this;
}
```

Matrix addition (and subtraction) is commutative, associative, and distributive; thus,

$$\mathbf{M} + \mathbf{N} = \mathbf{N} + \mathbf{M}$$
$$\mathbf{M} + (\mathbf{N} + \mathbf{P}) = (\mathbf{M} + \mathbf{N}) + \mathbf{P}$$
$$\mathbf{M}(\mathbf{N} + \mathbf{P}) = \mathbf{MN} + \mathbf{MP}$$
$$(\mathbf{N} + \mathbf{P})\mathbf{M} = \mathbf{NM} + \mathbf{PM}$$

Matrix Subtraction: The -= Operator

This operator simply subtracts the passed matrix from the current one on an element-by-element basis. For two matrices to be subtracted, they must be of the same *order*, that is, they must have the same number of rows and columns.

```
inline    Matrix3x3& Matrix3x3::operator-=(Matrix3x3 m)
{
    e11 -= m.e11;
    e12 -= m.e12;
    e13 -= m.e13;
    e21 -= m.e21;
    e22 -= m.e22;
    e23 -= m.e23;
    e31 -= m.e31;
    e32 -= m.e32;
    e33 -= m.e33;
    return *this;
}
```

Scalar Multiplication: The *= Operator

This operator simply multiplies each element by the scalar, s:

```
inline    Matrix3x3& Matrix3x3::operator*=(float s)
{
    e11 *= s;
    e12 *= s;
    e13 *= s;
    e21 *= s;
    e22 *= s;
    e23 *= s;
    e31 *= s;
    e32 *= s;
    e33 *= s;
    return *this;
}
```

The following relation applies for scalar multiplication (and division):

$$s(\mathbf{MN}) = (s\mathbf{M})\mathbf{N} = \mathbf{M}(s\mathbf{N})$$

Scalar Division: The /= Operator

This operator simply divides each element by the scalar, s:

```
inline    Matrix3x3& Matrix3x3::operator/=(float s)
{
    e11 /= s;
    e12 /= s;
    e13 /= s;
    e21 /= s;
    e22 /= s;
    e23 /= s;
    e31 /= s;
    e32 /= s;
    e33 /= s;
    return *this;
}
```

Matrix Functions and Operators

The functions and overloaded operators that follow are useful in performing operations with two matrices, with a matrix and a scalar, or with a matrix and a vector. Here, the matrices are assumed to be of the type `Matrix3x3` and vectors of the type `Vector` as discussed in Appendix A.

Matrix Addition: The + Operator

This operator adds the two matrices together on an element-by-element basis:

```
inline    Matrix3x3 operator+(Matrix3x3 m1, Matrix3x3 m2)
{
    return     Matrix3x3(   m1.e11+m2.e11,
                            m1.e12+m2.e12,
                            m1.e13+m2.e13,
                            m1.e21+m2.e21,
                            m1.e22+m2.e22,
                            m1.e23+m2.e23,
                            m1.e31+m2.e31,
                            m1.e32+m2.e32,
                            m1.e33+m2.e33);
}
```

Matrix Subtraction: The − Operator

This operator subtracts matrix m2 from m1 on an element-by-element basis:

```
inline    Matrix3x3 operator-(Matrix3x3 m1, Matrix3x3 m2)
{
    return     Matrix3x3(   m1.e11-m2.e11,
                            m1.e12-m2.e12,
                            m1.e13-m2.e13,
                            m1.e21-m2.e21,
                            m1.e22-m2.e22,
                            m1.e23-m2.e23,
                            m1.e31-m2.e31,
                            m1.e32-m2.e32,
                            m1.e33-m2.e33);
}
```

Scalar Divide: The / Operator

This operator divides every element in the matrix, m, by the scalar, s:

```
inline    Matrix3x3 operator/(Matrix3x3 m, float s)
{
    return     Matrix3x3(   m.e11/s,
                            m.e12/s,
                            m.e13/s,
                            m.e21/s,
                            m.e22/s,
                            m.e23/s,
                            m.e31/s,
                            m.e32/s,
                            m.e33/s);
}
```

Matrix Multiplication: The * Operator

This operator, when applied between two matrices, performs a matrix multiplication. In matrix multiplication, each element, e_{ij}, is determined by the product of the ith row in the first matrix and the jth column of the second matrix:

```
inline    Matrix3x3 operator*(Matrix3x3 m1, Matrix3x3 m2)
{
    return Matrix3x3(m1.e11*m2.e11 + m1.e12*m2.e21 + m1.e13*m2.e31,
                     m1.e11*m2.e12 + m1.e12*m2.e22 + m1.e13*m2.e32,
                     m1.e11*m2.e13 + m1.e12*m2.e23 + m1.e13*m2.e33,
                     m1.e21*m2.e11 + m1.e22*m2.e21 + m1.e23*m2.e31,
                     m1.e21*m2.e12 + m1.e22*m2.e22 + m1.e23*m2.e32,
                     m1.e21*m2.e13 + m1.e22*m2.e23 + m1.e23*m2.e33,
                     m1.e31*m2.e11 + m1.e32*m2.e21 + m1.e33*m2.e31,
                     m1.e31*m2.e12 + m1.e32*m2.e22 + m1.e33*m2.e32,
                     m1.e31*m2.e13 + m1.e32*m2.e23 + m1.e33*m2.e33 );
}
```

Two matrices can be multiplied only if one has the same number of columns as the other has rows. Matrix multiplication is not commutative, but it is assocociative; thus,

$$\mathbf{MN} \neq \mathbf{NM}$$
$$(\mathbf{MN})\mathbf{P} = \mathbf{M}(\mathbf{NP})$$

Scalar Multiplication: The * Operator

This operator, when applied between a matrix and a scalar, multiplies each element in the matrix, m, by the scalar, s. Two forms are given here depending on the order in which the matrix and scalar are encountered:

```
inline    Matrix3x3 operator*(Matrix3x3 m, float s)
{
    return    Matrix3x3(    m.e11*s,
                           m.e12*s,
                           m.e13*s,
                           m.e21*s,
                           m.e22*s,
                           m.e23*s,
                           m.e31*s,
                           m.e32*s,
                           m.e33*s);
}

inline    Matrix3x3 operator*(float s, Matrix3x3 m)
{
    return    Matrix3x3(    m.e11*s,
                           m.e12*s,
                           m.e13*s,
                           m.e21*s,
                           m.e22*s,
                           m.e23*s,
                           m.e31*s,
                           m.e32*s,
                           m.e33*s);
}
```

Vector Multiplication: The * Operator

This operator, when applied between a vector and a matrix, performs a vector multiplication in which the ith column in the matrix is multiplied by the ith component in the vector. Two forms are given here depending on the order in which the matrix and vector are encountered.

```
inline    Vector operator*(Matrix3x3 m, Vector u)
{
    return Vector(    m.e11*u.x + m.e12*u.y + m.e13*u.z,
                      m.e21*u.x + m.e22*u.y + m.e23*u.z,
                      m.e31*u.x + m.e32*u.y + m.e33*u.z);
}

inline    Vector operator*(Vector u, Matrix3x3 m)
{
    return Vector(    u.x*m.e11 + u.y*m.e21 + u.z*m.e31,
                      u.x*m.e12 + u.y*m.e22 + u.z*m.e32,
                      u.x*m.e13 + u.y*m.e23 + u.z*m.e33);
}
```

Quaternion Operations

This appendix implements a class called `Quaternion` that encapsulates all of the operations you need to handle quaternions when writing 3D rigid body simulations.

Quaternion Class

The `Quaternion` class is defined with a scalar component, n, and vector component, $\mathbf{v}$, where $\mathbf{v}$ is the vector $x\mathbf{i} + y\mathbf{j} + z\mathbf{k}$. The class has two constructors, one that initializes the quaternion to zero and one that initializes the elements to those passed to the constructor:

```
class Quaternion {
public:
    float       n;      // number (scalar) part
    Vector      v;      // vector part: v.x, v.y, v.z

    Quaternion(void);
    Quaternion(float e0, float e1, float e2, float e3);

    float       Magnitude(void);
    Vector      GetVector(void);
    float       GetScalar(void);
    Quaternion operator+=(Quaternion q);
    Quaternion operator-=(Quaternion q);
    Quaternion operator*=(float s);
    Quaternion operator/=(float s);
    Quaternion operator~(void) const { return Quaternion( n,
                                                         -v.x,
                                                         -v.y,
                                                         -v.z);}
};

// Constructor
inline      Quaternion::Quaternion(void)
{
    n   = 0;
    v.x = 0;
    v.y = 0;
    v.z = 0;
}
```

```
// Constructor
inline    Quaternion::Quaternion(float e0, float e1, float e2, float e3)
{
    n   = e0;
    v.x = e1;
    v.y = e2;
    v.z = e3;
}
```

Magnitude

The method, `Magnitude`, returns the magnitude of the quaternion according to the following formula:

$$|\mathbf{q}| = \sqrt{n^2 + x^2 + y^2 + z^2}$$

This is similar to calculating the magnitude of a vector except that for quaternions you have to take the fourth term, the scalar n, into account.

Here's the code that calculates the magnitude for our `Quaternion` class:

```
inline    float    Quaternion::Magnitude(void)
{
    return (float) sqrt(n*n + v.x*v.x + v.y*v.y + v.z*v.z);
}
```

GetVector

The method, `GetVector`, returns the vector part of the quaternion. This method uses the `Vector` class defined in Appendix A:

```
inline    Vector    Quaternion::GetVector(void)
{
    return Vector(v.x, v.y, v.z);
}
```

GetScalar

The method `GetScalar` returns the scalar part of the quaternion:

```
inline    float    Quaternion::GetScalar(void)
{
    return n;
}
```

Quaternion Addition: The += Operator

This operator performs quaternion addition by simply adding the quaternion, $\mathbf{q}$, to the current quaternion on a component-by-component basis.

If $\mathbf{q}$ and $\mathbf{p}$ are two quaternions, then

$$\mathbf{q} + \mathbf{p} = [n_q + n_p, (x_q + x_p)\mathbf{i} + (y_q + y_p)\mathbf{j} + (z_q + z_p)\mathbf{k}]$$

Here, $n_q + n_p$ is the scalar part of the resulting quaternion, while $(x_q + x_p)\mathbf{i} + (y_q + y_p)\mathbf{j} + (z_q + z_p)\mathbf{k}$ is the vector part.

Quaternion addition is both associative and commutative; thus,

$$\mathbf{q} + (\mathbf{p} + \mathbf{h}) = (\mathbf{q} + \mathbf{p}) + \mathbf{h}$$

$$\mathbf{q} + \mathbf{p} = \mathbf{p} + \mathbf{q}$$

Here's the code that adds the quaternion $\mathbf{q}$ to our `Quaternion` class:

```
inline    Quaternion    Quaternion::operator+=(Quaternion q)
{
    n += q.n;
    v.x += q.v.x;
    v.y += q.v.y;
    v.z += q.v.z;
    return *this;
}
```

Quaternion Subtraction: The −= Operator

This operator performs quaternion subtraction by simply subtracting the quaternion, $\mathbf{q}$, from the current quaternion on a component-by-component basis.

If $\mathbf{q}$ and $\mathbf{p}$ are two quaternions, then

$$\mathbf{q} - \mathbf{p} = \mathbf{q} + (-\mathbf{p}) = [n_q - n_p, (x_q - x_p)\mathbf{i} + (y_q - y_p)\mathbf{j} + (z_q - z_p)\mathbf{k}]$$

Here, $n_q - n_p$ is the scalar part of the resulting quaternion, while $(x_q - x_p)\mathbf{i} + (y_q - y_p)\mathbf{j} + (z_q - z_p)\mathbf{k}$ is the vector part.

Here's the code that subtracts the quaternion $\mathbf{q}$ from our `Quaternion` class:

```
inline    Quaternion    Quaternion::operator-=(Quaternion q)
{
    n -= q.n;
    v.x -= q.v.x;
    v.y -= q.v.y;
    v.z -= q.v.z;
    return *this;
}
```

Scalar Multiplication: The *= Operator

This operator simply multiplies each component in the quaternion by the scalar, s. This operation is similar to scaling a vector as described in Appendix A.

```
inline    Quaternion Quaternion::operator*=(float s)
{
    n *= s;
    v.x *= s;
    v.y *= s;
    v.z *= s;
    return *this;
}
```

Scalar Division: The /= Operator

This operator simply divides each component in the quaternion by the scalar, s:

```
inline     Quaternion Quaternion::operator/=(float s)
{
    n /= s;
    v.x /= s;
    v.y /= s;
    v.z /= s;
    return *this;
}
```

Conjugate: The ~ Operator

This operator takes the conjugate of the quaternion, $\sim\mathbf{q}$, which is simply the negative of the vector part. If $\mathbf{q} = [n, x\mathbf{i} + y\mathbf{j} + z\mathbf{k}]$, then $\sim\mathbf{q} = [n, (-x)\mathbf{i} + (-y)\mathbf{j} + (-z)\mathbf{k}]$.

The conjugate of the product of quaternions is equal to the product of the quaternion conjugates, but in reverse order:

$$\sim(\mathbf{qp}) = (\sim\mathbf{p})(\sim\mathbf{q})$$

Here's the code that computes the conjugate for our Quaternion class:

```
Quaternion operator~(void) const { return Quaternion( n,
                                                     -v.x,
                                                     -v.y,
                                                     -v.z);}
```

Quaternion Functions and Operators

The functions and overloaded operators that follow are useful when performing operations with two quaternions, with a quaternion and a scalar, or with a quaternion and a vector. Here, the quaternions are assumed to be of the type Quaternion, and vectors are assumed to be of the type Vector as discussed in Appendix A.

Quaternion Addition: The + Operator

This operator performs quaternion addition by simply adding the quaternion q1 to quaternion q2 on a component-by-component basis:

```
inline     Quaternion operator+(Quaternion q1, Quaternion q2)
{
    return     Quaternion(    q1.n + q2.n,
                              q1.v.x + q2.v.x,
                              q1.v.y + q2.v.y,
                              q1.v.z + q2.v.z);
}
```

Quaternion Subtraction: The — Operator

This operator performs quaternion subtraction by simply subtracting the quaternion q2 from quaternion q1 on a component-by-component basis:

```
inline    Quaternion operator-(Quaternion q1, Quaternion q2)
{
    return    Quaternion(    q1.n - q2.n,
                             q1.v.x - q2.v.x,
                             q1.v.y - q2.v.y,
                             q1.v.z - q2.v.z);
}
```

Quaternion Multiplication: The * Operator

This operator performs quaternion multiplication according to the following formula:

$$\mathbf{qp} = n_q n_p - \mathbf{v}_q \cdot \mathbf{v}_p + n_q \mathbf{v}_p + n_p \mathbf{v}_q + (\mathbf{v}_q \times \mathbf{v}_p)$$

Here, $n_q n_p - \mathbf{v}_q \cdot \mathbf{v}_p$ is the scalar part of the result and $n_q \mathbf{v}_p + n_p \mathbf{v}_q + (\mathbf{v}_q \times \mathbf{v}_p)$ is the vector part. Also note that $\mathbf{v}_q$ and $\mathbf{v}_p$ are the vector parts of $\mathbf{q}$ and $\mathbf{p}$, respectively, $\cdot$ is the vector dot product operator, and $\times$ is the vector cross product operator.

Quaternion multiplication is associative but not commutative; therefore,

$$\mathbf{q(ph)} = \mathbf{(qp)h}$$

$$\mathbf{qp} \neq \mathbf{pq}$$

Here's the code that multiplies two quaternions q1 and q2:

```
inline    Quaternion operator*(Quaternion q1, Quaternion q2)
{
    return    Quaternion(q1.n*q2.n - q1.v.x*q2.v.x
                         - q1.v.y*q2.v.y - q1.v.z*q2.v.z,
                  q1.n*q2.v.x + q1.v.x*q2.n
                         + q1.v.y*q2.v.z - q1.v.z*q2.v.y,
                  q1.n*q2.v.y + q1.v.y*q2.n
                         + q1.v.z*q2.v.x - q1.v.x*q2.v.z,
                  q1.n*q2.v.z + q1.v.z*q2.n
                         + q1.v.x*q2.v.y - q1.v.y*q2.v.x);
}
```

Scalar Multiplication: The * Operator

This operator simply multiplies each component in the quaternion by the scalar, s. There are two forms of this operator depending on the order in which the quaternion and scalar are encountered:

```
inline    Quaternion operator*(Quaternion q, float s)
{
    return    Quaternion(q.n*s, q.v.x*s, q.v.y*s, q.v.z*s);
}
```

```
inline    Quaternion operator*(float s, Quaternion q)
{
    return    Quaternion(q.n*s, q.v.x*s, q.v.y*s, q.v.z*s);
}
```

Vector Multiplication: The * Operator

This operator multiplies the quaternion q by the vector v as though the vector v were a quaternion with its scalar component equal to zero. There are two forms of this operator depending on the order in which the quaternion and vector are encountered. Since v is assumes to be a quaternion with its scalar part equal to zero, the rules of multiplication follow those outlined earlier for quaternion multiplication.

```
inline    Quaternion operator*(Quaternion q, Vector v)
{
    return    Quaternion(    -(q.v.x*v.x + q.v.y*v.y + q.v.z*v.z),
                             q.n*v.x + q.v.y*v.z - q.v.z*v.y,
                             q.n*v.y + q.v.z*v.x - q.v.x*v.z,
                             q.n*v.z + q.v.x*v.y - q.v.y*v.x);
}
inline    Quaternion operator*(Vector v, Quaternion q)
{
    return    Quaternion(    -(q.v.x*v.x + q.v.y*v.y + q.v.z*v.z),
                             q.n*v.x + q.v.z*v.y - q.v.y*v.z,
                             q.n*v.y + q.v.x*v.z - q.v.z*v.x,
                             q.n*v.z + q.v.y*v.x - q.v.x*v.y);

}
```

Scalar Division: The / Operator

This operator simply divides each component in the quaternion by the scalar, s:

```
inline    Quaternion operator/(Quaternion q, float s)
{
    return    Quaternion(q.n/s, q.v.x/s, q.v.y/s, q.v.z/s);
}
```

QGetAngle*

This function extracts the angle of rotation about the axis represented by the vector part of the quaternion:

```
inline    float QGetAngle(Quaternion q)
{
    return    (float) (2*acos(q.n));
}
```

---

* For a description of how quaternions are used to represent rotation, refer to the section entitled "Quaternions" in Chapter 14.

QGetAxis

This function returns a unit vector along the axis of rotation represented by the vector part of the quaternion, q:

```
inline    Vector QGetAxis(Quaternion q)
{
    Vector v;
    float m;

    v = q.GetVector();
    m = v.Magnitude();

    if (m <= tol)
        return Vector();
    else
        return v/m;
}
```

QRotate

This function rotates the quaternion **p** by **q** according to the formula

$$\mathbf{p}' = (\mathbf{q})(\mathbf{p})(\sim\mathbf{q})$$

Here, $\sim\mathbf{q}$ is the conjugate of the unit quaternion, **q**. Here's the code:

```
inline    Quaternion QRotate(Quaternion q1, Quaternion q2)
{
    return    q1*q2*(~q1);
}
```

QVRotate

This function rotates the vector **v** by the unit quaternion **q** according to the formula

$$\mathbf{p}' = (\mathbf{q})(\mathbf{v})(\sim\mathbf{q})$$

Here, $\sim\mathbf{q}$ is the conjugate of the unit quaternion, **q**. Here's the code:

```
inline    Vector    QVRotate(Quaternion q, Vector v)
{
    Quaternion t;

    t = q*v*(~q);
    return    t.GetVector();
}
```

MakeQFromEulerAngles

This function constructs a quaternion from a set of Euler angles.

For a given set of Euler angles, yaw (ψ), pitch (τ), and roll (φ) defining rotation about the z-axis, then the y-axis, and then the z-axis, you can construct the representative rotation quaternion. You do this by first constructing a quaternion for each Euler angle and then multiplying the three quaternions following the rules of quaternion multiplication. Here are the three quaternions representing each Euler rotation angle:

$$\mathbf{q}_{\text{roll}} = \{\cos(\varphi/2), [\sin(\varphi/2)]\mathbf{i} + 0\mathbf{j} + 0\mathbf{k}\}$$
$$\mathbf{q}_{\text{pitch}} = \{\cos(\tau/2), 0\mathbf{i} + [\sin(\tau/2)]\mathbf{j} + 0\mathbf{k}\}$$
$$\mathbf{q}_{\text{yaw}} = \{\cos(\psi/2), 0\mathbf{i} + 0\mathbf{j} + [\sin(\psi/2)]\mathbf{k}\}$$

Each one of these quaternions is of unit length.*

Now you can multiply these quaternions to obtain a single one that represents the rotation, or orientation, defined by the three Euler angles:

$$\mathbf{q} = \mathbf{q}_{\text{yaw}}\, \mathbf{q}_{\text{pitch}}\, \mathbf{q}_{\text{roll}}$$

Performing this multiplication yields

$$\mathbf{q} = \{[\cos(\varphi/2)\cos(\tau/2)\cos(\psi/2) + \sin(\varphi/2)\sin(\tau/2)\sin(\psi/2)],$$
$$[\sin(\varphi/2)\cos(\tau/2)\cos(\psi/2) - \cos(\varphi/2)\sin(\tau/2)\sin(\psi/2)]\,\mathbf{i}$$
$$+ [\cos(\varphi/2)\sin(\tau/2)\cos(\psi/2) + \sin(\varphi/2)\cos(\tau/2)\sin(\psi/2)]\,\mathbf{j}$$
$$+ [\cos(\varphi/2)\cos(\tau/2)\sin(\psi/2) - \sin(\varphi/2)\sin(\tau/2)\cos(\psi/2)]\,\mathbf{k}\}$$

Here's the code that takes three Euler angles and returns a quaternion:

```
inline    Quaternion    MakeQFromEulerAngles(float x, float y, float z)
{
    Quaternion    q;
    double    roll = DegreesToRadians(x);
    double    pitch = DegreesToRadians(y);
    double    yaw = DegreesToRadians(z);

    double    cyaw, cpitch, croll, syaw, spitch, sroll;
    double    cyawcpitch, syawspitch, cyawspitch, syawcpitch;

    cyaw = cos(0.5f * yaw);
    cpitch = cos(0.5f * pitch);
    croll = cos(0.5f * roll);
    syaw = sin(0.5f * yaw);
    spitch = sin(0.5f * pitch);
    sroll = sin(0.5f * roll);

    cyawcpitch = cyaw*cpitch;
    syawspitch = syaw*spitch;
    cyawspitch = cyaw*spitch;
    syawcpitch = syaw*cpitch;

    q.n = (float) (cyawcpitch * croll + syawspitch * sroll);
    q.v.x = (float) (cyawcpitch * sroll - syawspitch * croll);
    q.v.y = (float) (cyawspitch * croll + syawcpitch * sroll);
    q.v.z = (float) (syawcpitch * croll - cyawspitch * sroll);

    return q;
}
```

* You can verify this by recalling the trigonometric relation $\cos^2\theta + \sin^2\theta = 1$.

MakeEulerAnglesFromQ

This function extracts the three Euler angles from a given quaternion.

You can extract the three Euler angles from a quaternion by first converting the quaternion to a rotation matrix and then extracting the Euler angles from the rotation matrix. Let **R** be a nine-element rotation matrix,

$$\mathbf{R} = \begin{vmatrix} r_{11} & r_{12} & r_{13} \\ r_{21} & r_{22} & r_{23} \\ r_{31} & r_{32} & r_{33} \end{vmatrix}$$

and let **q** be a quaternion,

$$\mathbf{q} = [n, x\mathbf{i} + y\mathbf{j} + z\mathbf{k}]$$

Then each element in **R** is calculated from **q** as follows:

$$r_{11} = n^2 + x^2 - y^2 - z^2$$
$$r_{21} = 2xy + 2zn$$
$$r_{31} = 2zx - 2yn$$
$$r_{12} = 2xy - 2zn$$
$$r_{22} = n^2 - x^2 + y^2 - z^2$$
$$r_{32} = 2zy + 2xn$$
$$r_{13} = 2xz + 2yn$$
$$r_{23} = 2yz - 2xn$$
$$r_{33} = n^2 - x^2 - y^2 + z^2$$

To extract the Euler angles, yaw (ψ), pitch (τ), and roll (φ), from **R**, you can use these relations:

$$\sin \tau = -r_{31}$$
$$\tan \varphi = r_{32}/r_{33}$$
$$\tan \psi = r_{21}/r_{11}$$

Here's the code that extracts the three Euler angles, returned in the form of a Vector, from a given quaternion:

```
inline    Vector    MakeEulerAnglesFromQ(Quaternion q)
{
    double    r11, r21, r31, r32, r33, r12, r13;
    double    q00, q11, q22, q33;
    double    tmp;
    Vector    u;
    q00 = q.n * q.n;
    q11 = q.v.x * q.v.x;
    q22 = q.v.y * q.v.y;
    q33 = q.v.z * q.v.z;

    r11 = q00 + q11 - q22 - q33;
    r21 = 2 * (q.v.x*q.v.y + q.n*q.v.z);
```

```
r31 = 2 * (q.v.x*q.v.z - q.n*q.v.y);
r32 = 2 * (q.v.y*q.v.z + q.n*q.v.x);
r33 = q00 - q11 - q22 + q33;

tmp = fabs(r31);
if(tmp > 0.999999)
{
    r12 = 2 * (q.v.x*q.v.y - q.n*q.v.z);
    r13 = 2 * (q.v.x*q.v.z + q.n*q.v.y);

    u.x = RadiansToDegrees(0.0f); //roll
    u.y = RadiansToDegrees((float) (-(pi/2) * r31/tmp));    // pitch
    u.z = RadiansToDegrees((float) atan2(-r12, -r31*r13)); // yaw
    return u;
}

u.x = RadiansToDegrees((float) atan2(r32, r33)); // roll
u.y = RadiansToDegrees((float) asin(-r31));       // pitch
u.z = RadiansToDegrees((float) atan2(r21, r11)); // yaw
return u;

}
```

Conversion Functions

These two functions are used to convert angles from degrees to radians and radians to degrees. They are not specific to quaternions but are used in some of the code samples shown earlier.

```
inline    float    DegreesToRadians(float deg)
{
    return deg * pi / 180.0f;
}

inline    float    RadiansToDegrees(float rad)
{
    return rad * 180.0f / pi;
}
```

Bibliography

A wise old professor once told me that it is not important to know the answers to everything as long as you know where to find the answers when you need them. In that spirit, I've compiled a list of references to books, articles, and Internet resources that you might find useful when looking for additional information on the various topics discussed throughout this book. I've tried to categorize them as best I could. However, keep in mind that several references cover more than just the subject matter referred to in the category headings I've assigned.

General Physics and Dynamics

Anand, D. K., and P. F. Cunniff. *Engineering Mechanics: Dynamics*. Boston: Houghton Mifflin, 1973.

Beer, Ferdinand P., and E. Russell Johnston, Jr. *Vector Mechanics for Engineers*. New York: McGraw-Hill, 1988.

Dugas, Rene. *A History of Mechanics*. New York: Dover, 1988.

Ginsberg, Jerry H. *Advanced Engineering Dynamics*. New York: Cambridge University Press, 1995.

Lindeburg, Michael R. *Engineer-in-Training Reference Manual*. Belmont, Calif.: Professional Publications, 1990.

Meriam, J. L., and L. G. Kraige. *Engineering Mechanics*, Vol. 2, *Dynamics*. New York: John Wiley & Sons, 1987.

Rothbart, Harold A., ed. *Mechanical Design Handbook*. New York: McGraw-Hill, 1996.

Serway, Raymond A. *Physics for Scientists and Engineers*. New York: Saunders College Publishing, 1986.

Mathematics and Numerical Methods

Boyce, William E., and Richard C. DiPrima, *Elementary Differential Equations*. New York: John Wiley & Sons, 1986.

Kreyszig, Erwin. *Advanced Engineering Mathematics*. New York: John Wiley & Sons, 1988.

Larson, Roland E., and Robert P. Hostetler. *Calculus with Analytic Geometry*. Lexington, Mass.: D. C. Heath, 1986.

Press, William H., Brian P. Flannery, Saul A. Teukolsky, and William T. Vetterling. *Numerical Recipes in Pascal: The Art of Scientific Computing*. New York: Cambridge University Press, 1989.

Computational Geometry

Arvo, James, ed. *Graphics Gems II*. New York: Academic Press, 1991.

Bobic, Nick. "Advanced Collision Detection Techniques," *Gamasutra*, March 2000. URL: *http://www.gamasutra.com/features/20000330/bobic_01.htm*

DaLoura, Mark, ed. *Game Programming Gems*, Chap. 4.5. Hingham, Mass.: Charles River Media, 2000.

Foley, James, Andries van Dam, Steven Feiner, and John Hughes. *Computer Graphics: Principles and Practice*. Reading, Mass.: Addison-Wesley, 1996.

Glassner, Andrew, ed. *Graphics Gems*. New York: Academic Press, 1990.

Goodman, J. E., and J. O'Rourke, eds. *Handbook of Discrete and Computational Geometry*. Boca Raton, Fla.: CRC Press, 1997.

Heckbert, Paul, ed. *Graphics Gems IV*. New York: Academic Press, 1994.

Kirk, David, ed. *Graphics Gems III*. Academic Press, New York, 1992.

Mirtich, Brian. "Fast and Accurate Computation of Polyhedral Mass Properties," *Journal of Graphics Tools* 1, no. 2: 31–50, 1996. URL: *http://www.merl.com/people/mirtich/pubs.html*

Mirtich, Brian. "Rigid Body Contact: Collision Detection to Force Computation," MERL Technical Report 98-01, *Proceedings of Workshop on Contact Analysis and Simulation, IEEE International Conference on Robotics and Automation*, May 1998. URL: *http://www.merl.com/people/mirtich/pubs.html*

Mirtich, Brian. "Efficient Algorithms for Two-Phase Collision Detection," MERL Technical Report 97-23, *Practical Motion Planning in Robotics: Current Approaches and Future Directions*, edited by K. Gupta and A. P. del Pobil, 1998. URL: *http://www.merl.com/people/mirtich/pubs.html*

Mirtich, Brian. "V-Clip: Fast and Robust Polyhedral Collision Detection," MERL Technical Report 97-05, *ACM Transactions on Graphics* 17, no. 3: 177–208, July 1998. URL: *http://www.merl.com/people/mirtich/pubs.html*

O'Rourke, Joseph. "comp.graphics.algorithms Frequently Asked Questions," Copyright 2000 by Joseph O'Rourke. URL: *http://jupiter.felk.cvut.cz/FAQ/articles/a1834.html*

O'Rourke, Joseph. *Computational Geometry in C*. New York: Cambridge University Press, 1998.

Paeth, Alan, ed. *Graphics Gems V*. New York: Academic Press, 1995.

Projectiles

Power, H. L. and Iversen, J. D. "Magnus Effect on Spinning Bodies of Revolution," *AIAA Journal* 11, no. 4, April 1973.

Sports Ball Physics

Adair, Robert K. *The Physics of Baseball*. New York: Harper Perennial, 1994.

Davies, John M. "The Aerodynamics of Golf Balls," *Journal of Applied Physics* 20, no. 9, September 1949.

Jorgensen, Theodore P. *The Physics of Golf*. New York: Springer, 1999.

MacDonald, William M., "The Physics of the Drive in Golf," *American Journal of Physics* 59, no. 3, March 1991.

McPhee, John J., and Gordon C. Andrews. "Effect of Sidespin and Wind on Projectile Trajectory, with Particular Application to Golf," *American Journal of Physics* 56, no. 10, October 1988.

Mehta, Rabindra D. "Aerodynamics of Sports Balls," *Annual Review of Fluid Mechanics* 17: 151–189, 1985.

Shepard, Ron. *Amateur Physics for the Amateur Pool Player*, copyright Ron Shepard, 1997.

Watts, Robert G., and Steven Baroni. "Baseball-Bat Collisions and the Resulting Trajectories of Spinning Balls," *American Journal of Physics* 57, no. 1, January 1989.

Watts, Robert G., and Eric Sawyer. "Aerodynamics of a Knuckleball," *American Journal of Physics* 43, no. 11, November 1975.

Aerodynamics

Abbot, Ira H., and Albert E. Von Doenhoff. *Theory of Wing Sections*. New York: Dover, 1959.

Hoerner, Sighard F., and Henry V. Borst. *Fluid Dynamic Lift*. Bakersfield, Calif.: Hoerner Fluid Dynamics, 1985.

Hoerner, Sighard F. *Fluid Dynamic Drag*, Bakersfield, Calif.: Hoerner Fluid Dynamics, 1992.

Thwaites, Bryan, ed. *Incompressible Aerodynamics*, New York: Dover, 1960.

Hydrostatics and Hydrodynamics

Clayton, B. R., and R. E. D. Bishop. *Mechanics of Marine Vehicles*. Houston, Texas: Gulf, 1982.

Daugherty, Robert L., Joseph B. Franzini, and E. John Finnemore. *Fluid Mechanics with Engineering Applications*. New York: McGraw-Hill, 1985.

Gillmer, Thomas C., and Bruce Johnson. *Introduction to Naval Architecture*. Annapolis, Md.: Naval Institute Press, 1982.

Lewis, Edward V., ed. *Principles of Naval Architecture*, Second Revision, Vol. I, *Stability and Strength*. Jersey City, N.J.: The Society of Naval Architects and Marine Engineers, 1988.

Lewis, Edward V., ed. *Principles of Naval Architecture*, Second Revision, Vol. II, *Resistance, Propulsion and Vibration*. Jersey City, N.J.: The Society of Naval Architects and Marine Engineers, 1988.

Newman, John Nicholas. *Marine Hydrodynamics*. Cambridge, Mass.: The MIT Press, 1989.

Zubaly, Robert B., *Applied Naval Architecture*. Jersey City, N.J.: The Society of Naval Architects and Marine Engineers, 1996.

Automobile Physics

Beckman, Brian, *Physics of Racing Series*, Copyright 1991 by Brian Beckman, Stuttgart-West, 1998. URL: *http://www.autopedia.com/stuttgart-west/StuttPhysics.html*

Real-Time Physics Simulations

DaLoura, Mark, ed. *Game Programming Gems*, Section 2. Hingham, Mass.: Charles River Media, 2000.

Hecker, Chris. "Physics, The Next Frontier," *Game Developer*, October/November 1996.

Hecker, Chris. "Physics, Part 2: Angular Effects," *Game Developer*, December 1996/ January 1997.

Hecker, Chris. "Physics, Part 3: Collision Response," *Game Developer*, March 1997.

Hecker, Chris. "Physics, Part 4: The Third Dimension," *Game Developer*, June 1997.

Katz, Amnon. *Computational Rigid Vehicle Dynamics*. Malabar, Fla.: Krieger, 1997.

Lander, Jeff. "Collision Response: Bouncy, Trouncy, Fun," *Gamasutra*, February 8, 2000. URL: *http://www.gamasutra.com/features/20000208/lander_01.htm*

Lander, Jeff. "Crashing into the New Year," *Gamasutra*, February 10, 2000. URL: *http://www.gamasutra.com/features/20000210/lander_01.htm*

Lander, Jeff. "Lone Game Developer Battles Physics Simulator," *Gamasutra*, February 15, 2000. URL: *http://www.gamasutra.com/features/20000214/lander_01.htm*

Lander, Jeff. "Trials and Tribulations of Tribology," *Gamasutra*, May 10, 2000. URL: *http://www.gamasutra.com/features/20000510/lander_01.htm*

Lander, Jeff. "Physics on the Back of a Cocktail Napkin," *Gamasutra*, May 16, 2000. URL: *http://www.gamasutra.com/features/20000516/lander_01.htm*

Mirtich, Brian. "Impulse-Based Dynamic Simulation of Rigid Body Systems." Ph.D. thesis, University of California, Berkeley, December 1996. URL: *http://www.merl.com/people/mirtich/pubs.html*

Mirtich, Brian, and John Canny. "Impulse-based Simulation of Rigid Bodies," *Proceedings of the 1995 Symposium on Interactive 3D Graphics*, April 1995. URL: *http://www.merl.com/people/mirtich/pubs.html*

Mirtich, Brian, and John Canny. "Impulse-Based Dynamic Simulation," *Proceedings of Workshop on Algorithmic Foundations of Robotics*, February 1994. URL: *http://www.merl.com/people/mirtich/pubs.html*

Witkin, Andrew, and David Baraff. "An Introduction to Physically Based Modeling," 1997. URL: *http://www.cs.cmu.edu/afs/cs/user/baraff/www/pbm/pbm.html* (see also SIGGRAPH '95 course entitled "An Introduction to Physically Based Modeling").

Index

Symbols

* operator
  in matrix operations
    matrix multiplication, 301
    scalar multiplication, 301
    vector multiplication, 302
  in quaternion operations
    quaternion multiplication, 307
    scalar multiplication, 307–308
    vector multiplication, 308
  in vector operations
    scalar multiplication, 293
    vector dot product, 292–293
*= operator
  in matrix operations, 299
  in quaternion operations, 305
  in vector operations, 290
+ operator
  in matrix operations, 300
  in quaternion operations, 306
  in vector operations, 291
+= operator
  in matrix operations, 298
  in quaternion operations, 304–305
  in vector operations, 289
− operator
  in matrix operations, 300
  in quaternion operations, 307
  in vector operations
    conjugate, 290–291
    vector substraction, 291
−= operator
  in matrix operations, 299
  in quaternion operations, 305
  in vector operations, 289–290

/ operator
  in matrix operations, 300
  in quaternion operations, 308
  in vector operations, 294
/= operator
  in matrix operations, 299
  in quaternion operations, 306
  in vector operations, 290
operator, in quaternion operations, 306
^ operator, in vector operations, 291–292

A

acceleration
  angular, 4, 50–56
  centripetal, 52–53
  concepts, 27–28
  constant, 28–30
  equations for, 72–73
  linear, units and symbol for, 4
  nonconstant, 30–31
  relative, 55–56
  tangential, 52–53
  velocity and, 25–28
acceleration vector, in law of motion, 16
aerodynamic drag, 165–167
  in cars, 168
  components of, 165
  induced, 165–166
  momentum, 166
  viscous, 165
  wetted, 166–167
aerostatic lift, 163
ailerons, in aircraft, 131

G

GetScalar, in quaternion operations, 304
GetVector, in quaternion operations, 304
golf
    as collision example, 98–100
    as Magnus effect example, 116

H

Hamilton, William, 227
Hook's law, 64
horsepower, in cars, 169–170
hovercraft, 163–167
    aerodynamic drag, 165–167
        components of, 165
        induced, 165–166
        momentum, 166
        viscous, 165
        wetted, 166–167
    concepts, 163–165
        aerostatic lift, 163–165
        skirts for, 164
    2D rigid body simulation, 184–204
    linear collision response in, 206–211
    over water, 165–167
    resistance, 165–167

I

impact of collision, 89–95, 91
impulse
    angular, 88
    collision
        angular, 96–98, 221–222
        linear, 95–96, 209–210
    force, 88
    linear, 88
    torque, 88
impulse-momentum principle, 88–89
inelastic collisions, 90
inertia, products of, 20–21
inertia tensors, 19–24
    angular momentum equation, 19–20
    products of inertia, 20–21
    sample code, 23–24
    symmetry, 22
    transfer of axes, 21
instantaneous velocity, 27
    calculation for, 28–29
inverse, in matrix operations, 297–298

K

kinematics, 25–56
    angular velocity and acceleration, 50–56
    constant acceleration, 28–30
    2D particle, 31–33
    3D particle, 33–43
    local coordinate axes, 49–50
    nonconstant acceleration, 30–31
    particle explosion, 43–48
    rigid body, 49
    velocity and acceleration, 25–28
kinematic viscosity, units and symbol for, 4
kinetic energy
    collision impact and, 89
    concepts, 89
kinetics, 69–86
    2D particle, 70–75
    3D particle, 75–82
    problem solving guidelines, 70
    rigid body, 82–86
Kutta-Joukouiski theorem, 115, 125

L

length, units and symbol for, 4
lift force, 114–118
    in aircraft, 124–125
    equation for, 116
linear acceleration, 4
linear collision response, simulation, 206–211
    check for collision, 207
    collision impulse, 209–210
    determination of collision, 206–208
linear impulse, 88
    in collisions, 95–96, 209–210
linear momentum, in law of motion, 16
linear motion, defined, 5
linear velocity, 4

M

magnitude
    in quaternion operations, 304
    in vector operations, 286–287
magnus effect, 114–119
MakeEulerAnglesFromQ, in quaternion
        operations, 311–312
MakeQFromEulerAngles, in quaternion
        operations, 309–310
mass
    calculation of, 6–8
    defined, 6

About the Author

As a naval architect and marine engineer, **David M. Bourg** performs computer simulations and develops analysis tools that measure such things as hovercraft performance and the effect of waves on the motion of ships and boats. He teaches at the college level in the areas of ship design, construction, and analysis. On occasion, David also lectures at high schools on topics such as naval architecture and software development. In addition to his practical engineering background, David is professionally involved in computer game development and consulting through his company, Crescent Vision Interactive (*http://www.crescentvision.com*). Current projects include a massive multiplayer online role-playing game, several Java-based multiplayer games, and a couple of PC-to-Macintosh game ports. David is currently working on his Ph.D. in Engineering and Applied Sciences.

Colophon

Our look is the result of reader comments, our own experimentation, and feedback from distribution channels. Distinctive covers complement our distinctive approach to technical topics, breathing personality and life into potentially dry subjects.

The animals on the cover of *Physics for Game Developers* are a cat and a mouse. The age-old rivalry between cat and mouse has been the topic of many children's books and Saturday cartoons. From traditional folk tales, such as Aesop's fables and Grimm Brothers' fairy tales, to today's cartoons, such as *Tom & Jerry*, the cat has chased and bullied the mouse and the mouse has avoided becoming lunch. The cat may be bigger and stronger, but the mouse is small, fast, and can fit in tight spaces, so the end result is often a battle of wits.

Darren Kelly was the production editor, Barbara Willette was the copyeditor, and Donna Leik, Larry Hykes, and Charles Snyder were the proofreaders for *Physics for Game Developers*. Claire Cloutier provided quality control. Angie Wiley wrote the index.

Ellie Volckhausen designed the cover of this book, based on a series design by Edie Freedman. The cover image is a 19th-century engraving from the Dover Pictorial Archive. Emma Colby produced the cover layout with QuarkXPress 4.1, using Adobe's ITC Garamond font.

David Futato designed the interior layout. Techbooks, Inc. implemented the design. The illustrations that appear in the book were produced by Robert Romano and Jessamyn Read, using Macromedia FreeHand 9 and Adobe Photoshop 6. The tip and warning icons were drawn by Christopher Bing. This colophon was written by Linley Dolby.

Whenever possible, our books use a durable and flexible lay-flat binding.